Shakir M. Pashov.
History of the Gypsies in Bulgaria and Europe: Roma

Roma History and Culture

VOLUME 1

Shakir M. Pashov

History of the Gypsies in Bulgaria and Europe: Roma

Edited by

Elena Marushiakova, Vesselin Popov,
Lilyana Kovacheva

BRILL | SCHÖNINGH

The open access of this volume is possible thanks to funding from the European Research Council for the Project RomaInterbellum. Roma Civic Emancipation between the Two World Wars, ERC-Advanced Grant no.694656, hosted by University of St Andrews.

DOI: https://doi.org/10.30965/9783657790302

Bibliographic information published by the Deutsche Nationalbibliothek

The Deutsche Nationalbibliothek lists this publication in the Deutsche Nationalbibliografie; detailed bibliographic data available online: http://dnb.d-nb.de

www.schoeningh.de

Cover design: Celine van Hoek, Leiden
Cover illustration: “Down with racial differences!” Gypsy demonstration in front of the National Assembly after 9.IX.1944. Source: ASR, f. Photos
Bulgarian-English translation: Aleksandar G. Marinov
English language editing: Savelina Danova
Production: Brill Deutschland GmbH, Paderborn

ISSN 2702-5020
ISBN 978-3-506-79030-9 (hardback)
ISBN 978-3-657-79030-2 (e-book)

Content

Acknowledgement

This book is written and published as a part of the research project *Roma Interbellum: Roma Civic Emancipation between the Two World Wars*, which was funded by the European Research Council (ERC), under the European Union's Horizon 2020 Research and Innovation Programme (Grant Agreement No. 694656). The content reflects solely the authors' view, and the agency is not responsible for any use that may be made of the information it contains.

Foreword

This book is the first publication from the *Roma History and Culture Book Series.*

The Series's overarching goal is to incorporate Roma history and culture into the mainstream of European and global academia. To achieve this goal, the *Roma History and Culture Book Series* will publish books from a wide range of disciplines that offer innovative, critical, and, above all, reliable insights into the history and culture of the Roma (formerly known as 'Gypsies'), relying on critical rereading and rethinking of historical sources and existing research. This approach marks a critical turn in the academic studies of Roma history and culture. This scientific field had been blighted by myths, stereotypes and misinterpretations all too often in the past, which created serious obstacles for the development of modern academic knowledge as a field in its own right.

The Series challenges the prevailing academic narratives, which present the Roma as a disengaged, marginalised community, a passive object of governmental policies, by analysing and contextualising the agency of Roma as actors in their own right, with their own views and visions for the development of their communities. In this way, the books published in the *Roma History and Culture Book Series* contribute to making the Roma voices heard and to understanding the Roma views. This approach is conducive to the incorporation of the Roma past and present into the mainstream of European and global academia rather than the confinement of Roma history and culture into a narrow ethnic box as a kind of academic ghetto.

The Roma from Central, Eastern, and South-Eastern Europe are the academic focus of the *Roma History and Culture Book Series*. In addition, the Series aspires to cover the history and cultures of other communities that have historically been known under the general label 'Gypsies', such as the Sinti, Manush, Kale, Romanichals, Irish and Scottish Travelers, etc.

***

For us, the fact that the *Roma History and Culture Book Series* begins with Shakir Pashov's book *History of the Gypsies in Bulgaria and in Europe: Roma* is of particular, even symbolic, importance. Not only is this the first comprehensive book written by a Roma author and dedicated to the origin and history of the Roma, but it also has another, much more comprehensive and, above all, more significant meaning.

In recent years, a false stereotype has developed in academic work on the subject. It holds that for the history of the Roma, it is not necessary to know and use written historical sources because they are written by non-Roma and do not allow the voice of the Roma to be heard in history. The proponents of this theory insist on prioritising the oral history of the Roma. This mantra can be heard everywhere, and it is a direct consequence of another equally widespread false premise, namely that the Roma civil emancipation movement is a product of our time, and the Roma elite is a creation of the age of modern neoliberalism.

In previous publications, we have clearly demonstrated, based on a vast body of diverse historical sources written by Roma, that the movement for Roma civil emancipation is an integral part of the era of modern nationalism, and its origins can be traced back to the mid-19th century (Marushiakova & Popov, 2021; 2022). In the same way, the birth and development of Roma literature (in the broad sense of the word) is the product of this movement (Roman et al., 2021).

Against this background, and taking into account the existence of 22 Roma newspapers and journals as well as several dozen books by Roma authors published before the Second World War, it is absurd to insist on prioritising oral history in the study of the Roma (and yet, such views are dominating).

A leading position in the movement for Roma civil emancipation is held by the Roma civil elite, who generated and spread among their community the main ideas that shaped the movement. However, this Roma elite is not the outcome of social engineering, carried out through generous donations and dissemination of neoliberal ideas in the community by the respective donors (as they often like to point out) who eagerly play the role of the "big white brothers". On the contrary, the Roma elite emerged and developed over the course of generations in the Roma community itself. The present book by Shakir Pashov is one of the best illustrations in this regard.

During the preparation of this book, Dr Tomasz Koper, a member of the Romani Advisory Board of the *Roma History and Culture Book Series*, left us prematurely after a severe illness. We dedicate this first publication of the new *Series* to his memory.

Elena Marushiakova, Vesselin Popov, Sofiya Zahova
/Series Editors/

Preface

The present book is more or less unusual. Its core is an unpublished manuscript written by Shakir Pashov (1898–1981). Contrary to Mikhail Bulgakov's well-known dictum that "manuscripts do not burn", in practice, the discovery and publication of previously unknown manuscripts is a relatively rare phenomenon. Moreover, the book that we present is an unrevealed manuscript authored by a historical figure, relatively less known to the wide public but, at the same time, surrounded by various rumours, myths, and even mystifications.

It would be wrong to say that nothing has been written about Shakir Pashov so far, at least in the small circle of researchers of the Roma community in Bulgaria. His name and his activities for the civic emancipation of the *Gypsies* (*цигани* in Bulgarian, the official name of the community at the time, which was used by Shakir Pashov himself) in Bulgaria appear in academic publications – both in his country (Марушиакова & Попов, 1993; Мизов, 2006; Стоянова, 2017) and internationally (Marushiakova & Popov, 1997; 2017; 2021). These texts, however, feature Shakir Pashov's activities only as a fragment from the general historical study of the Gypsies/Roma socio-political movement over the years. The only exception in this regard is the book *Shakir Pashov – The Apostle of the Roma* by Lilyana Kovacheva (2003). Although this book is an important work, from today's point of view, it is incomplete and insufficient because it has not exhausted all available historical sources.

What was missing before the present edition was Shakir Pashov's own voice and narrative of the historical events in which he was not only an active participant but often the main driving force, i.e., his personal historical narrative. The purpose of this publication is to fill this gap by presenting Shakir Pashov's own texts and, most importantly, by making available to the public the manuscript of his book *History of the Gypsies in Bulgaria and in Europe: Roma.*

Shakir Pashov's present manuscript was preserved and provided to us by the late Gospodin Kolev, an important historical figure.

Gospodin Kolev was born in the town of Sliven in 1923 in a family of Roma textile workers (since the 19th century, many of the Gypsies in Sliven have been working in the local textile factories). When he was a high school student, he became a member of the Workers' Youth Union, a youth organisation of the Communist Party, and participated in the outlaw anti-fascist resistance (at that time, Bulgaria was an ally of Nazi Germany in World War II). He was arrested in 1942 and sentenced to eight and a half years in prison, serving part of his sentence in the prisons in Sliven and Varna. After September 9, 1944, when the Communist Party in Bulgaria took power, he worked as a member of the Regional Committee of the Workers' Youth Union in Sliven in 1944–1946 and as a Secretary of the City Committee of the Workers' Youth Union in Sliven in 1946–1947. He graduated from the Military-Political Academy and later from the Sofia University St Kliment Ohridski, Faculty of Law. Since 1947, he has been a political officer in the Bulgarian People's Army, where he reached the rank of lieutenant colonel. On March 18, 1958, he was appointed an associate in the Central Committee of the Bulgarian Communist Party, responsible for the work with the Gypsies in Bulgaria, and remained in this position (with short interruptions) until March 15, 1990 (Колев, 2003, 271–278).

Our conversations with Gospodin Kolev did not reveal how the manuscript of Shakir Pashov's book ended up with him. According to him, when he started working as an instructor (low nomenclature position) at the Central Committee of the Bulgarian Communist Party, the manuscript had already been in the archives of the Central Committee of the Bulgarian Communist Party. Presumably, Pashov had handed it himself in the hope that it would be approved and published. Currently, the archives of the Central Committee of the Bulgarian Communist Party are part of the Archives State Agency, but Shakir Pashov's manuscript is not there, and neither is it in the author's personal archive, which was preserved by his relatives. The manuscript was probably confiscated by the authorities because it seems unlikely that Shakir Pashov had not preserved a copy of his own work. It is not clear how many typewritten copies of Shakir Pashov's manuscript were printed out and where they can be found today (if they are preserved at all). In any case, Gospodin Kolev is the person who managed to preserve the text published here for future generations.

Shakir Pashov's manuscript *History of the Gypsies in Bulgaria and Europe: Roma* was written in Bulgarian. It is published in this edition in English translation, in its entirety, with minimal editorial abbreviations and corrections (corrected were only some typographical errors, grammatical and stylistic forms, and some repetitions were removed). In some cases, we made additions (in square brackets []) to clarify some words or expressions and indicate omitted text parts in repeated passages. We also changed the numbering of the individual chapters in the manuscript, as in the original, the listing is inconsistent.

The Bibliography prepared by Shakir Pashov as an integral part of his manuscript is quite far from the established academic standards used nowadays. We left it in its original form but complemented Shakir Pashov's references to authors in the text, with citations according to modern standards also in square brackets []. We included the cited titles in the general Bibliography.

The text is accompanied by short Comments, which explain some points that may not be clear in the manuscript of the book, as well as by some additional explanations of historical events and personalities mentioned in it. The academic credibility (from the point of view of the contemporary scholar achievements) of the stated facts and interpretations has not been commented on at all deliberately. The aim of the team that has prepared this publication is not to give an academic assessment of the work of Shakir Pashov but to present his reading of the history of the Gypsies, i.e., to publish the Gypsy historical narrative.

In the interest of a more comprehensive and thorough presentation of Shakir Pashov's written historical heritage, a number of documents have been added to his manuscript, in Annexe No. 1. He is the author of most of these documents or the main contributor to the documentation produced by organisations that he had established. These additional documents are accompanied by brief comments. Annexe No. 2 includes the text of Lilyana Kovacheva's book *Shakir Pashov – The Apostle of the Roma* in English translation, with some edits by the author. This text is important not only because it reveals some key aspects of Shakir Pashov's life and work but also because it testifies that Shakir Pashov's effort to create a genuine Roma historical narrative has been carried forward to the present day. Instead of a conclusion, this edition includes one of our works, which summarises Shakir Pashov's life and work and highlights his contributions to the Roma civic emancipation in Bulgaria.

It was very important for us to include below the words of Mrs Lilyana Kovacheva and Mr Aleksandar Marinov, who are representatives of two different generations of the new Roma elite. With their participation, this edition has given life to Shakir Pashov's hopes that the younger generations would continue his work.

We hope that our efforts in the preparation of this book have not been in vain and that the book will fill some significant gaps in historical knowledge of the past. Apart from the purely academic dimensions, this publication may have another, much broader social effect – to help the Roma in their civic emancipation movement, of which Shakir Pashov has been the forefather and which, unfortunately, has not yet fully accomplished the goals he had set. The future will show whether our aspirations were achieved.

Elena Marushiakova, Vesselin Popov

***

The memory of that day has faded. I was only five or six years old, and I vaguely remember the details, but I was very impressed by the excitement of my parents from the upcoming visit of a respected friend. They talked about him with the neighbours that he was a great man, and I expected to see a huge figure. I was surprised when I saw a very ordinary person who was not any different from the other Roma living in our mahala in Kyustendil. This ordinary man with an extraordinary soul was the famous Gypsy poet Usin Kerim. In his conversation with my father, the Roma activist Zhelyu Kovachev, he often mentioned the name Shakir Pashov. I hardly understood then what the adults were talking about, but I remembered his name as well as their words that "he was a great man".

In the 1990s, when I started teaching the Romani language at the school in our Romani neighbourhood, the mahala, in the town of Kyustendil, I was trying to find and give examples of successful Roma to my students. In the library, I found an issue of the newspaper *Nov pat* ('New Way', from Bulgarian) from 1974, published by the National Council of the Fatherland Front, with editor-in-chief Stoyanka Sokolova, in which there was an article about Shakir Pashov and a photograph of him (Вапирев, 1974, pp. 1–2). I asked my father if he knew Shakir Pashov personally, what he knew, and what he could tell me about him. That is how I found out that Shakir Pashov is from Sofia, that he has been a member of the National Assembly, the founder of the first Gypsy organisation *Ekhipe* ('Unity', from Romani language), and the founder of the Gypsy Theatre *Roma* and all this provoked my interest in Shakir Pashov's personality.

I asked for a meeting with Elena Marushiakova and Vesselin Popov, the authors of the book *The Gypsies in Bulgaria*, which is the first edition of this kind about the Roma in Bulgaria. They advised me where to find more information and documents about Shakir Pashov's work. And as the saying goes, appetite comes with eating, I was not satisfied with what I had collected, so I decided to look for his heirs and ask how they remember him as a father and a grandfather. I first met his son Neno in the Roma neighbourhood Fakulteta in Sofia, who spoke to me with details about the activities of the Gypsy theatre and the reasons for its closure. I was really lucky to find Neno and speak with him because shortly after that, he passed away. From him, I learnt that Shakir Pashov's archive and many of his photos are kept by Neno's niece, Shakir Pashov's granddaughter, Snezhana. She lived in Sofia with her grandfather till his last days, in Druzhba Housing Complex, Block 6, where many Roma still live today, and she had preserved his archive, which she gave to me, as well as many photos from her album. Snezhana also told me interesting stories about his life and work. I learned from her that Pashov had been interned twice and that his second internment in the village of Rogozino in the Dobrudzha region had been provoked by a report that he kept a photo of Tsar Boris III in his home, although a subsequent search did not discover the portrait. With tears in her eyes, she told me about Shakir Pashov's regret that he was respected by Bulgarians but betrayed by his people, i.e., the Roma. Snezhana also shared that Manush Romanov had asked her grandfather for forgiveness on his deathbed, and she wondered why he had not done so while Pashov had been alive.

After the meeting with Snezhana, I had with me Shakir Pashov's autobiography, his membership card for the *Union of Fighters against Fascism and Capitalism*, numerous newspaper clippings with his articles and interviews, posters and advertisements of performances at the *Roma* Gypsy Theatre, as well as many photographs from his social and family life. I also managed to collect stories of his contemporaries (Demir Aliev, Yashar Malikov, Sulyo Metkov and others), and that is how I got the idea of writing the book *Shakir Pashov – The Apostle of the Roma in Bulgaria* (Ковачева, 2003).

The book itself was dedicated to Shakir Pashov's 20th death anniversary. My idea was to show the life and work of a praiseworthy person who would serve as a role model for the Roma with his public activities; who laid the foundations of the organised movement of the Roma community in Bulgaria with numerous awareness-raising and educational initiatives and promotion of the Roma culture. The book is a fact-based scholarly work. In addition to the documentary materials, I also used stories about Shakir Pashov, and through the artistic style, I tried to take the readers to the times when Pashov was a child and a pupil, for which there is no other historical evidence.

While writing the book, I was impressed by the fact that despite numerous defamatory reports against Shakir Pashov from his "friends" who aimed at ruining his reputation and taking his place, he never responded with slander and defamation. He would endure the blows with dignity until the truth prevailed, and he was vindicated, albeit belatedly. I often remember the story told by Demir Aliev, a former school principal in the Fakulteta neighbourhood and a prominent Roma public figure, about how Shakir Pashov sold his personal motorcycle to finance the last performance of the *Rom*a Gypsy Theatre. The funding for the theatre was discontinued as a result of malicious reporting by people who were part of the theatre, which is so sad and unfortunate. It made a strong impression on me that Shakir Pashov successfully cooperated with both monarchists and communists in order to support the cause of the Roma, despite obstacles created by his colleagues. He was much envied, according to his granddaughter, because he was a well-set and handsome man with a stable family and enjoyed respect from Bulgarians. Pashov managed to overcome the hatred and the libels and established an organisation, a newspaper, and a theatre; he helped the establishment of schools and community centres in the Roma mahalas and organised football tournaments; these activities gave him the opportunity to attract followers and associates.

After the presentation of my book in Sofia, some Roma activists from Sofia were angry that a woman from Kyustendil took the liberty of writing about the great Shakir Pashov. I heard expressions: "Why should she write about Pashov, we know him better than her; it should have been us, not her; she should have written about the locals from Kyustendil". At first, it was difficult for me to comprehend such reactions, but eventually, I realised that the people who made the harshest critiques were among those who had written the defamatory reports against Shakir Pashov. My reply today is the same as it was before: The more books are written, the better; if I had not included, or if I had missed, due to ignorance, key moments of his life, they could also write; it is their right.

For me, Shakir Pashov is the Apostle of the Roma in Bulgaria -- an exemplary person who spent his life in dignity and active work for society; an activist in his heart and soul. He is a role model as a Roma activist for the younger Roma generation. I believe that the first book about Shakir Pashov had its impact because many students from the country and abroad who write academic works on topics related to the Roma community in Bulgaria contacted me to order copies of the book. Also, many Roma activists from other countries were interested in the book, which was published in Bulgarian and Romani. A Roma organisation from Albania contacted me with a request to translate the book into Albanian, to which I consented. In the last couple of years, many young Roma, especially those active in Roma NGOs, have been eager to find the book, which, however, is no longer available although it had a relatively big circulation. Often, when I meet Roma from other cities in Bulgaria, they greet me and say that they know me because they have read my book about Shakir Pashov. I remember once, while I was travelling by train from Sofia to Dobrich, a boy who passed by my compartment, looked at me, and after a while came back with two other girls and asked me if I am Lilyana Kovacheva – the author who wrote the book about Shakir Pashov. I will not hide that such events make me happy and proud.

On the eve of Shakir Pashov's 40th death anniversary and the 20th anniversary of my book about him, the *Initiative Group for Roma Culture*, of which I am a member, donated a portrait of him to Todor Kableshkov Primary School in the largest Romani neighbourhood in Sofia, Fakulteta. Shakir Pashov turned the first sod in the construction of the school. The Initiative Group intends to submit a request to the Sofia Municipality to rename Todor Kableshkov Primary School and the main street in Fakulteta after Shakir Pashov.

In the times after Shakir Pashov, many Roma activists have worked for the civic emancipation of the Roma community in Bulgaria. Following the publication of my book about Shakir Pashov, several other works dedicated to important personalities of the Gypsy/Roma movement were published: *A Gypsy in the Central Committee of the Bulgarian Communist Party* and *The Bulgarian Communist Party* and *the Gypsies in the Period 1944–1989* by Gospodin Kolev (2003; 2010), as well as my books *The Rom Knows the Way* and *The Kovachevs*

Family, Kyustendil (Ковачева, 2000; Kovacheva, 2000ab; Ковачева, 2020). However, these editions are by far sufficient. There are many other Roma whose life is worth writing about, including Rusi Zabunov from Shumen, Dimitar Golemanov from Sliven, Manush Romanov, Pavel Ivanov, and many others who have contributed to the Roma cause. I really hope that Roma university students, who are the future elite of our community, will understand the importance of such books and will write about the people who dedicated their lives to the advancement of the Roma community. These people have been forgotten; calling attention to their life and work would allow young people to learn about them and carry on their legacy. There is no better motivation for the young generations than the inspiring examples of the old generations of Roma activists. Such books challenge the long-standing negative stereotypes about the Roma; they reveal the authentic insights, values, and character of the Roma community. I believe and I am convinced that books written by Roma about Roma are very important for both Roma and non-Roma, for history studies, and for science in general.

I am happy that I had the opportunity to join the team who prepared the present book about Shakir Pashov. This edition of the book presents unknown until today historical documents that have complemented and enriched the first edition. I knew that Shakir Pashov had written a book entitled *History of the Gypsies,* but I was unable to find this manuscript. That is why I am glad that, thanks to Elena Marushiakova and Vesselin Popov, we have the opportunity to become familiar with this relic.

Good luck with the new book, and hopefully, it is not the last!

Lilyana Kovacheva

***

Shakir Mahmudov Pashov's (sometimes spelt as Pashev) *History of the Gypsies in Bulgaria and in Europe: Roma* stands out for many reasons and can have various interpretations depending on the audience. Before you, dear reader, start reading this historical work, I would like to share briefly the insights that I, a relatively young Roma academic, have about it. My own understanding is that the book aims to portray the Roma, referred as *Tsigani* (popularly translated as 'Gypsies'), as a group of people who have positive contributions to society, superb talents, honour, a dignified past, and a history that deserves to be told. Even though some of us might feel like hiding their Gypsy identity or adopting a different (non-Gypsy) identity, Pashov's work underscores that we should not be ashamed of who we are because the Roma possess valuable characteristics and they have an important role in our civilisation. Pashov had an optimistic view of the Roma and vested his hopes for a brighter future of the community in the young generations. On several occasions in the book, the author expressed his hope in the Roma youth and stressed the importance of working with them. He described them as progressive, brave, capable, and forward-looking, and believed in their potential to build a bright future for the Roma in Bulgarian society. He trusted that the young generation of Roma would have a better life.

The publication of this book aims to raise awareness among today's and future generations of Roma, scholars, and society as a whole, about Pashov's personality and legacy. Unfortunately, Shakir Mahmudov Pashov's personality and work for the advancement and emancipation of the Roma in Bulgaria are familiar only to a small circle of people. He is largely unknown and forgotten by the Roma, and especially by today's Roma youth and intelligentsia in Bulgaria. What is missing in the historical narrative is acknowledgment and respect for Shakir Pashov's role in Bulgarian history and especially in the history of the Roma in Bulgaria. Pashov was one of the earliest, most active and successful leaders of the Roma civic emancipation in Bulgaria and in Europe, and deserves to be remembered as such.

Pashov was working on his historical book for several years. In the beginning of his monograph, he explains that he had been discussing the idea of writing a book about 'the Gypsies' with his contemporaries for several years before he actually began working on it. In fact, even during the most difficult periods in his life, when he was struggling to secure the livelihood of his family, he did not stop talking with friends about his work and dedication to the educational advancement and development of the Roma. As he explains in the Foreword, even as a soldier in the First World War, in the trenches, under shelling and bombing, he kept talking about his favourite subject – the situation and the problems of the Roma in Bulgaria and the need to build an organisation. In this most difficult time of his life, he gave a promise to himself and to his friends to write a book about the history of the Roma, as it had been told among the Gypsies for generations and centuries.

Shakir Pashov's book aims to tell the history of the Gypsies in Bulgaria and in Europe but does not deal in depth with the history of the Gypsies in Europe. He writes about Gypsies in Austria, England, France, Germany, Greece, Italy, Romania, Spain, and the USA, among others, without providing a comprehensive historical picture. The lack of in-depth analysis of other countries is understandable given the limited written and oral historical sources at the time. Overall, Pashov's history book is a revolutionary work because it was written by a person who had dedicated his life to the emancipation of the

Roma in Bulgaria and advocated for their rights, interests, and public image, and ultimately for the improvement of their situation. My reading of the book is that it seeks to raise the spirit of the people who identify as 'Gypsies' and give them a sense of pride and dignity that they are not "a people without a history". The book focuses on a critical moment in the history of the Roma: the active formation of nation-states on the Balkans, after the First World War and the dissolution of the Austro-Hungarian, the Russian and the Ottoman empires. In this period, the process of nation building determined who does and who does not belong to the nation in the new nation-states. In this context, Pashov's work is unique and revolutionary because it seeks to disseminate knowledge, raise the spirit and pride of the Roma, and define a new, dignified position for the Roma in Bulgarian society.

I know about the personality of the Roma leader Shakir Pashov perhaps as much as someone who has made an effort to learn or a scholar who has taken interest in the history of the Roma mobilisation movement. Unfortunately, Pashov's name has been forgotten, and it could be brought to light only when someone studies historical sources and archives. For example, if someone seeks information about the Roma civic movement, political situation, and representation, at the birth of the modern Bulgarian state, they would come across some of Pashov's achievements and contributions in these areas. His legacy and contribution, however, have not been sufficiently publicised.

My research on the Roma civic organisations in Bulgaria in the interwar period has provided me with the opportunity to learn more about Shakir Pashov's tireless work and legacy (Marinov, 2020a, 2020b). While studying Roma newspapers and other editions, I learned about the organisation *Common Mohammedan-Gypsy National Cultural, Educational and Mutual Aid Union in Bulgaria*, which was headed by Shakir Pashov, and about its founding members listed in the Constitutive Meeting protocol of December 25, 1933 with their registered addresses (CSA, f. 264, op. 2, a.e. 8413, l. 28). To my surprise, these addresses are located in an area a couple of blocks away from where I grew up (Stamboliyski Boulevard), and close to my grandparents' old house and the birthplace of my father – Tatarli Street in today's Roma mahala *Konyovitsa* in Sofia. This fact sparked my interest and I made some inquiries with my grandmother and my father. My grandmother, known by most Roma in Sofia as Chala, easily recognised the names of the organisation's founding members, which I read to her. She told me that her family and Shakir Pashov's family knew each other because both families lived in *Boyana mahala* (today Gotse Delchev neighbourhood) in Sofia, and she remembered that he had led a Romani organisation. She told me that Shakir Pashov had bought her father's house, and she remembered his wife and his children. My father,

Georgi Marinov, remembered Shakir Pashov as a person who was extremely devoted to and honest about his work for the betterment of the situation of Roma in Bulgaria and in other countries. He was "always well-dressed and was respected by both Roma and non-Roma", my father explained. Interestingly, when Shakir's eyesight weakened with the age, he used to ask my father to come to his house and read newspapers to him. My father also remembered reading to him a passage in a newspaper about a Roma painter, reportedly from France, who had called for the formation of an independent 'Gypsy' state. Pashov was so much excited by this information that he asked my father to read it over and over again. A simple and quick inquiry like this, with the elderly people in my family, was enough to cast light on Pashov's personality and his genuine love and dedication to the Roma in his native country and beyond.

The more I learned about the turbulent past of the pioneer of the Roma emancipatory movement in Bulgaria; about the hardship in his life; his visionary hope to unite all Roma in Bulgaria, regardless of their beliefs, professions, affiliations or geographical location; and his passion, charisma, and drive, the more I wanted to tell everyone about Shakir Pashov. Incidentally, 40 years after his death, and about 64 years after he had written the monograph, which is presented in this edition, I was invited by Elena Marushiakova, the Principal Investigator in the project *RomaInterbellum: Roma Civic Emancipation between the Two World Wars*, to transcribe and translate his book in English. It was a real honour for me to undertake this task, and I did it with a great pleasure and love. This was my tribute to the continuation of Shakir Pashov's work (just as my father had helped him read in the later years of his life). Moreover, by joining the publication team, I helped with making the book accessible to a greater audience and had the opportunity to express in public my gratitude for Pashov's work for the Roma.

Shakir Pashov is largely unknown to the Roma in Bulgaria, but not due to restrictions on the freedom of speech as Tahir claims in one of the few articles written about him (Тахир, 2020). The responsibility for this situation is entirely ours, of the Bulgarian Roma and leaders, because his legacy could have been publicised through countless platforms and channels. Let us not leave our past in history and make sure that no Roma youth, anyone from the Roma intelligentsia in Bulgaria, or scholar in Romani Studies, is unaware of the lifelong contributions and sacrifices of the visionary Shakir Mahmudov Pashov. We hope that this first publication of Pashov's work would enlighten and inspire the Roma to live up to their potential, talents, and legacy of contribution to society.

Aleksandar G. Marinov

ШАКИР М. ПАШОВ.

починал на 73 год. възраст
на X. 984 год.
(роден 19[illegible])
в Соф[illegible]

И С Т О Р И Я
на
ЦИГАНИТЕ В БЪЛГАРИЯ И В ЕВРОПА.

"Р О М А"

СОФИЯ, 1957 ГОДИНА.

SHAKIR M. PASHOV

HISTORY OF THE GYPSIES IN BULGARIA AND IN EUROPE: ROMA

SOFIA, 1957

PREFACE

It is not an easy task to write a complete history of the Gypsies because the sources are very scattered, and it takes a lot of work to collect them systematically and precisely. That is why I worked for many years until I collected the materials. I would be happy if I achieved my task, at least to some extent.

There are no details about the exact place in Asia from which our compatriots started their trip to Europe. There are, however, indirect data that allow us to establish that with some approximation. Comparing the manners, customs, and way of life of some Indian tribes in general, we can already say with certainty where the Gypsies had come from because these manners, customs, religious and other beliefs have been preserved to this day among our compatriots. Even though everywhere in Europe, our compatriots were a minority element, they did not succumb to assimilation but firmly preserved their national character. Other nations were unable to make any impact on the spirit of our compatriots. The majority of the Gypsies converted to Islam and others to Christianity [1]. The Apostles and the Imams spread their religious enlightenment to our tribe, among others, which from times immemorial had its own written history whose origins are lost in the Biblical legend of the Flood and Noah's Ark that had stopped on Mount Ararat.

Regardless of whether they were free or enslaved, our compatriots' way of life and national character remained intact. They followed their customs, religious rites and national epic with amazing stamina, even though they went through burning hardship.

States emerged and disintegrated. Some peoples merged with others, adopting the language of one people and the state system of another. Our people, however, did not merge with others and remained as they had been when they left India. What must be strongly emphasised is the fact that our people never waged wars of conquest. They lived in peaceful co-existence with all nations. Settling in a country, our compatriots devoted themselves to peaceful and creative work. For centuries, we had lived amongst peasants and citizens in different countries, and our metal products brought benefits to them, especially to the peasants. In Europe, we found the wooden plough and made an iron tip on it that made it easier for the farmers to cultivate the land. Our compatriots made horseshoes for cattle, made various household tools such as axes, hoes, adzes, etc. We were the first to import bronze into Europe and begin its processing [2]. Gypsies were mainly engaged in tinsmithing, mining, comb-making, and basket-making, and they were one of the most active traders in metal products. They also made copper cauldrons and sold them to towns and villages. What makes the Gypsies distinctive is their peaceful spirit. They never fought wars of conquest; they were and remained peaceful and loyal citizens of the countries in which they lived. What is most characteristic of our compatriots, however, is their musical talent. Unattainable are also the Gypsy dances. The original music of the Gypsies is so powerful and captivating that even now, it is sought and listened to with great interest by all nations of the world. Our national songs inspired great composers and gave them a foundation on which they built their musical creations. There is almost no nation in the world that possesses songs as pleasing to the soul as the Gypsy songs.

My compatriots, who had heard from me the history of our tribe many times, insisted that I should write everything that I had learned from our centenarians and collect it in one book so that everyone could be enlightened about our history. Initially, I thought to do this only for Bulgaria, but when I started looking for and collecting materials, I realised that it would be better to expand my idea and give historical data about the Gypsies throughout Europe. This idea came to my mind one winter a few years ago during an incidental meeting at the Sofia train station. I had gone to the station to see a friend who had to leave for the countryside that evening. I was looking for him to borrow some money as I had no job and did not have a penny in my pocket. I was quite dispirited that I did not find him because I was hoping that he could and would help me with a small loan to meet my basic household needs. At home, my children were expecting me hoping that I would make them happy upon my return. The cold north wind was blowing relentlessly, and I felt as if a heavy stone was pressing my soul. Freezing on the platform, desperate that I had not found my friend, I walked to the station buffet to warm up. But what could I do at the buffet without a penny in my pocket? Deep in thought, I leaned against a pillar, and my eyes filled with tears. I was taken away by heavy thoughts. I did not even notice the excitement of the people on the platform at the arrival of the conventional train from Istanbul. Distracted and indifferent while watching the crowd, I took myself back to 1929 when I returned from Istanbul. I hesitantly headed for the exit. I raised my hands to warm them with the breath of my mouth and accidentally pushed a citizen who was coming out of the buffet at that moment. I was just about to say the usual "Sorry" when I recognised one of my very close friends.

"Oh, Ramcho ..."

And he called at me in a low voice.

"Oh, Pasha ..."

We greeted each other warmly and kissed brotherly.

We started a conversation on various topics, and soon we came to our favourite topic about our organisation, which took care of the cultural and educational enlightenment of the Gypsy tribe. We imperceptibly moved on to an episode from the last World War, when a large number of enemies were stationed against our army unit. In the trench, there were several of us -- Ramcho, Emcho, Bilalov, Naydo, Raycho, Bilal, Asen and Palyacho, as well as the writer of these lines. At one point, we noticed that a shadow was moving towards us from the opposite side. Ramcho was the first to open fire, and I followed him while Emcho, Bilalov, Naydo, Raycho and Palyacho loaded the bombs. The enemy's grenades started falling around us. At one point, Emin stood up and threw several bombs whose terrible crash tore the darkness of the night. An enemy grenade fell nearby and threw soil on us. We shook off and noticed that Emin was lying, squirming, and soon he started screaming in pain. I approached him and saw that he was wounded in the right leg above the knee. A strong stream of blood rushed from the wound. I called Bilalov, and we quickly bandaged the wounded comrade with a clean towel, which I tore from one of my shirts which I was carrying in my backpack. Emin was lifted and taken to the rear.

We gathered again and continued our conversation on the issue of organising our Gypsy minority. We always discussed at length this topic in our meetings, and my friends asked me to promise that if one day I returned home alive and well, I would write the history of the Gypsies as it was passed down from centenarian to centenarian, from father to son and from grandfather to grandson. I made a commitment because I realised that it would be good to gather all the materials on the history of the Gypsy minority in one book. I worked for many years because my task was not easy. I leave it for my readers to determine whether I have succeeded with this task.

I have taken all information in my current work from foreign and Bulgarian authors as well as from legends and myths that I struggled to assess so that they have real value. I have also used our national folklore – tales, songs, proverbs, riddles, customs, religious rites, and manners. I tried to give credibility to the information so that my work would be a real source tomorrow for those who would try to write something about the life of the Gypsy tribe. If I succeed in this task, I will be very happy. I have fulfilled my duty as much as my ability and knowledge allowed me.

The author

TO LOVE AND TO PRESERVE OUR NATIVE LANGUAGE

The Gypsy language ... It had come to us through the centuries – a lighthouse and a sword, sharpened and hardened in struggles, in spiritual battles. It is the shining shield of their thought.

Oh, you are beautiful, our native Gypsy language. You reflect the spirit, kindness, and nobility of our people, their temperament and life, their sense of simplicity and grace. You are playful, like the Gypsy songs, agile and lively like the Gypsy dances. Through you, oh sweet native Gypsy language, we dream, through you we express our deepest feelings, through you we love and adorn our beloved with the most tender names. You can encompass our whole life, all our reveries, dreams, and deeds.

You have gathered the charms of our original homeland India; the silence and the magical beauty of the jungles; the cheerful noise of the mountain streams; the quiet serenity of the lakes; the wonderful songs of the majestic forests; the azure of the transparent sky of India.

You are filled with the warmth of the south. But you, oh sweet native Gypsy language, also bear the harshness of the north.

The history of the Gypsy language is glorious, majestic, and enlightening because it is seven thousand years' old and although it was not written, it survived extinction. It is full of examples of the highest patriotism.

Solely through you, oh glorious native language, have we preserved our national identity. Solely through you did we glorify the name of the Gypsies throughout the world because through you, oh kind and dear native language, we captured the soul of mankind, singing our Gypsy songs with their unsurpassed beauty. Anyone who has heard our songs could never forget them because they are graceful, playful, cheerful, and lively, just as the Gypsy people themselves.

Language is the pride of every nation. It is one of its hallmarks and a celebration of the nation's cultural development. The love for the native language is an integral part of the patriotic upbringing of the people. And that is why our patriotic feelings oblige us to love and preserve our wonderful native language.

CHAPTER I
THE ORIGINAL HOMELAND

Until recently, there were different opinions regarding our original homeland. Some claimed that it was India; others, that we had moved with the troops of

Genghis Khan; and still others, that our origins should be sought in Egypt. It is interesting that each statement has its reason and arguments. The lack of clarity on this issue, is due to the lack of a Gypsy script. Our tribe did not leave written heritage to draw information from and to guide us to the acceptance of one of the three theories above. However, thanks to Gypsyology scholars, our origins have gradually become clear. Now, it can be stated with certainty that our tribe came from distant India. Prior to this determination, there were two opinions that competed for plausibility. One was that of Benaventura Vulcania (who died in 1614) who claimed that our origin was from Egypt, and the other was that of the German linguist A. F. Pott [Pott, 1845], who claimed, and rightly so, that the Gypsy origin was from India. As of now, Pott's theory is considered the most positive because he found that the Gypsy language is closely related to the Sanskrit language. That this is the case is proven by the language of the Gypsies from Sofia, which has a striking affinity with the Old, Middle and New Indian languages. Pott's claim is supported by the fact that some customs of the Gypsies from the recent past showed similarities with [those of] some of the tribes of India. For example, Gypsies had until recently the custom of vowing their newborn children to one another, i.e., they were engaged while still in diapers – something that still exists today in some Indian tribes. Indians also have the custom of making freckles on their foreheads. This custom has been preserved to this day among the Gypsies in Bulgaria and in Europe. In some Indian tribes, until today, weddings last for three days. It was the same in our country until a few years ago. Other arguments in support of Pott's theory can be found in the similarities of the Gypsy way of life as a whole as well as in the similarities with the Indian tribal names. The Italian name of the Gypsies is *Zingaro*, which is very similar to the name of a tribe on the river Ind – *Changer*, a wandering tribe. Already Pliny [the Elder] was familiar with the existence of the tribe *Singe, Singane, Singani* at the mouth of the same river, and with *Chingaleze* or *Lingaleze* on the island of Ceylon [3].

A comparison is drawn between the Indian castes *Paris* – the poor, the Armenian name for Gypsies *Posha*, and the Georgian *Bosha*, a despised, mixed caste with great musical inclinations, which we observe in all Gypsy tribes. All of this, no doubt, comes in an obvious way to confirm that Pott's theory of our origin is the most plausible. Indeed, the Gypsy language has some linguistic differences with the language of the Indian tribes. This circumstance, however, can in no way undermine Pott's theory because we must bear in mind the fact that thousands of years had passed since our emigration from India. We, unfortunately, have not lived as a compact group, at the same place; we did not have a Gypsy script; and finally, no matter how much we preserved our language, we did not shield it from some influences by the peoples among whom we lived temporarily or permanently; it is irrelevant. This is the explanation for the linguistic differences with some Indian tribes.

CHAPTER II
IMMIGRATION FROM INDIA

There are no precise and clear data from which to judge at least the approximate date of the immigration of the Gypsies from India. The information is quite contradictory, and anyone who takes a certain position on this issue does not provide convincing arguments. However, comparing the different opinions, one can come to some conclusions, at least approximately. The German, Hasse [Hasse, 1803], believes that we arrived in the south-eastern parts of Europe around the 5th century BC. The best Gypsyologist, Pott, however, believes that the Gypsies did not arrive in Europe before the 15th century because he considers all the data in this regard to be insufficiently convincing. He claims that the country they certainly passed through is Iran. Miklosich thinks that the Gypsies came to Europe around the 10th century. His assertion is based on linguistic and grammatical considerations. However, when he learned that the Gypsies had certainly lived here since the 7th century, he assumed that the immigration could have taken place earlier.

The Czech, P. J. Ješina [Ješina, 1886], insists that the Gypsy musicians moved from India to Persia around 420 AD and from there to Phrygia and Lycaonia in the 7th and 8th centuries.

There is evidence suggesting positively that the immigration of the Gypsies from India did not happen all at once. Another part of the Gypsies is known to have left their Indian homeland in the 13th century when Genghis Khan marched there. These Gypsies, according to Ješina, passed by the Black Sea and entered Moldavia and Wallachia, from where in the 14th century, they conquered Thessaly, Epirus, and Corfu. Here, as almost everywhere, they won the love of the local population so that Thessaly began to be called Great Wallachia.

Quite implausibly, some believe that the Gypsies immigrated from their original homeland of India by sea. In support of this view, an archbishop from York drew attention to the pirates, the *Chingalezes* of Ceylon, and the *Sinds* of the Sindhu River. He believes that the Gypsies left India by sea, heading to the east coast of Africa, to the Red Sea and Egypt, and from there scattered to the north and west. As much as we have reason to consider this view, we must refrain from accepting it as truthful because the observation of the spiritual aspirations of the Gypsies never revealed anywhere, even the slightest aspiration to the sea. Nevertheless, the Gypsies are known everywhere as honest and hard-working people without an affinity for adventure and piracy. In those times, when the emigration of the Gypsies took place, the transportation of such large masses of people required a large fleet, the existence of which in that epoch is out of the question. To transport 50–60,000 Gypsies by sea, a huge navy would be needed to carry not only the people but also the provisions needed for such a long sea voyage. On this basis, we will have to reject the opinion that the Gypsies emigrated by sea.

The Dutch scholar J. de Goeje [de Goeje, 1903] asserts that the Gypsies immigrated to Egypt, or to the west in general, through the Arab countries. Miklosich, while opposing such a view, acknowledged J. de Goeje's thesis. Among the numerous words that J. de Goeje translated from Arabic was the word *muhto* which means *suitcase* (*chest*) for the Gypsies from Sofia.

Bonaventura Vulcanius' [Vulcanius, 1597] theory about the Egyptian origins of the Gypsies has already been abandoned. He relied on the language, and his translation from, for example, the Nubian language, i.e. the Coptic language, found that the words were closely related to the respective Gypsy words. For example, the Nubian *dad* – father, the Gypsy *dad* – in the same sense; *yag* – fire, in Gypsy language *yag* also means fire. From this, Vulcanius concluded that the Copts and the Gypsies were one and the same people and that their homeland was Egypt. Later on, however, a basic study found that the "Nubian" words that were studied were not used by the Copts but by the Gypsies in the land of the Copts. Another reason to believe that the Gypsies came from Egypt is the name of the Gypsies which reminds us of the Egyptian people – for example, the Bulgarian *Agupti, Guptsi*. This assertion is objected on the grounds that no words in the Gypsy language are related to the Coptic language. The origins of our name may be related to the fact that the Gypsies had stayed in Egypt for some time.

Some others point to the similarities in the life of the Gypsies and the Egyptians. For example, in the Holy Scripture it is stated: "I (God) will scatter the Egyptians among all nations; I will scatter them in various lands". Proponents of the theory of the Indian origin of the Gypsies argue that the similarity in everyday life is not reliable proof, while the similarity of words in the Gypsy language and in the ancient Egyptian language could be just a game of chance.

Jacob Goar [4] believes that Egypt was only a station for the Gypsies during their immigration from India to Europe, but it is not in any way, nor could it be, their homeland. In this sense, there is a message from Vulcanius, which says that in the 15th century, the "Nubians", i.e. the Gypsies, moved from "lower Egypt", through Asia Minor, the Bosphorus, and reached as far as the Thrace and the lands around the Danube. The most authoritative Gypsyologist, Pott, however, believes that the Gypsy language does not give reliable and positive evidence that it resembles the Egyptian language. He also claims that the theory of the Egyptian origin of the Gypsies did not originate from the Gypsies themselves but was adopted by them.

According to the Indian theory of the origin of the Gypsies, on their way to Europe, they probably passed through Iran. This is what Pott concluded on the basis of the Gypsy language in which he established many elements of the Iranian languages: Old Bactrian, Persian, Afghan, Kurdish and Ossetian.

The Gypsies from Sofia, with some linguistic peculiarities, confirm Pott's opinion.

The residence of the Gypsies in Mesopotamia is presumed, especially recently, but it has not been unequivocally established. According to those who support Pott's theory, the Gypsies, in their wanderings from India to Europe, remained in Armenia for a longer time [5]. And for this theory, there are some linguistic data from the Gypsies in Sofia. For example, in Gypsy *vogi* means *soul, godi – mind, brain,* and in Armenian it is *vozhi, ozhi.* In Gypsy *tagar* [means] *king*, in Armenian [it is] *tagavor*; in Gypsy *gras* means *horse*, in Armenian, it is *grast*; and others.

It is believed that in the 7th century, the Gypsies moved from Armenia to Byzantium where we already find written data about them. The information refers to the period from the 7th to the 13th century. Thus, under Emperor Nikephoros (802–811), the Gypsies, as can be seen, paid attention to themselves; under Michael (811–113), the Gypsies were exiled; while under Michael II (820–829), the Gypsies, on the contrary, gained influence even in the imperial court. After that time, there is no information about the Gypsies in Byzantium.

Information about the residence of the Gypsies on the island of Crete has been preserved. Here, they were met by a Franciscan monk in 1322. They were a wandering tribe and considered themselves of the Ham kin; they had tents (çadır), in the Arabic model, which served as their home. They professed the Greek Orthodox faith.

From the same period, there is information about Gypsies on the island of Cyprus, who were known under the name of *kilindzhiridis* – masters of swords, and also on the island of Rhodes – *kalaidzhii* (tinsmiths).

Interestingly, although disputed, is the information that the Balkan Gypsies were known mainly as blacksmiths. It is also claimed that they have something in common with the old metallurgists in the Aegean Sea basin.

CHAPTER III
THE GYPSIES ON THE BALKAN PENINSULA

The Gypsies moved to the lands of the Balkan Peninsula probably, in the distant past. There is some confirmation of Miklosich's opinion about the migration of the Gypsies from Greece to western and northern Europe.

The borrowings in the Gypsy language from ancient Greek, and especially from modern Greek, have been studied by Pott and Miklosich. Miklosich, for example, lists 20–30 borrowed words that he has found in most Gypsy dialects in Europe. He has also noted the influence of Greek grammar on the Gypsy language.

A Gypsy, who has been a prisoner of war in Greece during the First World War, believes that the Gypsy language in Thessaloniki is an "old Gypsy" language.

Linguistically, the dialect of the Gypsies in Sofia is close to Miklosich's Greek-Gypsy language, but it is not far from the Czech-Gypsy language.

An edict of the Wallachian voivode, Mircea, from 1370, mentions *Atsigani*, who were given under the authority of the monastery of St Anthony in Voditsi.

There are also *Atsigani* in the Peloponnese [peninsula]; in 1398, the Venetian Governor of the city confirmed their privileges that had been granted by his predecessors.

A document by Catherine of Valois (1346) mentions *Vageniti* on the island of Corfu. Under Vageniti, it seems, would have to be understood Gypsies, who later, in 1370 and 1373, moved from the peninsula to the island of Corfu and, at the end of the 14th century, formed the nucleus of a piece of property, designated in 1386 as *Feodum Atsiganorum*.

All these sources do not refer to the Gypsies as newcomers in the [Peloponnese] peninsula but as sedentary inhabitants, serfs or people with certain privileges. However, when exactly did the Gypsies come to the Balkan Peninsula, from where and in which country first, these questions cannot be answered accurately and positively.

Paul Bataillard thinks that they first came to Moldova, Wallachia, Bulgaria and apparently to eastern Hungary, but does not say any date. Ješina holds the same opinion, adding that [from] Wallachia, they invaded the Peloponnese, Epirus, and Corfu in the 14th century, apparently influenced by the above-mentioned information about the island.

Miklosich, probably influenced by linguistic considerations, believes that the country in which the Gypsies first arrived was Greece, or rather Byzantium, where the Gypsies were known as early as the 7th century. It was not possible to consider another Balkan country because, in this case, it would have been difficult to explain the huge influence of the Greek language on the more recent Gypsy language. The Slavic borrowings in the Gypsy language, which are 649 words according to Miklosich, did not give complete proof that the Gypsies had borrowed from the Bulgarians, for example, because there was no specific Bulgarian connotation in these borrowings. The loan words were also found in Romanian, and one possibility is that the Gypsies borrowed them from that language.

The following circumstance is also important in determining when the Gypsies came to the Balkan Peninsula and whether they had been for a long time in the Balkan countries: the Gypsies have their names for almost all Balkan peoples, while the Turks, for example, have only one word – *raya*. The Gypsy word *das* means *Bulgarian, balamo* – means Greek, *Gadjo* – means Romanian [6], *khorakhai* – means Turk, *chindi-chibengoro* (with severed tongue) – means Albanian. There are also special relations between the Gypsies and the Balkan peoples: among Greeks, and especially among Romanians, the Gypsy feels at home; they are indifferent to the Turk; the Albanian is disgusting to him. There are also Gypsy local names: *Anatolate* – Asia Minor, *Poravdi* – the Bosphorus, *Kalo-Deryav* – Black Sea, *Parni-Deryav* – the Aegean Sea, *Tuna* – the Danube, *Polina* – Constantinople, *Moldova* – Moldova and others. Sofia, for the Gypsies is a *bari dis* (big city), Bulgaria – *Daskanipe*, but almost never used. The Gypsies treat Bulgarians as masters nowadays. They have a vague idea about the Wallachia: they often compare their language with *vlaxich/s/ski*, which seems to be not so much Wallachian but a name like *pavazas, burgudzhides, yerlides*. When it comes to the settlement of the Gypsies on the Balkan Peninsula, one should not forget the existing belief among the Gypsies themselves that they came here, supposedly brought by Genghis Khan. There are almost no Romanian elements in the Sofia Gypsy dialect; instead, there are many Turkish ones, which are also used to some extent in the Bulgarian vernacular.

CHAPTER IV
SETTLEMENT OF THE GYPSIES IN BULGARIA

What has been said so far about the settlement of the Gypsies on the Balkan Peninsula also applies to a large extent to Bulgaria. In this respect, of relevance is the information about the island of Corfu, according to which in 1370 and 1373 the Gypsies moved to the island from the neighbouring Slavic-Bulgarian region of Vagenecia.

Vulcanius claims that in the middle of the 15th century the Gypsies were expelled from Egypt, and they invaded Bulgaria. This information we put in question because the data on it is not definite.

Gypsy legends hold that the Gypsies came to Bulgaria almost simultaneously with the fall of Bulgaria under Turkish slavery. As this information has not been confirmed either, we consider it doubtful. In this respect, however, there is preserved information about the Gypsies from 1606 in the Vlach-Bulgarian charters, issued by [Yuriy] Venelin [Венелин, 1840]: *atsigani, tsigani* [i.e. Gypsies]. Later, already in the 18th century, the Gypsies are mentioned in the history of Father Paisius [7]. He considers that their origin is from the Hamites tribe of Canaan. It seems that Paisius probably knew about the Egyptian theory, whether directly from Vulcanius or indirectly. Soon after our national historian Paisius, the Englishman William Marsden [Marsden, 1875] compiled a small dictionary of the Gypsies in general in the then-Turkish empire.

The Franciscan Pizzicannella [8] gave information about the life of the Gypsies in the village of Ladzhene, Svishtov region, in 1825. They lived among Paulicians [Roman Catholics], Orthodox and Turks and practised mainly magic. This was the main occupation of the Gypsy women, who, together with their husbands, took care of earning money for their families. The Gypsy women carried around iron and copper products made by themselves and their husbands, as well as copper cauldrons. The Gypsy men themselves dealt mainly with blacksmithing and were of great benefit for the local Bulgarian agricultural population. They made hoes, iron elements for the wooden ploughs, and axes.

In more recent times, we already have written sources about the Gypsies in Bulgaria. For example, we have information about the Ottoman Gypsies in Mihail Kogălniceanu [Kogalnitchan, 1837], Ami Boué [Boué, 1840] and others. Linguistic and other folklore materials about the Thracian Gypsies were published in 1870 by the Greek A. G. Paspati [Paspati, 1870]. We have an ethnographic essay on the Gypsies in Bulgaria published by our compatriot S. P. A. Borov in the Constantinople Bulgarian magazine *Chitalishte* [Боров, 1870].

From what was left about the Gypsies by our national historian, Paisius, we see that he was a supporter of the theory of the Egyptian origin, while Borov supports Pott's theory of the Indian origin of the Gypsies. From these two comparisons, we can conclude that Bulgarian Gypsyology goes hand in hand with European.

Borov writes that "The Gypsies in Serbia, Macedonia and Bulgaria were settled near the big cities and villages, or they were travellers. In Wallachia and European Turkey, the Gypsies are Christians, while another part of them are

Muslims. In Bulgaria, the Christian Gypsies wrote in Bulgarian letters, read in Bulgarian and were settled."

This is a very interesting finding about the influence of the Bulgarian language at a time when the Bulgarians themselves were in slavery. This information, given to us by Borov, should be deepened and studied to clarify the extent of this influence.

Felix Kanitz [Kanitz, 1882–1887] gives us many interesting data about the Muslim Gypsies in Northern Bulgaria, again in ethnographic terms. He claims that there was a significant number of Gypsies in Bulgaria, around the Danube. He also claims that the Gypsies must have been in these lands for centuries. If we accept this statement of the Austrian Felix Kanitz as true, we will have to reject resolutely the theory that the Gypsies settled in our country almost simultaneously with the fall of Bulgaria under Turkish slavery. In all probability, Kanitz is right because, given the information about the presence of the Gypsies in the 7th century in Byzantium, it is obvious that from there, they could easily move to Bulgaria. It is not possible to believe that when they came to Istanbul, the Gypsies finally stopped here and did not take to the north again, to the Danube. This eternally mobile and tireless tribe would not stay in one place at that time. In smaller or larger groups, the Gypsies moved all over Europe, and in the early days of their resettlement, they did not settle for a long time almost anywhere. From this finding, we can draw the conclusion that since we know positively that the Gypsies were in Istanbul in the 7th century, we have every reason to assume that they could and did penetrate Bulgaria at the same time. So, for the settlement of the Gypsies in Bulgaria, we can say that they were here at the same time at which they were in Byzantium, i.e. in the 7th century. Starting from here, we can now definitely oppose the theory that the Gypsies resided in Bulgaria almost simultaneously with its fall under Turkish slavery. It is obvious that the Gypsies moved to Bulgaria much earlier, and from here, they continued their journey to the north and westwards to Europe. Perhaps, Bulgaria was for the Gypsies, like Egypt, a temporary station through which they passed and travelled further to Europe. Naturally, not all Gypsies who came to Bulgaria left it to continue their journey to Europe. Many of them stayed here and remained forever. This was undoubtedly influenced by the fact that they found here primitive farming, they found the wooden plough. For them as blacksmiths, there was a wide room for earning their livelihood, and they stayed in Bulgaria, probably welcomed with joy by the locals for whom the Gypsies were of great benefit because they made many of their agricultural tools. This explanation could be accepted because it corresponds to the then economic situation of Bulgaria.

Figures for the Gypsies in Bulgaria are given by St. Zahariev [Захариев, 1870]. They pertain to the first years after our liberation from Turkish slavery [9].

K. Jireček [Иречек, 1876] also gives us [figures] about the Gypsies in Bulgaria in the first years after the liberation.

In 1912, on the other hand, the British Bible Society published the Gospel in Bulgarian-Gypsy language, which appears to be in the Lom-Gypsy dialect, with a Latin transcription. This translation by an unknown author [10], is used today in the Lom region, and partly in the Kotel region. The publication of that Gospel [11] in the Gypsy-Bulgarian language marked the beginning of the Gypsy written works in Bulgaria, a fact that is known by few.

Subsequently, after the liberation, many works have been written about the Gypsies in Bulgaria.

There were explorations focused specifically on the language of the Bulgarian Gypsies. In this respect, the first one was Prof. St. Mladenov [in] *Introduction in the General Linguistics* [12].

Concluding the chapter on the settlement of the Gypsies on the Balkan Peninsula, I believe that the Gypsies moved to the Balkan Peninsula almost simultaneously with their arrival in Byzantium, that is, around the 7th century. All other theories, however widespread, are untrue. It is difficult to believe that, given the fact that there were Gypsies in Byzantium as early as the 7th century, they did not continue north to the Balkans immediately afterwards. This vigorous tribe that would not settle for long almost anywhere at that time, could not have settled permanently in Byzantium without making excursions to other countries, especially to the nearby Balkan Peninsula. And when they came here, on the Balkan Peninsula, and especially in Bulgaria, they found the promised land in which the locals had primitive farming. They then began to forge farming tools and were of great benefit to the local population, which in turn welcomed them warmly because the Gypsy blacksmiths made their work easier.

CHAPTER V
INFLUENCE OF BULGARIAN ON THE GYPSY LANGUAGE

The numerous borrowings from the Bulgarian language in the Gypsy language fall into two groups. One group contains words that have probably penetrated more recently. These are, for example: *bregos* – бряг (shore), *prahos* – прах (dust), *orlos* – орел (eagle), *makos* – мак (poppy), *paltos* – палто (cloth), *bikos* – бик (bull), *platos* – плат (cloth), *svetos* – свят (world), *koliba* – колиба (hut), *chavka* – чавка (jackdaw), *kana* – кана (jug), *lopata* – лопата (shovel), *masa* – маса (table), *boya* – боя (paint) and much more.

The other group contains words with a Bulgarian element, words that are more or less Gypsyfied. For example: *pishime* – written, *zagradime* – enclosed, *krastime* – baptised, *pozhaltisaylo* – yellowed, *sluchisaylo* – happened, *kupate* – together, and the like.

The large number of Bulgarian loan words in the Gypsy language, especially from the vernacular, testifies to the strong influence that the Bulgarian language had on the Gypsy, and more specifically, on the dialect of the Sofia Gypsies. There is, by the way, a reverse effect, of course, to a lesser extent.

Information about the Gypsies from Sofia is available from K. Jireček in his travel notes from Bulgaria 1878–1884. According to him, they lived in small houses, outside the city, along the road to Lom, today's Grobarska Street. In Bulgarian, they called themselves *tsigani*, in Turkish *çingene*, and earlier – *kıbt* (gyupti). Most of them were Muslims and spoke Indian language. They were engaged in blacksmithing, pottering and music-making. On holidays and official celebrations, along with the Bulgarian and Jewish craftsmen, there were also Gypsies, always with a red flag [13]. Most of them were Muslims, but their religious notions were not clear. They celebrated St George's Day and St Basil's Day very festively, and they also celebrated the God-Bearer [Theotokos], although they professed the Muslim religion.

We can judge about the extent to which the Bulgarian language has influenced the Gypsy language by the fact that when the Gypsies speak, a Bulgarian who listens can guess the meaning of half out of a dozen words and their speech becomes almost understandable. This is due to the great closeness that existed between the Bulgarians and the Gypsies and their almost friendly relations. The Bulgarian peasant farmer was grateful to the Gypsies for making tools and baskets for him; for shoeing his cattle; for supplying him with copper cauldrons; for making spindles and spoons; and treated them friendly. The Gypsies, on their part, had rightly assessed the fact that they found a livelihood in Bulgaria; they were grateful to the Bulgarians, and thus a friendship was established. In addition, due to the democratic nature of the Bulgarians in general, the Gypsies were placed here at almost the same level, socially almost no difference was felt, at least as far as this applies to the two nations themselves, and especially to the Bulgarian people.

CHAPTER VI
RELIGIOUS BELIEFS

The Gypsies profess mainly two religions – Muslim and Christian. Undoubtedly, the Muslim one is predominant. They came Muslims and Christians from their original homeland India. It is true that many of them were baptised here, in the states where they settled to live forever, but they practised these two religions while they were in India. Their religious concepts are not very clear even for themselves. As we mentioned above, the Gypsies celebrate, and very festively, St Basil's Day, St George's Day, the God-bearer.

They did and have been doing until today the so-called *peperuda* to stop the drought and bring rain [14].

They strongly believe in ghosts, *talasami* [goblins]. The national Gypsy folklore, especially their tales, are full *of samodivi* [fairies], *zmeyove* [dragons], *talasami* [Goblins], etc. [15]. They believe in the rebirth of the soul, even though they are Muslims. Those Gypsies who are Christians, bury the dead in a Christian way, in a coffin. *In Muslim burials, the corpse of the deceased is wrapped in a white cloth* [16]. They put stones on the graves that are usually without an inscription, *although inscriptions tend to appear of late* [17].

Neither Muslims nor Christians do attend mosques and churches. They have a Gypsy Imam (called *Hodja*) who performs their marriages or attends funerals, but there is no Christian priest. The Hodja performs the so-called *syunet* [circumcision] [18] for 10–12 year-old boys.

CHAPTER VII
SOFIA GYPSIES

K. Jireček says that during his trip around Bulgaria, he saw Gypsies near Sofia, living in small houses. Some of them had pitched tents that served as their homes. These tents were usually set up by the travelling Gypsies in spring and summer on the meadows near Sofia. In 1880 their number was 788, and in 1920 – 2,664 according to nationality, and 2,582 according to language.

The first mention of the Gypsies as inhabitants of Sofia dates from 1571. According to Jireček, they came to the Balkan Peninsula from India through Egypt, in the first half of the 14th century.

The Sofia Gypsies are not called *Gyuptsi* anymore; this name is used for the Macedonian Gypsies.

The Gypsies of Sofia do not use *Tsigani* as their tribal name. They say, "Our name is Roma". It feels as if they find something undesirable, even offensive, in the term *Tsigani*. And this is exactly how it shouldn't be. We, the Gypsies, have no reasons to be ashamed of our name because we have not tarnished it with anything. The Gypsy people are hardworking, peaceful, and progressive; they work hard and are not ashamed of doing any honest work that would ensure the livelihood of their family. The Gypsy is curious, naturally musical, and if so far he has not moved forward with other nations towards progress and civilisation, this is due to the situation in which our people have lived for so many years. In capitalist and bourgeois settings, the Gypsy had indisputably slavish conditions. Like the Bulgarian workers themselves, the Gypsies were subjected to cruel and ruthless exploitation. In this situation, although the Gypsies had the sympathy of the people, they were subjected to real discrimination by the bourgeois government, although according to the constitution they were equal citizens of the country. Naturally, in such situation, they were not able to unfold their national genius in its true breadth and power. The bright mind, the unbreakable vitality, and the cheerful disposition of the Gypsies are elements that open up an easy way to progress for them. In addition, their almost unmatched diligence enables the Gypsies to get involved in all areas of work. Gypsies have a tender attachment to their family, which is usually a numerous one. They have many children and caring for them takes up valuable time that they might otherwise devote to some cultural aspirations. And this is especially noticeable after the historical changes in Bulgaria after September 9, 1944. It is no longer a rare phenomenon to meet on the streets children, young and old Gypsies with books for reading in their hands.

Undoubtedly, the Gypsies in Bulgaria had given many valuable contributions, which, unfortunately, were not published in the press or made public by word of mouth so far. Even before the liberation of Bulgaria, the Gypsies, and especially the Orthodox ones, had made a great contribution to the national liberation movement of Bulgaria. During the establishment of the revolutionary secret liberation committees, Vasil Levski, Hadzhi Dimitar, Panayot Hitov, Georgi S. Rakovski and others, found great acceptance and protection from the Gypsy Orthodox minorities. It has been proven that when Vasil Levski came to Sliven to meet with members of the Secret Revolutionary Committee in the city, he slept over in a Gypsy house. The supporters of Panayot Hitov in the Sliven Balkan mountain were Orthodox Gypsies who had a sincere and deep commitment to the liberation movement. And Georgi S. Rakovski found refuge, protection, and faithful accomplices in the Kotel Balkan mountain among the Orthodox Gypsies. Hadzhi Dimitar was a close friend of the Orthodox Gypsies in Sliven and went to collect firewood with them in the Balkan mountain. We will talk about this activity of the Gypsies in a special chapter.

The Gypsy blacksmiths in Sofia have the name *burgudzhides*, and the tinsmiths – *pavazi*. Both the *burgudzhis* and the *pavazi*s seem different in language from the real Sofia Gypsies who also call themselves *yerlides*.

The Sofia Gypsies lived in the past and continue living to date, mainly on Zhdanov Street [19], on the main Tatarli Street and on its sections. In this place are nestled their small but tidy houses. It seems that in the past there were no other artisan shops except the farriers. Most of the Gypsies from Sofia work as bearers. Some of them are shoeblacks, but there are also merchants. However, they had, albeit rarely, a cart and horses. In the past, there were Gypsies with carts and horses who led a nomadic life, but gradually, over time, they settled with the rest of the Gypsies and stopped their *chergarstvo* [i.e. nomadism]. The term *chergarstvo* comes from the fact that travelling Gypsies made tents out of *chergi* [rugs]. In the Gypsy neighbourhood, the people speak Bulgarian, Turkish and Gypsy languages. The Gypsy language is spoken almost exclusively by women who are not very sociable; the Bulgarian language is very well-known, even by children, and only the older Gypsies speak Turkish. "We are *karmakarashık* [i.e. mixed]", the Gypsies themselves explain their ethnographic origins. This was, of course, years ago. Now the Gypsies have their own national language, their own national honour. Their children study in high schools and universities along with the Bulgarian youth. Officially, the Sofia Gypsies are Muslims, although Christianity is making serious conquests among them. For example, there are families in which the parents are Muslim, while their children are baptised Christians. In general, the Sofia Gypsies are at a crossroads. The men, who took part in the last war, noticeably have something like Bulgarian nationalism.

During and after the liberation, the Sofia Gypsies occupied the following neighbourhoods in Sofia:

1. Chaush-pasha mahala with about 60 houses in the today's area between St Sofia church and the former State Printing House.

2. Sheh-mahala also numbered about 60 houses, the inhabitants of which were mostly musicians. It was located in today's Slaveykov Square, as well as around the neighbouring streets.

3. Chukur-mahala with about 50 Gypsy straw houses. This mahala [neighbourhood] was mainly engaged in blacksmithing and tinsmithing. It was located in today's Georgi Dimitrov Square.

4. Mahala Hadji Manov's bridge, which had about 40 houses, was located in the area of the today's Lion Bridge. The population in it was engaged in blacksmithing and served the citizens and peasants with their metal products.

Prof. Ishirkov says that, according to all sources, the population of Sofia at the time of the liberation was very diverse. Apart from the native Bulgarians, there were also many Jews, Gypsies, Turks, and others.

In 1837, the French traveller, Ami Boué, counted about five thousand houses with a population of about twenty thousand inhabitants. The streets of Sofia were narrow and very crooked, but that did not prevent him from predicting the future of the city, which was the crossroad of more than six roads.

On January 1, 1881, the first census took place in Sofia. According to it, the population was about 21,000, including the garrison.

The composition of the population by ethnicity was the following: Bulgarians – 14,000; Jews – 4,274; Gypsies (Muslims) – 1,258; Gypsies (Christians) – 788; Turks – 535.

With this composition of the population, it is obvious that the Gypsies were able to serve very well citizens and peasants alike.

Our compatriots made mainly the following agricultural tools: ploughs, ploughshares, sickles, axes, adzes, hoes, and many other agricultural equipments. They were also very successful in assembling the iron parts of the carts. They made cart axles and other iron items. Some of the more famous masters in this field at that time were the following: Tossen, Becho, Kine, Rustem, Tule.

The master Bashko proved to be an artistic master of the bridles and stirrups, who, after making the mentioned objects, tinned them, and they looked as if they were made of silver.

Several of our compatriots proved to be masters of hand-made horseshoes: Salcho Durov, Yusein, Monge, Rashid and others.

Today, our compatriot Ali Saliev Bozhkov is a famous orthopaedist.

And in terms of the good workmanship of oxen's hand-made horseshoes, distinguished were: Mato, Zinko and others.

During the construction of new railways in the young Bulgarian state, after the liberation, our compatriots also took an active part, and some of whom showed such dexterity and knowledge that they were awarded. These are Kurtish Kalendarov, Mahmud Pashov [20], Yashar Baryamov and some others.

Our compatriots dealt with various crafts. For example, they made hand-made shoe pliers, grater sheets, hand hammers and scissors. In this area, distinguished were the following masters: Ali Ahmedov and Dumir Rustemov.

Our famous musicians from 50–60 years ago, who entertained Sofia, were the following: Kanbur Murat, with his orchestra; Gyoko Baryam, Denko, Vule, Mele, Enken, Ismail, Yashar and Kurtish.

Karlo [Aliev], on the other hand, became extremely famous, as he was one of the first to play Bulgarian folk songs on Radio Sofia.

In 1908, in Sofia, several persons were distinguished as clarinet players: Lolo, Demir Cholaka and Yashar.

Ibrahim was distinguished as a great flugelhorn artist.

In Sliven, Vratsa, Belogradchik, Kula, Kotel and Lyaskovets, our compatriots managed to create very good orchestras.

In Plovdiv, Kolarovgrad [today Shumen], and Pazardzhik are the best Alaturka orchestras.

With the naming of our compatriots, distinguished craftsmen and artists-musicians mentioned above, we want to point out that the Gypsies in Bulgaria have made every effort to catch up in every respect with their compatriots from other countries. They tried not to lag behind their compatriots in other countries.

In 1882, according to the regulation plan of Sofia, the Sofia City Municipal Council decided to move the Gypsy minority from all mahalas to one common neighbourhood, located in the area of today's customs office, next to Kozloduy Street. In 1906, i.e. 24 years later, due to the increased needs of the Bulgarian Railways, the Sofia Municipal Council decided to relocate the Gypsy population to another common neighbourhood, which today is called Konyovitsa, located between Konstantin Velichkov Street, Ilyu Voyvoda Street, Zhdanov Street and Dr Kalnikov Street. There, the Gypsy population was divided into eight units; families were provided with yards of 200 square meters and with notarial deeds for them, on condition that they paid back the property in the course of one year at the price of 0.80 levs per square meter. Each unit consisted of 50–60 houses. Due to the increase of the Gypsy population, in 1929, the Sofia Municipal Council had to buy plots in the following neighbourhoods:

1. [Fakulteta] – under the faculty in Suhodolska River (3rd District) [21].
2. Boyana Meadows in 4th District, this is currently Emil Markov neighbourhood [22].
3. Slatina (5th District) [23].

About 10,000 Gypsies currently live in Sofia. Their main occupations are bearers, cart drivers, shoeblacks, blacksmiths, traders, and employees of various public departments and enterprises.

CHAPTER VIII
THE NUMBER OF GYPSIES IN BULGARIA AND WORLDWIDE

The number of Gypsy minority in Bulgaria is about three hundred thousand people [24]. They are scattered in all towns and villages of the republic. The biggest number of Gypsies live in Sliven, almost equal to the number of the Bulgarian population. There are about 12,000 Gypsies there, almost all of whom are Christians. After [the town of Sliven], a large compact group of Gypsies lives in Sofia, where their number is, as we said previously, about 10,000.

In 1935, the number of Gypsies worldwide was about 5,000,000. This information is published in the Encyclopaedia *Der Gross Brockhaus* in Leipzig, Germany.

Given the fertility of our compatriots, we believe that the number of Gypsies worldwide has long exceeded five million.

CHAPTER IX
SLIVEN GYPSIES

There are about 12,000 Gypsies in Sliven. In their larger part, they are Orthodox. They are employed mostly in industry and have proven to be exceptionally capable and fast-learning workers. Many of them are involved in various enterprises and their work is highly valued. Sliven Gypsies, and especially the Orthodox ones, have a high patriotic sentiment and are at the forefront of the progressive citizenry. In the liberation struggles before 1878 and in those before 1944, the Sliven Gypsies made high-cost sacrifices.

The Sliven Gypsies, and especially the Orthodox ones, were one of the most active allies of the fighters for national liberation in the formation of revolutionary committees before the liberation from Turkish slavery. It is known for certain that Vasil Levski often spent the night in a local Gypsy's house when he stayed in Sliven. Panayot Hitov's supporters in the Sliven Balkan mountains were Orthodox Gypsies. Georgi S. Rakovski was sheltered by Orthodox Gypsies in the forests of the Kotel Balkan mountains. Older people said that Hadzhi Dimitar was friends with the Sliven Gypsies and often went with them to collect firewood in the mountains.

Everything said so far makes it clear that the Gypsy minority in Sliven was highly patriotic people imbued with a revolutionary spirit.

After the liberation, a large number of the Sliven Gypsies, perhaps the majority, had progressive socialist views and strongly supported the struggle of the working class for our liberation from capitalist exploitation. The success of the Workers' Party [25] in Sliven in elections before September 9, 1944, was largely due to the support that the Gypsy minority gave to the Party.

After the invasion of the German invaders in Bulgaria, when the partisan groups appeared and the resistance movement in Bulgaria began [26], the Sliven Gypsies sided with the resistance and made any effort to support the partisan struggle. They sheltered partisans, and some of them joined the partisan units. The partisan struggle in the Sliven Balkan mountains would have been almost impossible had they not found the unreserved support of the Gypsy minorities, both in the towns and in the villages. The Gypsy minorities supported the liberation struggles wholeheartedly, and anyone contributed as they could. They were couriers and carried valuable ammunition for the partisans, messages, and orders from the centre and warned whenever police launched raids against the people's sons who hid in the mountains to fight against the German invaders and the ruling bourgeois class at home. In this regard, the Sliven Gypsies created monuments of unprecedented heroism, self-denial, devotion to the national liberation movement and great sacrifices.

They also showed great vigilance and ingenuity, tracking the routes of the police that attacked the people's sons who fought in the mountains. Thanks to this activity of the Gypsy minorities from Sliven and the Sliven villages, many important fighters of the liberation struggle were saved. In this respect, the Gypsy minorities from Sliven and the region made a valuable contribution to the resistance movement as factory workers; they also participated in the sabotage operations, organised support for the partisans with funds and provisions, and supported political prisoners and concentration camp inmates. In short, they were actively involved in the struggle and did not give up until they brought the battle to a successful and victorious end.

CHAPTER X
CULTURAL, PATRIOTIC AND REVOLUTIONARY EVENTS OF THE GYPSIES

The cultural, patriotic and revolutionary manifestations of the Gypsy minorities are indisputable, both before and after the people's victory of the September 9, 1944.

Even before the Liberation, the Gypsies made a great contribution to the national liberation movement. When the revolutionary committees were set up with the task to organise the Bulgarian people and the other poor classes in the struggle for liberation from Turkish oppression, the Gypsies were always at the forefront of this struggle. Along with their Bulgarian brothers, they worked relentlessly to raise the revolutionary spirit of the masses.

When the Russian troops entered Bulgaria to liberate their younger brethren from slavery, the Gypsies also took an active part in the war [27]. More than 80 Orthodox Gypsies from the regions of Sliven, Kotel and Elena, who unfortunately did not call themselves Gypsies but Bulgarians because they were Orthodox, took part in the Battle of Shipka. After the liberation, these Gypsies broke away from the environment of their people; they became friends with Bulgarians, started marrying Bulgarian women and calling themselves Bulgarians. Great persons originated from them. After the liberation struggle of September 9, 1944, which ended with full victory of the workers, many people from the ranks of the Gypsy minorities rose to high positions. Some became officers, others participated in the leadership of enterprises that they ran with great professionalism, still others headed institutions with great organisational tact and skill.

Gypsies also took part in the Serbo-Bulgarian war in 1885. Here, they showed miracles of heroism. Many of the Gypsies were awarded orders of bravery for their heroic deeds at Slivnitsa, Dragoman, Tri ushi and elsewhere. Most of these Gypsy heroes remained modest Bulgarian citizens, who never made a profit from their heroic actions. They did not seek rewards, and when they returned home alive and well, they devoted themselves to their peaceful occupations.

In 1912–1913, more than 4,000 Gypsy volunteers enlisted in the army to fight in the Balkan War. Most of them were included in the Third Balkan Division and in the Sixth Bdin Division. Most of them came from the following districts: Sliven, Kotel, Elena, Polyanovgrad (Karnobat), Lom, Vidin, Kulata, Oryahovo, and Vratsa. There were also Gypsy volunteers from Tarnovo and Gorno-Oryahovitsa districts. They fought heroically, and some of them laid their bones for the freedom of Bulgaria. The then army commanders, Generals Mihail Savov, Radko Dimitriev and the Governor of Lozengrad, General Georgi Vazov, referred to the Gypsy volunteer groups, which were mixed with the Bulgarian ones, as the elite troops of the Bulgarian volunteer units because of their heroism.

Sanitary Colonel, D. Dagorov, said in his report that during the outbreak of major epidemics at the front such as plague and cholera, which were then the biggest enemy of the Bulgarian army, the Gypsy volunteers were least affected because they were resilient, which is why they gave the lowest percentage of casualties and resisted the front against the enemy. The same sanitary colonel referred to them as "Balkan Prussians and Japanese" in his report. He called the white Gypsies "Prussians" and the black ones "Japanese". What motivated the young Gypsies to volunteer in 1912, was solely their strong love for their homeland and desire to support the liberation struggle of the Bulgarian people, which had risen to salvage their brothers from the oppressive Turkish slavery in Trace, an area populated for the most part by Bulgarians at that time. In this war, for the honour and glory of the Gypsy minorities, no one resorted to desertion, betrayal or deception; actively and with incredible heroism, they threw themselves into the war to defend the interests of the Bulgarian people and Bulgaria. After the end of the war, many of them were awarded orders of bravery; with their inborn modesty, they never sought benefits from the state but were devoted to peaceful and creative work. All Gypsy minorities, Orthodox and Muslim, took part in the War of 1915–1918 [28] and fought bravely and devotedly on all fronts. In his report to Ferdinand, the then Commander-in-Chief, General Zhekov, said that of all the minorities who took part in the war, the most courageous was the Gypsy minority, which showed no weakness and was always strong-willed and firm in the struggle. They were unpretentious and modest fighters who had only one goal – to be good soldiers. No petitions were made for them to be released from the front or to receive any other privileges, as other minorities did. They have always been on the front line of the battle.

Apart from their patriotic actions, the Gypsy minorities also had indisputable merits in the creation of the workers' trade union movement. In 1903, the late socialist leader Georgi Kirkov, who laid the foundations of the socialist movement in Sliven, worked mostly among the Gypsy minority, most of whom were textile workers. Georgi Kirkov found an enthusiastic and great reception among the Gypsy minorities who actively supported the socialist movement. In the elections for MPs in 1905, Georgi Kirkov was elected Member of Parliament, with the dedicated and loyal support of the Gypsy minorities from Sliven. In 1908, in the elections for municipal councillors, 100 % of the Gypsies voted for the socialist candidate for municipal councillor, Georgi Kirkov's student and Orthodox Gypsy, Nikola Kochev. Subsequently, Nikola Kochev became a member of the Central Committee of the Bulgarian Workers' Trade Union. He died in 1923 in the town of Sliven. His followers were Gypsy combatants, loyal and devoted to socialism: Vasil Chakmakov, Georgi Zhelezchev, Nikola Terzobaliev and others. The latter is still alive and is a member of the Central Council of the General Workers' Professional Union. The Gypsies were at the forefront of the competition for MPs, district councillors and municipal councillors not only in Sliven but almost throughout Bulgaria and especially in Kotel, Polyanovgrad (Karnobat), Plovdiv, Popovo, Ruse, Gorna-Oryahovitsa, Lom and [Veliko] Tarnovo.

In 1918, a Gypsy woman was killed in the women's revolution in Sliven [29], while at the rally in Sofia in 1919, a Gypsy man was killed on the crossing of Kiril and Metodiy Street and Slivnitsa Boulevard [30].

One of the great Gypsies who played a major role in the Karnobat region, and who was wholeheartedly committed to the communist movement, was the prominent Zhelyu Koev, from the Galata neighbourhood in Karnobat. He had a high school education and as an enlightened man he had great influence on the Gypsy minority not only in Karnobat, but in the whole Burgas district. Thanks to his efforts and devotion to the Party, he managed to integrate into the Party the entire Gypsy minority. He was also an army reserve officer.

The Gypsies had an outstanding contribution to the Great September Uprising in 1923. The struggle of the Gypsy minority from the Lom district, including the village of Mladenovo [31], the town of Lom itself, Metkovets, Brusartsi and others, will be remembered for generations. During these memorable days, the Gypsy minorities threw themselves into the fight against fascism with unprecedented heroism and fearlessness. The Gypsies from the Berkovitsa region, as well as the Gypsy minorities from the Mihaylovgrad district, were no less heroic during these events. Many of these Gypsy combatants were mercilessly killed by the raging fascism after the uprising was put down, while others emigrated. Those who failed to emigrate were thrown into prisons.

In 1923, the Communist Party prevailed in the elections for municipal councillors in the capital. The bourgeoisie was hoping to grab by force the votes of the Gypsies, but these hopes were severely crushed because the Gypsy minority in Sofia overwhelmingly supported the Communist Party.

In February 1940, in the elections for the 25th Ordinary National Assembly, all minorities were intimidated into voting for the fascist candidates. Other minorities, and especially the Jews, were really scared and voted for the fascist General Lazarov. However, the Gypsy minority was not afraid of these fascist threats and supported the Communist Party's candidate Dr Lyuben Dyukmendzhiev, who was eventually elected, to the great surprise of the ruling fascist clique. The Gypsy minority also supported the Party's candidate, Dr Nikola Sakarov, who was also elected.

In all elections during the fascist regime, the Gypsies overwhelmingly supported the Labour Bloc's candidates [32]. This is also what the Gypsies in Plovdiv did in 1938, resolutely supporting and electing the communist candidate Todor M. Samodumov.

From what has been said till now, it is clear that the Gypsy minority has always been on the side of the Party. They consider the Communist Party as their own and closest to their interests; they see it as their sole protector and patron, and that's why they wholeheartedly supported the Party in the past in all its struggles. The Gypsy minority is progressive in spirit. It serves the Party with love and faithful devotion because they know that it is the only one that honestly caters for their interests.

Apart from merit, however, we must sincerely and honestly admit that the Gypsy minority also makes mistakes which they must eliminate once and for all, and sooner rather than later. They need to become aware of their mistakes, acknowledge these mistakes and take on a new path that would secure their cultural growth.

These mistakes are not insignificant, and their elimination requires, above all, a deep awareness of the Gypsies themselves in order to overcome and eliminate them. One of these mistakes is that some of the Gypsies, and unfortunately, they are not few, are not involved in socially useful work but are prone to nomadism, vagrancy and petty theft. In the new situation which has been established in our country, this will be eliminated soon because the factors which secure for the Gypsies, as well as for all citizens and workers in the republic, the right to work, are all present. The second mistake, which in the new political and economic situation will inevitably be eliminated, is that the Gypsies did not aspire to education. This is gradually being removed because we already witness that the Gypsies are becoming educated. They attend libraries in big numbers, where they find books to read, and take them from the community centres to read at home.

The other part of the Gypsies, those who are Orthodox, live a totally sedentary life; they are also extremely hardworking, and earn their livelihood solely by work.

The first textile workers in Sliven and Gabrovo were Gypsies. The Gypsies are also good farmers, excellent blacksmiths, tinsmiths, and horse-shoe makers.

In the past, the Gypsies were also very good horse traders and were called *dzhambazi*. Due to the new economic system, this craft is gradually disappearing, and Gypsy traders are looking for new forms of labour. They started working in the factories, the plants, and the cooperatives; in the villages they are members of the agricultural cooperatives, where along with the Bulgarians, they work on the vast economic units. This collective work will further strengthen the ties between Gypsies and Bulgarians and will create brotherly relations between them, side by side, laying the foundations of the new socialist edifice in our country.

They are also good miners. Many Gypsies work in all the mines of the Balkan Mountains, and they are considered to be among the very good miners. In this respect, they are unsurpassed as workers in the Rhodope basin at Madan, Rudozem and others, who have done for centuries; now that the Madan basin has grown and developed to such proportions, the Gypsies have found a large field for their labour and their love of mining.

The favourite profession of the Gypsies, which very much corresponds to their inclinations, is a musician. And this is not only in Bulgaria but all over the world. Gypsy musicians are greeted with great interest everywhere, and their music concerts are attended in large numbers.

After the people's victory on September 9, 1944, dozens of Gypsy amateur groups were formed in our country; they travel across the country bringing pleasure, delight, and amazement to their listeners. The amateur Gypsy groups spread the unsurpassed beauty of Gypsy dances, called *kyuchetsi*, they present plays and organise wrestling fights, which attract thousands of spectators. Through these amateur groups, the Gypsies contribute to the spiritual growth of their listeners as well as their own cultural and educational growth. The people's government shows affection for these Gypsy amateur groups and makes great sacrifices to secure support for their progress.

In the last 20 years, the Gypsies have brought great benefits to the national economy. In all parts of the country, and especially in large industrial cities, all members of Gypsy families – men, the elderly, women and children, are involved in the collection of waste, such as rags, glass, bones, old tires, hardware, paper waste and other valuable waste materials. These waste materials are processed and from them new products are obtained, which are absolutely necessary for our economic growth. In times of war and in times of an economic embargo, these waste materials bring great benefits to our national economy, supporting our industry and crafts. Two-thirds of these waste materials are being collected exclusively by the Gypsy minorities and they secure hundreds of millions of benefits for our national economy. The collection of waste material is a big challenge for the people's government, because the waste material provides us with items for which we would otherwise have to pay valuable foreign currency in order to import them from abroad.

Not minor is the Gypsies' contribution for collecting herbs for export. The majority of herbal collectors in our country are Gypsy men, Gypsy women and Gypsy children who, with their activity, bring great benefit to our state economy. By exporting herbs, we earn valuable foreign currency, which we need so much when buying other items needed for our industry and occupations. Organised at the village cooperatives [33], the regional cooperative unions, and the Central Cooperative Union, the Gypsies diligently carried out all their tasks. With the care of the people's government, especially the young Gypsies, dedicate to socially useful work by collecting waste and herbs, thus contributing enormously to the consolidation of our national economy. The collection of herbs and waste has an educational role for the Gypsies, because, through the socially useful work, which earned their livelihood, especially the young people, gave up heft, drunkenness, gambling and debauchery, and set out on a new path, the path of the working people which is glorious for every honest person.

Whereas in the past, the private buyers of waste and herbs exploited the Gypsies and purchased the waste and herbs they collected at insignificant prices, now, under the people's government, they are protected from any kind of exploitation.

CHAPTER XI
GYPSY MUSIC

If there is one thing that the Gypsies should be most proud of, it is the Gypsy music. The Gypsies have an innate talent for music. They are great masters of all musical instruments. In many ways, they are true virtuosos of various instruments. They are equally good as violinists as clarinettists, flugelhornists, flautists, accordionists, etc. They are truly great Masters of Music. They often play without music notation, only by ear, and yet their performance is so accurate and true that it is simply amazing.

Imre Magyar's famous Hungarian Gypsy orchestras, consisting of 60 people, mostly a string orchestra, spread the fame of the Gypsies not only in Hungary but also abroad and there is not a single major European stage on which Imre Magyar did not perform. He raised the Gypsy music to such a level that his orchestra became a favourite throughout Europe.

And we have other master musicians who cannot be forgotten. However, we will talk about them in another chapter of our book.

The innate musical talent of the Gypsies is so great that it is enough for a Gypsy child to hear a song only once and they can immediately reproduce without mistakes.

All Gypsyologists who study the history of the Gypsies, searching for their origins, unanimously concluded that the Gypsies were a people with innate musical inclinations that no other nation had. In this regard, they assert that the Gypsies are of Indian origin, because there were tribes with innate, astonishing, musical inclinations.

That is why we believe that the Gypsy minorities should not look lightly and indifferently at the musical talent of young people but they should encourage them decisively, and make them learn and develop their talent in its true breadth. The Gypsy minorities and their organisations have a duty, an imperative duty, to urgently find these young people, and give them all kinds of material and spiritual support to encourage them to develop their talent. In such cases, they can turn to the People's government, which would give them all the facilities and comprehensive support in this regard. The musical talents of the Gypsy youths should not be allowed to perish without being utilised.

CHAPTER XII
GYPSY DANCES

Along with the Gypsy songs, there are also Gypsy dances. They are also world-famous and are watched with great interest by connoisseurs. Their dances are lively, cheerful, voluptuous. The Gypsy dance, called *kyuchek*, is especially famous. It is a voluptuous dance, through which the dancing Gypsy woman expresses various voluptuous scenes, in which, however, there is no cynicism, but real plasticity.

The Gypsies do not have their own folk *horo* dances. They dance a lot, and love the *horo* dances, but they usually dance the *horo* dances of the countries where they live. They bring in the *horo* dances vivacity and temperament because the Gypsies perform them with their innate liveliness and add their Gypsy temperament and character.

On the other hand, they have special elements in their Gypsy dance *kyuchek*, which they call "throwing a *gyubek*". These are especially beautiful, flexible, and virtuoso curves, which make the *kyuchek* dance infinitely interesting, juicy, and insatiably beautiful.

The Gypsies have the so called "peperuda [butterfly]" ritual in dry weather. The peperuda's girlfriends sprinkle her with water and the wet girl, covered with flowers, performs a dance praying for God's mercy for rain. The people who had superstitions in the past, liked the peperuda ritual; they would welcome the dancers with love and treat them with foods, which the peperuda performers would eat afterwards. [34]. After the dance, they would gather and make a little mu-man, which they would bury to appease the Gods [35].

CHAPTER XIII
AGUPTI BLACKSMITHS IN THE TOWN OF MADAN

The Gypsies, known as Agupti, live in the Rhodope region and until recently they lived in the town of Madan.

When they came to Madan and whether they are from the same group of Gypsies who settled in Macedonia allegedly in the 15th century, cannot be said with certainty.

The fact that in the Rhodope region they are called Agupti and in Macedonia – Gyuptsi, speaks in favour of the opinion that the Gypsies from Macedonia and those from Madan are of the same group. The similar names suggest some historical proximity.

The time of the Gypsy settlement in the Rhodopes can be established with positivity after a complete and comprehensive study of the history of the Gypsies in our country, their material and spiritual culture.

A complete, historical, ethnographic and linguistic study of the Muslim Gypsies in the town of Madan, and in the Rhodope region in general, would probably lead us to interesting conclusions, relevant to other important issues from the distant past of the Rhodope region.

This task has gained relevance today, when this area of the Rhodope region, and precisely this population, are being decisively transformed.

If we assume that the migration of the Gypsies to Bulgaria dates back long before the 15th century, we will have to accept that the Gypsies Agupti came to the Rhodope region before that time. The fact that an Agupti's legend holds that they were brought to the Rhodopes as captives by the Romans to cultivate the mines in this area also confirms our view about the earlier settlement of the Gypsies in the Rhodopes. These hypotheses, however, are not yet supported by research and we cannot accept them as true without verification. Our only clue is the name of the Rhodope Gypsies, who are called Agupti (Egyptians).

Here, for the first time, we come across materials dealing with the main occupation of the Gypsies – blacksmithing. The research on blacksmithing among the Gypsies can lead to interesting and important conclusions about the emergence and development of blacksmithing in general in our country.

The Gypsies who lived for centuries in the Middle Rhodopes and dealt exclusively with blacksmithing, are called Agupti, similarly to those in Macedonia, Gyuptsi.

It should be strongly emphasised that the Gypsies themselves associated their origins with some Egyptian slaves brought to these lands before Roman times, in connection with the processing of metals, mainly lead and iron. Whether this is a plausible story or rather some propaganda among the Gypsies themselves will have to be studied and researched. It is a fact, however, that they differ both anthropologically and in everyday life from both the Christians and Muslim Bulgarians. The Agupti do not mix with them even though the Bulgarians speak the same ancient Rhodope dialect as the Agupti themselves.

Their origin aside, these ancient settlers of the Rhodope region had the same political destiny as the population of today's Bulgarian lands. They became 'Slavs' and after about a century, when the Turks invaded and occupied the Balkan Peninsula, they converted to Islam and became so committed to their new religion that no one could dissuade them that they are the most faithful Muslims and the most righteous followers of the "din Islam" [36].

Nowhere else in the Rhodope region but in Madan, Agupti blacksmiths are concentrated in such big numbers. This fact about Madan, which was until recently a quiet Bulgarian village, mostly Muslim, and now it is one of the centres of the Rhodope mining basin, deserves an additional discussion.

There was human settlement in Madan already in ancient times. Many mining traces, probably left by the Romans, tell us about it. Many legends have remained since then.

For example, Nikola K. Varadinov said, "I have heard that once upon a time, long time ago, when the Romans brought the blacksmiths to Madan to work the ores of "Pachinsko" [locality], there was a large factory for lead smelting. The bellows of the factory was very large, comprising 40 buffalo skins, and it was made by the Agupti – the Gypsies themselves who mostly worked in the factory. Other foundry tools were also discovered in this place."

From the time of Christianity, before the Bulgarian population was converted to Islam, many Christian relics and memories have been preserved. Many ruins of churches and chapels can still be seen in the vicinity of Madan.

The population still tells Christian legends from the time of the conversion to Islam. A living memory from the Christian era are the numerous names of places and neighbourhoods with purely Bulgarian Christian names.

According to legends and memories of old people, 200–250 years ago Madan had a much larger population than the population recorded before September 9, 1944. The centre of the village then was not today's market (Oryaha), but the place where the school is, the current premises of the District People's Council. Old people say even today that there was a "plague" in Madan three times: around 1750, around 1800 and around 1836–1838. The third "plague" was the most devastating and claimed the biggest number of victims. The population was so frightened by the plague, which killed "both young and old", that people did not dare to visit their former neighbours, who had settled across from them on the slopes, and communicated with each other by shouting and knocking on boards.

It was not only the plague that reduced Madan's population. At the end of the 18th century, Mehmed Sinap raged in the Rhodope region and set on fire all the villages that did not obey him. Madan was not spared, and was burned. Part of its inhabitants were killed, the others fled to the mountains.

The conversion to Islam of the Bulgarian population of Madan, the attack and destruction of the place by Mehmed Sinap, and the outbreak of the "third plague" (around 1840), all took place in a short period of time. These three crucial events for the once large population of Madan were the reason why the population fled, scattered in 19 settlements, and sought refuge elsewhere.

The conversion of Madan's inhabitants to Islam took place much later than the mass conversion to Islam of the population in the other villages (1655–1661). Madan's inhabitants were converted to Islam mainly in the second half of the 18th century with great resistance on their part. Some fled far from their homeland, already terribly ruined; a larger part went to today's Devin district and, together with other settlers from the Aegean Sea, mostly from Drama, gave rise to today's village Shiroka Laka; while a third group was hiding for a long time in near and far places and forests.

Again, according to stories of old people, Madan had a very developed industry by 1850. There were about 150 workshops working with hydropower. These workshops produced various types of rifles (*tyufetsi*), knives and especially *karakulatsi* (large knives with black bone handles), mills for coffee and black pepper, hoes, shovels, nails, various types of knives, wrought iron bells (*tatralki*), and large wrought iron bells (*tyumbeltsi*), which were much needed for sheep-breeding and other agricultural tools. Until then, Madan was the industrial centre of the Middle Rhodopes. Today, only the memories of these industries have remained. By 1933, only the Zaimovi family, father, and son, from the Karyak mahala, dealt with it.

Against the background of Madan's history as a flourishing production centre in the first half of the 19th century, the fact that must be emphasised is that the main workers in this Rhodope's industrial centre were the Gypsies. They were excellent craftsmen and the main driving force of the production process at that time. Both the foundries and the workshops for rifles, knives, hoes, shovels, nails, and wrought iron small and big bells were occupied mainly by Gypsies. Their products were made and spread on all corners of the then-vast Turkish Empire – south to the Aegean Sea and north to the Danube. Experienced and skilled workers in the industry, the Gypsies have played a major role in the prosperity and development of the town of Madan. They also prepared weapons for the Wallachian army because the fame of the Gypsies as weapon masters transcended the borders of the Turkish Empire.

The *afuz* [37] Salihmed Gerchekov, a native of the village of Elhovets (Enuzdere), Rudozem municipality, and Imam in the town of Madan, tells the following about the industry in Madan and the vocations of the population by 1850:

> In Madan, a hundred years ago, many rifles and knives were made and sold to the Bulgarian population in old Bulgaria: in Sofia, Ruse, Varna and Vidin, on the opposite corner. The weapons were transported by a dozen mules and sold on the market within one hour. The Bulgarians bought it for the uprisings. I heard this from the old ones: from Mollahmed Ushev, from the mahala of Ardashla (Maglishta), and from Hasan Ushev, from the same mahala who died at the age of 110. At a young age, Hasan Ushev himself brought rifles and knives to old Bulgaria to sell them to the Bulgarians for the uprisings. Then they made mills for coffee. They wove different fabrics and sold them in Thessaloniki, Drama, Kavala. The fur was bought from the Aegean Sea as well as from here. And there were a lot of goats here then.
>
> The population, which was mainly Agupti, worked also in agriculture, but rarely; they sowed rye and maize. They were engaged in cattle breeding – sheep, goats, cows, mules. That was a hundred years ago.

Until the September 9, 1944, the population of Madan, which was majority Gypsies, was engaged in agriculture, cattle breeding and wage labour at the mines of the then Granostoid Company.

It is interesting to note, comparing the current size of the workforce in the Rhodope Basin, particularly in Madan, that until August 1, 1934, 80 Bulgarian Muslims worked in Granostoid Company, and after that August 1, there were 300 Muslims, mostly Agupti.

When we talk about Madan, about the inhabitants, about their occupations and their livelihood, we will have to focus on blacksmithing in the first place.

Until today, there are about 40 families of blacksmiths or about 200 people in Madan. They make a living mainly from blacksmithing, although they have small property -- one or two acres of weak, infertile land.

The Agupti blacksmiths live together, grouped in a neighbourhood located on a sunny hill facing the East. At the top of this hill chaotically perched are their huts, and at the bottom are their workshops, which form a whole bazaar, now mockingly called "the industrial neighbourhood".

The blacksmith's shop resembles a simple hut built with *chatvo* (plastered fence, covered with stone slabs (*tikli*). The blacksmith's workshop is usually 2 to 4 meters wide and 4 to 6 meters long. The workshops have no ceiling. They only have a roof. The doors are usually only on the West side. In most workshops, there is a "window" next to the door, i.e., an opening with a shutter. On the opposite side, usually in the East, there is one large hole (with a shutter) or two smaller ones. These windows do not have glass as they are not adapted for it, and are closed with wooden shutters. The workshops are not always covered with stone plates. Some of them are covered with planks, others – with various tins and boards, while some others – with straw.

The population of the Rhodope mountains calls these workshops *kuzni* [smithies]. That is also how the blacksmiths themselves call their workshops.

The interior of the workshop is also very simple. On the southeast side, in the corner, is usually the *odzhak* [fireplace], which occupies about a third and sometimes half of the workshop. The *odzhak* consists of bellows, an anvil, and a pit. The pit is a small trap with almost square dimensions: 50 by 60 cm deep and with the same width. The *odzhak* does not always have a pit. It is needed when the *odzhak* in the workshop is at the level of the ground. This way, the master does not have to bend too much when working on the anvil. In some smithies, such as those in Ustovo, where the *odzhaks* are built about one meter above the ground, there are no "pits". The pits are probably an indication of the antiquity of the blacksmith's trade, of course, in the Rhodope region.

The most important tools in the blacksmith's workshop are:

The anvil, which is called by the Turkish name *yorz*.

The bellows, which blacksmiths call *meh*. It was *aysty* in the old time. In old times, it was also called *kyuryuk*, in Turkish.

Some of the blacksmiths make their own bellows, but most of them order from local bellow masters.

Pliers, which are of several types: straight and curved, small and large. In most cases, blacksmiths make them themselves, but mostly they are bought ready from the market.

Scissors for cutting iron. The masters make them themselves too. They are made of steel; they are 30–32 cm long and 5–6 cm wide. They weigh about 2 kilograms.

Tongs. It is used for making nails. It is 21 to 24 cm long.

Gvozdilnitsa, or as blacksmiths call it *mohtach,* is the most important tool in making nails. The *gvozdilnitsa* is 25 to 30 cm long and weighs about one kilogram. It has the shape of a pipe. It is perforated at the twisted end. On the front part, where the nail is placed, the hole is wider, and on the other side it is smaller.

A small anvil (small *yors*) and a chopper. At the lower end of the ordinary anvil, the blacksmiths place a small steel rectangle, 3 to 5 cm long, 1 to 1.5 cm wide and up to 2 cm high. This device is called a small anvil (small *yors*) because the nail is hammered on it.

Chopper. Next to the "small anvil", the blacksmiths put a blade with the same length of the small anvil, but sharp – 1 mm. The blade is made of steel and is called *sechilka* [chopper] because the nails are cut on it.

Big hammer.

Small hammer.

Baksiya, a hammet with which axes are made.

A very large hammer with which the apprentice stands against the master.

A cutter, used to cut iron.

A small hammer with which the master hits.

Proboy, with which hole openings are made.

Nail pliers.

Extinguisher – a whisk with an iron rod. It is an iron whisk that ends in one of its ends with a vice. The length of the whole extinguisher is 25–36 cm.

Different types of rasps. They are used for sharpening axes, carpenters, hoes, knives, etc.

Gribach – an iron shovel. It is used for clearing fire.

Water trough filled with water for hardening the products.

In addition to the tools listed above, a blacksmith's workshop has other secondary tools and accessories, such as drills, various brooms, augers, shovels, coal cans, small hammers, etc.

CHAPTER XIV
BLACKSMITH'S WORKS AND THEIR MANUFACTURING

1. Nails (*gozde*). Used for livestock shoeing.

The nails are one of the most characteristic works and they give a "look" to the blacksmith's trade of the Rhodope Agupti – Gypsies.

2. Hoes or *motıki*, as the locals call them. They are made mostly in the spring, when the hard work begins, which is impossible without a hoe. There is no other tool in the agricultural work of the Rhodope population as necessary as the hoe. The Rhodope soil also contributes to this: on the one hand it is poor and sandy, and on the other hand it is steep, a plough cannot pass through it and therefore the soil is dug up and generally worked exclusively with a hoe, by hand.

3. Axes. The axe is the most needed blacksmith's work at any time of the year, especially in the autumn, when firewood should be secured for the winter and the leaves should be cut for the cattle.

The axes are usually made by two masters: one who works and directs, and the other who performs – he is the *chikidzhiya* – a worker who turns a big hammer.

The process of making the axe is the same as with the hoe, only it is slower. In one day, two masters can make two to three axes.

4. Horseshoes. Other blacksmith's works, which are very popular among the Rhodope population, are the horseshoes or, as the blacksmiths – Agupti call them, *petali*.

The blacksmiths Agupti work mainly the following three types of *petali*:

a) *petali* for donkeys which usually have the following dimensions: length 7–8 cm and width 5.5–6 cm. These horseshoes have two holes on each side for shoeing.

b) *petali* for mules. The usual length of these horseshoes is 10–12 cm and their width is 7.5–8.5 cm; the horseshoes for mules have six holes – three on each side.

c) *petali* for horses. They are wider than those of the donkeys and the mules. And they have six holes – three on each side. In the middle they have a hole 7–10 mm wide in diameter, which serves to "ventilate" the dead part of the hoof, in order not to become hot in the summer.

5. Ploughshares. In spring and autumn, the Agupti-blacksmiths also make ploughshares for the ploughs. They are mostly made of steel, called *chilik*.

In addition to the most important blacksmith's works, the master blacksmiths Agupti also make smaller objects such as: shovels for kneading trough; door latches; wide nails for decorating doors; various trivets and chains for cooking, trestles for lining wood (jack-horses); long nails (Agupi's nails) – in the past, used for nailing beams in house construction; various types of rings (for children's swings), for hanging meat and other objects; large rings for ploughs, rings for scythes and various other small and large devices related to agriculture, sock-breading, crafts and everyday life.

CHAPTER XV
LEGENDS ABOUT THE AGUPTI'S ORIGIN AND STATE

The blacksmiths Agupti are very rich in legends, tales, proverbs, and sayings, which are primarily related to their past, crafts and life.

The Agupti from the Rhodope mountains tell, for example, the following legend about the Agupti, about their former state and king, "It has been a long time ago – the old people tell it as a dream. The Agupti from Masır (Egypt) had a big and strong state. Firvalyu ruled, an evil and mean king. Everyone screamed, cried and ran away from him. Even the unborn children were screaming. He tortured his people. But Allah punished him, took his soul, and put him in hell. Our Agupte are also from this offspring."

There are many legends about the Agupti's origin:

a) "The Agupte – Egyptians. They brought them from Masır (Egypt) to these places. They were brought from Arabia. After the breakdown of the Roman state, they remained here and have worked as blacksmiths ever since. From Egyptians they became *Agupti*."

b) "The Romans conquered Egypt. The Agupti were brought as slaves by the Romans. This was many years ago, long before the emergence of Islam ... They are very emotional. They explode suddenly. Their blood is not like ours ... They are smart people. Smarter than the Jews. They are very capable working with iron – they have no equal. They can work in factories ..."

c) "Old times. We learned the craft from our fathers, they from theirs. That is how we found it and that is how we will leave it. Our people have come here a long time ago, it was like a dream. They were brought from Egypt."

d) "We are Egyptians. When the Egyptians fought in this place, they brought us and put us here and there to guard, as soldiers."

e) "As we hear from old people – we are from Egypt. We moved from there. We were brought in Roman times."

f) "We are Egyptians, an old tribe. The Romans brought us."

This legend has passed down to the Christian population too:

a) "The Agupti, these are the oldest inhabitants of Madan, and they themselves say this, I have asked them many times why they are called Agupte, and they answer that their ancestors and grandfathers were from Egypt. And since then, they have been practising this craft, blacksmithing. They are honest people, hardworking. They work from morning till night. There were no lies or thefts from them. This is about the past when Madan was a village and there were no outsiders yet."

b) "The Agupti are remnants of Egyptian troops brought from Egypt to fight in Greece and along Bulgaria's southern borders."

CHAPTER XVI
BLACKSMITHING IS FROM GOD

There are many legends about the Agupti, about their origin, date of settlement in Bulgaria and in the Balkan Peninsula, as well as about their main craft, blacksmithing. The following tales, which the Agupti blacksmiths tell, come to show us the affection and hope they have for their craft:

> Our craft, blacksmithing, is the most important and without it nothing can happen. Therefore, before the world was created, God created our craft, because nails are needed everywhere for hammering and for building. Shovels and hoes are needed to dig and plough the ground. *Petali* are needed to shoe the animals. Axes are needed to cut wood. Adzes are needed to make barrels and build houses. Knives are needed for everything. God left blacksmithing as a gift to man. Nothing can happen without blacksmithing.
>
> Our craft does not make a person rich, but it does not leave them hungry. Put the copper vessel on the fire and the hominy will come. Our craft is blessed by God because you only rely on your own hands.

CHAPTER XVII
AGUPTI'S WAY OF LIFE AND CULTURE

The Agupti blacksmiths not only sing ancient Bulgarian songs but also speak the same Rhodope dialect as the local Bulgarian Muslim population, the only difference being that they pronounce the words more protractedly, more slowly.

Although the blacksmiths have had a sedentary life for centuries, their material culture differs significantly from that of the local population. It is at a far lower level than that of the Bulgarian Muslims. The reasons for this are many: poor financial situation, lagging cultural development, the absence of whatsoever appropriate attitude on the part of the state before the September 9, 1944, religious fanaticism, and others.

"Everything is weak in our people. I do not remember an old person from us. One has tuberculosis, another one has pleurisy, and they all die early. When I was young, our house had no ceiling and no roof. At night, we watched the sky and the stars through the roof, and in the morning – the daybreak. We all die young. Here, I suffer from heart issues. You will rarely see one of us who is older than 70 years."

The Agupti's households are poor.

Their food is weak, insufficient, and poorly prepared. Therefore, along with the care for improving their material conditions, there is a need to increase their domestic and material culture.

Before September 9, 1944, illiteracy was high, especially among the older Agupti. Now, it almost does not exist.

They live well with the local Bulgarian Muslim population. In family law relations, they have preserved their racial purity. The blacksmiths Agupti from Madan, as well as from the other Rhodope villages, marry mainly within their group. If a boy or a girl cannot find a suitable partner in Madan, they resort to the small tribal groups in the village of Srednogortsi (Totoklu), the village of Smilyan, Smolyan region, the village of Beli Izvor, Ardino region and others.

If the candidate for marriage cannot find a spouse among them either, they turn their feelings and attention to the local Bulgarian Muslim population. But the young Agupti man meets strong resistance here. Fanaticism and prejudice, for many centuries, have undoubtedly done their part. No matter how friendly they had lived for centuries and are still living with fellow men, the Bulgarian Muslims in Madan and the nearby Rhodope villages do not want to marry the Agupti. It is very rare for a young and beautiful Bulgarian Muslim girl to agree to marry an Agupti boy. If this happened sometimes, albeit in exceptional cases, the Agupti would be very happy and would make fun of the Bulgarian Muslims. It happens, however, that sometimes a widowed woman or a maiden who is not young and has a serious physical disability, decides to take a companion from among the Agupti blacksmiths. Even in these occasions, however, marriages between Bulgarians and Agupti are very rare. Only one Bulgarian Muslim woman from the village of Varbina (Syudzhuk), Ardino region, has agreed in the recent years to take an Agupti man as her husband.

Talking about family and marital relations, it is noteworthy that until now, the Agupti have not given any of their girls to marry a Bulgarian Muslim.

The difference that is made between the blacksmith Agupti and the local Bulgarian population is noticeable not only in the family law relations but also in the funeral, i.e., in the cemetery. No matter how diligently the Agupti blacksmiths practice Islam, and even though they do not have their own separate cemeteries (mezarlık), they are buried in the same cemetery, but at one end.

In principle, the wedding of the Agupti is a religious Muslim wedding. When marrying, especially when the bride is from another village, the Agupti like to go to the wedding with horses or mules. If the wedding guests do not have their own livestock, and in most cases they do not, then they hire it from someone else. The bride also rides a horse. Her horse must be a white one, led by her father. At wedding ceremonies, they like to shoot, especially when they lead the bride and approach the boy's village.

Because of the centuries-old coexistence with the Bulgarian Muslims, who in their way of life and culture have preserved many Christian features and peculiarities, the Agupti have taken some rituals from the Bulgarian wedding. For example, when taking the girl from her father's house, the boy's relatives sing, "Get up and startle, mother of the maiden, because we've got your girl" [in Bulgarian].

The wife addresses her husband as *chileku* [man], while the husband calls his wife *babitse* [Grandma], no matter how long they were married. Even if they got married the day before, the husband still addresses his wife with *babitse*.

Family law relationships are not very sophisticated. Of course, this depends on many factors, their poor culture and poor financial situation, in the first place. It should be noted that spouses often quarrel and abandon each other once or twice, and then reunite again. Nevertheless, it should be noted that there are also exemplary families, and they are not uncommon.

What must be highly emphasised here is the extreme diligence of the Agupti blacksmiths. Besides, they are impeccably honest. This can be seen both in their actions as masters (they sell all works very cheaply) and in their daily lives.

In their daily needs, they do not demand much, they are satisfied with little, and they are not greedy at all.

CHAPTER XVIII
THE AGUPTI'S MERITS

As traditional founders, who once dug and smelted the ore, and their descendants are now skilled blacksmiths, the Agupti have had and still have an undeniable contribution to the creation of the material culture of the Rhodope region in the past. There was a time when the population not only in the Rhodope region but also in the entire Thracian plain, relied on their supply of agricultural tools. With axes, hoes, ploughshares, nails, wedges, and other economic and handicraft tools, they supplied the Rhodope region almost regularly until the First World War, and the appearance of the factory production of some of the above tools.

Even during the World War, when European factories manufactured military production and horseshoes did not reach the Rhodope region, Agupti blacksmiths supplied horseshoes and wedges to almost all southern Bulgaria. The distributor of this "smithing production" was then the "cooperative" of the old Aguptin, Hasan Hasanov Dzhilyanov.

The old Agupti are very religious. They follow the precepts of Islam with great fanaticism. They do not miss a single prayer in the Mosque.

For their religious holidays – Sheker Bayram and Kurban Bayram [38] – they keep one, two, three rams for *kurbanlok*, for sacrifice. The *kurbanlok* is slaughtered, both for the health of the living, and for the souls of the dead.

The Agupti slaughter *kurbanlok* also for the health of their wives.

As we have said, the Agupti are excellent masters and have no equals in this respect. These abilities are generally recognised. Had young Agupti blacksmiths been qualified in special technical schools and mining colleges, they would have been excellent technicians and first-class mining workers.

We cannot omit noting, however, that even now many young Agupti work in the mines and are excellent miners.

The merits of the Agupti blacksmiths, as well as of the Gypsy blacksmiths in general in Bulgaria, in supporting agriculture, cattle breeding, etc. are indisputable. Their economic activity has contributed immensely to the easier cultivation of the land and to the increase of the yield.

The axes made by them, played a huge role in the timber industry and this merit must be universally acknowledged.

As regards cattle breeding, without their horseshoes or as they call them *petali*, the cattle, both in the Rhodope region and in the whole country, would be in a miserable condition.

CHAPTER XIX
THE SAMOKOV GYPSIES

The Samokov Gypsies, like the Agupti blacksmiths from the Rhodope region, are mostly founders and blacksmiths. Both the Agupti blacksmiths and the Samokov Gypsies are extremely skilled founders and blacksmiths. Their ironworks were famous and in-demand across the country.

They made anvils, which they cast themselves, each one weighing from 20 to 100 kg. They sent the anvils to be sold all over the country. Their works were highly valued in their time because they were artfully crafted, durable and very cheap.

Apart from anvils, the Samokov Gypsies also made other iron works, such as hoes, sickles, axes, ploughshares, iron ploughs, horseshoes for horses, oxen, donkeys, and various other iron works, which were of high quality and were in-demand in the whole country.

Their most masterly work, however, were the horse-nails, or as they called them, *mıhya*. The cattle were shod with these first-class horse-nails and the nails were famous for their durability. The skilful and masterful creation of horse-nails earned the good name of the Samokov Gypsies, and their anvils certainly confirmed it.

In the primitive setting in which they cast and forged their hundred-pound anvils, it took great skillfulness to perform this difficult task and produce high-quality anvils, the durability of which was recognised by all blacksmith masters. With their ironworks, the Samokov Gypsies have left a deep mark as excellent founders and blacksmiths.

Their location in the middle of the country, in Samokov, allowed them to expand their trade to the south – to Thrace, and to the north – to the Danubian plain and Dobrudja. Therefore, their role in developing and facilitating agriculture and cattle breeding in these areas is of undeniable importance. From this point of view, they undoubtedly have great merits in strengthening agriculture, cattle breeding, and timber-industry.

The Samokov Gypsies also had shops where they sold their ironworks.

The most famous masters, whose names are still remembered in Samokov, were Usta Ali, Usta Pehlivan.

CHAPTER XX
THE PLOVDIV GYPSIES

Plovdiv has the biggest number of Gypsies. Here, they form the most compact minority group. According to the latest census, there are about 18,000 Gypsies in Plovdiv.

Here, as in the whole country, they are mostly blacksmiths. Like the Samokov Gypsies, they also make various agricultural tools, such as hoes, sickles, ploughshares, axes, as well as horseshoes for horses, oxen and donkeys, nails for them and the famous Gypsy nails. The Gypsy blacksmiths from Plovdiv were also famous as masters of blacksmithing.

Under the new conditions, however, with the emergence of competition from the factory production of the above agricultural tools, the Gypsies had to reorganise themselves to meet the new demands of life and to provide for themselves and for their families. Because of this, they gradually abandoned their small iron and crafts workshops and went to work in the tobacco industry, in plants, factories, craft and production cooperatives, and agricultural cooperatives.

Back in these days, when factory production was still unknown in our country, the Gypsy blacksmiths in Plovdiv had their small iron and craft shops, which were mostly on the hill *Bunardzhik* and there they made, in addition to agricultural tools, the famous awls (chisels) for pavement, in the Izida quarry.

The Plovdiv Gypsies, like the Samokov ones, also had their own shops in which they sold their works.

Like the Samokov Gypsies, and the Agupti in Madan, the Plovdiv Gypsies also have great merits for the rapid development of agriculture, cattle breeding, and logging in our country.

They were also skilled craftsmen and their good reputation transcended the boundaries of Plovdiv.

In political and social terms, the Plovdiv Gypsies have always followed the progressive political trends in our country, and in the first place, the Communist Party. With the emergence of socialism in our country, they were the first to join its ranks, and despite all the threats, pressure and promises of the bourgeois and fascist governments in our country, they have remained loyal supporters of the Communist Party to this day. With their flexible minds and intuition for the right decisions, the Plovdiv Gypsies as well as the Gypsies throughout the country, realised that the Communist Party was their only faithful defender and therefore wholeheartedly supported it until its complete victory on September 9, 1944.

CHAPTER XXI
THE GYPSIES ALONG THE DANUBE

The Danubian Gypsies inhabit the towns of Vidin, Lom, Oryahovo, Nikopol, Svishtov, Ruse, Tutrakan and Silistra. They live both in the cities and in the villages along the Danube.

There were Gypsy blacksmiths here as well, but their number was not as large as in Madan, Samokov, Plovdiv, Sofia, Pleven, Pazardzhik and elsewhere. Many of the Danubian Gypsies, and especially those who inhabited the villages, were engaged in agriculture; some were working their small fields, while most of them were hired as agricultural workers. This was the occupation of most of the Gypsy women. The Gypsy women performed small services to the population, for which they received flour, vegetables, cheese, etc.

The Gypsy men, who lived in the cities along the Danube, usually had one craft, porters. They earned their living mainly as porters at ports and railway stations. The younger men, who lived in cities, were also shoeblacks. They are porters and shoeblacks in the cities even now.

Many of the Gypsies along the Danube, who practised the porter's occupation, were socially insured and organised at the time, and today they receive pensions and have stopped working. They are especially grateful to the People's Government, which secured them in old age by granting them a pension.

Here, there were also Gypsy blacksmiths, and especially in the villages, however, their number was small. Nevertheless, they gave a big support to the population by supplying them with agricultural tools, and especially by repairing the latter.

By religion, the Danubian Gypsies are mostly Muslims, but there are also Christians, significantly smaller in number. They are not fanatics in their religious beliefs.

After September 9, 1944, the Gypsies, both in the cities and in the villages, entered the agricultural cooperatives and, along with the Bulgarians, were active cooperative workers.

The Danubian Gypsies, perhaps due to the good livelihood they had as porters, are culturally at a higher level than, for example, the Madan Gypsies. They have nice, albeit small, but neat houses in which they maintain very good cleanliness. Therefore, when the Gypsies celebrate their religious holidays – St George's Day, St Basil's Day and the God-bearer, the Bulgarians visit their houses quite commonly and they stay there for lunch or dinner. The same is observed at the Gypsy weddings. The latter never take place without visits by Bulgarian men and women.

It is noteworthy, as a characteristic and beneficial fact, that after September 9, 1944, the interest among the Gypsies in education has increased, especially among the youth. It is not uncommon, for example, to meet almost every day, young Gypsies on the streets of the city with books in their hands, which they have borrowed from local community centres. They are among the very good clients of the community centres.

Their children, on the other hand, attend the schools where the Bulgarian children study.

The Danubian Gypsies are renowned as hardworking and honest people. That is why the population loves them very much.

The Danubian Gypsies, like the rest of their compatriots all over the world, are musical. There is almost no town along the Danube, and in the larger Danubian villages, without musical bands. In addition to the purely Gypsy music groups, in many places, Gypsy musicians make music together with Bulgarian musicians.

After September 9, 1944, many of the young Gypsies graduated from high schools and entered government offices and cooperatives, where they proved to be good workers.

Politically and socially, the Danubian Gypsies have progressive views.

During the People Uprising in 1923, the Gypsies of Lom were at the forefront of the uprising and many of them fell from the bullets of the fascists.

CHAPTER XXII
GYPSY CAULDRON-MAKERS AND TINSMITHS

Some of the Gypsies, in addition to blacksmithing, were also engaged in making copper cauldrons, which they sold to the population in towns and villages. These cauldrons were handmade; they were very strong because they were wrought, not extruded, and were preferred by many people. In addition to cauldrons, they made pots, pans, coffee pots and many other copper products and cutlery.

They also tinned these copper products. Tinning took place either in the small tinsmith workshops, which were in the homes of the tinsmiths or in the homes of the clients themselves.

Some of the masters worth mentioning, who have proven themselves to be great in their craft, and whose names are remembered by the generations, are Dimir, Murat, Osman and Yashar. These masters left many worthy successors, who to this day successfully continue their craft.

The Gypsy blacksmiths, coppersmiths and tinsmiths usually worked in their workshops with their whole families. All family members helped with the work. Women had the task of selling the works of their husbands, and they often collected orders for new work.

CHAPTER XXIII
ARTISTIC-CULTURAL WORK

The first manifestations of artistic, cultural, and musical work took place in 1902, in Sofia. Our talented musicians and artists then organised an art theatre and performed several plays with great success, including *Ibish Aga, Kuklik, Leblebizhi* and others. These plays were very successful, and this success greatly encouraged the initiators to continue this work. Outstanding were several of our compatriots: Amet (Babushka), Muto (Koko), Aisha, Ali (the Rabbit), Dzhemila and Akila, and the violinist Yanchev was no less successful. During the Bayram, Ramadan and other religious and patriotic holidays, they performed artistic programmes almost every night, which were a great success.

During the Turkish occupation, our compatriots had become very famous for the special tricks they performed like walking on a rope known as *ibzhanbaz*. In addition, our compatriots performed various scenes during the holidays, and during these parties our compatriot Dingel Ahmed excelled the most.

They made the performances in the present-day Lozenets area, by the river, where there were many willows, and around the *Roman Wall*, which was then called the *Namazyah*, where the *hadjis* went to pray after their return from the hadj pilgrimage.

The talented Hungarian Gypsy violinist, Oskar Egon Halmi, played in Rodopi pub fifty years ago; the orchestra of the Serbian Gypsy Vuleto played in other restaurants; and all this is described in the book by Georgi Kanazirski-Verin, entitled *Sofia 50 Years Ago* [Каназирски-Верин, 1947].

It is obvious that the cultural awakening among the Gypsy minority began more than half a century ago, but due to the specific living conditions of the Gypsies, they could not develop and engage in activities with results. Cruelly exploited and totally discriminated against, despite the legal requirements of the Tarnovo constitution providing that all Bulgarian citizens are equal, the Gypsies could not develop their theatrical, musical, and artistic geniuses in their breadth. Crushed under pressure to think every day and hour about their livelihoods, they abandoned these cultural aspirations in order to meet the basic needs of their families.

It was only after the people's victory on September 9, 1944, that the Gypsies were liberated from oppression and discrimination, and devoted themselves to the mainstream culture, and theatrical, musical, and educational activities in general. In our country, since September 9, 1944, many Gypsy amateur groups were created, the success of which is undoubtedly great. They are moving only forward, and we have every reason to hope and believe that these groups will grow into real cultural centres opening space for the Gypsies to develop their talents. In this respect, they have the full support – moral and material, of the people's government.

CHAPTER XXIV
EDUCATIONAL WORK

The Gypsy students, before the Liberation and soon after that, even up to 1905, used to study in Sofia in the Turkish school whose *moalim* (principal) used to be Osman Efendi. More than a hundred Gypsy pupils used to study in this school, five of which were sent to study with a scholarship at the University of Istanbul [39] by the Turkish Religious Council. Their names were: Kocho Ramadanov, Malik Omerov, Sadik Sefidov and Ibrahim Kokov.

In 1905, due to the expulsion of the Turkish population from Sofia and Bulgaria, the number of Turkish students decreased and those who remained were mainly the children of our compatriots. The members of the new Turkish

Board of Trustees who were angry about this fact, closed the school and our children massively went to the Bulgarian schools in 1906. After September 9, 1944, on the initiative of our organisation, a Committee was founded, which asked the People's authorities to build a separate school. The Committee was composed by the following people: Shaban Yushniev, Meto Bilalov, Demcho Blagoev and the then Member of Parliament Shakir Pashev. The members of the Committee managed to explain our need for a Gypsy school, and as a result, our People's authorities built a separate, new school. The newspaper *Rabotnichesko delo*, issue 263, published on November 10, 1948, informed about the launching of the first Gypsy school. The description is accompanied by a photograph which shows how the then Member of Parliament from the Gypsy minority, Shakir Pashev, turns the first sod.

In 1906, the newly created Gypsy gymnastic societies, performed day and evening programs and organised excursions to Knyazhevo and Vrazhdebna.

According to our social order, and similarly to the European Gypsy minority groups, we had a leader, called *Muhtar* (*Cheribashiya*), who represented the Gypsy minority in front of the official authorities [40]. The *Cheribashia* was elected voluntarily, and he made sure that the moral norms and order were observed by the population.

In 1919, after they came back from the war, the Gypsies gathered in a meeting in which we already had young, intelligent people; during a stormy meeting the aforementioned elders (*cheribashii*) were ousted and replaced by Committees with five to seven members which represented the Gypsy minority in front of the authorities and cared after the re-education of the minority. The committees were composed of a President, a Secretary, and Members. Besides the committees, there were also associations for the support of the socially weak which had existed since old times. These were called 'londzhi' [41]. The latter continued their work. They helped those who are most in need while alive and in cases of death. Each *londzha* was composed of between 30 and 50 members. They used to organise outings in Knyazhevo (Bali Efendi, Bali Baba) [42] and other places, where they organised musical parties with horo and other dances throughout the day. The leaders of the *londzhi* were called Usta Bashi and Egit Bashi.

In 1920, the Gypsy youth substituted these *londzhi* with associations, which were managed also in a new, modern way. Their management was composed of a President, Vice-President, Secretary, and Members of the Managing Board, while their statutes were approved by the Ministry of Internal Affairs. These Committees had the same task as the *londzhi* – to give out aid and to be vigilant in preserving good morals.

CHAPTER XXV
EGYPT

Having talked so much in this book about Egypt and India, I cannot resist be it a cursory description of these two wonderful countries, which raised disputes with regard to the origins of the Gypsies.

For Egypt, I will give excerpts from the wonderful travelogue of Totyu Belchev *Days and Nights by the Nile: A History Lesson*, published in newspaper *Otechestven front*:

"I crossed far and wide a dozen of countries; I learned about the way of life and culture, the achievements and struggles of many people, but what I learned and saw near the Nile, I had never met anywhere. It grabs the person, conquers them with terrible force, excites them and gives them no peace, clenches their fists in an angry protest against colonialism and the enslavers who made millions of people live in indescribable conditions.

The Egyptians, who in ancient times stopped in north-eastern Africa between the Mediterranean Sea to the north and the Red Sea to the east, have a millennial history. They sought happiness in the spills of the full river Nile, which in summer, due to the melting ice and heavy rains in the mountains from which it springs and in its upstream, comes out of its bed and floods with its murky waters thousands of acres and sands for hundreds of miles, before flowing into the sea not far from Alexandria. The Nile silts are blessed – lush greenery gushes as the river recedes, and the people who survived the floods, swarming like ants, gather rich harvests – up to three, and sometimes four per year. And if the Egyptians still live in bad conditions, we cannot blame them or their present leaders, who are searching a way to a better future and have fought life-and-death battles against barbaric colonialism.

Egyptian history is full of lessons. Let's turn some of its pages.

In the middle of the fourth millennium BC, Egypt was formed as a slave-owning state. Already in ancient times, the country became a centre of highly developed science, art, construction equipment and music. The flourishing of the Egyptian material and spiritual culture in ancient times is evidenced by the preserved pyramids, sphinxes, obelisks, parchments, various handicrafts of ivory, stone, gold, silver, wood, etc. It is not only these works that fascinate our contemporary fellow men. Many centuries ago, the Egyptians created the mummies with remarkable mastery, that inspires and delights the visitors to the museum of Cairo, who cannot take their eyes off the man-made monuments of the ancient Egyptian civilisation, savagely crushed by the "civilisation" of the colonialists, who trampled in the mud the flowers of the once flourishing culture. The Egyptian people are especially proud when they talk about the historical monuments in Giza, Luxor, and Cairo. Many of them are from the time of Ramses II, Cheops and other pharaohs. The ancient ruins are still carefully preserved to tell to the generations what Egypt had been before it lost, towards the beginning of our era, its power and independence.

Dressed in their old Egyptian costume, the dry, tall cicerone from the luxurious Luxor Hotel takes us a long way between the obelisks dotted with arabesques and the ancient 17–18-meter-high columns of Luxor historical monuments. His olive-black eyes now gleamed with joy, now sparkled with hatred as he spoke of the bright days of his people's lives or the gloomy, long years of bloody colonial oppression. The hours passed imperceptibly; countless electric lights started shining on the Luxor. The great river, which had witnessed so many events, was slowly dragging its waters to cut through the sands of the Libyan desert, before reaching the Mediterranean Sea. And Mahmoud went on talking and talking ... As if every corner, every stone became a living thing who spoke about the days and nights along the Nile, by the date palms, by the dunes in the desert, on the banks of the Suez Canal, and about the short-lived joy of the Egyptian past. About the days and nights in the impenetrable darkness of long slavery.

In 332 BC, Alexander the Great's hordes occupied the country with bloody battles, and after that, it fell under Roman rule for three centuries. In the middle of the 7th century, Egypt entered the Arab Caliphate after the conquest by the Arabs, who assimilated the ancient Egyptians, and the latter accepted Islam and the Arabic language. In 1517, in the hands of Ottoman Turkey, Egypt was turned for about 500 years into an Ottoman province, oppressed and plundered, just like our homeland during the five-century Turkish yoke. The terrible Turkish plunder ruined the Egyptian peasants and Egyptian agriculture, which perished soon afterwards. The irrigation system was destroyed, the cultivated areas were limited, the crafts declined, and the trade was ruined. The unbridled Ottoman cruelty and exploitation led the Egyptians to poverty and disbelief, which other people rarely experienced. Death by malnutrition and unbearable slavery reigned in the Nile Valley, and Egypt's population quickly began to decrease. People died like flies – without care from anywhere – in darkness and ignorance. For centuries, they lived in holes dug in the ground which was thrown away during the digging of the irrigation canals; in roofless huts; under the open sky; without a loaf of bread all day, ragged, skinny, deadened by incurable stomach, lung and skin diseases. Misery and destitution, which one cannot imagine that ever existed or still exist; misery and destitution in front of which the heart's rhythm breaks; misery and destitution that leaves you breathless. This misery and destitution pushed the population to rise in uprisings for freedom and independence.

And that was not enough. At the end of the 18th century and the beginning of the 19th century, the European coloniser set foot on Egyptian soil. Napoleon Bonaparte occupied Egypt in 1798. At the foot of the hills of the low Mokattam Mountains, from which the city of Cairo begins, rises the Citadel with its majestic fortress walls and the mosque, built 148 years ago. Traces from the cannonballs of Napoleon's troops, who captured the Egyptians, can still be seen on the walls. And something else reminds of those times: the clock tower donated by Bonaparte, stolen from who knows which other enslaved country, and brought here as a sign of "mercy" and "friendship" by the conqueror, who seized the wealth of the country. The people, however, did not reconcile with the French rule and after years of hard and fierce struggles, they forced them to leave the borders of Egypt. England's attempts to settle in the Nile Valley in 1807 were unsuccessful.

The Western colonisers, who knew Egypt's price as the centre of Europe's roads to Asia and Africa, did not give up their intentions to conquer it. The rich country of the Egyptians, located around the stream and delta of the water-full river Nile, would not escape the dangers. The colonisers knew about Egypt's favourable climate conditions, about its natural resources, about the infinitely cheap labour, which they could find there for processing cotton, wheat, corn, rice, sugar cane, legumes (beans, peas, etc.), tangerines, oranges, bananas, and many other agricultural fruits that the country is famous for. Their wolfish appetite was aroused by the deposits of oil, iron ore, lead, zinc, nickel, tungsten, gold, and marble in the earth, which bespoke innumerable gains and made the thieves of the peoples' happiness rub their hands in delight. Why should it matter that a few thousand years before our era, one of the first hearths of human civilization went ablaze in Egypt, a country of world importance then?

After all, the interests of the colonisers suggested that the country must be conquered in order to exploit its people and its enormous wealth, to plunder with impunity, to suck its life juices.

And as they could not enter through the doors, they crept in through the window. British merchants, using the Treaty of Turkey imposed in 1838, flooded all the provinces of the Ottoman Empire, including Egypt, with goods, suffocating the nascent Egyptian national industry. Assisted by Turkey, the English bourgeoisie gradually conquered all branches of the Egyptian economy. Seizing the lands of the Egyptians, the colonisers imposed enslaving loans on the country and that is how the influence of foreign capital, mainly French and English, became dominant.

The struggle for colonies and sea routes between England and France became extremely fierce at the end of the 18th century, as a result of which France lost its possessions in India, in the western hemisphere, and decided to replace this loss by strengthening its position in the Eastern Mediterranean and North Africa. As early as the occupation of Egypt by Napoleon's troops (1798–1801), the French developed a plan to dig the Suez Canal, but their expulsion thwarted their intentions.

In 1802, Egypt again fell under the vassal dependence of Turkey. Anarchy and economic decline began to reign in the country; violent peasant uprisings broke out; and the starving people rose to fight for bread and independence. A few years later, in 1805, the Turkish sultan's representative in Egypt received the title of pasha and became a full-fledged unlimited ruler of the country, which was turned into an absolute feudal state of large landowners. Taxation and other reforms deepened the enslavement of the population.

Our footsteps echo on the stone courtyards; the alabaster-lined walls of the mosque; in the rooms of Mohammed Ali's harem of more than 150 women; in the ceremonial hall with antique chests and carpets from ancient times; between the columns of the Citadel. In front of us are Hindus who have come to see the sights of Cairo. We stop in front of every corner to hear the explanations of our companion Georgi Isaevich (one of the four Isaevich brothers who came here from Bulgaria 25–30 years ago), who knows every important area of the city, and the streets which he walked many times. In the ceremonial hall of the mosque, built by Mohammed Ali, with its minarets in the Mokattam Hills towering above the other mosques, Bai Georgi stops us to recall what happened to the Mamluks, the rulers of the districts.

[...]

The years were flying by, the slavery continued ... Mohammed Ali, who ruled Egypt after 1805, contrary to what has been previously stated, did not feel he had solid ground under his feet and cunningly decided to get rid of the Mamluk tribal chiefs. At the opening of the mosque in the Citadel, he invited all the Mamluk feudal lords, gathered them in the ceremonial hall, and when they were waiting for his appearance, tough executioners with yataghans jumped out of the chests, and began a slaughter in which 365 people died and only one managed to escape. The land of the Mamluk feudal lords was confiscated by Mohammed Ali. Since then, he had suddenly become incredibly rich. At the same time, the extermination of all Mamluks continued. Having settled his accounts in this way, he created a European-style army and navy, and fought for a long time.

The blood and tears of those years had not yet dried, when in 1854, the French capitalists, through the French General Consul in Alexandria, F. Lesseps succeeded in concluding a concession agreement with Egypt for the construction of the 168 km long Suez Canal, with a width on its surface of 80–135 meters, and at the bottom 45–100 metres, and depth of 11–12, meters, which connects the Mediterranean with the Red Sea. The Egyptian viceroy from 1822 to 1863, Said Pasha (Mohamed) after whom was named the town of Port Said at the entrance to the Suez Canal, became a shareholder in the so-called stock company *Universal Company of the Maritime Canal of Suez*. Under the terms of the concession, Egypt provided the company with the land through which the canal would pass free of charge and, most importantly, undertook to give the company, free of charge, four-fifths of all workers needed to dig the canal. The tragedy of the Egyptians became enormous. Under unbearable weather conditions, under the scorching sun, hungry, often without a drop of water, all day in arid, completely uninhabited areas, 40,000 people, mostly ragged and skinny peasants, began slave labour on the facilities of the canal. Separated from their families, who were brought to the sites to evade heavy taxes and other levies, the fellahs and the other martyrs of the Suez Canal died of starvation and illnesses on the routes of the canal. No wonder that 120,000 Egyptians left their bones fighting with the sands, rocks, and land under harsh conditions, digging the Suez Canal, which has brought the colonisers billions in profits since those days.

If the traveller set foot on Egyptian soil, they would learn what the suffering was, how widespread the poverty was, while on the bones of the Egyptian people, the Suez Canal stretched from the Mediterranean to the Red Sea to shorten the way for the colonizers' ships carrying goods from distant Asian, African, and other coasts.

A black, pitch-dark night fell over the land of the freedom-loving Egyptian people – the night of ruthless and cruel barbaric colonial exploitation. The defeats of the past are still visible, and they have left their mark on the days and nights along the Nile.

The government is making efforts to erase them; the people struggle to overcome their backwardness and to come out on a straight road; to live more humanely because they have the right to do so. But is it easy to recover the economy which was robbed for centuries, and the people who were oppressed for hundreds of years, groaning under the yoke and scythe of more than one enslaver?

It takes an enormous effort by the population and a heavy strain on the resources of the state to move the country uphill.

We detest imperialism and colonial slavery, which is shameful for mankind, and which many peoples are courageously fighting to overthrow. However, we could hardly perceive the hatred of the Arab peoples and other oppressed peoples towards imperialism and the colonizers.

[...]

When I set foot on Egyptian soil for about a month during these years, the root of evil, which infuriated the Arab peoples to the bottom of their hearts, flashed naked in front of me. From Upper Egypt, along the Nile and through the deserts, I reached Lower Egypt, descended from the Red Sea along the Suez Canal, and set foot on the Mediterranean coast of Alexandria, from where I returned after a short stay along the straight as a string road through the Cairo desert.

I enjoyed the ancient Greek culture, whose monuments are preserved in Cairo, Luxor, Giza with the majestic Pyramid of Cheops and its two cousins; the miracle of Egypt, the 73 meters long sphinx, carved from stone, stretching its huge torso on the sands, which has endured the storms of the desert and the bloody invasions."

CHAPTER XXVI
INDIA. THE ROAD THROUGH THE MILLENNIA

We give the present notes on India from the book of the Austrian Harry Sichrovski, who has lived in India for many years and knows it intimately.

> India, which occupies a key position in Asia, is getting closer to the centre of the world events day by day. However, very little is known in Europe about this huge country, and even that little knowledge often has nothing to do with reality. [44]

The author of this book has lived in India for many years. He is a young Austrian who has personally come to know the colourful mix of peoples there as well as the social relations in this subcontinent.

In connection with his book, a contemporary Indian writer wrote to the author the following:

> A deep-rooted belief and a traditional legend exist in Europe, and they are limited to several fantastic concepts: fabulously rich maharajas, also fabulously beautiful *bayaderki* [Shamakhi dancers], the hunting of tigers and elephants, snake tamers, rope players, yogis and fakirs who sleep on nails, and finally mystical, mysterious rites and customs, and a deep, abyss-like, unknowable soul that an ordinary mortal does not hope to reveal. This is the veil that traditions, biased reports, and sensational journalism have thrown at my homeland. Your book will show what treasures of culture and knowledge India has given to the world, how its people actually live, what path its history has taken, what is the significance of the religion and the nationalities, and what is the state of other problems that are abundant in India and waiting for a solution. I am sure that the light you spread about India and its place in the modern world will help dispel the darkness and tear the veil.
>
> Yours sincerely: Mulk Raj Anand. [45]

Indian history begins in the dark and passes a long way through thickets, forests, and jungles, through the darkness that has not been completely penetrated today by the light of research. There is not much information about the prehistoric people in India. Parts of the petrified jaw of the Sivapithecus, an extinct ape that lived 20 million years ago in the forests of the southern slopes of the Himalayas, have been found in the rocks of Sivalik Hill in Kashmir and Bilaspur. Fossils of the Dryopithecus (an ape living in the trees, a monkey of the oak forests) reveal characteristics which are similar to the humans. Fossil cranial types with a wide nose, a slightly protruding face, a strongly reclining forehead, and protruding bones under the eyebrows have been found from the Older and Younger Stone Ages. This Aditanalur man, as he is called by his whereabouts, does not resemble the Negroid Grimaldi man of France and the African Bushman. The discovery of tools made of flint, quartzite, basalt, and hardened lava, as well as engravings, carvings on the rocks and drawings on the caves (by the way, images of a rhino and a giraffe), allows us to conclude that the settling in India by prehistoric people occurred about 400,000 years ago. Between that period and the appearance of certain tribes, there are big gaps in the research. The descendants of the oldest inhabitants of India are considered to be the tribes of Mon-Khmer, Munda, Santal, Naga, and others. Later came the Dravidians, whose descendants today are the South Indian peoples of Telegu, Tamil, Malayali, and Kannadiga. And finally came those who decisively influenced the fate of India and perhaps half the world, the Aryans.

Where did the Aryans come from? Opinions vary widely.

From Siberia?

From the Volga region?

From Persia?

An Indian nationalist was trying to prove that the ancestral home of the Aryans was the Arctic.

It is more likely that the Aryans had no homeland but lived scattered across the European steppe from where they emigrated to Europe, Asia Minor, and India. This process must have lasted from 3,000 to 1,000 years before our era.

Why did the Aryans move?

They were probably forced to do so by some natural disaster, perhaps by a flood. Besides, as nomads, they had to look for new pastures, new food. Maybe they were driven out by enemy tribes. That is how they came in small and larger groups with their entire families, not as conquerors but as vagrants and settlers in Kashmir, Punjab and through the Khyber passage.

Over time, due to rapid reproduction and environmental exhaustion, the tribe was not able to find conditions for life in its previous habitat. In search of new places to live, one part separated, a new tribe emerged and developed new habits, manners, and a different language. It happened that natural disasters, droughts and floods destroyed the food, livestock, and household goods of the tribe. With this, new factors came in the primitive society – the war, the struggle for water, for cattle, for pastures. The wandering horde attacked other clans in order to secure the conditions of life it needed but had lost; or after a long journey, the tribe finally found a comfortable pasture or a hunting ground, which had already been inhabited by others and thus it set out to conquer the land.

The pastoral tribes separated from the rest of the barbarians: this was the first great social division of labour. The pastoral tribes not only produced more means of subsistence than the other barbarians, but they were also different. They had not only milk, dairy products, and meat in larger quantities, but also hides, wool, fur and yarns and fabrics (which have been increasing along with the mass of raw material). That's how regular exchange became possible for the first time.

The second great division of labour occurred when agriculture was separated from crafts. In India, the first artisans were the foundry workers, who mined and processed copper, tin, bronze, and weavers.

With the increase of goods and the complexity of the social production process, the social division of labour also expanded. There was a need for people to deal with rites and prayers, with predicting the time and the future, and with healing the sick.

There was a need for strong, battle-tested men to take on the constant protection of the community.

This is how the castes of the Brahmins (the priests) and that of Kshatriya (soldiers) originated, while all the others – the peasants, the craftsmen, the stockbreeders – represented the caste Visha (later Vaishya). The captives, who served as lawless helpers in agriculture, cattle breeding, crafts, etc., formed the fourth caste Shudra (the slaves).

Around the same time, when Attila's hordes invaded the Roman Empire, India experienced its first Hun invasion. The Huns, also a nomadic tribe from Central Asia, flooded all of North and Central India. For fifty years, India was under the rule of the Hun king Toramana and his son Mihirakula.

The Huns were followed by Harsha-Vardhana, who founded one more time an empire from the Ganges to the Kathiawar Peninsula. He remained in history as one of the last rulers before the great Muslim invasions and as the last significant Buddhist king of India.

A new historical period began in India after Harsha's death. Arab tribes attacked and occupied Sindh. They brought Islam within India's borders for the first time. Once again, the South Indian states stood out at the forefront of historical events. The most beautiful and richest of the colonies of these countries was today's Indochina.

About 1000 AD, Mahmoud of Ghazni invaded Afghanistan with fire and a sword and conquered Punjab. In Somnath, 50,000 people fled to the temple, hoping that the gods would not abandon them and make some miracle. However, their hopes were in vain. They were all killed. Mahmud's hordes were Turkish-Mongol tribes from Central Asia. The living conditions in these steppes determined the history and customs of their inhabitants. They were mainly shepherds, nomads, whose economic bases were the flocks of horses, sheep, and camels. Along with this, hunting played a big role, while agriculture – almost none. The blacksmith occupies the first place among the craftsmen. The search for comfortable pastures was the main concern of the tribe; the horse, as a means of transport, was man's most important companion.

This nomadic economic form did not allow the formation of larger social communities. The norm was the small independent community, which comprised only one tribe.

CHAPTER XXVII THE ESTABLISHMENT OF THE SOCIETY *EGIPET* [EGYPT] AND ITS MERGING WITH THE COMMUNIST PARTY

The Society *Egipet* [Egypt] was founded in Sofia in 1919. A major part of the Gypsy intelligentsia and all progressive youth were members of the Society. The task of the society was to raise the cultural and educational level of its members and of the Gypsy minority itself, and most of all – to work for the political and civic awakening of the Gypsy minority. This work was extremely hard because the backwardness of the Gypsies in every respect was a generally acknowledged fact. With great enthusiasm, the society's initiators got ready for work. Through lectures, personal conversations, excursions, etc., the aim was to persuade the Gypsy minority to adopt a more cultured life. And much has been done in that respect, too.

A few months after the formation of the Society *Egipet*, following a decision of the General Assembly, with great enthusiasm and political consciousness, the members made a decision to merge the society into the Communist Party (formerly 'Narrow Socialists') [43]. On the day of the merger, a solemn assembly took place; among the invited were Dr Valcho Ivanov, secretary of the third district, attorney Dr Alexander Lambrev, and others. The merging of the Society *Egipet* into the Party took place in the most solemn setting, in the club of the society, at 51 Tatarli Street.

At the time of the merging, the management of the organisation consisted of the following nine members: Assen Totev, Shakir Pashev, Yusein Bilalov, Mancho Shakirov, Mustava Saidiev, Demir Yasharov, Mancho Arifov, Ali Yasharov and Ramcho Shakirov. The last three are now dead.

In its initial composition, the society comprised about 50 members.

In 1920, the society, which was already fully incorporated into the Communist Party, was provided with a wine-red flag that was safely kept by Comrade Yusein Bilalov. Carrying the flag, the society members departed from the club on 25 Tatarli Street, passed through the streets of Sofia and headed to the Party's regional club on Tsar Simeon Street, where the then-young railwayman Shakir Pashev gave a speech.

Carrying the same flag, the society participated in the manifestation on the 1st of May, passing through the whole city.

When the founder of Communism in Bulgaria, Grandfather Dimitar Blagoev, died on May 7, 1924, most of the Gypsy minority participated in the funeral of the beloved leader of the workers' movement in Bulgaria. Gypsy tobacco-workers wore and handed over giant wreaths of real flowers that they laid on the grave of the unforgettable and beloved Grandfather Blagoev.

All Gypsies at the funeral were dressed in national Gypsy clothes, *shalwars*.

CHAPTER XXVIII
STRUGGLES FOR CIVIL AND POLITICAL RIGHTS

At a meeting in 1921, the progressive youth decided to set up a committee with the task of securing political and civic rights for the Gypsy minority. Despite the constitutional provisions, [Prime-Minister Petko] Karavelov, who was dissatisfied with the Gypsy minority because they had not supported him but had given their support to [Vasil] Radoslavov, deprived the Gypsies of their electoral rights. Karavelov's blatantly unconstitutional act was received with pain by the Gypsy minority, who believed that he had no reason to do that [44].

Considering the numerous youths who took part in the 1915–1918 war and those who left their bones across the Balkan Peninsula, the Gypsy minority felt that there was every reason to claim equality before the laws of the country. The Prime Minister then was Aleksandar Stamboliyski.

The elected Committee members included Yusein Balilov, Shakir Pashev, Rashid Mehmedov, Redzheb Yuseinov, Muto Bialov, Yusuf Mehmedov, Bilal Osanov.

Shortly after it was set up, the Committee appeared before Prime Minister Aleksandar Stamboliyski, who listened intently to the Committee's requests and then promised that these rights would be granted. He kept his promise. At the first meeting of the next National Assembly, he submitted a proposal for the restitution of the voting rights of the Gypsies and with the support of the Communist MPs, the law was passed [in 1923] [Дневник, 1923].

In 1925, the Gypsy minority elected a school Board of Trustees, consisting of President Rashid Mehmedov, Vice-President Redzheb Yuseinov and Secretary Shakir Pashev; Members: Mustafa Enkekov, Malik Omerov. The school Board of Trustees was approved by the Sofia municipality, but the Turkish religious community, which was required by law to guarantee for the school board, refused to do so. The Muslim Gypsies at that time fought to have the right to be elected to the Waqf Board of Trustees [45]. The statute of the Muslim community required the presence of 40 families as a condition for the Gypsies to have the right to elect, and since the Gypsies did not fulfil this condition, the Muslim community did not agree once again. This action on the part of the Muslim community has greatly aroused the Gypsy minority. All Gypsies united and soon obtained certificates from Sofia municipality for more than 40 families that they are Mohamedans and that they are Turks. The Muslim community, however, resisted and did not want to acknowledge the certificates as credible. The struggle reached the Supreme Administrative Court, but here again the case was decided in favour of the Muslim religious community. The Gypsies were left with undisputed documents that they are Turks.

Once, before elections, Nikola Mushinov appointed a three-member commission including Yusein Papukchiev, president; Hyusein Bilalov, Secretary and Malik Eminov, Member. After the elections, however, there was no chance for this commission to take their place because Shumkov, Nikola Mushanov's private secretary, had issued an order preventing the aforementioned three-member commission to take over the responsibility of the Waqf Board of Trustees from the old members; as is also now, the few Turks who had remained, prevailed over the majority [46].

The Gypsy minority has not despaired even this time, and they devoted themselves to organisational life. As a consequence, on May 7, 1929, the first organisation of the Gypsy minority in Sofia was founded, which united all former societies (*londzhi*) in the *Istikbal* (Future) organisation, which had the significant, for that time, number of 1,500 members, with President Yusuf Mehmedov and Secretary, Shakir Pashev, and Member, Yusein Bilalov.

In that same year, the Association *Vzaimopomosht* (Mutual Aid) was founded, with President Rashid Mehmedov, whose members were part of the former *londzhi*. Thus, the Gypsy minority created two large organisations – *Istikbal* and *Vzaimopomosht*.

Besides these two large organisations, the Gypsies also had other professional associations of blacksmiths, tinsmiths, and traders who were members of *Istikbal*.

There were also youth cultural and educational associations with very progressive trends: the Society *Naangle* [Forward] [47] and the Sports society *Egipet* [Egypt]

In 1930, the progressive youth united the two large organisations of the Gypsy minority in one single organisation, called 'Istikbal' (Future), with President Shakir Pashev, two Vice-Presidents, namely: Redzheb Yuseinov and Rashid Mehmedov and Secretary: Ahmed Sotirov and Ramcho Shakirov, and Members: Yusein Bialov, Emin Eminov, Raycho Kochev and others.

In 1931, following the proposal of the President of the organisation, Shakir Pashev, a decision was made for the publication of a Gypsy newspaper, entitled *Terbie* (Upbringing). His first editor was Shakir Pashev. The newspaper had distribution throughout the country. For that purpose, many people were organised in Vratsa, Lom, Oryahovo, Pleven, Plovdiv, Kyustendil, Stara Zagora, Rousse, Shumen, Burgas, Pernik, Sliven and in many villages.

The task of both the united organisation *Istikbal* and the newspaper *Terbie* was the upbringing and the enlightenment of the Gypsy population in Bulgaria through culture and education.

On May 7, 1932, the First Gypsy Conference took place at Mezdra station. This Conference was held thanks to the initiative of the Gypsy organisation in Vratsa. Organisers of the Conference were our compatriots Nikola Palashev and Sando Ibrov. Delegates from the whole Vratsa region, including from the villages, were present. Mihailovgrad, Oryahovo and the villages around it, Byala-Slatina, Pleven, Lom, Cherven-bryag and Sofia were also presented here. The Sofia delegation was headed by the President of organisation *Istikbal* in Sofia – Shakir Pashev, and also included Emin Eminov, Naydo Yasharov and Ali Yasharov. The conference took place near the Mezdra fortress, and it decided that all Gypsies in Bulgaria should be led by the organisation *Istikbal*. It was also decided that the *Istikbal's* organ, the newspaper *Terbie*, would spread as an enlightening beam to the last Gypsy hut in Bulgaria.

On May 7, 1934, a wreath was laid at the tomb of the deceased activist of the organisation, Redzheb Yuseinov, who had generously contributed to the school and to the Gypsy children. He was Vice-President of the Gypsy organisation for a long time. He was born on May 10, 1879 and died on December 30, 1933. On behalf of the leadership of the organisation, Shakir Pashev and the Secretary Ramcho Shakirov joined the ceremony and made a short speech. Since then, on May 7th the Gypsy minority paid tribute to the honoured Gypsy activist, Redzheb Yuseinov, at his grave.

The *Istikbal* cultural and educational organisation became a legal representative of the Gypsy minority in Bulgaria. The organisation kept a register for the births and deaths only for Sofia. It had its own funeral car. *Istikbal* issued official notices for our compatriots, without which the Sofia Municipality did not issue the necessary certificates. The organisation used to present to the municipality a list of poor Gypsy families based on which the families received material assistance.

In short, *Istikbal* played the role of the only official institution representing the Gypsy minority before the legal authorities in Sofia.

The newspaper *Terbie*, on the other hand, played the role of an educator of the Gypsy minority. Its task was to raise the cultural and educational level of the Gypsies, to work towards their political and civil education, and to guide the Gypsy minority towards progressive political ideas, which guarantee the equality of all nations in the country. This task was executed with passion and enthusiasm and the leadership of the newspaper was truly happy when they found out that the newspaper was raising the level of the Gypsies in all aspects. Hyusein A. Bilalov was one of the closest associates in the newspaper and he was in the Editorial Board. He was really enthusiastic, he loved the newspaper and with his work he was the right arm of the editor, Shakir Pashev. Both of them, joining forces, and wasting no time, energy, and money, made concerted efforts to improve the pages of the newspaper and make it lively, luscious and interesting for its readers. They were aware that a newspaper could become attractive for the readers when it advocates for their material well-being as well as when it reflects their thoughts, desires, aims and ideals. In that respect, they made anything possible to satisfy the numerous requirements of their readers. Also, they were proud because *Terbie* was the first newspaper in Europe which was published with the goal of raising the cultural and educational level of the Gypsy minority. Before the creation of the newspaper *Terbie* and long after that, nowhere in Europe there was a newspaper for the Gypsy minorities [48]. That was a huge advantage for the Bulgarian Gypsies, and the newspaper initiators, especially the Editorial Board, took justified pride in this fact.

In its columns, the newspaper reflected the everyday concerns of the Gypsy minority; it covered the comprehensive and fruitful work of the organisation *Istikbal*; reflected the realities of the other Gypsy organisations – those of the youth, of their sports clubs, of the craftsmen; and communicated all events which took place in the lives of the Gypsy minority. It encouraged the young and enthusiastic Gypsies to improve as much as possible their cultural and educational level; it worked tirelessly towards the overall development of the Gypsy minority; it encouraged the people for progressive political and civil activities; it fought against prejudices, rigid and dying traditions, and in that respect, it had an undoubted success. For example, it was at the forefront in the fight for the abandonment of the *feredzhe* [49] and shalwars, and in that respect, it helped the struggles of the organisation *Istikbal*. Looking at the fruits of its work, the Editorial Board was happy because there was consent that without cultural and educational development of the Gypsy minority, without abandoning the harmful, rigid prejudices, superstitions and norms, a nation cannot make progress. The editorial board was aware that, above all, the Gypsy minority had to get rid of all harmful prejudices, and take a new road towards re-education, to accept the new progressive political and civil ideas; and in a word, to be in harmony with all other civilised nations.

The newspaper *Terbie* was published in the Bulgarian language.

By a decision of the first national Gypsy conference in Bulgaria, which took place at the Mezdra station, near the fortress, on the initiative of the Gypsy minority in Vratsa, the newspaper *Terbie* was declared the newspaper of the Gypsy minority in Bulgaria. The Conference recommended that it should reach even the last Gypsy hut in order to work for the re-education of the minority. The Conference also decided that the Sofia organisation *Istikbal* should be representative of all Gypsies in the country.

The newspaper *Terbie* was welcomed with exaltation, enthusiasm and unheard excitement, by the Gypsies from Sofia and from the country alike. It was in demand. Everybody promoted it. Each Gypsy and especially the youth, became a promoter for the widespread distribution of the newspaper among the Gypsy minority. The pride and happiness of the Bulgarian Gypsies were for a true reason because the newspaper *Terbie* was the first newspaper in Europe, which was issued on behalf of the Gypsy minority. It was a pride for the Gypsies themselves and even more so for its initiators. Shakir Pashev, who was among the first people to come up with the idea of the Gypsy newspaper in Bulgaria and his first assistant Hyusein A. Bilalov, had all the reasons to be happy that their idea was welcomed with such excitement by their compatriots. They made every effort to improve the content of the newspaper so that it became a true educator of their compatriots. Whether they were successful with this task remains to be judged by those who assess the results from the newspaper. As for the initiators, they fulfilled their obligation towards their nation.

The fact that the demand for the newspaper increased each day; the fact that everybody was eager to regularly receive it, shows us how relevant the idea of issuing a Gypsy newspaper has been.

The results from the educational role of the newspaper, as well as the results from the work of the organisation *Istikbal* soon became obvious. There was no doubt about the role and influence of the newspaper *Terbie* and the organisation *Istikbal*.

The editor of the newspaper, Shakir Pashev, and his first assistant Hyusein A. Bilalov invested all their energy, desire, strength, and knowledge to fulfil the tasks of the newspaper. They worked with youthful enthusiasm and with the belief that their deed was right. They did their best to raise the patriotic feeling of the Gypsy minority, but they did not aim to foster chauvinistic and ignorant fanaticism; through the columns of the newspaper, they propagated that all people and nations are brothers, that there is space for everyone on the earth and under the sun, to live in peace and understanding.

The newspaper *Terbie* truly raised the national patriotic feeling of the Gypsy minority, but it fought resolutely and convincingly against its chauvinistic feelings. The newspaper was working towards an enlightened patriotism and stood against uneducated fanaticism and chauvinism.

In that respect, too, the newspaper *Terbie* was a standard of a truly progressive democratic organ whose task was to spread love, not divisiveness among people. It was against the brotherly humiliating wars – it was for peace and understanding between all nations in the world. The main stimulus of the newspaper *Terbie* was the love between people and the understanding between the nations. It was a firm enemy of the hatred between people and the animosity between the nations. With these main slogans, which were embedded in its program, the newspaper was welcomed with joy by all, and especially by the Gypsy minority.

That is why its success was so big.

CHAPTER XXIX
HABITS AND CUSTOMS, AND THE FIGHT AGAINST THE HARMFUL ONES

Up until 1920, the Gypsies used to have marriage customs, which were harmful, often quite offensive for the girl and very harmful for the creation of truly happy Gypsy families. That was the custom *Baba-hak* [50], according to which the boy's parents had to make a costly payment to the father of the girl in order to consent to the marriage. This harmful and utterly offensive custom had to be eliminated by all means as it created motivation for making marriages based not on love and mutual attraction, but marriages in which the young bridegroom, through bidding, could dissuade a girl from marrying the one, whom she truly loved. This *Baba-ak* (father's merit) was undoubtedly a remnant of the times when women were traded as a commodity, like cattle, for example. This anachronism and harmful custom had to be abolished by all means, and the organisation *Istikbal* as well as the newspaper *Terbie* resolutely revolted against it. The struggle was not easy, because the biases and the stubbornness, especially of the elderly, were not easy to overcome. Nevertheless, with systematic explanatory work, both in general meetings and in domestic and personal conversations, this custom was slowly wiped out opening the gates for the creation of a truly happy Gypsy family.

With the abolition of this custom, divorces in the Gypsy families have greatly diminished, because the marriages were no longer based on interest but on attraction. Strengthening the family, which is the basic unit of every nation, means strengthening of the nation itself. In this respect, the fight of the organisation *Istikbal* and the newspaper *Terbie* against the abusive *Baba-ak* custom will have to be judged correctly and fairly; they should be applauded with the achievement of a true national victory for the Gypsy family, with great difficulty and in the face of serious resistance. The *Baba-ak* custom, involved money giving, and in kind gifts such as clothes, shoes, cows, rams, flour, etc. The young girl was sold as mere cattle, and the bargaining for her was done without asking her whether she was attracted to the bridegroom who was offering a rich ransom. In this way, familymaking had nothing to do with mutual attraction; the families were an artificial construction that disintegrated at the slightest collision. That is why the struggle of both the organisation *Istikbal* and the newspaper *Terbie* was just, because it aimed to create a true relationship based on mutual love, attraction and understanding so that the Gypsy family would not fall apart with the slightest problem. With this, the struggle of the organisation *Istikbal* and the newspaper *Terbie* gained the significance of a huge national benefit.

Weddings once lasted for four days (from Tuesday to Friday). This custom, however, was increasingly vanishing because of the new economic situation. Nothing justified the custom of having four-day weddings, wasting a lot of means for celebrations, exhausting both the young family and their relatives by four-day fests, and being forced to seek money for the most urgent family and domestic needs a few days after the wedding was over. The unimaginable costs of these weddings often deprived young families of the opportunity to furnish their places and have normal living conditions in their homes. This tradition, against which the Organisation conducted explanatory work, gradually, by virtue of the circumstances, became obsolete, and today's weddings last one day.

In the weddings, the new family received gifts from their close relatives, usually rams, wine, *rakiya*. This custom still exists today, but it has changed and the young spouses receive as gifts various kinds of household goods such as cauldrons, pots, jugs, wardrobes, buffets, etc., things that their new life requires.

It was also common for the bride to put on white cream as makeup and stick various ornaments on it. The girl's face was covered in a thick layer so that it could hold the decorations glued to it. Some makeup artists (called *teleziyki*) used to apply on white cream other colours, and special pellets (called *pulcheta*).

Muslim Gypsies carried out their marriage ceremonies at home, with an Imam, and the Orthodox Gypsies carried out theirs in the Orthodox Church without making up the bride. After the ceremony, the customs were the same as with the Muslim Gypsies.

When there was a serious confrontation in the family, a special department of the organisation *Istikbal* intervened to settle the dispute. This department was called the Conciliation Council of the Gypsy Minority. It managed to settle the controversial issues and bring peace and reassurance to the family in most of cases. Based on this, we can see how comprehensive and fruitful the activities of the organisation *Istikbal* were.

When we talk about the activities of the organisation, we have to note the huge work that Hyusein A. Bialalov did in it. He was the secretary of the organisation and took care of its multifaceted activities. He was the soul of the organisation because he was absorbed exclusively by its multifaceted work. He kept the registers of the organisation and issued the notices that we mentioned above, without which the Sofia Municipality did not issue any certificates to the Gypsies.

The organisation *Istikbal* had a weekly conference of each group separately, which discussed the enlightening of the Gypsy minority and its cultural, political and social rise. These conferences also led a systematic struggle against the shalwars, which were soon removed from the Gypsy minority. In addition, the *Istikbal* organised [...] [51]

Another custom, existing among the Gypsies, is the so-called *syunet* – circumcision. The young boys, when they reach a certain age, are circumcised in a special solemn ceremony that resembles very much that of weddings. A specially trained barber performed the circumcision.

The organisation *Istikbal* had a comprehensive activity. In its educational work, it managed to eliminate many unnecessary and even harmful and expensive customs.

On the insistence of the organisation *Istikbal*, the makeup at the bride's marriage was abolished, and *Baba-ak* was also removed. Weddings became more modest. People can understand these gains, if they realise the harm of all these customs.

Shalwars have ceased to be the daily clothing of the female Gypsies; they have remained a museum item and are worn only on special occasions when the national character of a party has to be emphasised.

CHAPTER XXX
HOLIDAYS

Legend has it that soon after the Gypsies moved to Europe, on a cold winter night, when there was no food in the Gypsy tents and there was no opportunity to get it from anywhere, incidentally, frozen wild geese came in large numbers around the Gypsy tents. It was as if the Gods had sent these frozen wild geese to feed their starving followers. According to the legend, this happened on St Basil's Day and that is why it has become a national traditional Gypsy holiday since then. Unlike the Bulgarians, the Gypsies celebrate St Basil's Day for three days instead of one. During this time, the geese are cooked and roasted. All relatives and friends go to visit each other "za proshka" [for forgiveness] while bringing with them *rakiya*; their hosts serve roasted or cooked goose, and lots of wine and *rakiya*. This tradition is still alive today although the conditions have changed significantly.

The other Gypsy national traditional holiday is *Hederlez*.

During this holiday, the Gypsies slaughter a lamb for a sacrifice. This holiday coincides with the Christian holiday St George's Day. This holiday is also celebrated for three days, unlike the Bulgarian one. On this holiday, people make great feasts, parties, and *horo* dances. There are solemn celebrations; no one does any works; and everybody enjoys the parties and visits relatives and friends.

The other Gypsy holiday is *Meerem*. It is celebrated in a similar solemn way, on August 28, and it coincides with the Christian holiday of the Gods' Mother.

According to the Muslim religion, the Gypsies have two major holidays, which are also celebrated for three days: Ramadan Baryam and Kurban Baryam [52].

During these holidays, especially on St Basil's Day and St George's Day, Gypsy families are visited by many Bulgarian families who stay for lunch at the Gypsy homes, have fun with them, dance horo, etc. This shows the close relationship between Bulgarians and Gypsies and also their mutual respect and esteem.

CHAPTER XXXI
THE GYPSY HOUSE OF CULTURE IN SOFIA

In 1906, the Sofia Municipality granted the Gypsy minority two hundred square meters of space for building a Public Cultural House of the Gypsies in Sofia.

This gift inspired the entire Gypsy minority in Sofia to proceed faster with the construction of the Public Cultural Gypsy House. Everybody got down to work, and everybody helped as they could in the building of the House. Indeed, thanks to these efforts, the public house of culture was built on 175 Naycho Tsanov Street, exclusively with the resources, efforts, and labour of the Gypsies.

Subsequently, the organisation *Istikbal* accommodated 5–6 homeless old Gypsies in this building until 1934.

In June 1934, the organisation *Istikbal* was dissolved by a written order; its publication, the newspaper *Terbie* was suspended [53].

The same thing happened with all political parties in Bulgaria as well.

On March 6, 1936, the sanitary authorities blocked the Gypsy neighbourhood because there was a false allegation about an epidemic among the Gypsies, which later turned out to be a lie. Although the sanitary authorities provided food to the people in the locked-out neighbourhood, the blockade did not appeal to the Gypsies, and they set up a committee in order to lift it. Members of the Committee included: Shakir Pashev, Ahmed Sotirov, Hyusein A. Bilalov, Emin Eminov, Raicho Kochev, Shakir Mestamov, Ismail Shakirov (Tolio), Yashar Mustafov, Nayde Yasharov, Asan Osmanov, Muto Bilalov, Asan Osmanov, and others who, after long negotiations managed to favourably settle the issue and the blockade was lifted.

The committee also arranged for the compensation of those Gypsies who, due to the blockade, had lost their wages. The state paid them their lost wages.

CHAPTER XXXII
THE FIRST GYPSY BALL IN SOFIA

On March 3, 1938 [54], the Gypsy minority organised the first Gypsy ball in Sofia with oriental Gypsy musical performances and scenes from *One Thousand and One Nights* at the City Casino. Citizens from Sofia who visited this first of its kind Gypsy ball, continuously acclaimed all the performances in the superb programme and were amazed by the gifted Gypsy artists and musicians.

The Bulgarian newspapers did not miss this first cultural event and came out with enthusiastic articles and comments about the Ball, writing extraordinary praises for both the artists and the musicians.

The author of the artistic plays and scenes from *One Thousand and One Nights* was Shakir Pashev, Director was Emin Eminov, and the ballet master, Hyusein A. Bilalov.

This first Gypsy ball marked the beginning of the Gypsy minority theatrical performances. It was our first, albeit timid, step towards a cultural expression in which we could demonstrate the gifts of the Gypsies.

The warm reception by the audience and the press in Sofia gave us the courage to continue this tradition, which we have commenced and which, for our joy and pride, has turned out to be so successful.

CHAPTER XXXIII
THE RESTORATION OF THE GYPSY ORGANISATION IN SOFIA

In 1945, when people had their freedoms restored, the Gypsy minority, on the initiative of the dissolved organisation *Istikbal*, convened a large meeting on March 6th, at 18 Tatarli Street. This was a constitutive meeting, which unanimously decided that the organisation of the [Gypsy] minority should be restored in order to continue the enlightenment of the latter.

The meeting unanimously elected the following leadership of the organisation: President – Shakir Pashev, Vice-President – Ramcho Kochev and Bilal Osmanov, Treasurer – Demir Rustemov, Secretary – Tair Selimov, Members: Emin Eminov, Hyusein A. Bilalov, Sulyo Metkov, Resho Demirov, Ramcho Totev, Demcho Blagoev, Naydo Yasharov, Asan Osmanov (Palyacho), Asan Somanov, Ismail Shakirov, Shakir Meshanov, Ali Mehmedov, Izet Salchov, Tseko Nikolov.

The organisation involved about 3,000 members.

The leadership established local organisations in all neighbourhoods, which held regular meetings and conferences. The task of these meetings was to work more and more persistently for the comprehensive cultural, educational, political and social rise of the Gypsy minority.

After the People's Victory of September 9, 1944, new bright horizons of full political, cultural, and national freedom opened for both the Bulgarian people and the Gypsy minority. The Gypsy minority enthusiastically congratulated the People's victory because it opened the doors of freedom, previously tightly locked for them. With the Victory of September 9, 1944, the discrimination against the Gypsy minority, previously imposed by the bourgeois-fascist governments, was abolished. The wide route for cultural and educational work was open for the Gypsy minority, and it did not hesitate to take full advantage of it. The amateur artistic and musical groups which were created all over the country, were accepted everywhere with great interest, general approval, and enthusiasm.

Due to the rightful leadership of the organisation, which strictly observed the material and cultural-educational interests of the Gypsy minority, and persistently took care for the enlightenment of the people, a meeting in 1946 made a decision to extend the organisation's term without new elections. With this act, the assembly demonstrated its satisfaction with the work of the committee and, thanking it for its work until that moment, continued its mandate emphasising the trust for this committee among the Gypsy circles.

At this meeting it was also decided to resume publishing a Gypsy newspaper with the title *Romano esi* (Gypsy Voice). At the same meeting, an editorial committee was elected with the task to make the newspaper, to organise its distribution among the Gypsy minority, to inform them about all political and cultural events, both inside and outside the country, without giving up the task of enlightening the Gypsy minority. Shakir Pashev was elected editor of the newspaper, and members of the editorial committee included: Sulyo Metkov, Tair Salimov, Mustafa Aliev, Hyusein A. Bilalov and others.

The assembly decided to convene a general Gypsy national conference in Sofia on May 2, 1948. The conference was convened, and it took place on the appointed date in the hall of Vasil Levski school, on Dimitar Petkov Blvd., with the participation of representatives of the Fatherland Front -- comrade Georgi Dimitrov's secretary, Pachevski; MP Yanko Petkov; Dobri Bodurov; and other public figures.

Greetings on behalf of the Armenians and the Jews in Bulgaria were addressed at the conference. They were accepted with great joy. It was obvious that the discrimination against the Gypsies was eliminated and thrown into the archives from where it would never come out again.

Delegates and guests of the conference took part in the May 1st manifestation.

The conference decided that the leadership of the Sofia organisation should operate as the Central Initiative Committee of the Gypsy Minority in Bulgaria and elected Mustafa Aliev as the first secretary of the Committee. The conference made this decision in accordance with Circular Letter No. 18 of the Fatherland Front.

After this conference, other organisations of the Gypsy minorities were formed in the country and they convened their own regional and district conferences, which were attended by representatives from Sofia almost every time.

The conference that took place on May 2, 1948, played the role of a congress of the Gypsy minorities in Bulgaria and will be remembered by all those who took part in it as well as by the Gypsy minorities in general.

It marked the beginning of a new organisational life, which aimed to do persistent and devoted efforts for the enlightenment of the Gypsies in the country and for their cultural-educational and political-social development.

CHAPTER XXXIV
CREATION OF THE *PHARAOHS* ART AND MUSICAL COLLECTIVE

In 1945, Shakir Pashev gave the initiative and provided material assistance for the creation of the artistic and musical collective called *The Pharaohs*.

The enthusiasm for this collective was indescribable, especially among the younger Gypsies. With joy and great enthusiasm, they joined the collective and everyone tried to be as helpful as they could. Musicians, artists, dancers – all of them were full of enthusiasm and determined to demonstrate the Gypsy talent. They developed their talents and everyone who participated in the team made sure to uphold their reputation, guarding against the slightest frivolousness that could damage the name and honour of the collective. Everyone did their best to safeguard and increase their reputation. And indeed, the collective became famous; the Bulgarian public greeted it with astonishment and surprise and at the same time with joy and enthusiasm. Praise and encouragement came from everywhere, and everyone wanted to guide the collective along a truly artistic path so that it could fulfil its tasks. Distortion was inadmissible.

The collective worked tirelessly. Everyone was aware that the theatre and the music would contribute to the cultural and educational rise of the Gypsy minority. And because of this, everyone worked with love, selflessly, putting all their efforts into their work. This activity of the members of the collective gave brilliant results: the Bulgarian public welcomed the performances of the ensemble with great interest and could not find words to express their admiration of the artistic play and the magnificent musical performance.

Everyone gave a great reception to the two performances of the collective in *Slavyanska beseda* community centre.

In addition, the team visited wounded soldiers from the Fatherland War in schools and hospitals. The soldiers joyfully greeted these performances and applauded them constantly.

The two performances in *Slavyanska beseda* community centre were an unprecedented and surprising success. These two performances are unforgettable and everyone will remember them; they demonstrated the capabilities of the Gypsy.

The collective performed in schools and hospitals where soldiers in the Fatherland War were treated, hoping to bring a little joy to the soldiers' souls and hearts. The performances were expected, welcomed, and sent away from the wounded soldiers with joy and true satisfaction. The soldiers appreciated the masterful artistic and musical performance and applauded unceasingly.

The Gypsy minority both in Sofia and in the whole country appreciated the activities of the collective because it raised the national feeling of the minority and strengthened the awareness that when the Gypsy has freedom, they can develop their power and show their worth, which until recently no one thought the Gypsies possess.

CHAPTER XXXV
THE CREATION OF THE THEATRE *ROMA*

The Member of Parliament, Shakir Pashev, gave the initiative for the establishment of the Theatre *Roma*. The theatre, however, needed funds. Shakir Pashev met with the parliamentary committee and comrade Georgi Dimitrov, and after making the case for the establishment of a Gypsy theatre, Pashev asked for a subsidy from the state to furnish and develop it. Both the parliamentary committee and comrade G. Dimitrov immediately responded to the request of MP Shakir Pashev and the National Assembly unanimously granted the amount of two million levs subsidy to the theatre. When Shakir Pashev announced the subsidy at a meeting, the whole minority enthusiastically applauded the Government, and nominated their own people to manage the theatre. They were Emin Eminov, Neno Shakirov Pashev and Sulyo Metkov.

The reformed Theatre *Roma* performed *Gypsy Rhapsody* by Al[exander] Girginov with great success [55]. Everyone was delighted with the unprecedented success of the theatre and the performance of that play.

The newspaper *Otechestven front*, issue No. 1147 of May 28, 1948, made a detailed report of the premiere and gave very good reviews. It was obvious that everyone was delighted with the performance of the play and publicly expressed their enthusiasm. The newspaper described the premiere in detail and gave excellent reviews of the performance.

Young Gypsy women, men, and talented musicians performed all roles. The artists performed their roles very well, with full awareness of the artistic play. For the most part, illiterate, they memorised their roles and played without prompters. This fact made obvious, even to the biggest sceptics, that the Gypsy man and the Gypsy woman are capable of great deeds as long as they have the opportunity to express freely their gifts and talents. The musical performance was simply virtuoso because if there is one thing that the Gypsy soul likes, it is undoubtedly the music.

Under unceasing applause, to the delight and astonishment of the Sofia audience, the Theatre *Roma* made its performances with great success in May and June 1948. The performances were a real celebration for the Gypsy minority; they could not have been pleased more with their compatriots, who had demonstrated the Gypsy abilities and gifts so well.

On July 6, 1948, the Theatre *Roma* started a country tour in response to invitations from all over the country. It visited the following cities: Plovdiv, Stara Zagora, Yambol, Sliven, Burgas, Kolarovgrad [today Shumen], Tolbuhin [today Dobrich] and Varna. Everywhere the Theatre *Roma* invoked only admiration and amazement. Everyone admitted their surprise by the highly artistic performance. The audience welcomed this Gypsy cultural, artistic, and musical show with enthusiasm everywhere.

The performances of the Theatre *Roma* actors and musicians fully justified the government subsidy.

Undoubtedly, Ali Metov stood out among the best male actors, and Asiba Alieva, among our best female actors.

The best musicians in the Theatre *Roma* were Peyu Budakov, Yashar Agaliev and Iraim Chinchiliev.

These artists and musicians brought fame not only for themselves but also for the Gypsy minority. With their artistic performance, with masterful musical performance, our artists and musicians affirmed the fame of the Gypsy minority for high artistic and musical gifts. When we talk about them, we should express not only gratitude but also warm praise.

CHAPTER XXXVI
SINGERS IN RADIO BROADCASTS

We cannot fail to point out the names of our good singers, such as Gugulya and Amida Shakova, who sang on the radio. They usually sing the songs of our famous composer Yashar Malikov, which are also on gramophone records and are often broadcast on the radio, and which everyone listens to with pleasure and delight.

In 1946 and 1948, on *Vasilyovden* (St Basil's Day), the orchestra of Yashar Malikov with Asiba Hyuseinova and Metova performed great musical shows on Radio Sofia.

The programmes were preceded by a short speech by the then MP Shakir Pashev, as well as by Hyusein Bilalov.

The performances of the Theatre *Roma* will be remembered and cherished, especially by the Gypsy minority. They were, in fact, a great cultural celebration for the minority, which, after so much oppression and discrimination, finally received the opportunity to express freely its great and undeniable talents. The Gypsy minority owes this jubilation exclusively to the people's Government and the Communist Party because without them these gifts would have remained suppressed and dormant in the souls and hearts of every Gypsy man and every Gypsy woman. The monstrous and unjustified discrimination against the Gypsy minority was eliminated once and for all, and the Gypsy minority has got open doors for cultural growth and artistic and musical creativity. That is exactly why every Gypsy man and woman carries in their souls and hearts a warm and unquenchable gratitude to the people's Government and the Bulgarian Communist Party.

CHAPTER XXXVII
SPARKS OF DISSATISFACTION AND A SEVERANCE ATTEMPT

Despite the enthusiasm of the Gypsy minority; despite the exaltation with the activities of the amateur artistic and musical collective; despite the wonderful work of the Gypsy organisation, which established itself as a true official representative of the minority; and despite the endless successes of the Theatre *Roma*, some members of the minority, unfortunately young ones, expressed dissatisfaction with these activities, pretending to have a higher culture. Their behaviour undermined the general enthusiasm and planted a bomb under the feet of this activity threatening to destroy everything created so far with so much effort.

In July 1950, on the insistence of the dissatisfied young people, and in order to prevent the division in our circles, the Sofia organisation and the Central Committee of all organisations were handed over to these dissatisfied young people. The same, of course, happened with the Theatre *Roma*.

Without any reason, these young people rushed to give a new name to the newspaper, now entitled *Nevo drom* (New Way), despite the will of the conference of May 2, 1948. This newspaper published only three issues because the leadership and the Editorial Board lost the sympathy of the minority from Sofia and the whole country.

The Central Committee was headed by Nikola Terzobaliev and Tair Selimov.

Demcho Blagoev led the Sofia organisation, and Lyubomir (Mustafa) Aliev and Sulyo Metkov became the leaders of the Theatre *Roma*.

The mentioned new leaders failed to cope with the public work among our compatriots as a result of which, our organisation, along with the theatre, ceased their activities.

In this way, young people, driven by personal rather than social ambitions, ruined a deed that had taken so many sleepless nights and exertion to succeed.

This was, and will remain, a dark spot in the history of the Gypsy organisation and the Theatre *Roma*; it is also a lesson for those who envy others for their work, but once they take their place, are unable to sustain their predecessors' work and to achieve success.

CHAPTER XXXVIII
REVIVAL OF THE AMATEUR ARTISTIC AND MUSICAL COLLECTIVE

It took six full years of oblivion and indifference for the cultural and educational work among the minority, before the amateur artistic and musical collective *Roma* resumed its old but proven path towards progress and creativity. In 1956, with the help of the old leadership of the organisation, an amateur artistic collective for music, songs and dances was created under the leadership of Yashar Malikov [56]. He began working with the familiar old enthusiasm and ardour.

Our compatriots Sabria Nenova Pasheva and Asiba as well as our well-known and beloved artist Ali Metov distinguished themselves as its champions.

Speaking of this activity, we cannot miss the name of our first playwright from Pleven, Mustafa Aliev [57], who staged the play *Koshtana* [58] in Sofia.

Other compatriots who already had higher education were the following:

Demir Aliev, who graduated in Russian philology and is a teacher at the first Gypsy school, named after Makarenko, in Sofia.

The son of Dankolov from Samokov graduated in medicine.

Asan, from the village of Chorlovo, Lom region, graduated in engineering.

Bena Minova, who has been studying medicine for three years now, and Asen Demirev.

There are many more of our youth, men and women, who pursue their education and who will be tomorrow's pride of the Gypsy minority.

In 1958, our compatriots Sabria Nenova Pasheva and Asiba Ilieva, together with our compatriot Ibro Lolov, visited Germany at the Leipzig fair and performed Gypsy dances before the Germans with great success, energetically applauded by the audience. They stayed there for a whole month.

The cultural activities of our compatriots have become increasingly important. They are enrolled and study in all secondary and graduate schools, and we firmly believe that it won't be long before the intelligentsia would flood our circles and start leading the minority on new paths of genuine culture, progress, and prosperity.

CHAPTER XL
GYPSY COMMUNITY CENTRE IN SOFIA AND ITS TASKS

Today, the Gypsy Community Centre *9th September*, located in the Gypsy House of Culture, has a good library, which is widely used by all our compatriots from Sofia. The primary concern of the community centre is the enlightenment of the Gypsy minority. It does a great job in that direction. Through discussions, personal meetings, through the amateur artistic collective, through the theatre, etc., the management of the community centre makes great efforts to raise the Gypsy minority in Sofia to a higher cultural level. And we can state, with joy and pride, that the efforts of the community centre management are not in vain.

We should note that in 1956 a delegation of MPs from the People's Republic of China visited our House of Culture and expressed interest in our lives because our people are one of the oldest nations in the world. We learned from them that our compatriots in China are called *Chi*.

The Gypsy House of Culture in Sofia is a centre where each of our compatriots feels at home.

The large number of books that our community centre owns is widely read by our minority. You will often see in the community centre our compatriots who have come to get books, to exchange thoughts on the books they have read, to draw conclusions from them and to recommend each other a good read. This creates close brotherly relations between them and brings them closer to each other. The Gypsy House of Culture, created with so much effort, now plays the role assigned to it – to educate and enlighten, and to do everything possible for the cultural rise of the Gypsy minority and for fostering brotherhood relations among the Gypsies.

The rehearsals of the theatre, of the amateur artistic and musical collective, and the meetings of the Gypsy organisation all take place in the community centre.

CHAPTER XLI
GYPSY SCHOOLS IN SOFIA AND IN THE PROVINCE

In Sofia, there are currently two Gypsy schools, called First and Second, which educate 1,200 Gypsy children. In the Emil Markov neighbourhood, there was a Gypsy class in the Bulgarian school; and there was another Gypsy class in the Bulgarian school in the Slatina neighbourhood. Apart from Sofia, there are Gypsy schools in the following towns in the country:

In Stara Zagora, we have a separate school in the Chadar Mogila neighbourhood.

In Nova Zagora, we have a Gypsy school and a community centre.

In Vidin, Berkovitsa, and Kyustendil we have separate schools.

In the latter city, the school was built in 1957.

There are Turkish schools for Gypsies in Plovdiv, Ruse, Varna and Pazardzhik. In these cities, the Gypsies are trying hard to pass for Turks.

There is a Gypsy school in Sliven.

In Sliven, Yambol and other places, where our compatriots study in Bulgarian schools, they want to pass for Bulgarians.

The People's Gypsy Community Centre *9th September* in Sofia selected an Editorial Board that publishes the newspaper *Neve Roma* (New Gypsies). The composition of the editorial board is as follows: Sulyo Metkov, Yashar Al. Saliev, Shakir M. Pashev, Tair Selimov, Asan Demirov, Bena Minova and Yashar Malikov.

From year to year, the number of our children attending various schools is increasing. They study in high schools, in various types of technical schools and the [Sofia] University, and we can realistically expect that it won't be long, only about ten years, before our minority would be enriched with an intelligentsia that would push its development in cultural terms far ahead.

CHAPTER XLII
HISTORY OF THE GYPSY MINORITY ACCORDING TO FOREIGN AUTHORS

The Gypsies are a nomadic people scattered throughout all European countries, in western Asia and Siberia, in northern Africa, in Egypt and mainly Algeria, in America, and even in Australia.

Accurate data on the number of Gypsies outside Europe, or even in Europe, cannot be provided because the data from official statistics is often contradictory and unreliable.

Nevertheless, the number of Gypsies worldwide is estimated at approximately 5,000,000. This figure, however, is approximate, and we cannot accept it as reliable.

The Gypsies have kept their old characteristics despite the different circumstances in which they were placed. In this respect, the Gypsies, like the Jews, have not lost their characteristic national features, customs and manners and have not succumbed to assimilation.

CHAPTER XLIII
NAMES BY WHICH THE GYPSIES ARE KNOWN

They are known mainly by two names according to one or another heritage. The first group, which comprises the majority of the Gypsies in Europe and includes the compact masses living on the Balkan Peninsula, Romania and extending to Germany and Italy, is known as *Atsigani*, which sometimes changes to *Çingene* in Turkey and Greece; *Цигани* in Bulgaria; *Ţigani* in Romania; *Czigany* in Hungary; *Zigeuner* in Germany; and *Zingari* in Italy.

The other name by which the Gypsies are better known in the East is the *Egyptians*.

In England, the Gypsies are called *Gypsy*, probably named after Mount *Gyp* in the Peloponnese, Greece, where a large tribe used to live long before moving to England.

In some German documents, they are called *Aegypter*, and in Spanish – *Gitano*; in modern Greek – *Gyptos*. They are also known by the terms *Pharaohs* in Romania and *Faraonepek* in Hungary (or the people of the Pharaoh), which are variations related to their residence in Egypt.

The habit of attributing Egyptian origins to this people, known for possessing magical powers, had lasted for a long time.

The name Egyptians come from a strange tale that the Gypsies spread when they appeared in Western Europe. They said they had come from a small country called Little Egypt, which was due to their misconceptions about Egypt, Armenia, or the Peloponnese.

In the Syrian translation of the apocryphal book of Adam, known as *The Treasure Cave*, which was probably combined in the sixth century, there is a passage: "And they are of the seed of Canaan, as I said, the Egyptians; and of course, they were scattered all over the earth and served as slaves to slaves" (Bezold, p. 25) [59].

Although Canaan is the old name of the old western Palestine, the above quote refers to the Gypsies probably because they lived there for a long time. No other source mentions about the wandering and slavery of the Gypsies. This may have been a legend known in Asia Minor and from there, perhaps, attributed to the Gypsies.

In France, the Gypsies are known as *Bohemians*, after the old name of today's Czechia (Bohemia), where they had lived for a long time before going to France. There are other names that are attributed to them, such as *Vlachs, Saracens, Hagrites, Nubians* and others.

In Germany, quite wrongly and absolutely incorrectly they were originally considered Tatars, although they had nothing to do with this people.

In the beginning, the Gypsies were also called *Heyden*, which means unbelievers (non-religious).

As for the origin of the word 'Atsigan', Miklosich believes that it came from 'atinganoi', a name that originally belonged to a special pagan sect that lived in Asia Minor and was also known as 'melki-zedekaitos'. The members of this sect followed very strict rules, which in their eyes had been desecrated. That is why they were given the name 'atinganoi', which means people who should not be touched by people of other nationalities.

Byzantine historians of the 9th century describe them as fortune-tellers, sorcerers, and snake charmers.

On the question of the origin of the word Gypsy, there is still an unresolved dispute t. Some historians support the aforementioned German author. Others side with Bataillard, a French researcher of the history of the Gypsies. He claims that the Ligurians mentioned by Herodotus, who lived near Masali, used to refer to the merchants as 'singines'. The Cypriots, however, used this term to name the spears, and since the Gypsies at that time were constant producers of arms and metal products, the term *tsigani* is of Greek origin because the modern Greek word 'atsinkanos' seems to be a translation of 'sigines' from the old Empire. The Cypriots refer to the Gypsies as 'kilindzhirides', a Turkish word with a Greek ending that cannot mean anything else but sword- makers.

Everything known about the Cabeiri associations [60] in which the Sinti and Siginesti took part is incredibly reminiscent of today's Gypsy metallurgists. "And don't the strange Greek prophetesses, the sibyls, resemble the Gypsy fortune-tellers in name and character?" And out of these reflections, Bataillard has built a broader assumption concerning Europe's prehistoric past.

The European Gypsies, who had left the old Byzantine Empire, travelled west, and settled in Europe, America, and Australia, call themselves *Rom* while the woman is called *Romni*. There are many ways to explain the word *Rom*.

Miklosich attributes it to 'doma' and 'domba', a low caste in India.

This coincides with the view that the language of the European Gypsies shows great closeness to Hindu tribes such as 'doms'.

The language of the Gypsies in Europe is in any case closer to that of the farthest part of North-Western India, except for those who stayed only for a short time in this part, such as the Armenian Gypsies, whose language is very close to Hindi.

Most of the Gypsies arrived in Europe speaking a language slightly altered by the tribes through which the ancestors of the *Romanian Chali* have passed and stayed [61]. Another view, supported by careful phonetic research, is that the language originated in the central group with a clear influence from the north-western group of Sanskrit languages in India.

Gaster [Gaster, 1883] suggests that the Gypsies, who had no home or homeland, because after separating from India, they did not intend to conquer other peoples and therefore did not have political traditions and literature, identified themselves with the people in whose environment they lived and called themselves *Rom* (*Romanoi, Romaion*), a name that satisfied their vanity.

This origin of the word explains why it is limited only to Europe.

The Gypsies refer to each other using the name for 'people' in their language: *Rom, Manush, Gadzho* [62].

The names that are very popular and suitable for them are *Tsygani* and *Rom* [63].

CHAPTER XLIV
HISTORY. APPEARANCE IN EUROPE

The first mass appearance of the Gypsies in Europe cannot be identified before the beginning of the 14th century. They began leaving India several centuries earlier (the year 1000).

The similarity of their language with Hindi led historians to trace the origins of the Gypsies in India.

Dr Kopernicki in Bucharest [64], who managed to collect 20 skulls of Gypsies, found that even today they are completely similar in a positive way to the Hindus, who have a special shape. It should be accepted, according to A. A. Hovelacque [Hovelacque, 1874], that the Gypsy race emerged in India from two groups consisting until today of one fine and one rough model. It is quite possible, however, that they may have mixed in Europe. It remains indisputable that the Gypsy language is related to the seven New Hindu dialects (Hindi, Marathi, Punjabi, Sindhi, Gujarati, Bengali, Oriya). It does not approximate any of these specifically.

It was difficult to identify the Gypsies with certainty, with one single people from the peoples in present day India.

Bataillard claims that it is not possible to track down the traces from their first settlement in southeastern Europe. He mentions a faint trace of them in Mesopotamia. However, he maintains that they had settled, since times immemorial, in Eastern Europe, the Caucasus, Asia Minor, and the Mediterranean islands. He is convinced that the Sigines mentioned by Herodotus and these Sinti from the time of Homer were the ancestors of our Gypsies.

Bronze production in Europe is widely recognised today as originating in India. It was introduced gradually through itinerant metalworkers. And it is known, namely, by the shape of the handle, that their producers had small hands.

At least three centuries before history recorded the emigration of the true Gypsies, there were itinerant ironworkers who travelled from one country to another. It is believed that the Gypsies assimilated them and adopted their craft, but Bataillard claims that they were the actual ancestors of our Gypsies.

The name by which the people called the first blacksmiths, ironworkers and street vendors from the East or from Greece, was also attached to the newcomers.

Hopf has proven that the Gypsies were in Corfu 1326 years ago. In 1346, Empress Catherine de Valois gave the governor of the island of Corfu the right to keep under his dependence some wanderers who had arrived from the continent.

They must have settled on the Balkan Peninsula and in the countries north of the Danube, such as Transylvania and Wallachia, quite sometime prior to the end of the 15th century and must have been enslaved like the Gypsies on the island of Corfu in the second half of the 14th century. At that time, there must have been Gypsies settled in Wallachia, who were treated as slaves; and there were newcomer Gypsies who were ironworkers, musicians, dancers, horse sellers, etc., because we find that the Voivode of Moldavia allowed these Gypsies in 1478 "to freely light fires for their smithies". However, a certain part, perhaps the larger one, fell into slavery and thus, the Gypsies were sold, exchanged, and inherited.

Many of them were tied to the land, and their situation was different from that of the Gypsies who headed west and who did not get the right of permanent residence or home anywhere and were treated very badly, except for a period of a very short time.

Their appearance in the West was first noted by chroniclers in the early 15th century. It is mentioned that in 1414 they were in Hessen. In 1418, they reached Hamburg, in 1419 -- Augsburg, and in 1428, they were already in Switzerland. In 1427, the Gypsies entered France, mainly in Provence. One group is said to have arrived in Bologna in 1422 during a pilgrimage on the way to Rome.

After this first settlement, a second one took place, however, on a larger scale, led by Elder Zumbel [65].

The Gypsies spread throughout Germany, Italy, and France between 1438 and 1512. Probably by the year 1500, they headed towards England.

In Europe, the Gypsies divided into twelve groups. The language of all these groups contains Greek words. It can be inferred from this circumstance that all these twelve groups had the same starting point and that this original centre must have been, as mentioned earlier, some Greek state.

Turkey was another centre from which many Gypsies made their way to Europe. In Turkey, they became mostly Muslims, although there were many Christians among them, who came to Turkey from Greece, where they had converted to Christianity. Of the total number in Turkey at the time (107,000 people), only 2,600 were sedentary. One part of the latter had completely forgotten their native language.

The Romanian Gypsies were the second group. They were more numerous. There were about 300,000 Gypsies there. Their language contains Greek and Slavic elements.

The third group formed in Hungary. Their language testifies about their previous stay in Romania. From Hungary, they scattered to Moravia and Bohemia.

The language of German Gypsies, an addition to Greek, Slavic and Romanian, contains also traces of French and Italian, which shows that many of them were previously in France and Italy.

The language of the Gypsies in Poland (15,000 people) and those in Lithuania (10,000 people) contains elements of Greek, Romanian, Hungarian and German.

The Russian Gypsies, who more than four centuries ago numbered about 48,000, one-third of whom were in Bessarabia, came from Poland except for those from the south, who came straight from Romania.

The Gypsies in southern Italy had lived in a Greek and in a Slavic country.

The Gypsies in Spain have passed through Romania and France. Those in England have travelled through Germany and France.

For all Gypsies, the last stage of their dispersal was Romania, except for those from southern Italy.

Albert Krantz [Krantz, 1580] says that the Gypsies first appeared in Germany in 1417 and they were called *Ciani*. They had a chief and a few well-dressed horsemen while the others went on foot. The women and children travelled in carriages.

The Gypsies carried letters of trust from Emperor Sigismund and other princes.

They lived carefreely and gathered other homeless people around them. Their wives practised fortune-telling, and Krantz called them in Italian *Ciani*.

CHAPTER XLV
LATER HISTORY

At the end of the 15th century, many countries issued orders obliging the 'Egyptians' to go into exile under the threat of death.

They were hanged in Edinburgh in 1611 for disobeying the order and staying in the kingdom, being 'Egyptians', and in 1636, in Haddington, orders were issued "to hang Egyptian men, to drawn women, and to beat others with their children until they leave the city and to burn them on the cheeks".

Burning the sides of their faces and stamping the backs of Gypsy men and women with red-hot iron was a common punishment, which was applied very often and ruthlessly.

In 1692, four Gypsies [in Hungary] were accused of cannibalism; the Inquisition forced them to admit that they had eaten a monk, a pilgrim, and even a woman from their own tribe, and sentenced them to death.

The Gypsies faced persecution, especially in 1725, by the Prussian King Friedrich-Wilhelm, because they did not have their own military organisation and were peaceful in nature. He was the only monarch who did not allow his wife to have a housemaid or a seamstress. He made her cook, wash the dishes, wash the clothes, clean and sew her own clothes and those of her children. He reduced the maintenance of the palace five times compared to his predecessor; in addition, he was very rude to the footmen, beat them with his cane, and never refrained from hitting any of his ministers. Historians of the Great French encyclopaedia characterised him as very limited and stubborn. Upon issuing an order, he would take to the streets to check its execution. All the Germans ran into hiding because he had indeed instilled great fear in them. The Gypsies were the easiest target for his anger.

In 1782 [66], Hungarian Gypsies were accused of similar crimes as in 1692 and when the alleged victims of the alleged murder were not found at the places indicated by the Gypsies, the Gypsies confessed to having "eaten them" after being subjected to torture by stretching.

It goes without saying that they were immediately beheaded or hanged.

Emperor Joseph II (1765–1790), author of one of the first decrees in favour of the Gypsies, appointed an investigation into this case. The investigation established that the Gypsies had not committed any murder and had been the victim of this monstrous accusation. Joseph II's mother, Maria Theresa, was also favourable to the Gypsies.

In 1904, the Prussian Landtag (State Diet) unanimously accepted the proposal to consider granting permits for peddling to the German Gypsies.

On February 17, 1906, Prussia issued special orders for the persecution of the Gypsies, and a special register in various places in Germany and Austria recorded the origins of Gypsy families with an unidentified place of residence.

In 1907, in Germany, there was a proposal for the persecution of the Gypsies.

In Romania, they were divided mainly into two classes:

First, slaves were tied to the land and deprived of any personal liberty, owned by the nobles, churches or monasteries; and the second class – wanderers.

According to their occupation, they were divided into four classes:

1. Such as *Lingurari* (those who worked with wood, spoon-makers).

2. *Kaldarashi* (ironmongers, tinsmiths, blacksmiths, and horse-makers).

3. *Ursari* (bear leaders) and

4. *Rudari* (miners), also called *Aurari* (gold diggers), who extracted gold from the golden sands in Wallachia.

Another group, separate from the previous ones, consisted of Gypsies who are called *Laeshi* or *Vatrashi* (settled in one place with a home and a fireplace) [67].

Each tent or Gypsy community was governed by a judge or leader while they were subordinated to the *byulyubashi* or voivode who, in turn, was under the direct control of the *yuzbashi* (or governor) appointed by the prince from among his nobles.

The *yuzbashiy* was responsible for the tax revenues from the Gypsies who were treated as the property of the prince. The soldiers or *yuzbashis*, who were not Gypsies by origin, often treated the Gypsies cruelly. Slaves could be sold and bought, freely exchanged, or inherited, and were treated like the Negroes in America until 1856, when their freedom in Moldavia was declared.

The abolition of slavery in Hungary and Transylvania, in 1871–1872, also affected the abolition of the slavery of the Gypsies [68].

In 1866, the Gypsies became Romanian citizens. Two years earlier, some had become farmers, but they were not able to work and preserve the land for a long time. Many of them rented their two hectares to Romanian villagers for an annual instalment. In this way, the Gypsies became workers on their former property.

Their inclination for wandering is strong and insurmountable. They were not willing to stay in one place, and that is perhaps the reason why they sold their land or rented it out. This passion among the Gypsies can still be noticed today, although it has already significantly decreased. It could also be noticed that there are Gypsies who settle down permanently when they find a job. They usually live with their families in tents or huts. In these tents or huts, they live half-dressed and raise pigs, and there are mules and donkeys around them. The Gypsies are peaceful by nature, but that does not stop them from exploding easily. However, they are easy to deal with when one treats them humanely and well, especially when they are offered *rakiya* and small services.

They are a noisy tribe. They speak loudly, and their way of speaking seems like a quarrel to those who listen to them and who do not know them well. They tend to live happy, carefree life. They are satisfied with very little. In addition, they are not very picky about food. They eat whatever they find, but despite their poor diet, they are still a healthy tribe. However, child mortality among them is not small. They have no sense of cleanliness. They do not maintain almost any hygiene, and that is why their morbidity is not small.

Their wives are beautiful, and their dark complexion makes them especially attractive. However, their wives are not sociable and communicate exclusively in the Gypsy language. Due to this circumstance, perhaps, the Gypsy language has been preserved to this day, although they lived in different countries between different peoples and in small groups, which otherwise would lead to their fast assimilation. This could not happen, however, due to the unsociable character of the Gypsy woman and the fact that she preserved the Gypsy language in the family. From this point of view, the Gypsy woman undertook a great role in the preservation of the language and hence – in the preservation of the national identity of the Gypsies. They almost never marry a man from another tribe, although young Gypsy men often marry women from other nations.

Usually, the chief of the Gypsies bargained for them during the grape harvest or the work on the land; he took care of their subsistence, and in the end, he paid the difference in money.

The Gypsies liked to have a chief to lead them, to rule them. People elected and accepted the leader voluntarily. His word was a law for every Gypsy in the group. The Gypsies obeyed the will of the chief even if they were not pleased with some orders. The chief represented his group to the authorities.

In Romania [69], the chief was called *vataf*. When the severity of the *vataf* diminished, the whole tribe rose as one; this happened on some Bacchus feasts, especially when the weather portended a storm; the previous chief was replaced and the tribe proceeded immediately with the election of another one who instilled a greater fear in them, as Obédénare [Obédénare, 1875] describes.

The Gypsies are primarily violinists, but they are also engaged in ironwork, blacksmithing, horseshoe-making, making copper cauldrons, making wooden spoons, spindles, baskets, etc. They are cooks, washers of golden sand, and other occupations that are less common among them.

However, what is most attractive for the Gypsy, it is undoubtedly the music. In Romania, Gypsy musicians are mostly violinists, and they are in great demand, both in restaurants and in various family celebrations such as weddings, baptisms, etc. The Gypsy violinists play without notes – by ear, but still, they are great performers of musical pieces. Their music is emotional, warm, and has great depth. Although the Gypsies are, by nature, cheerful and carefree people, their music is sad. The dances of the Gypsy women, on the other hand, are spirited, erotic and cheerful. Gypsy women always dance willingly and are carried away in their dances. They perform usually during home celebrations such as weddings, engagements, baptisms, circumcisions of young people and at their holidays – especially on St Basil's Day and St George's Day. When they dance, they play the so-called *daare* [daire] in the rhythm of the dance. On their hands, they put *dzilove* that they beat in the rhythm of the dance, and these *dzilove* create a special liveliness, beauty and plasticity of the dance.

The Gypsies were especially useful in agriculture because long before the establishment of today's plants and factories, they made all agricultural tools. With this activity, they contributed greatly to simplify the farmers' work. They made hoes, sickles, iron ploughshares for ploughs, axes, etc. They also repaired these agricultural tools, and made the farmers' work easier by improving their agricultural tools. In addition, they made horseshoes for horses, cattle, donkeys and mules and thus contributed greatly with their support to cattle breeding and agriculture. By making these agricultural tools, they came in close contact with the rural population and established good, friendly relation with them.

The Gypsies also like to wash sand to extract gold.

Some of the Gypsies are the only great masters of metal spoons, in addition to wooden ones. They also make various pots, pans and *krini* [bushels]. Some of them are bricklayers. In addition, there is a special group of Gypsies who are masters of copper cauldrons, pans, etc.; usually, women would distribute these cauldrons in Romania and sell them to the public.

As strange as it may sound, the Gypsies were the first workers who made, in those primitive times, the Romanian artillery.

In Romania, they also had superb sergeants in the army. One of them was even promoted to lieutenant for his outstanding activity.

Mention is also made of the son of a Romanian Gypsy cook who had become a physician.

Some Gypsies in Romania are, in addition to coppersmiths, tinsmiths. Coppersmiths make copper candlesticks.

From Turkey, a separate group went to Romania, called *Turkiti* or *Spoitori*, who dealt only with tinsmithing. Their migration from Turkey took place in the early 19th century. This group was then about 5,000 people. In winter, these tinsmiths live in huts, which are made deep in the ground. When the weather is favourable, in early spring, they set off to travel with all their accessories in a tall wagon. They settle down in tents near the cities and search for work there.

Women help their husbands by cleaning the pots and pans with sand, before the tinning itself, by rubbing them with their feet.

These Gypsies do not work iron. They are recognised as belonging to the Muslim religion but are essentially without any religion.

Unlike the Gypsies who claim to be Christians, according to Obédénare, they enjoy greater respect because none of them has committed theft. They maintain cleanliness and order which are their usual features. They also elect a chief; they marry only each other and until recently, they have practised circumcision. The young girls marry at the age of 12–13. Then, they take her for a walk around the village in a wagon, her head covered with a veil.

As we mentioned above, they have good music. Their songs resemble the Turkish ones; they perform music with a flute-like instrument and a flattened drum. As we have said already, in 1866, the Romanian Gypsies became Romanian citizens.

We know from Paspati that there are Gypsies in Turkey who married poor Greek girls in the vicinity of Istanbul. These Gypsies once entertained the Turks and Christians at their celebrations, festivities and banquets. The Gypsy nomads deny them.

These unsettled Gypsies could be found especially in the north and mostly in Bosnia. One of their tribes, the tribe of the *Zapari*, was particularly wild.

They usually bury the dead at night.

Metalworkers, blacksmiths, horseshoe-makers and coppersmiths for the most part, they have a holiday of the copper which seems to be their only distinctive holiday. Gypsies from Asia Minor sometimes come to visit the vicinities of Istanbul to see their compatriots who live here.

On January 6, 1906, the first Gypsy congress in Europe, which took place in Sofia, demanded political rights for the Turkish Gypsies or, as they call them, the *Gopti* [70].

It seems that the Gypsies in Bulgaria enjoy the best cultural and educational life, because apart from the fact that the first Gypsy Congress took place in Bulgaria, the first Gypsy newspaper in all of Europe was also published here. This shows that the Bulgarian Gypsies are relatively more cultured compared with their compatriots in other European countries, and they are more enterprising; they have a developed socio-political consciousness and an aptitude for public expression.

In Hungary, on the other hand, the Gypsies have a very strong tendency to make tours with all their belongings. In the 19th century, they even went to France, from where they returned only after 2–3 years. They had the best reception during their touring in Romania.

CHAPTER XLVI
RELIGION, CUSTOMS AND CHARACTER

The Gypsy religious views are a strange mixture and a variety of local faiths that the Gypsies had embraced everywhere they went, along with some world-famous old superstitions that they share with many other peoples. This uncertainty in religion and in their religious views is characteristic not only of Romanian Gypsies but of all Gypsies in Europe. This impasse explains why they celebrate holidays that are otherwise purely Christian, such as St George's Day, St Basil's Day, and God's Mother, which, of course, they call by other names, but cannot explain why they celebrate.

Among the Greeks, the Gypsies belonged to the Greek Church; among the Muslims, the Gypsies were Muslims; and in Romania, they belonged to the national Church. In Spain and Hungary, most Gypsies are Catholics according to the official faith of the country in which they live.

The Gypsies do not recognise the Ten Commandments.

The Gypsies are very optimistic in life, and they are desperate fatalists.

There is nothing special of Eastern origin in their religious vocabulary.

In general, their beliefs, customs and tales, etc., belong to the common folk works of the countries in which they live, and many of their symbolic expressions find an exact copy in Romanian and modern Greek and are often retold as if they were a translation from these languages.

Despite this religious syncretism and that their language is often a mixture of the language of the country in which they live, the Gypsies have retained their national identity intact and are strictly characteristic as a tribe. No one can deny that. They are not chauvinists, they do not preach any racism, but they strictly preserve their national identity and do not allow their girls to marry youths from another nation. They do this somewhat instinctively, without injecting any national or religious fanaticism into it.

The Gypsy superstitions are widespread. They are afraid of goblins, vampires, mermaids, and ghosts. When they are sick, they would rather see quacksalvers than seek medical help. The only explanation for this is their cultural backwardness. For example, the Gypsies cannot explain where their fear of goblins comes from, etc.

A special phenomenon is observed among the wandering Gypsies: Due to their mobility, they cannot be covered by smallpox vaccinations, which is why we meet many of them with scars on their faces and not a few who lost one and even both of their eyes and remained blind forever because of this insidious disease. This is exactly because they had no vaccination. In Europe, except for the Gypsies, almost no one else suffers from this disease thanks to the vaccine.

The Gypsy nomads practice the old craft, and they are copper-smiths or metalworkers in general. They also make sieves and traps, but in the East, they are rarely horseshoe-makers or horse sellers.

What is their pride, and a deserved one, is their music in which they are unsurpassed. The Gypsy musicians were the troubadours, or the travelling musicians, of Eastern Europe. The great composer Liszt even accredits the origin of Hungarian music to the Gypsies. Perhaps Liszt is right because it is hard to distinguish Gypsy from Hungarian music; there is such a great similarity between them.

The profession of musician has also been very successfully practised in Russia with great benefits. Their musical services were sought all the time for the numerous feasts of the former high society there.

It is the place to note here that the Gypsies have something else to be proud of, and rightly so. The Gypsy women are remarkably beautiful. They have a particularly emotional temperament, they are temperamental, and one can hardly withstand the pressure of their charm. Many Gypsy women became famous as talented singers and married rich people. A Gypsy woman from Moscow, specially gifted with both physical beauty and great voice, became the wife of Prince Galitzin. This allegedly true case was described in detail by Dixon. The charm of the Gypsy woman was so powerful that otherwise strong personalities gave in, abandoning everything in order to win her love.

The situation with the Gypsy women in Spain is the same except that there they are famous dancers; however, they carefully avert any attempt for marriage with rich Spaniards. In his case, they demonstrate nationalism for which there is no explanation.

Somewhat weaker, but similar is the success of the Gypsy women in Egypt.

The Gypsy woman is famous for her mystical practice – fortune-telling, exorcism, etc. She knows the means to hurt and avenge the enemy and to attack the friend. She can break magic done by others. In this direction, too, she is so convincing that naive people cannot resist her exhortations. In this way, the Gypsy woman earns her living and supports her family, to which she feels cordial and firm attachment. She loves her children, and she gives birth to many ones, although she does not show much interest in raising them. She takes care of her child with an instinct, similar, for example, to the animal one, without demonstrating any special cultural or pedagogical aspirations.

In magic, the Gypsy women use either the local language of the population or a slightly changed Romanian or Slavic, or Greek language.

The old Gypsy woman is also known for her skill in telling the future by cards, the well-known Gypsy Tarot.

The Gypsies have a lot of enchanting fairy tales, which are similar in every respect to the popular local tales.

CHAPTER XLVII
PHYSICAL FEATURES

The Gypsies are small in stature. Their complexion varies from the black colour of the Arab to the white of the Serb or the Pole. However, there are also white Gypsies, especially in Serbia and Dalmatia, who often cannot be differentiated from the local population except that they are more flexible, more temperamental and more muscular, with a better physique and more agile compared to the plump and phlegmatic Slavs and the mixed Romanian race. They are recognisable by the shimmer of their eyes and the wonderful whiteness of their teeth. Many of them have very good physiques, while others are similar to the mixed races, which is undoubtedly due to their marriage to outcasts from other races.

The Gypsy women are very agile, cheerful and carefree. They love performances and oriental exhibitions. They also love wrestling, which they watch with insatiable joy and attention and which they discuss for a long time afterwards. The Gypsy women love to dress colourfully in fabrics with screaming colours. She loves very much to adorn herself, and she does it with abundance and joy. The favourite colours of the Gypsy woman are red, yellow and green, and these colours are especially preferred by the Gypsy women from the East.

The Gypsy woman also wears a colourful headscarf with which she covers her head. She loves to wear a gold coin around her neck. The Gypsy woman usually wears a *festa* (skirt), and although many of them are Muslims, they have thrown away their *feredzhes* long ago. The Gypsy woman is freedom-loving in her spirit; however, she does not allow flirting with her. She maintains her morality when it comes to men of another race, but she is loving and sweet to her countrymen. She is ready to give everything for her love. However, she insists on getting the same in return. She is jealous and vigilantly protects her beloved one from the temptations of other female compatriots.

CHAPTER XLVIII
SOCIAL ORGANISATION

There is ample evidence that among the English Gypsies, there were many groups with matriarchy while others with patriarchy.

Their marriage system did not prevent marriages with nieces, granddaughters, or half-sisters, although common kinship was an obstacle for them for many years. Marriages with aunts and nephews are rare. Marriages between cousins, however, are something normal and very common. Marriages with relatives are strictly defined in a material respect. In marriages with female cousins, the one with the uncle from the mother's side was preferred to that with the uncle from the father's side.

Polygamy has recently been abandoned, probably due to the new economic structure, which does not allow support for a big number of women.

The sisterhood was respected.

It is usually the rule that the older sister should marry before the younger ones, but sometimes this rule is broken.

At the marriage, the man was supposed to prove his capability, and the woman – her virginity.

The marriage took place with *pristavane* [71], which was approved at a ceremony by the chief. The ceremony consisted of arms-crossing; or eating a loaf of bread with blood from the couple; or jumping on a branch or broom made of sticks; or jumping on a pair of tongs.

The man picked up the woman and carried her to the tent in his hands, symbolising the perfection and the permanence of the marital union.

These rites could be explained by their similarity to the Indian ones and elsewhere and are partly rites of fertility and protection from misfortune.

Their weddings usually lasted for three or more days. They were accompanied by much noise, fun and big feasts. The whole tribe took part in the wedding celebrations, and they were held in such ways that resulted in the creation of a unique festive character in the Gypsy settlement.

The girl's father received the so-called *Baba-ak* in money and other gifts.

CHAPTER XLIX
AMERICAN GYPSIES

Even though many of the descendants of the Gypsies who emigrated to America from England, the Netherlands, Germany, and France during the time of colonialism assimilated, in 1928, in America, the number of the Gypsies was probably 50,000 to 100,000, and they were called 'Roma'. Their number, due to their renowned fertility, is constantly increasing. Most of them went to America in the last quarter of the 19th century. In the United States and Canada, the English Gypsies are pretty numerous, and they differ little from the European ones.

Due to the decline of the horse trade, their main livelihood in America was fortune-telling. Others have established themselves as farm workers, while some sold oilcloths, baskets and old things.

Some Hungarian Gypsy immigrants in America live in homes. These are primarily musicians whose livelihood is secure because their music is highly valued and sought by Americans.

Most of them speak Romanes as their mother tongue.

The largest group could be found in Braddock, Pennsylvania.

It is rare to come across Gypsy violinists from Romania and Russia in America.

The families of Russian, Syrian, Bulgarian and Spanish Gypsies are pretty scattered.

There are mainly two types of Gypsies that are known in America:

The smaller group is *Karavachs* (black Vlachs) or *Bayash* (gold washers). They speak the Romani language, which is also the language of the Anglo-American Gypsies. Romanian is their "secret" language, although they lived in Serbia for some time before settling in America. Almost all of them are fortune-tellers.

The second group, which forms the majority of the American Gypsies, due to the lack of a more appropriate term, will be called here 'Travelling people'. Among themselves, they speak a pure Romani dialect, but the percentage of Romanian words in their vocabulary indicates that they were once in Wallachian countries. They are everywhere from China to Africa, however, not as many as in the United States.

There are many of them in South America.

They are divided into the following tribes:

Machvaia – named after an area in northern Serbia;

Kalderashi – blacksmiths, from their traditional profession;

Rusore, Ungeresore, etc. – related to the countries where they lived before migrating to America.

Despite the slight differences in their dialects and customs, these tribes are homogeneous, and they do not mix with other groups, even with those of the *Bayash* group.

They have their own court (Romano-Kris), which is run in the same way as the Hindus' court in India. Taboo (something forbidden) is strictly observed and is punishable by a fine or by expulsion from the tribe (*mahrime*).

The big silk handkerchief on the head of the married Gypsy woman, the necklaces with gold coins, and the clothes with gay and glaring colours are their distinctive features.

They travel by train or car and make their living on fortune telling, which is done by the Gypsy women. Before that, most of them were blacksmiths. Few of them are professional musicians, although almost all of them are musically inclined and talented musicians. They have managed to preserve tales and songs in their native language. They live in tents in the summer, but when it gets cold, they go to the cities where they live in houses.

The comfortable life there seeks to Americanise them, but like all *Romeni*, they easily return to their old habits.

CHAPTER L
MUSIC

Music is the only art that has been much loved and respected by the Gypsies, who are quite sensitive, full of imagination and inspired by nature. Gypsy music is unsurpassed in its power, appeal, and charm. Often, it is genuine and original and betrays its Eastern origin.

It is difficult to build a theory about Gypsy music because tonal relations barely exist; its modulation is full of fantasy; and the observance of the harmonic rules is a recent practice. One of the peculiarities of their music is the frequent change of the fourth and the minor chord, while the key does not have a determined character. This minor chord, so preferred by the Gypsies, is none other than the Persian, called "oriental in semitones", however, in reverse order -- it has an augmented fourth, the sixth is diminished, and the seventh is augmented.

Other characteristic features of Bohemian music [72] are its special rhythm and its free decoration – the two four time and the common time are very common.

From an aesthetic point of view, it can be said that Gypsy music is extremely easy-going, with instruments created for bohemian musicians, and especially the violin, along with other instruments, expresses their feelings.

The Bohemian composes all the time; they never review their musical creation and are inclined only to mnemonic rehearsals (those that exercise the memory).

In the various countries where they settled, the Bohemians retained their physical characteristics but not the distinctive features of their art.

Their music has been preserved mostly in Hungary and Bohemia.

Hungarian music was created by the Gypsies, although the vocal element in it is larger than the one in the bohemian music.

Less gifted with vocal cords, the bohemians rarely practised singing. Only a small number of ballads or war songs are mentioned. It seems that nature wanted them to express themselves mainly through instruments. The violin is the most important instrument in Gypsy or in Hungarian orchestras. The conductor is unnecessary, or rather, a violinist replaces him, while the other musicians, their imagination released, follow him without mistakes, if not in detail, then in the general spirit of the piece while they are inspired and guided by his great talent. After the violin, we must mention the *zymbola* [cymbal], a kind of table streaked with strings, which are struck with wooden hammers.

In its flexibility and imagination, the cymbal rivals the violin. Then come the other violins, the cello, and a few wooden musical instruments.

The special Gypsy musical performances are divided into two parts; each of them is formed by two dances, one – slow, the other – lively. The first, called *lasan*, is very melancholic; the second, called *friska*, moves from moderato to prestissimo.

In Ukraine, the Gypsies have a significant repertoire of songs of their own, but they also sing Russian folk songs, and their dances are called *zhyumki propoki* [73].

In Turkey, Moldova and Wallachia, the bohemian art has changed a lot. The energy of the rhythm has deteriorated significantly. The flute plays an important role, and a wind instrument similar to the flute of Pan augments the orchestra.

In Spain, the Gitanos (Gypsies) compose in line with the themes and rhythm of the Spaniards.

The best bohemian musicians are Syukeva, Barlea, Bihari, Syuzor, Badzhar, Sarközi, Kedzhkemeti, Cinka Pana, a cellist who was quite successful in Vienna.

The most famous, however, among all Gypsy musicians was Bihari (1827–1858), who knew how to shine and win the hearts of the audience with both Gypsy and classical music.

Today, in the Soviet Union, Lyalya Chernaya who plays in the State Gypsy Theatre *Romen* is known as a good actress.

The Gypsies have every reason to be proud of their compatriots Lebedov and Romel [74], who are well-known in the Soviet Union for their stage plays.

CHAPTER LI
INFLUENCE OF THE GYPSY MUSIC

Many famous composers, such as Beethoven and Schubert, have used Gypsy music in Bohemian themes to create examples of classical music, which humanity still appreciates with amazement and admiration.

Brahms, on the other hand, created ingeniously supported Gypsy dances.

Franz Liszt, however, was the one who understood them best, reviving the familiar vigour of the music and their vivid, inspiring fantasy. His *Hungarian*

Rhapsodies are unsurpassed, and one of the best that humanity has ever created.

Therefore, Gypsy music, along with Gypsy dance, played a huge role in the development of classical music.

Many classical works and the works of the most ingenious musicians have embedded motifs of the unsurpassed in its power, vitality, and dynamics of Gypsy music.

CHAPTER LII
MOVIES ABOUT GYPSY LIFE

The Gypsy life, so cheerful, carefree, and various; full of deep experiences and tender love, has been reflected in many films. Film directors make films about the life of the Gypsies with love because they can free their imagination and unfold it in its breadth.

The life of the Gypsies – eternally wandering, eternally dancing their dances under the open sky, eternally devoted to music, is a prolific source overflowing with lusciousness, life, and sensitivity, which makes the film infinitely interesting.

The exoticism that comes from the Gypsy life; the mysticism with which they explain all things in life; their devotion to the woman they love; their deep superstition and their special religiosity, which is not based on any lasting and healthy traditions, are all elements that make the films infinitely interesting. These themes also enable the director to create in an original way, without norms, because the Gypsy life itself does not recognise any norms.

The wild, passionate love dominates in the Gypsy character; this love knows no boundaries, no limits. The Gypsy loves selflessly, infinitely, and tempestuously. They completely devote themselves and seek complete devotion in return; they would do anything to have their loved one's full fidelity. Cast in a film, all these experiences make it dynamic, juicy, fresh, mysterious and, therefore, very interesting. That is why the Gypsy life has always been a favourite subject for film-making. There is no slowness and sluggishness in Gypsy life. It is lively, playful, noisy, and cheerful, but it often brings along sorrowful grief for the unattainable, and so much dreamed of, happiness in life. All this, cast in a film, grabs the audience from the first moments and keeps it in a dream until the last moment.

Such films are the French film *The White Truck*, the Spanish film *Carmen*, the Czech film *My Friend Fabian*, the Yugoslav film *Koshtana*, the Hungarian film *Gypsy Baron*, the Russian film *Gypsies* based on the novel of the Russian classical writer A. S. Pushkin, and many others.

CHAPTER LIII
GYPSY FOLKLORE TRADITIONS, FAIRY TALES, PROVERBS, SAYINGS AND EXPRESSIONS

The Gypsies have wonderful fairy tales, which they listen with great interest because these stories are full of unexpected fiction, and superstitions and usually have an equally unexpectedly interesting ending.

These tales are told in the evening, by the tent's fire, under the open starry sky, or at home in wintertime. The old Gypsy men and women fill the long winter nights with long, infinitely interesting, and surprisingly orderly tales about dragons, goblins, mermaids and fairies [75], as well as about the deep but unhappy Gypsy love. These tales are full of mysteries, mysticism, and fearful stories in which a Gypsy was a victim.

Sitting in the corner, the old Gypsy woman would tell stories which she had heard from her mother or father, and then she passed them on to her children and grandchildren. They would listen, be overwhelmed, and try not to miss a single word from their mother or grandmother. These tales are about the son of the king who has fallen in love with the beautiful white Gypsy woman, who, however, has a dear lover whom she cannot replace because she loves him deeply and to whom she remains faithful even when the cruel king's son, who is not able to achieve his aspirations, severely punishes the stubborn girl. She becomes a victim of the ruthless cruelty of the king's son but keeps her heart pure and devoted entirely to her beloved.

After the grandmother finished her story, the children kept looking her mouth, their small and bright eyes still longing to hear more.

And the grandmother or mother would begin again, a new tale, "Once upon a time ...".

This is how their stories usually start.

This time she tells the story of the *zmey* [dragon] who fell in love with the most beautiful Gypsy woman in the tribe and who came every night and secretly sneaked into his beloved's bed. Every night, the dragon lay down next to her, drank the juiciness of her lips while the girl, dying with fear, stood still and shook under the terrible and insatiable caresses of the dragon. The dragon did that every night until he finally drank the last juice of life from the body of the beautiful young white Gypsy woman who, on the other hand, was afraid to tell her relatives about the dragon's visits because he threatened to kill her.

And then, one evening, the brother of the unfortunate girl came and accidentally saw the dragon in the bed next to his sister; the blood boiled in her brother's Gypsy veins, he pulled out a knife and pierced the heart of the insatiable dragon. Black blood gushed out from the dragon, and suddenly, a horrible thunderstorm started raging outside. The relatives of the dragon, who sensed the death of their loved one, got so angry that they sent a terrible storm, which broke the branches of the trees that held their small houses and scattered the cloth sheets of their tent on all sides. Despite everything, the young Gypsy woman was saved. The dragon would no longer come to drink her blood. She slowly recovered and life returned to her. Her beauty was growing until one fine day, she found her beloved with whom she lived happily ever after …

The themes are endless, and the tales are wonderful. Such tales would fill the souls of the children with indignation against the cruel king's son or the ruthless dragon; their eyes would twinkle with joy when the grandmother told how the brave brother killed the dragon and saved his beloved sister.

The grandmother would start again, "Once upon a time …".

By this time, however, the children's heads were drooping, and their eyes were closed because they had fallen asleep. She would get up carefully, put each child to sleep, and then curl up next to them to warm them with her breath and her body …

CHAPTER LIV
TALES AND LEGENDS OF THE RHODOPE GYPSIES

[…] [76]

CHAPTER LV
SAYINGS

[…] [77]

CHAPTER LVI
SONGS

The Muslim blacksmiths – the Agupti, do not have their own songs. They use the songs of the Rhodope population, of the Bulgarian Christians and of the Bulgarian Muslims. During holidays, the Agupti blacksmiths visit each other and there, when they are together, they sing ancient Rhodope songs. Although they do not have their own Gypsy songs, they perform the songs of the Rhodope population so beautifully, so touchingly, with zeal and with temperament, that they captivate the soul of the listener. Musically inclined themselves, true to their Gypsy race, they invest so much liveliness and warmth into the songs that the latter, performed by them, have a charmingly good meaning. The Agupti blacksmiths spend their whole life in misery and hard work; however, they never stop singing. While singing, they express their misfortunes, their sorrows for dear love, or their joy at the little happiness that sometimes shines upon their poor huts. They are happy when they sing the excitement of their souls and hearts, whether sorrow or joy. Their grief is deep because they are sensitive and emotional people. They can best express the thrill in their souls in the song. It is undoubtedly a loss that the Agupti did not create their own songs. Their songs could have guided us to reveal the thoughts, desires, aspirations, and ideals that excite every Gypsy soul. Overworked and worn-out in the recent past, their lives were consumed by the worries of earning a living for their family and they did not have time for creativity. Let us hope that they will fill this void now when a new life has opened for the Gypsy Agupti. This new life is characterised by full equality with all other citizens in the republic; it is free from the offensive and unjustified discrimination to which they were subjected 14 years ago; and the doors of schools and universities are wide open to them. If they manage to do that, let us be sure that their songs would not be inferior to any other song creation. It is because the Gypsies are musical by nature and because mentally, they are not lagging behind any other nation. If until now, the Gypsies felt oppressed and outcast by society, this was not their fault but the fault of those who, until fourteen years ago, had treated them almost on an equal footing with the animals. However, in this new life, they will rise up and stand firmly on their feet; and they will contribute to the common song treasury of the Bulgarian state.

Here, I will present some of the songs that are mostly sung in the Rhodope region by the Gypsy blacksmiths [...] [78]. In the evening, when the voice of the Gypsy man and the Gypsy woman echoes over the dark cliffs of the Rhodope mountain and the sounds of their songs are carried from peak to peak, from rock to rock and echo through the valleys, some thrill overtakes everyone and despite their will, they stop to listen, overwhelmed by the fabulously magical performance of these simple but sweet folk motifs. This performance reveals the power and the magical sweetness of the Rhodope folk song. When a Gypsy man or a Gypsy woman performs the song, it sounds a thousand times better because they sing their souls, hearts, thoughts, sadness, or joy – anything that torments, saddens or cheers their souls. That is why when a Gypsy performs a Rhodope song, it sounds incredibly beautiful to us, and we cannot have enough of it.

CHAPTER LVII
SONGS BY THE SOFIA GYPSIES AND BY OTHER GYPSIES IN THE COUNTRY

Unlike the Agupti blacksmiths, the Gypsies from Sofia, and those from other parts of the country, have their own songs. This is due to many reasons, but the main one is the fact that the lives of the Gypsies in the country are better and therefore they have more time to think about problems of life, other than making ends meet, as is the case with the Agupti blacksmiths.

That is exactly why the Gypsies in the rest of Bulgaria, although not so widespread, have their own songs.

They also have poets who are not inferior in talent to many of the Bulgarian poets. One of them, and the most prominent, is Usin Kerim, who has created a collection of poems [Керим, 1955] which finds excellent acceptance among all circles. No one who has read the songs of Usin Kerim felt anything but fascination because they are unsurpassed in imagery, in the musicality of the verse, and in the depth of the poetry. They greatly excite the souls of the readers who keep reading them over and over again with pleasure and joy and admire this great native Gypsy talent. Usin Kerim is a rarely gifted poet; his songs are filled with so much vitality and passion, love, and faith in the goodness of people, all of which make his songs such pearls.

[…] [79]

A new phenomenon, unknown to the Gypsies 14 years ago, could recently be noticed among the Gypsies in Sofia, and in Bulgaria in general. This is the aspiration of some Gypsy poets to create their native songs in the Gypsy language. Along with the most talented of them, Usin Kerim, who writes mainly in Bulgarian, the little sparks of new Gypsy poets are visible; they are growing and building the foundations of the native Gypsy song. Such are Angel (Demcho) Blagoev, Shakir Pashev and others. We have every reason to hope that the fertile ground created for the Gypsy minority by the Government of the people will be meaningfully and systematically used to create a genuine Gypsy song.

EJ, ROMALEN

Ej, Romalen, mere tume,
phralalen, but durol tume alien.
Cela Azija tume phirgen,
o Egipet tume resken.

HEY, GYPSIES

Hey, Gypsies, my brothers,
you came from afar.
You roved all over Asia,
you have reached Egypt.

Trin dariava tume nakhlen,
andi Evropa tume resken.
E gilenca e bukasa,
celo Dunias tume phirgen.

You have passed through three seas,
you reached Europe.
Singing and working,
throughout the world you went.

Avdise ame e gilenca, e bukiasa,
e romen ka podvazdas,
o socializam ko resag.

Today with songs and work,
we raise up the Gypsies,
to reach the socialism

Shakir Pashev

ROMA

Phiren roma ke droma cahrenca,
bi bukjako gonime, nange, ne čhavenca.
Kaj džan save givesa si naangle ni dikhen.

Roma are roaming the roads with tents,
without work, naked, with their children.
As they walk, they don't see ahead of them [a road].

Roden drom životoske,
po nasvalo vogi te phenen,
phirde but breša ke droma bi džande,
but džene ke roma dikhe gurva,
čhave, roma, merenas sar makhja,
i khonik ni vakiarelas,
kaj e roma si manuša ...

They are searching for ways to survive,
and to share the pain in their hearts,
many years have passed in unknown routes,
many people see Gypsies as cattle,
children and adults died like flies
and nobody said,
that the Roma are humans ...

Avilo o nevo, lačho, sveto give,
čindas sosi šele sastrune,
phutardas sosi vogja savorenge,
e lačhe, česnone, bukjarne, manušenge.

A good, bright day arrived,
the heavy chains tore,
the hears of everybody opened up,
of the good, diligent, and fair people.

Di o Jašar, o xamali,
i sar leste but džene,
čhivte o šele, ta o phage moxte,
ando zavodja die sar savorende,
norme phagen, staxanovci ačhile.

Yashar the porter goes,
and many others like him,
they threw away the chains and the old chests,
they went to the factories as all the rest,
fulfilling norms and becoming stakhanovies [80].

Dikhen i Ajša, taj e Kalisko čhavo,
i sar leste but džene,
inžinerja, doktorja, studenta ačhile,
o nevo životos, socializmi kheren.

Look at Aysha, and the son of Kali,
and how many like them,
have become engineers, doctors, students,
they are building the new life, socialism.

Šunen čhavalen, taj phralalen,
den tumen vasta sar ekh, romalen,
te vazdas but učheste, o nevo životos,
e trudoskoro socializmi,
taj e mireskoro.

Listen, children, brothers,
hold each other's hands like one people,
to raise up high the new life,
and workers socialism,
and peace.

Angel Blagoev (Demcho) [81]

A TALE ABOUT THE BELLOWS

In old times, masters of various crafts used to gather for a chat and soon, they would start arguing about who was a greater master. The leatherworker said to the blacksmith that he was a greater master because if he didn't tan the fur, the blacksmith couldn't have made the bellows for fanning the fire and heating the iron. The blacksmith got angry and said to the leatherworker that if he took away his tools, the leatherworker would not be able to work on the leather. And so, it went until they became so infuriated that they made a bet. Thus, the blacksmith took all the tools and nails from the leatherworker, and the latter ceased working because he had no tools. The blacksmith, on the other hand, was left without a bellows because the leatherworker took away the tanned fur. The blacksmith started thinking and came up with the following idea: he took the raw furs, dipped them in wax, and thus managed to make new bellows, fan the flames, and forge the hot iron. All the masters gathered to see how the blacksmith made his fur without having proper materials; when the blacksmith told them how he had made his bellows, everybody recognised him as the greatest master of all masters. In addition, the blacksmith began making hoes, iron ploughshares for the wooden ploughs, as well as other agricultural tools such as axes, sickles, etc. That is why the blacksmith was acknowledged as the greatest master by all other master craftsmen.

A TALE ABOUT THE PLIERS

Blacksmiths used to hold the burning iron with their bare hands to forge it. At the time, they did not have pliers, as they did not know about that tool.

At that time, the masters used to have apprentices who, in addition to working in the workshop, worked in the night, bringing food to the master's house, meat to the master's wife so that she could cook, water to drink, etc. One day, the master sent an apprentice to bring meat to the master's home. The custom was to hang the meat on a wooden finger near the front door because by tradition, the apprentice should not see the master's wife. One day, the apprentice did not find the wooden finger in its usual place and wondered where to hang the meat. At that moment, he noticed a nice golden finger and hung the meat on it. On his way back to the workshop, the apprentice wondered whether that finger belonged to the master's wife and how beautiful she must have been if she had such beautiful fingers ... When he entered the workshop, the apprentice saw that his master was very angry but did not know why. The master was angry because he could no longer hold the iron with his bare hands. He asked himself what sin he had committed that Allah punished him so cruelly to hold the burning iron with his hands. Thinking, the master looked out of his shop where a dog lay with paws crossed. When the master saw the crossed legs of the dog, it immediately occurred to him that he could make iron pliers, like the dog's crossed legs and hold the iron with them. He immediately got to work and made the pliers that blacksmiths still use to this date [82].

CONCLUSION

We can draw some positive conclusions from what we presented above. We can now take a firm stand on many issues concerning the Gypsies around the world, namely: whether the Gypsies come from, Egypt or India; approximately when they began their journey; how long did it last; did all Gypsies leave their original homeland at once, or in waves and at different times; what was the reason that forced the Gypsies to leave their original homeland and move to Europe, America, Asia Minor, etc.; when did the Gypsies arrive in the Balkan Peninsula and when in Bulgaria; was Egypt the original homeland of the Gypsies or a temporary station; did they pass through Persia, did they settle down there for a long time; what role did they play in the Romanian army; were they the first to import bronze processing in Europe; did the Rhodope Agupti come as slaves, brought by the Romans to cultivate the rich deposits of Madan, or did they come alone, or were they sent here by the Egyptian pharaohs to guard the northern border of the Egyptian state; were they beneficial to the local population with their blacksmithing, making agricultural tools for them; what was the journey of the Gypsies – did they fight with other countries or did they travel peacefully; did the Gypsies ever have conquest goals in their movement towards Europe; for what reason the Gypsies in some countries were put under exceptional laws and ill-treated – was this a matter of prejudice or slander, or was it caused by evil deeds on the part of the Gypsies themselves; where does the innate gift of the Gypsies for music come from; what could explain the Gypsy frivolous and light-hearted worldview; what is the reason for the their discrimination in many countries; are the Gypsies a progressive people in their nature; why the Gypsies were accused of not having aspirations for work; is this prejudice or reality and what is the reason for it; do the Gypsies have vicious tendencies and what are the reasons if they do; whether the Gypsy is capable for science and what conditions would stimulate them to education, good hygiene, cultural rise, and enlightenment in general.

ORIGIN [AND] ORIGINAL HOMELAND

From the data that we presented in our work so far, researched by great scientists, the original homeland of the Gypsies is, undoubtedly, India. The similarity with the customs of some tribes that still live in India, such as the Sanskrit and the tribes living along the Ganges, makes it obvious that the original homeland of the Gypsies is, and this can already be positively confirmed, India. The theory that the Gypsies come from Egypt can no longer withstand even the slightest critique. We can already consider this theory completely irrelevant. Our opinion is that the Gypsies originate from India, and it is their original homeland.

Their journey to Europe began about five thousand years BC. There is evidence for this, as it is known that the Gypsies appeared in Persia and in Egypt five thousand years BC.

The journey of the Gypsies from their original homeland India did not begin and end in one go. We can positively state that they moved out gradually, in groups. It is known that the largest group, consisting of about 300,000 people, was led by Elder Zyumbyul. They set off in groups. The reasons for leaving their original homeland were: sometimes devastating floods, sometimes great droughts, which ended in a long famine among the peoples of India; another part emigrated when Genghis Khan invaded their homeland and ravaged their settlements, enslaving them, taking them in captivity and forcing them to work without being paid.

We can assume that the Gypsies left their original homeland of India because of an epidemic, which at the time had been quite common in India.

The data that we have from Byzantium show that there were Gypsies in Constantinople in the 6th century. Since they were there at that time, it should not be difficult to guess that this, already mobile and unrestrained tribe could not remain permanently fixed in Constantinople and moved north – to the Balkan Peninsula – respectively towards Bulgaria. Therefore, we claim that the Gypsies in Bulgaria, and in the Balkans in general, did not arrive, as claimed by some, together with the Turks, or approximately before or after them, but the Gypsies settled here long before the invasion and the settlement of the Turks on the Balkan Peninsula; the Gypsies had been here for a long time.

We also claim that Egypt, as well as Persia, two of the countries where the Gypsies stayed for a longer period of time, were only temporary stations for the Gypsies from which they moved north, north-east and north-west – to the Balkan Peninsula, Russia and Europe. It can be affirmed that the Gypsies passed through Persia, as the shortest route from India to Russia, as well as through Egypt, as the shortest route to Europe.

After their settlement in Romania, the Gypsies were held in high esteem because they were the main weapon masters who made weapons for the Romanian army. Here, the Gypsies played a great economic role in agriculture because, with their trade as blacksmiths, they made agricultural tools for the Romanian farmers, helping for easier and quicker work with the soil.

Nevertheless, we can already positively say that the appearance of the Gypsies in Europe marked the beginning of bronze processing too. From this, we could judge that the Gypsies were the first to begin bronze processing, which gave a new and strong impetus for the progress of the European peoples. Excellent in the blacksmithing craft, in which the Gypsies demonstrated their national genius, they also proved to be good masters in bronze processing. Here, their art has reached its height; they simply reached perfection. Along with iron processing, they proved to be such complete masters in bronze that they surpassed all others. Undoubtedly, this is a great merit of the Gypsies that no one would dare dispute.

The question also arises: Were the Rhodope Gypsy blacksmiths, known as the Agupti, brought to the Rhodope Mountains by the Romans as slaves to cultivate the rich Rhodope basin, or were they sent there as soldiers by the Egyptian pharaohs to guard the northern borders of the great Egyptian state? In this regard, although we have no certain data, we must assume that they were brought as slaves, together with their families, because it is known that the Gypsies have never been soldiers. Even in their journey to Europe and America, they moved peacefully without fighting, and when they passed through a certain country, they left many of their compatriots, who would dedicate themselves to peaceful and creative work, which provided a livelihood for themselves and their families. That is why, in terms of the question from which state the Gypsies came to the Rhodope region, we are inclined to believe that they were brought there by force as slaves of the Romans. We claim this, although we do not have any certain data about it. This conclusion could be made only by logical reasoning.

The Gypsies have invaluable merits for developing the national livelihood of the local population in all the countries in which they settled and for advancing the agricultural production of these peoples because with their crafts as blacksmiths, they supplied the local population with agricultural tools and made it easier for them to cultivate the land, to raise their income, and hence, to increase their subsistence. They supplied the people with hoes and sickles. They were the first to make the iron ploughshare, which substituted the wooden one; at the time being, this was an economic revolution because, with this iron ploughshare, they not only increased the life of the plough but also helped for a deeper ploughing, and therefore, for higher yields. In addition, by making horseshoes for horses, oxen and donkeys, the Gypsies contributed quite a lot to the consolidation of cattle breeding. In that respect, their merit is undeniably invaluable. By supplying the cattle with horseshoes, the Gypsies protected the animals' hooves from injury on longer trips and helped them work for a longer time than before.

This also explains the peaceful coexistence of the Gypsies with all the peoples in the places where they settled permanently. They lived in good coexistence with the peoples; because they contended themselves with small incomes and did not aim for large profits, the Gypsies made agricultural tools and horse, ox, and donkey horseshoes accessible to everyone, even to the poorest farmer.

The journey of the Gypsies to Europe during their emigration from their old homeland India was a peaceful one. They moved peacefully. During their travels, they did not fight with any of the nations that they met on their way. On the contrary, they passed through these countries as peaceful travellers, and when some of them found a livelihood in these countries, they abandoned their countrymen, settled down permanently, and left their brethren to continue their journey peacefully and quietly to Europe, Russia, England and even America. The Gypsies never demonstrated ambition for conquest, and they never aspired to get foreign lands. It was enough for them to be accepted in the country they passed through, and for some of them to settle down forever, and that was more than enough for the Gypsies. As soon as they settled in a land, they devoted themselves to peaceful and creative work, without great pretensions, except the desire to find a livelihood for themselves and their families. They were content with just a little, their expectations were not big, and once they found modest means of subsistence in those countries, it was sufficient for them. Although they were good blacksmiths of military equipment, which we know from the fact that they provided weapons forged by themselves to the Romanian army, they never used these weapons for military purposes. They never fought with any nation; instead, they lived peacefully and quietly in the countries through which they passed and in which some of them settled down forever. Besides establishing themselves as craftsmen-blacksmiths in the countries through which they passed and remained, they also participated in the celebrations and festivities of these peoples, entertained them with their innate musical genius, and their dances made these holidays even merrier.

It was once believed that a celebration would lose its cheerfulness and exuberance if the Gypsies did not take part in it with their music and dances. Therefore, they were in great demand and were highly valued. Their songs were attractive to everyone because they have spirit, sweet bliss, playfulness and gaiety as much as deep sadness at times. This great variety of the Gypsy song made them extremely interesting, and that is why the Gypsy musicians were in demand everywhere.

With their songs, independent and carefree life, the Gypsies have given an opportunity and impetus to great musicians to create music, which has not lost any of its charms until today. With their dances, unsurpassed in playfulness, the Gypsies won the hearts of all the peoples whose lands they passed through.

Their breath-taking and cordial love has inspired many great classics to produce novels, short stories, dramas, etc., that, in their artistic sense, have not been surpassed by anyone. Their love is thrilling, pure, and full of deep and heartfelt experiences. The Gypsy man is ready to sacrifice everything, even his life, for his beloved Gypsy woman. For her love, the Gypsy woman is ready to give such emotional gestures that amaze with their originality and sincerity. She would defend her love with passion and may even take revenge – ruthless and cruel, in order to keep her beloved only for herself. This genuine love of the Gypsies has been reproduced in dozens, or hundreds, of works by the old classics and these works have not lost their liveliness, originality and high artistic value until today.

Spending their lives under the open sky, under their tent, which they set up here today and elsewhere tomorrow, close to nature, their love is simple and strong as nature itself. Their love is deep and real because it is cultivated in the bosom of nature; and nature teaches us to be sincere and alienates us from everything that is pretentious, artificial and false. Only in this way can be explained the cordiality, depth and strength of Gypsy love.

Although the Gypsies lived in peaceful and friendly relations with the peoples among whom they settled down, they were often discriminated and severely, heartlessly and ruthlessly persecuted by some ruling circles in various countries. Thus, for example, in Germany, they were outlawed and ruthlessly burned or killed when captured on German soil. The Gypsies have not experienced such cruelty in almost any other country, although they were placed in extremely difficult conditions in various countries. These reactionary circles and governments, contrary to the sentiments of their own peoples who were living in peace and friendship with the Gypsies, persecuted the Gypsies without knowing why and attributed to them acts they had never committed. These reactionary circles created legends about the Gypsies and slandered them in order to have a reason for their persecution. They claimed that the Gypsies ate children, killed the inhabitants of these countries, committed thefts, etc. These things turned out to be fabrications and disgusting slanders, invented with the only purpose to to justify the ruthless and cruel discrimination against the

Gypsies and their brutal persecution. The Gypsies, however, did not respond with a vengeance because they did not have such feelings. Painfully, the Gypsies endured all the tortures, and not knowing any other way of resistance, they surrendered to their peaceful, creative aspirations, carrying the pain of their unjust suffering deep in their souls.

The question has been raised what could explain the carelessness of the Gypsies and their light-hearted approach to the problems in life. This seems to be an innate feature of the Gypsies, and it can only be explained by the fact that they had to do little work for their living in their old native India. Under the blessed sun of India, where all kinds of fruit grow and where the game is plentiful, they did not have to work hard to provide for their families because they had almost everything at their disposal. They had plenty of fruit, and the game that supplied them with meat was so much that the Gypsies put little effort into having it on their tables. This is the only explanation for the bohemian, carefree life of the Gypsies. Moreover, they were devoted to their songs, led by their musical genius, and with these songs in their mouths, they survived even the most horrible hardship and times when they could not give even a piece of bread to their children. It is strange, indeed, that thousands of years since they emigrated from their original homeland, they have changed almost nothing in their character. Only recently that there is a new aspiration among the Gypsies to work and reflect on the problems of life. This is explained not only by the influence of the peoples among which the Gypsies have settled but also by the fact that they already have an intelligentsia that has different views and that seriously focuses on the great problems of life. This is especially noticeable in our country, especially after September 9, 1944. Liberated from the discrimination under the bourgeois governments before September 9, 1944, the Gypsies appreciate the benefits they received after September 9, 1944, in our country. That's why they try to thank the people's government by contributing with their labour to all areas of economic life, and they stand on an equal footing with the other citizens of the republic in creating goods for the whole nation.

The Gypsies have always been progressive people. They have proven this in various ways so far. They took an active part in our Liberation, and it is known that Vasil Levski, when he was in Sliven, was hiding in Gypsy houses. After the Liberation, and especially after the establishment of a Socialist Party in our country, the Gypsies joined its ranks and supported its cause. In the elections before 9th September, despite attempts to make them vote with threats and bribes, they did not give in; on the contrary, they always supported the Socialist Party and not once were they subjected to persecution by the fascist governments before 9th September.

We can now say with certainty that those who consider that the Gypsies are a nation that does not like to work, have a prejudice, and as such, it does not correspond to the truth. The Gypsies love to work. This could be proven by their activities after September 9, 1944. Placed on an equal footing with everyone else in the republic, the Gypsies happily embraced labour and invested their creative forces in all industrial areas of our economic life.

After the liberation of the Gypsies from total discrimination under the fascist governments in our country, the doors of schools, technical schools and universities were wide open for Gypsy children, and they rushed in eagerly. Today, the Gypsies who have secondary or higher education are not few. They are among the good pupils and students. We already have Gypsy doctors, engineers, technicians in various fields, and officers in the army and in the police, and they are as good, conscientious, and diligent in their professions and with their activities, as other citizens are. The Gypsies already have about 60 schools across the country. They have many amateur groups, both musical and artistic. They are wonderful miners, as well as excellent blacksmiths. They are moving forward and only forward, and the day will not be far off when the Gypsies will not be weaker than any other nation in terms of culture and education. We believe in this firmly and without a shadow of a doubt, and this will happen because the Gypsies possess all the necessary talents.

BIBLIOGRAPHY

The following authors have been used as sources in this study:

Д-р Шейтанов. [83]

Примов. [Примовски, 1955]

Британската енциклопедия. Том XI. [Encyclopædia Britannica, 1910–1911, Vol. 11]

Батайар. "Последни проучвания, отнасящи се до бохемите". Париж, 1872. [Bataillard, 1872]

"Как се поставя въпроса за древността на циганите в Европа". Париж, 1877. Extracts from his presentation at the Anthropological Congress in Budapest in 1876. [Bataillard, 1876]

Потт. "Циганите в Европа и Азия". 1845. [Pott, 1845]

Паспати. "Проучвания на циганите". Цариград, 1870. [Paspati, 1870]

Миклошич. "За музикалното изкуство и странстване на циганите по Европа". "Антропологичен преглед". Виена, 1873. [84]

Диксон. "Свободна Русия". "Тур дю Монд", 1872. [Dixon, 1872]

Батайар и Обеденар. "Бюлетин на антропологичното дружество в Париж", 1873 and 1875, pp. 548, 557. [Bataillard, 1875a; Obédénare, 1875]

Батайар и Коперник. "Злотарите и джовонкарите". "Спомени на антропологичното дружество", 1878. [Bataillard, 1878]

Е. Р. Пенел. "Към циганската земя". 1883. [Pennell, 1893]

Бери. "Американския циганин в списанието на Франк Сесли". Народно месечно списание, No. 111, pp. 560–572. Ню-Йорк, 1902. [85]

Вестник за фолклора на циганското общество, Нова серия, Том VI, No. 4 (1912–1913); Том VII, No. 2, No. 3 (1913–914). [86]

А. Т. Синклер. "Американо-романи речник". 1915. [Sinclair, 1915]

"Американските цигани". Published by Library in New York, 1917. [Sinclair, 1915]

Й. Браун. "Дни и нощи по циганските следи". 1922. [Brown, 1922]

"Циганските огнища в Америка". 1924. [Brown, 1922]

С. Ж. Лиланд. "Циганите". 1924. [Leland, 1924]

Х. В. Шумейкър. "Цигани и цигански фолклор в Пенсилванските планини". Published in "Таймс трибюн" in 1924, USA, Altona. [Shoemaker, 1924]

"Произход на езика на Пенсилвано-германските цигани". 1925. Published in "Сървей График" – Том 12, No.1, Октомври, 1927 (one issue entirely dedicated to the Gypsies). [Shoemaker, 1925]

Ф. Лист. "За бохемите и тяхната музика". Париж, 1855. [Liszt, 1859]

Усин Керим. "Цигански песни". A Collection of Poems in Bulgarian. [87]

Comments

1. This finding refers specifically to the situation in Bulgaria when the manuscript was prepared (the 1950s) but is not valid on a more global scale.
2. Here and further down in the text, Shakir Pashov repeatedly develops in detail the naive and eccentric thesis about the Gypsies as the first bearers of the Bronze Age in Europe, first expressed in the 19th century (Bataillard, 1875ab; 1878).
3. Sri Lanka today.
4. Shakir Pashov does not cite this author in his Bibliography. He probably means here Jacques Goar (1601–1653), a French Dominican and Hellenist, but it is unclear to which of his books he refers.
5. Handwritten note in the margin of the manuscript: "300 AD". It is unclear who made the handwritten notes here and below, but they are not by Pashov himself; perhaps the manuscript has gone through some review/editing (unclear when and by whom).
6. It is unclear why Shakir Pashov translates the word *gadzho* as 'Romanian'. One can only find such a meaning of *gadžo* in Romania. In the various dialects of the Romani language (both in Bulgaria and around the world), *gadžo* usually means 'a person who is not Roma'.
7. Father Paisius, also Paisiy Hilendarski (1722–1773), was a clergyman and the author of Историѧ славѣноболгарскаѧ [lit. Slav-Bulgarian History]. He is considered in Bulgaria as the forefather of the Bulgarian National Revival.
8. Shakir Pashov means here Jeronimo Pizzicannella, a Franciscan priest in the Nikopol Diocese, and his work *Бележки върху Никополската епархия в България от о. Йероним Пицинанелла 1825–1834/1836–1866* (see Марков, 1947).
9. It is not clear what exactly Shakir Pashov had in mind, but there is a clear error because Stefan Zahariev's book (Захариев, 1870) refers only to the Tatar-Pazardzhik district, and he himself died in 1871 (i.e. before the Liberation).
10. This refers to Bernard Gilliat-Smith's translation of *The Gospel of Luke* (Gilliat-Smith, 1912).
11. Shakir Pashov means here the translations into the Romani language of two other Gospels in the 1930s (Сомнал евангелие, 1932; 1937).
12. This author is quoted directly in the text (Младенов, 1927, pp. 169, 254, 292).

 | DOI:10.30965/9783657790302_003

13. This refers to the flag of the Gypsy guild in Sofia, which was carried during various festive processions. In the 19th century, under the conditions of the Ottoman Empire (later also in the new Bulgarian state), ethnically demarcated guilds (professional associations), including Gypsy ones, were common occurrences; according to established tradition, they had their own guild flags (see Marushiakova & Popov, 2016a for more details).
14. For the Peperuda [Butterfly] rain custom, see further in the text and in the comments.
15. So-called 'самодиви' (Fairies), 'змейове' (Dragons), 'таласъми' (Goblins) etc. are supernatural creatures from Bulgarian mythology; the English translation is approximate.
16. Crossed out, possibly by Shakir Pashov.
17. Added by handwriting by Shakir Pashov.
18. Added by handwriting by Shakir Pashov.
19. Today Pirotska Street.
20. This is the father of Shakir Pashov.
21. The lands are located near the land parcels owned by the Faculty of Agriculture of the Sofia University St Kliment Ohridski, then outside the city's boundaries (today the Fakulteta neighbourhood).
22. Today, the Gotse Delchev neighbourhood. The former Gypsy mahala Boyana no longer exists today. In the second half of the 1960s, its inhabitants were displaced due to the growth of the city and the new housing construction, and most of them (including the family of Shakir Pashov himself) received apartments in today's Housing Complex Druzhba (then Iskar Station).
23. Today, Hristo Botev neighbourhood, the so-called Abyssinia.
24. According to the data from the Population Census conducted in 1956, total of 197,865 Gypsies were counted in Bulgaria (Илиева, 2012, c. 67). Because in these Censuses, it is a relatively common phenomenon (both in the past and nowadays) for parts of the Gypsy population to declare another (most often Turkish or Bulgarian) ethnic identity, Shakir Pashov's assessment of about 250–300 thousand people of Gypsy origin living in Bulgaria at that time does not seem inflated, but rather realistic.
25. This refers to the Workers' Party, which for a certain period (1927–1934) was the legal name of the Bulgarian Communist Party (since 1919); subsequently (until 1948), the Bulgarian Workers' Party (Communists) and then again, the Bulgarian Communist Party.
26. In fact, the Bulgarian Workers' Party (Communists) announced the course towards armed struggle on June 24, 1941, immediately after the German attack on the USSR.

27. This refers to the Russian-Turkish war (1877–1878), as a result of which Bulgaria was liberated from the Ottoman empire. The term Liberation in the book refers to the outcome of this war. Further, it refers also to the outcome of WWII.
28. This refers to Bulgaria's participation in the First World War.
29. This is about the so-called Women's Riots in Sliven, during which the Gypsy woman Tyana Malakova (also known as Tyana Neva) and the Gypsy man Peyo Dimitrov Yonkov (known as Peyu Dachev) were killed on May 17, 1918 (see Marushiakova & Popov, 2022, pp. 80–81).
30. It refers to the Gypsy man Ibrahim Kerimov, killed by the police in Sofia during a demonstration organised by the Bulgarian Communist Party in 1919 (his name is specified by a note in the margin of the manuscript, although according to other sources, his surname is Kyamilov).
31. Today, Mladenovo neighbourhood in the town of Lom.
32. It refers to the Labor Bloc (also known as the United Front) – a political coalition between the Bulgarian Communist Party and the left in the Bulgarian Agricultural People's Union, created in the fall of 1923.
33. 'Selkoop' – Rural Consumer Cooperative.
34. The case of the *Peperuda* rain custom is a typical example illustrating how the Roma have taken up traditions that were forgotten or preserved only as a cultural heritage among other peoples. The 'Butterfly' (*Paparuda, Dodola, Dudula,* and other similar names) custom was actively practiced by Bulgarians, Serbs, Romanians and other Balkan peoples in the second half of the 19th century. In the first half of the 20th century, however, in the process of modernisation, villagers gradually stopped performing the custom themselves but encouraged the Gypsies to continue doing it (Marushiakova & Popov, 2011, pp. 3–4; 2016b, p. 48).
35. This refers to the rain custom *German* (*Dzherman, Kaloyan,* and other names), the development of which is similar to that of the 'Butterfly' custom.
36. In the sense of 'true Islam'.
37. 'afuz' – a title of honour given to those who have memorised the Qur'an.
38. Muslims in the Balkans (including Roma Muslims) usually celebrate two major religious Islamic holidays, which they call 'Bayram' – the so-called Sheker Bayram (Eid al-Fitr or Ramadan Bayram) and Kurban Bayram (Eid al-Adha or Eid Qurban).
39. It is not clear what Shakir Pashov means by the designation 'Istanbul University'. At that time (late 19th and early 20th century), no university existed in Istanbul (except Robert College); it probably refers to the

Islamic Theological School, which in 1933 was transformed into Istanbul University.

40. It is not clear why Shakir Pashov associates the presence of a *Muhtar* (*Cheribashiya*) with "European minority Gypsy groups", although this is a legacy from the times of the Ottoman Empire (this is clear even from the terms used).
41. In the original, Shakir Pashov writes "lonzhii".
42. Knyazhevo (Bali Efendi, Bali Baba) village is a popular place for excursions for the Sofia Gypsies. It is also a sacred place in which there is an Orthodox Church and the grave of the Muslim saint Bali Efendi. Sofia Gypsies make ritual oaths on the grave of Bali Efendi (called by Roma also Ali Baba) as well.
43. In 1919, the Bulgarian Workers' Social Democratic Party (Narrow Socialists) was renamed the Bulgarian Communist Party.
44. Shakir Pashov refers here to the changes in the Electoral Act in 1901, which deprived Muslim Gypsies and nomadic Gypsies of the right to vote; as a response to this discriminatory act, the so-called Congress of Gypsies convened in Sofia in December 1905 (for more details on these events, see Marushiakova & Popov, 2021, pp. 33–69).
45. Waqfs are immovable properties granted to Islamic religious institutions at the time of the Ottoman Empire, the income from which is used for their maintenance as well as for other religious and charitable purposes.
46. The exact chronology of these events is not entirely clear. In all probability, this happened after the elections in 1931, which were won by the so-called People's Bloc (a political coalition dominated by the Democratic Party), and in the new government, Nikola Mushanov is the Minister of Internal Affairs and Public Health, and subsequently Prime Minister.
47. In his text, Shakir Pashov separates the two societies (*Naangle* and *Napred*), which is probably a typographical error because it is the same word in two languages (Romanes and Bulgarian).
48. Shakir Pashov's statement is not accurate. Gypsy newspapers and journals in Europe were published decades before the newspaper *Terbie* (see Roman et al., 2021); moreover, *Terbie* is not even the first Gypsy newspaper in Bulgaria (see Marinov, 2021 for more details).
49. 'feredzhe' is a type of niqaab (women's veil). Shakir Pashov crossed out the word 'feredzhes' in the text, probably because the Gypsies in Bulgaria did not have the custom of veiling even during the time of the Ottoman Empire.
50. In the original, Shakir Pashov writes 'baba-ak'. From Turkish, in meaning 'father's right' (translated by Shakir Pashov as 'father's merit').

51. An omission in the original text.
52. For the celebration of the two Bayrams among the Gypsy Muslims in the Balkans, see above.
53. Shakir Pashov's statement is not accurate. The organisation *Istikbal* was not disbanded and continued to exist after 1934, repeatedly communicating with the local authorities in Sofia, using its letterhead and seal in correspondence with the Sofia municipality (see the published archival documents below).
54. Regarding the year of the Gypsy Ball, there is clearly an error in Shakir Pashov's memories. According to him, the ball was held on March 3 (Bulgaria's national holiday) in 1938 (see also Neve Roma, 1957f, p. 4), but in fact, the ball took place in 1937, as evidenced by the numerous materials published in the Bulgarian and foreign press.
55. The premiere play of *Gypsy Rhapsody* is actually a free theatrical adaptation of the famous poem *Gypsies* by Alexander Pushkin, with many Gypsy songs and dances.
56. This refers to the *Roma* Music and Dance Group at the Gypsy National Community Centre *9th September* (today the Community Centre *Aura*) in Sofia, 175 Alexander Stamboliyski Boulevard.
57. Mustafa Aliev (later known as Manush Romanov) worked at the Pleven Theatre at that time.
58. The play *Koštana* by the famous Serbian writer Borislav Stanković, which has a Gypsy theme, is one of the most famous and performed plays in Serbia (and later in Yugoslavia).
59. It is not clear to which of the publications of the famous German orientalist Carl Bezold refers Shakir Pashov.
60. Religious associations in antiquity connected with the cult of Cabeiri.
61. The author's thought is not very clear, probably Shakir Pashov mixes the Roma in Romania with the Romanichals in the United Kingdom.
62. It is not clear why Shakir Pashov included in this series of names by which "Gypsies call each other", the term 'gadžo' (i.e. non-Gypsy).
63. It is not clear why here Shakir Pashov uses 'Gypsies' (plural) and 'Rom' (singular in his native Erlia dialect) as equivalents; the plural in this dialect is 'Roma', and the form 'Rom, Rrom' for the plural is used in the so-called New Vlax (or North Vlax) dialects of the Romani language.
64. Shakir Pashov refers to Isidor Kopernicki, who is a Polish author (Kopernicki, 1872).
65. Probably, the author means the so-called Gypsy King Sindel.
66. The original has the year 1882, which is probably a typographical error.

67. The source of the Gypsy slave categories in Romania (more precisely in the principalities of Wallachia and Moldavia) is not clear; the description provided has serious errors, e.g. Lâeshi (Gypsy nomads) and Vatrashi (sedentary Gypsies) are two different categories (cf. Marushiakova & Popov, 2009, pp. 89–124).
68. It is not clear what Shakir Pashov meant by "abolition of slavery" in Hungary and Transylvania (at the time, part of the Austro-Hungarian Empire).
69. In the original, it is written France, which is clearly a mistake because what is meant is Romania.
70. The congress in Sofia took place in December 1905, and the participants in it, continuing the established administrative practice from the times of the Ottoman Empire, defined themselves as 'Kopti', i.e. 'Copts', in the sense of 'Egyptians' (see the published materials from the congress in Marushiakova & Popov, 2021, pp. 33–69).
71. The term 'pristavane' is a form of marriage in which the girl went to the boy's house alone, taking only her most necessary things with her.
72. Here and below, Shakir Pashov uses the notions 'Gypsy music' and 'Bohemian music' (respectively 'Gypsies' and 'Bohemians', 'Gypsy musicians' and 'Bohemian musicians') as synonyms, influenced by the use in the Middle Ages of the appellation 'Bohemians' for the Gypsies.
73. It is not clear what Shakir Pashov means by the name 'zhyumki propoki'.
74. In all probability, 'Lebedov and Romel' is Ivan Rom-Lebedev, the leading artist and dramaturg of the Gypsy Theatre *Romen* in Moscow.
75. In the original, the authors used the terms from Bulgarian folk mythology: 'zmey', 'talasam', 'rusalki' and 'samodivi'.
76. This Chapter is omitted because it repeats almost verbatim Chapter XV of the manuscript (see above).
77. Parts of this Chapter are omitted because they repeat almost verbatim Chapter XVI of the manuscript (see above).
78. Here, we omitted three songs from the original manuscript, written in the local Bulgarian dialect.
79. There are some minor deviations (probably unintentional errors) in the texts of the poems by Usin Kerim in the Bulgarian language included in Shakir Pashov's manuscript, compared to their publications in the press and in the editions of Kerim's poetry collections. These poems are not published here, as they have been published many times, it should only be noted that among the poems included in Shakir Pashov's manuscript, there are also those that are not present in Usin Kerim's first collection of poems (Керим, 1955), but only in the second (Керим, 1959). This means

that Shakir Pashov was familiar with the poems even before their publication (his manuscript is from 1957), i.e. he was on close terms with Usin Kerim and was familiar with the first versions of his poems.

80. The term 'stakhanovets' (stakhanovite) – from the name of the Soviet miner Alexey Stakhanov. A title of honor given to shock workers, i.e. workers who regularly overrun their production plan.
81. In Shakir Pashov's manuscript, the poem by Angel Blagoev (Demcho) is only in the Romani language. The translation from Romani language is by the editors and Sofiya Zahova.
82. This is a famous legend about St Atanas, who invented the blacksmith's tongs, which was widespread among various Balkan peoples (Попов, 1991). In this case, another motive (about the 'golden finger') is woven into it, probably a confusion with some other fairy tale.
83. A blank space is left after the name of 'Sheytanov'. It is not clear what Shakir Pashov had in mind here – one or more of Dr Nayden Sheytanov's publications (Шейтанов, 1932; 1941; Мир, 1934) or his manuscript *The Gypsies in Bulgaria. Materials on their Folklore, Language and Way of Life* (AIEFEM, No. 295 II) from 1955 (for him, see further below).
84. It was not possible to guess to which work of Miklosich the author referred.
85. We were unable to discover the quoted article.
86. *Journal of the Gypsy Lore Society*, New Series, 1911–1912, 6 (4); 1913–1914, 7 (2, 3).
87. Shakir Pashov referred to Usin Kerim's poetry collection *Песни от катуна* [Songs from the Tent] (Керим, 1955).

ANNEXE NO. 1

Historical Evidence

1. Autobiography (1967 – ?)

[AUTOBIOGRAPHY]

[...] [1]

In a meeting held at the Renaissance theatre (now Georgi Dimitrov cinema) [2], our party group decided to give a modest sum to the party club [on the square next to] Lavov most (Lion's Bridge), which the bourgeois authorities had burned. The party group took part in the congress [3], which took place in the Renaissance theatre, where I was a delegate in 1922. The congress was attended by international figures of the Communist movement, such as Clara Zetkin and others.

In 1923, during the September events [4], agents and the police searched for me. That is why I decided to escape to Kyustendil, where I got involved in the construction of the Popular Bank as an ironworker, and I left my wife and three children without any funds. After the suppression of the uprising and when the construction of the bank was finished, I returned to Sofia; I got back to work and met Valcho Ivanov. We started illegal work and restored the party groups. Because of my merits and struggles in 1924 in creating a united front between Communists and the Bulgarian Agricultural People's Union, Valcho Ivanov put my candidacy forward in the parliamentary elections, and I was elected MP from the Bulgarian Communist Party [5].

On April 15, 1925, in connection with the bomb explosion at the St Nedelya cathedral, I was arrested again in the police station, then in the 6th regiment, then in the Police Directorate and in Konstantin Fotinov School, where I stayed for three months. Due to constant persecution and house searches by police officers and agents, I decided to emigrate to Turkey. For this action, I took the consent of the comrades, the lawyer Aleksandar Lambrev, Nikola Milev and Angel Boyadzhiyata, who told me, "If you manage, run away because the situation is bad and the police already know you as a Member of Parliament". After my return from Turkey in 1929, I again joined the ranks of the Bulgarian Workers' Party [6].

After the restoration of the Party group, which was named the Gypsy Party group, by the comrades Asen Boyadzhiev, Aleksandar Naumov, Petko Stoev and others, the members of the Party Group took active participation in all Party activities and in all elections. We were acknowledged as the champions of the 3rd Region. In 1931, I joined and became Chairman of the Gypsy Cultural and Educational Organisation in Bulgaria [7], and later I founded the first Gypsy newspaper in Bulgaria, *Terbie* (Upbringing), which advocated for the cultural and educational enlightenment and the rise of the political consciousness of our tobacco workers in Bulgaria [8]. In 1933, the Sofia Party Organisation of the Bulgarian Workers' Party, with headquarters on Positano Street 7, included me in its leadership [9].

After the dissolution of the Party in 1934, I was involved in an illegal activity carried out by the comrades Ivan Dyulgerov, Vasil Garvanov, Ivan Rakhov and other Party leaders. From them, I received materials for the newspaper *Terbie* (Upbringing), which was published illegally [10], and I helped raise funds for the political prisoners by distributing stamps which I received from the comrades Gologanov and Ezekiev, as well as from the Party Secretary Ivan Dyulgerov. I participated in the Party's activities; on comrade Ggeorgi Dimitrov's proposal, I got involved in all actions and electoral struggles, and I gave reports most regularly. Before September 9, 1944, as a group machine mechanic in the municipal technical workshop in 1934, I was fired on January 1, 1935, due to a [participation in] strike led by the Party, and I was without a job for the whole winter. From 1920 until 1944, I took part in all of the Party's actions, I was arrested and kept for months, but I remained loyal to the Party. In 1944, I moved from the 3rd district to the Brick Factories neighbourhood, in the Gypsy quarter in the 4th district Emil Markov [11]; at that time, I met with comrade Alexander Naumov, and we had agreed to hold a conference of the Gypsy population on September 5–6, but the events of September 9, 1944 [12] changed this plan.

WORK AND ACTIVISM
of SHAKIR MAHMUDOV PASHOV for the period from 1944 till today, then living at 163 Emil Markov Street

On September 10, 1944, I went to the temporary club of the Fatherland's Front and Bulgarian Communist Party at 1 Vrabcha Street together with several old comrades, members [of the Party] from the Gypsy population. I met the comrades Yanko Petkov, Alexander Naumov, former MP Kalaydzhiev and others there. I received instruction from the Party to set up a Fatherland Front organisation among the Gypsy population. Party representatives participated in the event of founding the organisation and the election of its leadership, [...] and I was elected Chairman of this organisation. I also participated in the temporary militia vigil in the 10th precinct, 3rd district, for a whole month, with comrades Ivan Stefanov – Tsereto, Micho and others, and reported about the consolidation of the authority and the organisation among the Gypsy population in all neighbourhoods, but mainly in Konyovitsa [and] Tatarli [neighbourhood], where the population is the largest.

After September 9, 1944, I restored the organisation of the Gypsy population for cultural and educational advancement in Bulgaria. I was the editor-in-chief of the newspaper *Romano esi* (Echo) [13], which aimed to raise the Gypsy population in Bulgaria to a higher cultural and political level and to stimulate their mass entry into the Fatherland Front organisation. With all my Party and social activities, I promoted the Party's interest above everything else. For my activities on behalf of the Party, I was elected a representative to the Great National Assembly [14]. This high post was the highest distinction for the Gypsy population and myself. The Member of Parliament Petar Terziev invited me to the local Fatherland Front organisation in Pazardzhik for a meeting of the Gypsy population. The comrades Valko Chervenkov and Elena Gavrilova also sent me to appease the tensions between the Turkish minority and the Gypsy population in the city of Ruse [...], I managed to reconcile them because the Turks did not recognize the Turkish Gypsies as Turks, and there was a dispute between them about the Waqfs of the Turkish municipality.

In 1947, the Party sent me to subdue the scandal in the village of Golintsi (now Mladenovo) [15]. At the behest of Todor Pavlov, the elected representative from the town of Lom, and priest [Konstantin] Rusinov (the Red Priest), also elected from the town of Lom, I successfully reconciled the misunderstandings. One day I was called by the editorial office of the newspaper *Rabotnichesko delo* to meet with the editor Koshnicharov [?], because visiting foreign students – journalists were interested in meeting with me and through our translator from French or English, they [wanted] to get acquainted with our customs. I was called to comrade Valko Chervenkov's office to report and answer their questions with a foreign language translator.

In 1947, I created a Gypsy Artistic and Musical Theatre *Roma* and became its chief director. As an MP, I went to comrade Georgi Dimitrov's office in the National Assembly. I asked him if it was possible to include a subsidy for our theatre in the budget in order to support the creation of a theatre similar to the Romen theatre in the USSR. He gladly accepted my proposal and sent me to the budget committee, which introduced us to the legislative assembly, after which two million BGN were voted. He sent his secretary, the honoured

Chairman of the Presidium of the National Assembly, Mincho Neychev, and Valko Chervenkov and other party figures to the theatre's premiere, and they enthusiastically, together with everyone present, acclaimed the presented program. In 1947, comrade Zhelapov was sent to me, and I helped him set up a professional organisation of carters and porters from the Gypsy population in Sofia, which all members accepted unanimously and became good organisers.

In the same year, 1947, progressive comrades decided to build a school for Gypsy children in the Fakulteta neighbourhood, for which I acted before the Sofia City People's Council in my capacity as an MP and succeeded in having the school built. I made the first sod as a representative and Chairman of the Gypsy minority in Bulgaria. Now, hundreds of children from the Gypsy population study there, and every year a good cadre of school teachers, professional school teachers, and others, graduate from that school.

For two years, between 1941 and 1943, the couriers of the Central Committee of the Bulgarian Communist Party used to leave packages with illegal materials and weapons in my blacksmith iron-forge workshop at 28 Serdika Street. I handed them over to comrade Asparukh Dimitrov. I had known him as a comrade since 1925, when we were detained for the bomb explosion in St Nedelya cathedral, in the Directorate of the Police and in School [Konstantin] Fotinov [16].

In 1923, during the parliamentary elections, a candidate was also comrade Georgi Dimitrov, who visited the ballot boxes of the 3rd District polling station at the Vasil Levski school on Dimitar Petkov Street and in a moment, the opposition group attacked him with fists. Our party group, which was there as promoters, immediately reacted and took comrade Dimitrov out of their hands, with other comrades joining. We accompanied them to the tram, and he said to me, "Shakir, one day, when we come to power, you will be the greatest man, and for me, people will lay a carpet from the train station to the palace." When the glorious date, September 9, 1944, came, I became a Member of the Grand National Assembly, nourished by the ideas of the Party, because I spent my whole life fighting for the victory of the Marxist ideas and in anti-fascist activities since 1919. I have been doing it until today in the capacity of Chair of the 18th Fatherland Front organisation, 2nd section, Druzhba Housing Complex, Iskar station, Vasil Levski neighbourhood, 5th District.

With comradely respect: ... [Signature] (Shakir Pashov).

My Autobiography is from 1919 to this day. [17].

Notes

1. The first page of the Autobiography is missing.

2. After 1948, Georgi Dimitrov trade union house of culture, and after the changes in 1989, the Sin City music club.

3. This refers to the 4th Congress of the Bulgarian Communist Party, held in 1922.

4. Shakir Pashov meant here the September uprising in 1923.

5. There were no parliamentary elections in 1924. Perhaps Shakir Pashov is referring to the local elections in Sofia, held on May 4, 1924. We could not find any other information about his participation as a candidate for municipal councillor in them.

6. The Bulgarian Workers' Party was established in 1927 as the legal entity substituting the Bulgarian Communist Party, which was banned in 1924.

7. Here, Shakir Pashov writes neutrally, 'Gypsy Cultural and Educational Organisation'. He doesn't give the exact names of the organisations he means, namely the Sofia Common Muslim Educational-Cultural and Mutual Aid Organisation *Istikbal – Future* and the General Mohammedan-Gypsy National Cultural-Educational and Mutual Aid Union in Bulgaria. This omission of the exact names of the organisations is apparently deliberate in order to avoid the definition 'Muslim/Mohammedan' in their titles.

8. There is no evidence that any materials dedicated to tobacco workers in Bulgaria were published in the newspaper *Terbie*.

9. There is no other historical evidence to support the claim of Shakir Pashov's participation in the city leadership of Bulgarian Workers' Party; on the contrary, in the various biographical references for Shakir Pashov, there is no mention of such participation anywhere (ASR, f. Shakir Pashov).

10. We could not find any other historical evidence that the newspaper *Terbie* was published illegally. The purpose of this statement is to suggest that the newspaper propagated communist ideas (which is not supported by available historical sources either).

11. Today, the Gotse Delchev neighbourhood.

12. Shakir Pashov's statement cannot be confirmed by other sources, but it seems unlikely that a Gypsy conference would be organised in the political situation at the time.

13. It is unclear why Shakir Pashov translates *Romano esi* (Gypsy Voice) as 'Echo'.

14. For Shakir Pashov's election as a member of the Great National Assembly, see further on.

15. Today, Mladenovo district in the town of Lom.

16. Konstantin Fotinov school became a place for detention of people who were arrested after the bomb explosion at St Nedelya cathedral.

17. The Autobiography is not dated. In all probability, it was written in 1967, when Shakir Pashov was already living in the Druzhba Housing Complex and when he submitted documents for rehabilitation and restoration of his membership in the Bulgarian Communist Party.

Source: ASR, f. Shakir Pashov.

2. Statute of the Organisation Istikbal – Future (1919)

I affirm [1]. Ministry of Internal Affairs and National Health.
No. 14300, from August 2, 1919.
Statute Transcript.

STATUTE
of the Sofia Common Muslim Educational-Cultural
and Mutual Aid Organisation Istikbal – Future

1. Headquarters of the organisation is the Capital Sofia.

2. The aim of the organisation is to organise the Muslims in one common organisation, which should help the poor in times of illnesses, accidents, death, and others, and fight for their moral, material, and educational-cultural upbringing.

3. [These aims] the aforementioned [organisation achieves], through discussions and lectures, organises classes etc. It supports a *Hodzha* [2] (Orthodox Priest) and a *Bula* [3] which are needed in our religious ceremonies. The support comes from membership fees, 5 levs per month, from morning and evening parties, entertainments and from various donations.

4. All Bulgarian citizens at the age of 20 and above shall have the right to be members, and shall not be elected [for leadership positions] for three months from the day of their membership.

5. Meetings shall take place each month while the General meetings are held every three months.

6. The organisation shall be strictly non-partisan, and, in its meetings, it shall forbid the discussions of any political matters.

7. Everyone shall obey the orders of the Board of Trustees and those who do not obey the rules shall be prosecuted and those who insult the leadership, or the organisation shall be prosecuted according to the law of our country.

8. The organisation owns movable and immovable properties, ownership of professional associations, which have joined the organisation. Burial items shall be used by members only, while non-members shall pay a pre-determined fee at the common cash register.

9. The Chair shall have an obligation to take care for the proper execution of all tasks of the organisation; when there is a minority, the Chair has an equal vote.

10. When the Chair is absent, he shall be replaced by one of the Board of Trustees [4] who shall have responsibility.

11. The Secretary shall maintain all paperwork and shall be subjected to the Chair.

12. The Treasurer shall take care of the membership fees and keep in the safe no more than 1,000 levs while the rest of the money shall be deposited in a bank on the organisation's account.

13. The Councillors shall hold consultation with the Chair and form the Board of Directors.

14. The Control Commission shall control the actions of the Board of Trustees as well as the accounting books of the Secretary and the Treasurer; as soon as it finds irregularities, it can lay off the accused and call for a meeting to report about their deeds.

15. The Board of Trustees shall be elected with a mandate of one year. The Board of Trustees can be censured when a 1/3rd of the Members hand in their resignations or when it is accused of wrongdoing in a General Meeting.

16. The organisation shall have a stamp with the same name.

17. The organisation has an office, which shall be used also for the purpose of meetings and when the organisation's capital increases, it could buy or build their own home which will host poor and disabled widows and orphans, and also dejected Muslims from all across Bulgaria.

18. The organisation shall provide support to the poor for *Bayram* [5] every year and in wintertime – wood, coal, etc.

19. The organisation shall advocate for Muslims who need to receive loans for improving their homes in order to have a more hygienic way of life, in accordance with the levelling of the town.

20. At times of death, [the organisation] shall give out a certain amount of money for the burial and the organisation shall accompany the deceased to their eternal home.

21. Members, who have not paid their dues for three months, shall be excluded from membership and all their rights shall be revoked.

22. The branches of the organisation shall be managed by a representative – a delegate who is a member from the branch and who has all the powers as a delegate and as a member of the Board of Trustees; the representative passes

the decisions of the organisation to the branch members, and they shall respect them.

23. Members can re-elect their delegate when the latter is accused of something and shall replace the person with a newly elected one with a power of attorney.

24. To advocate for the interests of its members at times of illnesses. Free medical help shall be provided as well as free legal defence and consultation.

25. The organisation will advocate before the office of the Main Mufti for a new life or the Muslim religious parish, which is governed [now] by the Sofia Mufti without law and statute.

26. The organisation shall help the administrative authorities and others.

27. The organisation shall mediate between its members who have arguments, etc.

28. In the case of liquidation, the real estate shall be transferred to the Board of Trustees of the Religious parish.

Chair: (Signature) ... Yusein Mehmedov.
Secretary: (Signature) ... Shakir M. [6] Pashev.
True with the original, Secretary: ... [Signature].
Management Body of the Organisation: ... [Illegible signatures of 7 people].

Notes

1. The resolution, "I affirm" of the Minister of Internal Affairs and National Health means that the Statute of the organisation is approved by the authorities and that it is already legally registered.

2. 'Hodzha' is the term used in Bulgaria for Imam; in this case, the term is used to refer to a person who was chosen from the folks in the mahala to perform the functions of an Islamic cleric during certain customs (first and foremost at funerals); this person is not the Imam in a mosque. Such forms of folk Islam are widespread among the Gypsies in Bulgaria to date.

3. 'Bula' is the term used to refer to the Hodzha' female assistant in folk Islam, who takes over some of the Hodzha's functions among the women. This form is also widespread among the Gypsies in Bulgaria; in some communities, there is solely a Hodzhakinya (female Imam).

4. In the original, it is 'one of the Chairs', which is an obvious mistake.

5. The Muslims in the Balkans (including Muslim Gypsies) celebrated two big religious holidays under the name 'Bayram' – *Kurban-Bayram* (Eid al-Adha or Eid Qurban) and Sheker-Bayram (Eid al-Fitr or Ramadan Bayram).

6. In the original, it is 'Shakir N. Pashev', which is a typographical error – Shakir Pashov's second (patronymic) name is 'Mahmudov'. He himself spells his family name in many documents as 'Pashev', and that is the case here.

Source: CDA, f. 1 B, op. 8, a.e. 596, l. 69.

3. Attitudes and Truths Poster (1930)

Sofia Common Muslim Cultural-Educational Organisation *Istikbal – Future* [1]

ATTITUDES AND TRUTHS

To the Attention of Our State, the Sofia Municipality, and the [BULGARIAN] Society

One of the new newspapers, *Naroden priyatel*, in its issues from February 24 and March 11 this year, as well as the newspaper *Utro* in its issue from February 28 of this year, published opinions that sound as definite decisions such as "the relocation of the Gypsy neighbourhood", i.e., the dispersal of about 80–100 families who are old Muslims, natives of Sofia. These newspapers, incompetently, with bad language and unverified data, embarrass a minority of a foreign religion in Sofia, only to prepare the public opinion and create the grounds for lawless acts against the minority. These acts satisfy thievish appetites for vacant spots within the bounds of the city and, if possible, for plots with construction on them, even if they are, today, by virtue of the laws in our country, in the hands of good-faith purchasers.

We draw the attention of the institutions in our Country, of the Honourable Sofia Municipal Administration and the society of Sofia in response to the dishonest and shoddy writers in the cited [above] newspapers and we present the following truths:

1. There is nothing true in the claim that the "Gypsy neighbourhood", the Muslim neighbourhood in the capital, is a hotbed of various diseases because this statement is most certainly refuted by the fact that in the hospitals of Sofia, there is not a single Muslim with any disease, let alone a contagious one, who comes from this neighbourhood. What is true is that the relevant authorities do not fulfil their duties to pick up the rubbish from our neighbourhood, inhabited by Muslims, on purpose, in order to maintain an unsightly appearance there, regardless of the fact that the Honourable Municipal Administration collects from us, just like all other citizens, fees for garbage and water.

2. In moral terms, we, the poor Muslims, the so-called "Gypsies" (pariahs), are the strictest, and only one fact is enough to convince you that this is the case: The Morality Bureau at the Police Directorate has registered prostitutes from diverse, and even prestigious in the past, social ranks, however, not a single "Gypsy" woman among them.

3. Regarding the hygiene of our streets and yards, we have already stated that this is due to the criminal negligence of the municipal officials responsible for the public hygiene in our neighbourhood, who fulfill their duty only about a week before some election, out of demagoguery, and led by their appetite for about a thousand electoral votes in our neighbourhood.

Perhaps, someone has raised this issue before the Honourable Municipal Administration or other authorities, and if this is the case, we are convinced that the relevant authorities and people will not succumb unreservedly to shoddy writers who want to fish in troubled waters by disseminating disinformation disregarding the laws of our country.

"Expel, chase away the old native Muslim owners who had set up their family hearths long ago so that we can rob them – we, invisible and dishonest shoddy writers".

It is known to the Esteemed trustworthy authorities that we are an obedient *rayah* [members of the flock] of about 80–100 families, old Muslim natives, who practice skilled labour, proven and used daily by the citizens of Sofia: blacksmiths, tinsmiths, basket-makers, *dzhambazi* [horse-traders], musicians, porters, shoe-shiners and others. We, as equal citizens of our dear homeland Bulgaria, participated heroically and courageously in both wars that Bulgaria fought, and along with everybody else, we gave beloved victims -- fathers, sons, and brothers. Many of the members of our small society are disabled; they have sacrificed their arms, legs, eyes, etc., for the FATHERLAND; many mothers, women and children still wear black, mourning their loved ones, who were lost in the battles.

If so, if Art. 57 of the Constitution of the Bulgarian Kingdom states that "all Bulgarian subjects are equal before the laws of our country", Art. 63, "the real estates in the Kingdom are subjected to the rule of the Bulgarian laws", and Art. 67, "the rights and the property are inviolable".

Why should we be treated as equal only when it comes to our obligations and never when it comes to our rights, sanctified by the constitution of our Kingdom?

Is it not for safeguarding our sound customs and our rights, protected by the laws in our country, that we gave, once again this year, 200 volunteers from our members in the Bulgarian Army?

Our modest, short, and fair request is that the Honourable Municipal Administration and any other authorities, if they are to take decisive steps for the reconstruction of our neighbourhood, should act, taking into account the following:

To accept the cooperation of a commission (consisting of three or five members) who come from our circles of the native Muslims of Sofia, who would bring to their knowledge the following:

1. The [information about the] families who lived for the longest while in the neighbourhood with regulated property rights.

2. A list of the people who live in the area from Pirotska Street to Knyaginya Klementina Street [2], between Konstantin Velichkov Boulevard and Indzhe Voyvoda Boulevard. This list contains data and instructions about those who are not natives of Sofia or craftsmen but internal migrants from the villages of Bulgaria, such as comb-makers, sieve-makers, beggars, etc., who are not settled down and live in a single plot shared by several families, and who, despite the control of the administration, may have no idea, since their birth, about the rules of hygiene in life. We can identify such people who would be subject to eviction.

3. We will assist them in establishing for each individual family how they have furnished their homes in terms of construction and hygiene; who needs certain small renovations in accordance with the modern ways of living. Instead of depriving us of our properties in the places where we have been residing since the liberation of Bulgaria to this day, we ask the authorities to assist us with some state mortgages so that we can meet the requirements of the modern day.

4. We will provide information about our homeless compatriots who were provided with empty municipal places and who gave up these privileges. They sold them and returned to our neighbourhood, causing its overcrowding. They could be punished by eviction from the neighbourhood, and we could give, if necessary, all other necessary information because the technique of any eviction requires both tact and great justice.

We firmly believe in the healthy public and state institutions of our Kingdom, we believe that the attitude of people with interest who wrote in the [newspapers] *Naroden priyatel* and *Utro* should not be the lead thread in resolving such an issue, but it should be the truth and the wisdom of the ruler.

Sofia, March 6, 1930.
By the Sofia Common Muslim Cultural-Educational Organisation *Istikbal – Future.*
Sofia. [Seal]

Notes

1. In the original, it is written 'Istigbal', which is clearly a typographical error.
2. Today Alexander Stamboliyski Boulevard.

Source: DA Sofia, f. 1 К, op. 2, a.e. 831, l. 1–10б.

4. Statute of the Common Mohammedan-Gypsy Union (1934)

STATUTE
of the Common Mohammedan-Gypsy National Cultural-Educational
and Mutual Aid Union

Headquarters of the Union – Capital Sofia.

Art. 1. Aims of the Union: To organise all Gypsies (Mohammedans and others) on the basis of their national belonging to Bulgaria in order to nurture among them educational, professional and general culture; based on the laws of Bulgaria, to strengthen their religious lives with valuable moral principles; to create an organisation for the preservation of the material and spiritual interests of this nation in the country, but also a mutual aid establishment.

Art. 2. Resources of the Union: membership fees of Union organisations from all places inhabited by Gypsy minorities; public lectures and courses for enlightenment and professional education; health civil learning for the cultivation of civil virtues in the motherland Bulgaria; raising the religious way of life of their members; and, if the laws permit, opening of private schools.

Art. 3. Regular Members of the Union could be all our fellow countrymen in Bulgaria and in other countries, who belong to associations, but also those who do not belong to any but are members of their professional guilds [of]: the blacksmiths, the tinsmiths, the basket-makers, the horse-dealers, the intermediary horse-dealers [1], the porters, the musicians and the others. The professional guilds or organisations shall be represented in the Union by one delegate authorised by their association or organisation.

As Honorary Members of the Union shall be proclaimed all donors regardless of the form of their donation -- cash, real estate or material support of the Union.

Art. 4. Material Resources of the Union are the means acquired from membership fees as determined by the Supreme Council of the Union, which meets annually; from donations; parties; social events; picnics; fines by the Union's leadership imposed on members; from print publications and badges. [...] [2]

Art. 5. Rights of the Members. All organised Members of the Union have equal rights and have the right to vote in all meetings of the Union. Each member of the Union is obliged to obey the ordinances of the Board of Directors, which do not contradict the current Statute; to work towards the success of the Union; to enrol new members; and to propagate among our national minority the educational and cultural goals of the Union, and in general to propagate the aims of the Union.

Art. 6. The Organisation of the Union. [...] Each provincial organisation, which is in the Common Union, shall elect and send, with a regular authorisation letter, their delegates to the Congress [...] The Congress of the Union elects a Supreme Union Council. The Congress may be attended also by willing guests, who shall not have the right to vote or to be elected. The Union will work for the acquisition of all rights, which are enjoyed by all other similar unions, in accordance with the laws of the country.

Art. 7. The Union will also aim to create, through its Members, the following cultural undertakings: 1) establishment of educational and professional community centres; 2) establishment of national private schools in the larger towns; 3) establishment of regional religious parishes; 4) appointment of teachers-specialists who will initially provide literacy training to the illiterate; guide the Members to acquire professional education and rights; canalise their religions lives and in general, prepare them for good citizens of Bulgaria.

Art. 8. Duties of the Union Members.

Each Union member shall subscribe to the official Union publication as well as secure new subscribers among non-members.

Each member shall wear the special Union badge at all events of the Union, as well as sell those badges to the unorganised.

Union members who do not pay regularly their fees via the treasurer of their own organisation or directly at the Union treasurer's office will be expelled from the Union, after notification to pay off their duties within a certain deadline.

Also, a Union Member who does not safeguard the image of the Union, propagates ideas that are harmful to the Union, or to the country, against its aims and ideals will also be excluded.

Also, entire associations shall be excluded if they, in their capacity as full members, commit any of the above-mentioned.

Art. 9. Governance and Rights of the Supreme Union Council. The Congress shall elect a Supreme Union Council from among the member organisations from all over Bulgaria; the Council shall convene in its full composition only by a majority decision of the Board of Directors and only in case of very important issues which the Union has identified. The Supreme Union Council hall convenes only once per year.

The Board of Directors has the following composition: a President, two Vice Presidents, a Secretary and a Treasurer. The Board of Directors is the permanent governing body of the Union during the organisational year. The Board shall be elected by the congress delegates, including the delegates of the professional associations. [...] The elections of the Supreme Union Council, the Board of Directors and of the Congress Bureau shall be conducted in accordance with the rules described in the current article in a secret ballot. A three-member control commission shall be elected with the ballot-paper for the Board of Directors. [...]

Note I: Before the end of the annual congress, the Supreme Union Council shall appoint eight-member committees from among the attending regular delegates of the Congress, with the following tasks: a) Cultural-Educational; b) Religious; c) Settlement and Infrastructure. [...]

Note II: The Cultural-Educational committee, as a subsidiary body to the Board of Directors, shall take care and bear responsibility for all undertakings described in the Aims of the Union. It sets up the Entertainment Commissions at each organisation, which collect material support for the Union from the following activities: sports, tourist, gymnastic, lectures, artistic groups, musical tours, selling of published materials, badges etc.

The Religious Committee, as a subsidiary body to the Board of Directors, shall take care and have responsibility for the moral and religious rise of the Union members; their religious representation and organisation according to their confessions; the punishment of those couples who live together illegally and legalisation of such cases. The Committee represents the co-religionists in Union to the respective authorities in procedures of appointment, discharge, etc., of all religious staff at the respective religious body. The Religious Committee is a body which plays the role of a conciliation board for all family conflicts which threaten to destroy the established family. This Committee shall create, together with the Board of Directors, the necessary conditions for the formation of a national religious community wherever it is needed in the Kingdom. [...] The Religious Committee shall organise all charity activities of the Union as well as those activities which preserve the religious traditions: engagements, weddings, birth celebrations, death, burials, etc.

The Settlement and Infrastructure Committee has the following duties: to protect vis-a-vis the respective authorities the rights of the Union Members to real estate ownership whether it is covered or not; in the towns specifically, the Committee shall oversee Union members' constructions that are included in the wider neighbourhood and make sure that these are built in accordance with the law and do not disturb the Union members' settlement. The same Committee, regardless of the authorities of the country, shall make sure that each Union or non-Union Member of the nation strictly observes all public hygiene requirements; to advocate before the respective state and council authorities for the development of the neighbourhoods where the national minority lives sedentary and to manage, on the whole, all settlement and infrastructure issues concerning its own nation.

Art. 10. Structure of the Union.

Each national association consisting of 20 or more members shall elect for a three-year term their own Board of Trustees, composed of President, Vice President and a Secretary-Treasurer. It shall be elected at the annual conference by a majority vote, and the minutes from the meeting shall be signed by the electoral bureau of the Board of Directors of the Sofia Union, which shall verify and approve the minutes for publication in the Union's edition. [...]

Art. 11. Rights and Obligations of the Members of the Board of Directors of the Union except the ones mentioned here.

The Board of Directors shall issue regulations on the organisation of the Union's life, and they shall be made public in the Union's edition.

Only the following positions from the Board of Directors shall be paid: President, Secretary and Treasurer, while the rest are honorary. [...]

Art. 12. The Union shall rent an office space in Sofia, which shall also be used for meetings. When the Union has good financial resources, its first task shall be the purchase and building of its own place, owned by the legal entity or by a cooperation. This space shall also serve as a school; *chitalishte* [3]; a hotel for poor Union members; a Union University training the youth in all kinds of crafts; a shelter for war invalids, people who had accidents, and old and handicapped people; for our nation across Bulgaria.

Art. 13. One of the Union's main charitable tasks is, on a certain day of the year, for all Union departments to have a Day of Charity for the Bulgarian Gypsy in order to support all our poor and deprived compatriots.

Art. 14. The Union's office shall keep the following books: a register book for incoming and outgoing correspondence; a protocol book for all Union's institutes according to this Statute, a cash book and other accounting books. [...].

Art. 15. The Stamp of the Union has a circular form with the inscription: "Popular Gypsy National Cultural-Educational and Mutual Aid Union" with a star in the middle [4]. [...]

Art. 18. For the immediate start of the mutual aid function of the Union, a Mutual Loan Association has been already established, whose books are kept by the general treasurer of the Union. It has the following aims: to assist poor people and people with urgent needs among the Union Members, following a motivated request; to help members at times of illness, unemployment, death, accident, etc.; to set up temporary shelters for elderly, handicapped and lone persons amongst our compatriots; to support poor, talented children for finishing lower secondary school, upper secondary school, and university or professional college; to support the burials of very impoverished male and female Gypsies. At such extreme cases, the Union organs shall also resort to individual one-off help from well-to-do members.

Art. 19. The Union's Patron Holy Day is St George's Day [5], which shall be celebrated each year.

Art. 20. The Congress of the Union shall convene each year on Bulgaria's Liberation Day [6] and shall be preceded by an evening party, multinational propaganda [7] and a manifestation.

Art. 21. This Statute may be amended and complemented by the Union's Congress.

The Statute was created, accepted, and approved by the General Constitutive Meeting of the established Union, which took place on 25 December 1933, in Sofia.

Of the Common Mohammedan-Gypsy National Cultural-Educational and Mutual Aid Union,
Director: ... [Signature]. Secretary: ... [Signature]. [Stamp of the Organisation].

Notes

1. It is not clear why the societies of 'horse-dealers' and 'intermediary horse-dealers' are divided because the names refer to the same occupation (the horse-dealers are always intermediators). It is possible that two such associations existed in Sofia at that time.

2. Here and below the general administrative details of the Statute are omitted.

3. In Bulgaria, the system of the so-called *chitalishte* (community reading centre) has been widespread since the time of the Ottoman Empire. They also perform broader functions as cultural and social centres in a settlement or in an urban neighbourhood.

4. In the text of the Statute (Art. 15), the inscription of the stamp bearing the name of the Union does not include the word 'Mohammedan', while the stamp itself, placed at the end of the document, lacks the word 'Gypsy'. Similarly, there

are discrepancies between the texts found in the Statute and in the stamp with regard to the symbols of the Union. The text of the Statute (Art. 15) states that the stamp has a star in the middle while the stamp actually has a crescent and a star (i.e. the typical Islamic symbolism). It cannot be established whether these are unintentional errors or deliberate omissions in the Statute.

5. It is interesting to note that the Statute uses the term 'Patron Holy Day' (Art. 19). The same term was used for the annual celebrations of the patron saints of various Esnafs (Guilds). For example, in Vidin, St George's Day was proclaimed as a Gypsy Holy Day, i.e. this traditional holiday became a national symbol for the Gypsies.

6. The designated Union's Congress date is March 3, the date of Bulgaria's National Holiday (Liberation Day). This choice makes an explicit emphasis on the fact that the Gypsies belong to the Bulgarian civic nation.

7. In this case, 'multinational' propaganda means propaganda among the Gypsy community itself.

Source: CDA, f. 264, op. 2, a.e. 8413, l. 7–12, 15–20, 21–26 (three copies).

5. Clarification by the Istikbal-Future Organisation (1938)

Sofia Common-Muslim Educational, Cultural and Mutual Aid Organisation Istikbal-Future – Sofia. [Form]

No. … . Sofia, March 16, 1938.

CLARIFICATION

From the Muslim Cultural-Educational Organisation ISTIKBAL (Future) – Sofia

Regarding the incorrect and inaccurate information in the newspaper *Dnevnik*
Concerning the appearance of the typhoid fever disease among the Gypsies

It is evident, even from the very statements of the sanitary authorities, that there is no typhoid fever in the Konyovitsa neighbourhood. Except for a single case on Indzhe Voivoda Street, this disease has not been found anywhere. Although this was a single case in which the disease was brought from the village of Vrabnitsa, or the town of Pernik, the sanitary authorities rightly undertook a thorough cleaning of all Gypsies and established that no parasites were found almost anywhere. By bringing this to the attention of all citizens of the capital, we ask them not to be afraid of the Sofia Gypsy workers, such as porters, shoe-shiners, basket-makers, florists, and so on, who should not be unjustly exposed to unemployment and hunger.

It is worth mentioning that all the alarms [1] and irresponsible writings in some newspapers have caused excessive damage and loss not only to us but also to the conduct of the population's daily life in the town. These alarms date back to 1929 when a committee in the Konyovitsa neighbourhood started fighting against the Gypsies in order to evict them from their homes. As a result, many of our compatriots sold their houses for nothing, moved out and exposed themselves to even greater misery. Even today, in our neighbourhood, there is a committee called *Podem* [Upsurge], which has the same tasks as the one in 1929 and which relies on alarms like the ones published by the newspaper *Dnevnik*. This, in our opinion, is dishonest and unjust; it is inflammatory and creates resentment that no one needs. Rather than support and guidance on how to be good Bulgarian citizens, we receive the above-mentioned treatment.

We are Bulgarian citizens with a Bulgarian spirit, and we left the bones of our fathers and brothers on the battlefields in both wars and today we are ready to make sacrifices for the good of our homeland Bulgaria where we were born, live and enjoy all freedoms.

Chairman: ... [2]
Secretary: ... [3]

Notes

1. This is a reference to the series of Applications and Petitions filed in the period 1937–1938, with complaints concerning the proximity of the Gypsy quarters (see more detail below).
2–3. The copy of the document does not have signatures.

Source: DA Sofia, f. 1 K, op. 4, a.e. 531, l. 5.

6. Letter to the Director of the Police (1939)

The Istikbal Common Muslim Cultural-Educational and Mutual Aid Organisation of Sofia.
July 18, 1939, Sofia.

To: Mr Director of Police, Here [Sofia].
[Stamp]: Directorate General of Public Health. 23 July 1939. Case No. 31.

Mr Director,

Observing that instead of moving forward, the Gypsy population goes to moral and material decline day by day, and in order to raise them in cultural, educational, moral and religious terms, we have founded the association of all Gypsies in the capital. Its task is to work for their material and spiritual rise and bring their lives closer to the rest of the capital's population because their present condition cannot and should be tolerated any longer.

In order to achieve our goal, however, we need full support from all responsible factors in the country within the existing laws because, without such support, the realisation of our task is impossible, especially for preserving the morality among the Gypsies.

While it takes years of hard work to raise them culturally and educationally by giving lectures and talks, as well as opening evening courses for adults, our task to preserve the morality among the Gypsies is quite difficult, and without the support of the authorities, it would be impossible to achieve.

In the first place, measures are needed to preserve their morality – the most valuable foundation on which family happiness and the future of a nation are based.

To our great disappointment, depravity and immorality not only do not decrease, but they are increasing day by day and have taken alarming dimensions. It is a common thing to see in the late hours of the night drunken men and women walking in the streets of the neighbourhood [1] and in obscure places, where shameful acts are being committed, as a result of which the most dangerous diseases for humanity are spread. At the same time, many women and children fall asleep hungry because their father eats and drinks up in the night everything that he has earned during the day, without returning to his home where his hungry wife and children are waiting for him.

Instead of rigorous measures to eradicate this great evil, unfortunately, we see that the family beer houses in the neighbourhood, which are nothing else but typical cabarets [2] and nests of immorality, have increased from one to three. These cabarets are the sole and greatest reason for the increase of immorality; shameful things are being done in them, and often by children under the age of 14, the description of which is impossible. The saddest thing is that these night houses are visited by many prominent people from the centre of the city [3] who, with their behaviour, set a bad example for the ordinary Gypsy population, while fights are not uncommon between these eminent persons.

If the drunkenness and the depravity among the Gypsy population were constrained, their material situation would improve, for which no resources would be needed by the authorities, but only a tighter control and measures to eliminate the reasons for the increase of immorality.

That is why we kindly ask you, Mr Director, to order through your subordinate police authorities the following:

1. Take the most stringent measures against all Gypsy men and Gypsy women who roam in the neighbourhood during the night without any reason, especially those in an intoxicated state.

2. Take due measures to close the Gypsy cabarets – the nests of immorality that demoralise the Gypsy population and have a bad effect on the upbringing, especially of the youth and of the children in the neighbourhood.

With the conviction that you will pay serious attention to these demands and that you will do everything in your power, showing attention to the Gypsy population, which has always been and continues to be of benefit to the state, we remain with great respect.

Secretary: ... [Signature] (Rashid Mehmedov),
Chair: ... [Signature] (Shakir Pashov). [Stamp].

Notes

1. This is a reference to the two Gypsy neighbourhoods, Konyovitsa and Tatarli (de facto united into one). They were then located on the outskirts of the city (around today's Aleksandar Stamboliyski Boulevard and Konstantin Velichkov Boulevard).

2. The most famous of these cabarets was *Pri Keva* (At Keva), where the popular singer of Gypsy songs Keva (originally from Vidin) used to sing. She had several phonograph records in the 1930s for the Record Company *Balkan*, which included the song *Telal Avel* (She Comes from Below), performed in the Romani language. This was the first record of such kind in Bulgaria.

3. The cabaret *Pri Keva* was especially popular and frequently visited by the Bohemians in Sofia (Тенев, 1997, pp. 225–227). According to widespread urban

rumours at the time, a frequent visitor to the cabaret was also Prince Cyril, brother of the Bulgarian King Boris III and, after his death, a regent of the Crown Prince Simeon II, sentenced to death by the People's Tribunal in 1945.

Source: DA Sofia, f. 1 K, op. 4, a.e. 683, l. 93.

7. Statute of the Organisation Ekhipe (1945)

STATUTE
of the United Cultural and Educational Organisation
of the Gypsy Minorities in Bulgaria Ekhipe [Unity]

Chapter I. Nature, Aims, Tasks and Structure

Art. 1. The United Gypsy Organisation in Bulgaria [ETsO] includes in itself all Gypsies who belong to the world Gypsy movement and are members of some of the local associations of the United Gypsy Organisation in the country to which they pay a membership fee.

Art. 2. The United Gypsy Organisation in Bulgaria is the legitimate representative of the Gypsy movement in the country and in the World Gypsy Organisation [1]. Eligible members are Gypsies at the age of 18 and above, regardless of sex and social status. Members can also be all Gypsies with Mohammedan and Christian Orthodox religions without any differentiation.

Art. 3. The United Gypsy Organisation in Bulgaria has the following tasks: a) To fight against fascism, anti-Gypsyism and racial prejudices; b) To raise the Gypsy national feeling and consciousness among the Bulgarian Gypsies; c) To introduce the Gypsy language among the Gypsy masses as oral and written language; d) To familiarise the Bulgarian Gypsy minority with the Gypsy culture; e) To familiarise the Bulgarian Gypsy community with their spiritual, social and economic culture; f) To raise the economic status of all Gypsy strata in Bulgaria; g) To make the physical condition of the Gypsy youth in Bulgaria; h) To make the Gypsy masses productive; i) To consolidate and set up Gypsy institutes in Bulgaria; j) To inform the general Bulgarian opinion about the needs of the Gypsy population; k) To foster an aspiration among the Gypsies for building a national hearth in their own land.

Art. 4. The bodies of the United Gypsy Organisation in Bulgaria are determined by the Conference of the ETsO, and they are the following: a) Local united Gypsy associations; b) Conference of the United Gypsy associations in Bulgaria; c) Supreme Council; d) Central Committee; e) Main Control

Commission; f) Chief Commission of the Gypsy Fund for Agricultural Preparation; g) Supreme Court of the organisation.

Art. 5. The Conference, as well as the present Statute, determine the functions of each of the above-mentioned bodies of the United Gypsy Organisation in Bulgaria and their relationships. The Conference has the power to create new bodies with specific tasks if that would be needed at a certain time.

The Conference could merge some functions of these bodies and delegate some of their tasks to the Central Committee of the United Gypsy Organisation in Bulgaria.

Art. 6. The central bodies of the United Gypsy Organisation in Bulgaria are elected by the Conference in accordance with Chapters ... [2] of the current Statute.

Art. 7. The United Gypsy Organisation in Bulgaria shall be represented to the authorities, the state-institutions, and private bodies by the Central Committee, which is selected by the Conference, respectively by the President of the Central Committee or his representative, together with the Secretary or by himself.

Art. 8. Within the United Gypsy Organisation, the separate Gypsy societies have the right to organise separately with their own governing bodies and statutes that do not contradict the Statute of the United Gypsy Organisation in Bulgaria. These societies can have independent organisational lives.

Chapter II. Local United Gypsy Organisations

Art. 9. Local united Gypsy associations can be formed by at least 15 members of the United Gypsy Organisation in Bulgaria who live in the same place, are over 18 years of age, respect the current Statute and regularly pay their membership fees.

Art. 10. Each Gypsy, who meets the terms of Art. 9, has the right to be a member of a local association. For that purpose, he shall submit a relevant declaration, and if the management of the local association rejects it, he has the right to refer the matter to the first general meeting of the local association.

Art. 11. Each *tabor* [3] shall have only one local Gypsy association. Each local Gypsy association shall have their own statute, which does not contradict to present one. The statute of the local Gypsy association is affirmed by the Central Committee. [...] New associations are accepted by the Central Committee and their acceptance is confirmed by the Conference.

Art. 12. Each local united association is autonomous within the framework of the present Statute. The local united association shall obey the decisions of the supreme Gypsy institutions and their ordinances. [...] [4]

Art. 13. The General Meetings are regular and special. The regular General Meetings are convened every six months for hearing the report of the Board and the other bodies of the association. The special General Meetings are convened by the Board when they consider it necessary and also when this is requested in writing by 1/5th of the members of the association; respectively, by 1/10th of the members of the local association in Sofia or upon request of the Central Committee of the United Gypsy Organisation in Bulgaria in order to review emergency matters.

Art. 14. The Board of the local united Gypsy association is its Supreme Executive Body. [...] The Boards of the local Gypsy associations are affirmed by the Central Committee. [...]

Art. 17. Each local association, respectively its Board, presents to the Central Committee of the ETsO annually a written report for its activities for the past organisational year.

Art. 18. The members of the Central Committee, as well as the members of the other central institutions of the United Gypsy Organisation in Bulgaria, have the right to be present and have the right to vote in the meetings of the Board of the local association.

Chapter III. Rights and Obligations of the Members

Art. 19. Each member of the organisation has an active and passive voting right for each of the electoral institutions – local and central, as long as they satisfy the following conditions: to be a member of a local united Gypsy association, to have paid their membership fee and for the elected – to have seniority [5] in the organisation for a year.

Art. 20. Each member of the organisation shall be enrolled in the local united Gypsy association; shall respect the present Statute, as well as the statute of the local association; pay his/her membership fee; respect the rules of the organisation; and carry out the orders and the decisions of the local and central bodies of the United Gypsy Organisation in Bulgaria.

Art. 21. The Conference of the United Gypsy Organisation in Bulgaria is the supreme body of the organisation. Its decisions are compulsory for all local united Gypsy associations and for each member of the organisation. The conferences are regular and special.

Art. 22. The regular Conference of the organisation convenes every 3 years and if possible after each World Gypsy Congress. [...]

Art. 23. The regular Conferences of the organisation listen to, discuss, and give opinion about the reports of all bodies elected during the previous Conference of the United Gypsy Organisation in Bulgaria. These bodies report to the Conference. The Conference determines the future activities of the organisation, approves its budget, and elects five delegates for the World Gypsy Congress. The Conference has the power to make changes to the present Statute and to the election rules. [...]

Art. 26. Each local united Gypsy association has the right to at least two delegates, regardless of the number of its legitimate members. Local associations with more than 100 regular members have the right to an additional delegate for every additional hundred members or part of 100 regular members. The regular members of a local association are determined based on the number of people who were regularly reported by the local associations to the Central Committee.

Art. 27. In the Conference, apart from the regularly elected delegates of the local association, with rights of regular delegates are the Presidents of the Central Committee; all members of the other institutions take part in the Conference in an advisory capacity. When the reports of the Central institutions are discussed, the persons in charge do not have the right to vote. [...]

Art. 30. The meetings of the Conference are open to the public unless the Conference itself decides that discussions should take place behind closed doors. The meetings take place according to the regulations determined by the Conference itself.

Chapter V [6]. Supreme Council of the Organisation

Art. 31. The Supreme Council is elected by the Conference and is composed of 35 people. In it, with equal rights, are delegated two representatives from the Central Committee. The Supreme Council is elected for three years. Members of the Supreme Council can be elected from different *tabors* (settlements). [...] [7]

Chapter VI. Central Committee

Art. 34. The Central Committee is elected by the Conference or, in special cases, by the Supreme Council of the organisation. It is composed of a President, two Vice-Presidents, two Secretaries and Treasurers, eight Councillors, all residing in the same town. The President of the Central Committee is appointed by the Conference itself, while the other positions are determined at the first meeting of the Central Committee. The President of the Central Committee is the President of the United Gypsy Organisation in Bulgaria. [...]

Chapter VII. Chief Control Commission

[...]

Chapter VIII. Supreme Court of the Organisation

[...]

Chapter IX. Budget, Accounting and Control

[...]

Chapter X. Disciplinary Rules

[...]

Chapter XI. Official Publication of the Organisation

Art. 47. The Official Publication of the United Gypsy Organisation in Bulgaria is the newspaper *Romano esi* (Gypsy Voice). It is compiled by an Editorial Board under the guidance of the Central Committee.

Art. 48. The organisation's Publication is primarily informative. It gives information on public and political issues as well as on the activities of organisations in Bulgaria. The newspaper shall educate all members with articles and reports in the spirit of the Fatherland Front [8] and advocate for the building of socialism in Bulgaria.

Art. 49. The format of the newspaper, the price, and the publication procedure shall be determined by the Central Committee. [...] The newspaper is supported by its own revenues and by subsidies envisaged in the budget. [...]

Chapter XII. Electoral Institutions and Conducting of Elections

[...]

Chapter XIII. General Regulations

Art. 58. [...] The stamp of the United Gypsy Organisation in Bulgaria is circular with the following text: 'United Gypsy Organisation in Bulgaria – Central Committee–Sofia' which is written in Bulgarian and in Gypsy languages [9]. The stamps [10] of the local united associations are similar to the Central Committee.

Art. 59. The organisation's holiday is May 7 [11.] The organisation's flag is red with two white fields and with a triangle in the middle [12].

Art. 60. The Conference of the Organisation is solely authorised to make amendments to this Statute.

Art. 61. This Statute was adopted by the Second Regular Conference of the United Gypsy Organisation in Bulgaria on ... [13], in Sofia.

The Second Regular Conference of the United Gypsy Organisation in Bulgaria on ... [14] in Sofia, which adopted and approved this Statute, was attended by the following delegates, representing local united Gypsy associations [15].

Notes

1. There is no historical record of the existence of a 'World Gypsy Organisation' anywhere in the world at that time.

2. An omission in the text. Apparently, the numbering of the chapters was made post-factum.

3. Here, as well as below (Art. 31), the term 'tabor' is used in the sense of 'settlement', which is rather unusual because in Bulgaria as well as in the former USSR (except for the Transcarpathian region which was annexed to the USSR after the end of the WWII), this term has always meant a specific Gypsy group who led a nomadic life. What is even more puzzling is that the whole phrase is, in fact, a loan translation from the Russian language (in Bulgarian, another preposition would be used). We could not offer a satisfactory explanation for this.

4. The detailed procedural regulations were omitted from the text.

5. The implication is that they were already elected to a leading position in the organisation.

6. Chapter 4 is missing from the text, which is probably an error in the numeration.

7. An ellipsis is marked in the text, probably for some text to be added.

8. This is a reference to the new Government of the Fatherland Front of September 9, 1944, which radically altered the country's political course and declared war on Germany.

9. Various stamps were used in the official documentation of the organisation over the years, but in all versions, the inscriptions are only in Bulgarian.

10. In the original, it is 'the seal' (singular), which is a mistake.

11. For the organisation's holiday, see more details later.

12. There is no record of the existence of a flag of the organisation in the format described. Its symbolism is not clear, but we can assume that the red colour of the flag is a continuation of the tradition of the Gypsy guilds' flags (cf. Иречек, 1899, Vol. 2, p. 33 for the participation of the "Gypsy guild" with its "red banner" in festive processions on official holidays). On the other hand, the use of this colour can be interpreted as a curtsey to the new political authority in the country, dominated by the Communist Party.

13–14. The text ends with an ellipsis which indicates that the Statute was ready before the second regular conference of the organisation and the insertion of the exact dates was supposed to be done after its adoption by the conference.

15. Shakir Pashov's manuscript reveals that the Statute was written after March 6, 1945 (i.e. before the end of WWII), following the constituent assembly of the new organisation (in fact, the restoration of the old organisation *Istikbal* under a new name). The Statute was supposed to be adopted by the National Conference of the new organisation, which took place no sooner than May 2, 1948. As we can see from Shakir Pashov's manuscript, the conference neither discussed nor did it adopt this Statute. It remained illegitimate and never entered into force due to the change in the Bulgarian political situation in 1948, when the Statute was no longer up-to-date or valid. As the Statute was never formally approved, it is understandable that the delegates' signatures are missing from it. Nevertheless, at least according to the newspaper *Romano esi*, the Statute was approved already in 1945 or 1946 by the then Minister of Internal Affairs, Anton Uygov (*Romano esi*, 1946c, p. 2). No historical record of this fact, however, has been preserved.

Source: CDA, f. 1 Б, op. 8, a.e. 596, l. 50–52.

8. Information (1946)

INFORMATION [1]
by Comrade Shakir Mahmudov Pashev, from the city of Sofia

I became a member of the Workers' Party – Communists [2] in 1918, and during that time, I worked in the Bulgarian State Railways, railway workshop.

I took an active part in 1920 in the rail workers' strike, and I was a striker. And at that time, I was arrested and taken to the barracks, and there I was dressed as a military railwayman [3].

After the strike failed, I quit my job and started working for my father, who had a blacksmith shop.

I am an organiser in the Gypsy neighbourhood of the first activity for the Workers' Party – Communists, and during that time, we made a red flag with the name "PROGRESS", during which time I knew the following comrades from the Workers' Party:

1. Georgi Dimitrov Kirchev; 2. [Vasil] Muletarov [and Hristo] Kabakchiev; 3. Alexi Lambrev – lawyer; 4. Nikola Milev; 5. Valcho Ivanov, secretary of the Workers' Party – 3rd district; 6. Angel Boyadzhiya in the Engineering Workshop.

When comrade Dimitar Blagoev died, our group in the Gypsy neighbourhood took part in his funeral; we went to the Yuchbunar garden to give last respect to the diseased who was placed in the orphanage, and from there, with wreaths from our group, we went to the cemetery.

I was included in the Workers' Party – Labor Bloc [4] list by Comrade Valcho Ivanov for my good deeds.

During the events in the fall of 1923, I was chased [5] and escaped to Kyustendil, where I worked [on the construction of] the Popular Bank, which was then under construction. In 1925, I was detained in the school [Konstantin] Fotinov for 70 days and was persecuted. After that, I escaped to Istanbul, and 2–3 years later, I returned and restored the all-Gypsy organisation, and in 1930, I became its leader. I entered the municipal workshop during the rule of the liberals [6]. I became a member of the Workers' Party, which was located on Positano Street, together with the whole group of 60–70 people [Gypsies]. I know the following comrades:

1/ Asen Boyadzhiev, now a colonel; 2/ Petko Napetov; 3/ Alexander Naumov and other former MPs. When the building of the club was underway, next to the Coloured Bridge [6], we collected about BGN 1,000 from the group and contributed this money to the building of the club.

I also know Comrade Yanko Petkov – now Mayor of the 3rd District, Georgi Chureto, Micho – Group Chief of the 10th Precinct, and other comrades. Now I am the founder of the General Gypsy Organisation and its Chairman, a member of the Workers' Party, 4th district.

The above confirms that I am a member of the Workers' Party.

I confirm this with my signature.
... [signature]

Sofia, September 5, 1946.

Notes

1. This autobiographical information was prepared by Shakir Pashov when he was nominated for a deputy in the Great National Assembly (for more details, see below).

2. At that time, the official name was the Bulgarian Workers' Party (Communists).

3. This means that he was forcibly mobilised so that he could not participate in strikes.

4. The Labor Bloc, also known as the United Front, is a political coalition between the Bulgarian Communist Party and the left wing of the Bulgarian Agricultural People's Union, established in the fall of 1923. As stated above, there is no other historical record confirming that Shakir Pashov was included in the lists of the Labor Bloc (United Front) for the parliamentary elections in December 1923 or for the municipal elections in Sofia in May 1924, except his own words. In any case, he was not elected either as a deputy or as a municipal councillor in these elections.

5. It is probably meant after the parliamentary elections in 1931.

6. Today *Lavov most* (Lion Bridge).

Source: CDA, f. 1 Бор. 6, a.e. 235, l. 6–7.

9. Speech on the occasion of 14 January (1948)

SPEECH

By the Chairman of the Gypsy Minority in Bulgaria and Member of Parliament SHAKIR M. PASHEV, on the occasion of the traditional holiday VASILOVDEN – January 14, 1948, in the studio of Sofia Radio, with the participation of the musical-artistic group of the organisation with the solo singer Pama Agova.

Dear fellow countrymen, fellow countrywomen, comrade-men and comrade-women, from all over Bulgaria.

For the third time, such freedom is given to us, the Gypsy minority, with the full right as citizens to participate in the cultural-economic and political life of the country in which we live – it is our homeland, and we do not know another. Today, we can stand in front of the microphone of the Sofia Radio to send our warm greetings and wishes to our compatriots on behalf of our United Cultural and Educational Organisation of the Gypsy Minority in Bulgaria, in my capacity as its Chairman and Member of Parliament for the Gypsy Minority in the Grand National Assembly.

Dear fellow countrymen, fellow countrywomen, comrade-men and comrade-women, Gypsy Christians and Muslims, on the occasion of our traditional holiday 14 January 1948 – VASILOVDEN, *O Baxtalo Vasili* [1], I wish you prosperity in 1948, which will be happier for our Gypsy minority as well as more fruitful. The Organisation will convene its first congress this year in Sofia, which will plan the future work for raising the cultural level of our minority, which according to the data collected by us, numbers nearly 500,000 people [2].

Three and a half years have passed since the bright historical date – September 9, [1944], a date which is recorded with the blood of thousands of people who perished [in the struggle] against the oppression and the injustice of the common enemy of mankind – fascism.

Thanks to this heroic struggle in which our compatriots, such as guerrilla fighters, supporters of the partisans, concentration camp inmates, political prisoners and fighters in the Fatherland War, took most active part, we, the Gypsies, liberated from the chains imposed on us by the last dictatorial authority – today, when we live in a new era of equality, given to us by the people's Government, apart from proving ourselves as champion workers in factories, workshops, labour brigades, etc., we, work tirelessly for the cultural and educational rise of our compatriots across the country.

Our Organisation, which has been affirmed by the people's Government, unites its compatriots in cultural and educational associations, many have already been formed throughout the country, and in the Vratsa region, there is no village or town where such an association has not been created and affirmed by our central leadership. The Organisation spreads light among its compatriots through its organ, *Romano esi* – the newspaper *Gypsy Voice*.

Many Gypsy schools, as well as evening literacy courses, have opened doors in the country. The first building for a Gypsy school is under construction in Sofia; for it, the state has allocated the sum of 3,156,000 levs, for which we must also thank the Government of the Fatherland Front, headed by the unmatched so far fighter for freedom, democracy and human rights, comrade Georgi Dimitrov. Gypsy schools are under construction in the country, while other similar projects and community centres will start in the next season.

In a few days, the first Gypsy orphanage will open its doors in Sofia, and it will house orphans of Gypsy origin.

The state takes care of all minorities in the country. In its budget for 1948, it voted the sum of 3 million levs, especially for the Gypsy National Cultural Theatre, where our compatriots can show their artistic and musical talents and art.

Our minority has lived in Bulgaria since the seventh century, where our ancestors were accommodated by the then leader of the Gypsies around the world, Berko, a very dangerous opponent of Abdurahman, the Indian Emperor at the time [3].

Until now, all Gypsies in Bulgaria have earned their living from their crafts – horse minders-*dzhambazi*, blacksmiths, tinsmiths, basket-makers, musicians, farriers, and other professional skills, as well as workers in the tobacco and textile factories. In the future, many of our compatriots will earn their living as farmers thanks to the fact that, according to the agrarian reform law and the labour land ownership law, they received plots of land to build their own houses as well as land for cultivation.

Dear fellow countrymen, fellow countrywomen, comrade-men, and comrade-women all over the country, I have the great honour to stand in front of the microphone of the Radio *Sofia* and to wish you, on behalf of the Organisation and on my behalf, a happy and cheerful *Vasilovden* [St Basil's Day]. I invite you all to become members of your Organisation, which will only bring you happiness, progress and cultural rising because the leadership of the Fatherland Front supports the Organisation. I also appeal to all my compatriots, who have so far been ashamed to call themselves Gypsies and have converted to the Turkish minority, while others have adopted Christianity, to take the masks off their faces, raise their heads and prove that they are Gypsies – descendants of the greatest fighter for freedom, democracy, and human justice – the Gypsy leader of the 7th century, Berko. Unite with your minority because, as I said above, only this Organisation will bring you progress and will protect your interests where necessary.

Each and every Gypsy person must become member of the Organisation and subscribe to its only newspaper, *Romano esi – Gypsy Voice*, which is always full of news, historical works and information about our minority. In the forthcoming publication of our Calendar, you will find not only the image of our Organisation and the two historical dates, May 7 and September 9 [4] but also the photos of our compatriots who excelled themselves as champion workers – miners who tirelessly dig out our black gold.

Dear fellow countrymen, fellow countrywomen, comrade-men and comrade-women – *romalen, romnjalen, amalinjalen, avdies si amaro baxtalo Vasili, kaj ame o roma keras avdies xamnasa, piimnasa adavka breš xariesa, dži breše bare džumbušesa.* [Roma men, Roma women, and friends, today is our holiday Vasili that we, the Roma, celebrate with food and drink. This year with less, next year with more fun.]

Long live the Fatherland Front with its new declaration and reform, which will bring only happiness and prosperity.

Long live the Bulgarian People's Republic.

Long live the first Bulgarian republican – founder of the fatherland and proven fighter, Prime Minister, the Comrade Georgi Dmitrov.

Long live the Gypsy minority in Bulgaria.

Notes

1. 'O baxtalo Vasili' in Romani language means 'The Happy Vasili'; this is a way to address St Basil which is widely used in the ritual songs and blessings of the holiday.

2. The number (500,000) of Gypsies is undoubtedly vastly inflated. According to the data from the population census conducted in 1946, the number of Gypsies in Bulgaria was 170,011 (Илиева, 2012, p. 67). Normally, we should bear in mind that it is a relatively common phenomenon (both in the past and nowadays) that in these censuses, parts of the Gypsy population would declare another ethnic identity (most often Turkish or Bulgarian). Still, the discrepancy in the figures is too drastic. Shakir Pashov himself, in his manuscript, is much more restrained and close to reality with regard to the number of the Gypsy population in Bulgaria in the 1950s (see above).

3. This is a reference (developed by Shakir Pashov in quasi-historical terms) to the legend of the Gypsy leader Berko. According to it, the Gypsy leader Berko travelled all over Europe, and when he reached the place of the present-day town of Berkovica, he saw that there were many chestnuts and said that it was an excellent place to settle. That's how the town, named after him, had originated (Романо еси, 1948b, p. 4).

4. In the original, the date is November 9, which is clearly a typographical error. It refers to September 9, 1944, when the Communist Party came to power in Bulgaria.

Source: Романо еси, An. 3, No. 9, January 14, 1948, pp. 1–2.

10. Statement (1949)

[To:] Bulgarian Communist Party, 3rd District Committee.
Copy: Central Committee of the Bulgarian Communist Party.

STATEMENT

From Primary Party Organisation *Saliko* [1].
3rd district, Gypsy minority, Sofia.

Comrades,

In view of the lessons learned from the historical decisions of the 5th Congress of the Bulgarian Communist Party [2], our Party organisation which did not have influence among the Gypsy minority until recently, thanks to the immediate help by the 3rd District Committee of the Bulgarian Communist Party and responsible communist comrades at the National Council of the Fatherland Front, managed to take over the leadership of the Central Gypsy Theatre *Roma*, by uniting all honest and non-partisan actors among our minority and thus became a leading factor in the socio-political life of the Gypsies in Sofia.

This activity of the Party organisation received the approval of all honest Gypsies, but it also embittered our class enemies, who immediately made an attempt to stop its development.

Our member of parliament, Shakir Mahmudov Pashov, considering that the United Cultural and Educational Organisation of the Gypsy Minority in Bulgaria and the Central Gypsy Theatre *Roma* should be led exclusively by the personality of Pashov and not by the Party organisation, and not being able to work with the latter, looking for support in circles that uncritically approve of his personal politics, has put himself in the position of a unifier of anti-communist sentiments among our compatriots.

In our judgement, he became delirious after his election as a member of parliament. In support of the above, we cite the following facts:

A few months ago, the Central Gypsy Theatre *Roma* was under the leadership and direct control of the United Cultural and Educational Organisation of the Gypsy Minority led by Pashov, and he had shaped the management of the theatre according to his requirements. He proclaimed himself the chief director of the theatre. He appointed his son Mahmud Shakirov Pashov as the treasurer of the same, his other son ASEN and his daughter-in-law TSVETANKA ASENOVA as artists, as well as many other friends of his. In this way, the theatre was created not for an idealistic purpose but rather for a career opportunity. In order to make sure that his actions are uncontrolled and surrounding himself with his loyal friends, he raised a barrier for the entry of party activists into the theatre.

Seriously committed to the creation of a high-art Gypsy theatre, the National Council of the Fatherland Front – Minority Commission, together with representatives of our Party organisation and the leaders of the Cultural and Educational Organisation, at a joint conference, condemned the entire activity of the theatre, and decided:

1. In order to make sure that the theatre will carry out its future activities in a proper way, it should be attached to the Minority Commission at the National Council [of the Fatherland Front], under its direct assistance and control, and personally to comrade Dobri Bodurov.

2. In order to increase the quality of the theatre productions and select the best of our artistic and musical personnel throughout the country, we should conduct examinations.

3. In order to help the theatre start its activity immediately, the Committee for Science, Art and Culture should be asked to provide material assistance.

With the attachment to the National Council of the Fatherland Front, the theatre has been placed on sound planning foundations. The previous ignorant, unaccountable and irresponsible state of the overall theatre activity was discontinued. Comrade Pashov did not like all this, and as he was not a part of the theatre's management, he launched insidious action aiming to undermine the theatre's new leadership.

On 15 January this year, Shakir Mahmudov Pashov organised a delegation that went to Comrade Dobri Bodurov and maliciously tried to defame the new management of the theatre, consisting of Communist comrades and those recommended by the National Council of the Fatherland Front.

The facts about the proper management of the theatre refuted all their slanders.

He has incited the spreading of the chauvinist and evil slander that we have "handed over the theatre to the Bulgarians" – what is meant here is the National Council of the Fatherland Front. Shakir Mahmudov Pashov and Mahmud Shakirov Pashov believe that as long as they are not in the theatre, it has become "Bulgarian".

They have spread the slander that the National Council of the Fatherland Front "imposed" its own people in the theatre while at the Constituent Conference, they themselves signed the protocol for the new reconstruction and management of the theatre.

One of their actions is bashing. They often resort to threats and beat anyone who disagrees with their views, especially if the latter are communists.

The son of the MP, Mahmud Shakirov Pashov, during the extended plenum of the Central Initiative Committee, on August 21, last year, in the club of the Gypsy minority, beat our party member comrade Tsvetan Nikolov Koev with a chair in the head, and as a result he lay in bed for a whole month. The purpose of the beating was to demoralise all the delegates.

During the meeting, Mahmud Shakirov Pashov also beat party member Angel Blagoev Sotyrov. He attends all our sessions without right and always provokes scandals. His father does not take any measures, despite repeated warnings from various sides.

Once, when Shakir Mahmudov Pashov's son had to hand over the theatre documents to the new theatre management, he even raised a chair to hit a member of the admissions committee.

Mahmud Shakirov Pashov's provocations in the rehearsal hall during working hours have become more frequent in recent time, for which the Board of Directors of the theatre notified the Minority Commission at the National Council of the Fatherland Front in writing.

Using his father's position as a Member of Parliament and acting on his behalf and according to his instructions, Mahmud Shakirov Pashov began obsessively collecting signatures from the artists for a statement to the National Council of the Fatherland Front with a copy to comrade Valko Chervenkov [3], aimed at defaming the theatre. He went several times to artist Nina Elmazova' home and forced her to sign a statement in which he slandered the new management of the theatre. In the end, the woman was forced to sign. He also offered ballet dancer Gorcho Petsev Krustev to sign the statement, promising him recruitment in the "new theatre" that his father would establish. Gorcho Petsev's wife kicked him out of her home.

Recently, Shakir Mahmudov Pashov offered the Artistic Director of the theatre, comrade Zhecho Yanev Zhechev, to accept his two sons and daughter-in-law in the theatre as a condition to stop the intrigues against the theatre.

Considering the above facts, our Party Organisation decided:

1. To demand the immediate labour mobilisation of Mahmud Shakirov Pashov, in order to guarantee the peaceful work of the theatre and the United Cultural and Educational Organisation of the Gypsy Minority.

2. To make a request to an authority in charge to persuade MP Shakir Mahmudov Pashov to stop the intrigues against the theatre and to eliminate the anti-communist sentiments among the Gypsy minority, which in our opinion, he is able to do.

We remind you that these intrigues have become increasingly acute in recent time. All members of the Party organisation ask that the resolution of this serious matter be speeded up because the annual meeting of the Gypsy minority is about to be held, and there is a danger that Shakir Mahmudov Pashov will escalate his actions to undesirable extremes. The comrades who worked directly among the Gypsy minority and knew well the contradictions existing in the organisation are familiar with the above cases in detail, namely:

Krum Ivanov – Instructor at the 3rd District Committee of the Bulgarian Communist Party.

Anton Antonov – Secretary of the Minority Commission at the National Council of the Fatherland Front.

Dobri Bodurov – Secretary of the National Council of the Fatherland Front.

Gocho Grozev – Secretary at the National Council of the Fatherland Front.

With this statement, we ask for the decisive opinion of the Central Committee of the Bulgarian Communist Party regarding the Member of

Parliament Shakir Mahmudov Pashov, as the main leader and instigator of all intrigues and struggles, to guarantee the proper development of the United Cultural and Educational Organisation of the Gypsy Minority, its offspring – the Central Gypsy Theatre *Roma*, and the Primary Party Organisation *Saliko* of the Gypsy minority.

Cheery Bolshevik greetings!

Sofia, 25 February 1949.

On behalf of the Party organisation:
Secretary: ... [signature] (Tair Selimov).

Members:
1. ... [signature] (Lyubomir Aliev).
2. ... [signature] (Sulyo Metkov)
3. ... [signature] (Angel Blagoev).
4. ... [signature] (Asan Osmanov).

Notes

1. The Primary Party organisation of the Gypsy minority from the 3rd district of Sofia was named after Saliko German (Yasharov), a young Gypsy from Sofia who died in the front in the so-called Fatherland War (Bulgaria's participation in the military actions against Germany during the WWII on the territory of Yugoslavia and Hungary after September 1944. (Неве рома, 1957e, p. 2).

2. This refers to the Fifth Congress of the Bulgarian Workers' Party (communists), held in December 1948, at which the Party re-adopted the name Bulgarian Communist Party.

3. Valko Chervenkov at that time headed the Bulgarian Communist Party.

Source: CDA, f. 1 Б, op. 8, a.e. 596, l. 39–41.

11. Plan for Operational Intelligence Work (1950)

Strictly confidential! I confirm.
Inspector Department 'A' (...).
March 28, 1950.

To: Comrade Inspector Department 'A' – Department 1.

PLAN

[...]

For the operational intelligence work among the Gypsy minority with objects Central Committee of the Gypsy organisation for the fight against racism and war [1], Theatre *Roma*, newspaper *Novo drom* [2] (New Way), Sports society *Naangle*.

The Gypsy minority in our country represents an impressive mass of 160,000 people, the majority of whom have relations to the Turks in our country by language, religion, and others, and have some common interests with the Turks. The phenomenon of the end of last year and the first quarter of this year is particularly characteristic with regard to the immigration of the Turks. A large part of the Gypsies in the districts of Plovdiv, Stara Zagora, Haskovo, Ruse, Pleven, and others, along with the Turks, have submitted applications for immigration carried away by the general psychosis of departing for Turkey. In this regard, they are helped by the action of the Turkish teachers, who agitate them to go to Turkey and persuade them that they are not Gypsies, but Turks. The Gypsies feel more Turks, which is why they appear as Turks on documents.
[...]

The desire of part of the Gypsies to immigrate to Turkey is characteristic of the Muslim Gypsies. The rest of the Gypsies are included in their *Organisation to Fight against Racism and Fascism* [3], and there are efforts to integrate them fully into the Fatherland Front. However, the leadership of this organisation has two rival groups that hinder the organisation's right course. The Chairman of the organisation, Shakir Pashov, created a group of Emin Eminov, Raycho Kochov, Naydo Yasharov, Demir Rustemov, Ismail Shakirov and others, who started a factional struggle against the better members of the organisation – Lubomir Aliev – director of the Theatre *Roma*, Sulyo Metkov Mutev – councillor in the Dimitrovsky District Council, Tair Selimov – instructor at the National Council of Fatherland Front, and others, accusing them of having sold out to the Bulgarians, [and] of betraying the interests of the minority. This division in leadership had its impact on the minority and often led to fights.

This state of hostility between the Gypsies [was] well used by the reactionary elements to discredit the Fatherland Front and the Bulgarian Communist Party. Given the lack of systematic and thorough work with the Gypsy minority in the entire country [4], the following more urgent tasks are planned for this quarter:

1. To create an intelligence and information apparatus that will serve the management of the Gypsy organisation, the management of the Theatre *Roma*, the editors of the newspaper *Novo drom*, the management of the *Naangle* sports society and other enemy elements.

2. To investigate the heads of the organisation, place them under surveillance and ON [5] of those for whom there is information of conducting enemy activities.

3. To send a special letter to the county authorities alerting them to take measures for conducting intelligence service to the minority. The following activities are planned for carrying out the above tasks:

I. WITH REGARD TO NEWLY OPEN INTELLIGENCE SURVEILLANCE RECORDS

1. Active surveillance 'DURAK' [6] – Sofia. The person Shakir Mahmudov Pashov, before September 9, 1944, was the head of the Muslim organisation *Istikbal*, which was under the patronage of the then Turkish reactionary circles. The purpose of this organisation was to educate the Gypsies in the Turkish spirit: he opened a school for learning the Turkish language, reading and writing, for which he was also paid a sum of money. He himself passed for a Turk. Before September 9, [1944], he fled to Turkey for unknown reasons. According to the secretary of the City Leadership of the Gypsy organisation [7], Pashov was a conspiracy-Mihailovist [8]. In 1933, during the elections, he held public meetings and campaigned for General Lazarov, Smilo and Doncho Arsov. After the death of the Coburg, [Tzar] Boris, Pashov organised the Gypsies and led them en masse to honour the mortal remains of the same.

After September 9, [1944], Pashov was smart to accustom himself to the new situation and managed to become an MP. As such, he passed among the Gypsies as their "King" [9]. He ordered the clubs of their organisations to place his portrait between the portraits of comrades Stalin and Dimitrov. After he was not elected as an MP in the last elections [10], he was embittered and started instigating a schism in the Gypsy organisation. For this, he was summoned and punished with a final warning.

Given the facts mentioned above, the same should be placed under active surveillance with a plan envisaging measures.

Deadline for implementation – the May 10, 1950.
Responsible – OR [11] (...).
[...]
Agreed, [Head] of the Group: (...).
Compiled by: OR (...).

Notes

1. The United Common-Cultural Educational Organisation of the Gypsy Minorities in Bulgaria *Ekhipe* (as is the name of the organisation according to its Statute – see above) is presented with different names in documents and in press publications (including in the Gypsy newspapers) at that time, e.g. General Organisation of the Gypsy Minority for the Fight against Fascism and Racism (CDA, f. 1 B, op. 6, a.e. 235, l. 5) and alike.

2. In this document, the Gypsy newspaper *Nevo drom* (New Way) is misspelt as 'Novo drom'.

3. See Note 1.

4. From this, it becomes clear that until the beginning of 1950 (i.e. more than five years after the seizure of power by the Communist Party), State Security did not actually pay any particular attention to the Gypsy population.

5. ON – operational intelligence surveillance.

6. 'durak' – 'fool' in Russian.

7. The secretary of the Gypsy organisation is Tair Selimov (see Pashov, 1957, p. 121). 8. This refers to the Democratic Alliance – a political coalition created in the 1920s.

8. It refers to the Democratic Alliance, a political coalition formed in the 1920s.

9. According to widespread rumours, at a celebration in the *Fakulteta* quarter, Shakir Pashov was declared the "king of the Gypsies" and was presented with an iron crown made by local blacksmiths, which after his arrest was kept in the Museum of the Ministry of Internal Affairs.

10. Reference to the parliamentary elections held on December 18, 1949.

11. OR – operational intelligence worker.

Source: AKRDOPBGDSRSBNA, f. 13, op. 1 a.e. 774, l. 26–29.

12. State Security Report (1950)

Strictly confidential! I confirm.
Inspector Department 'A' (...).
June ..., 1950.

To: Inspector Department 'A'

REPORT
From the operative worker (...) – Department I, Department "A", 5th group
The second quarter of 1950 from 1 April 1950 to 30 June 1950 with regard to the Gypsy minority

1. OPERATIONAL SITUATION
In the second quarter of 1950, no acute enemy activity was detected among the Gypsy minority. Rumours were spreadp in most cases expressing dissatisfaction with the allocated duties. What is characteristic for this quarter is that on April 7 of this year, the Central management of the United Cultural and Educational Organisation of the Gypsy Minority in Bulgaria had a meeting in which the activities of Shakir Mahmudov Pashev were examined, and the following decisions were made:

For his demonstrably anti-people activity before September 9, 1944, as an associate of the police [1], and for destructive activity after that date, the leadership of the Gypsy minority punished Pashov by removing him from his position of Chairman of the [United] Cultural and Educational Organisation of the Gypsy Minority in Bulgaria and excluded him forever from the ranks of the organisation. Nikola Petrov Terzobaliev [2] from the city of Sliven was elected as the Chairman of the [United] Cultural and Educational Organisation of the Gypsy Minority in Bulgaria.

Embittered by his expulsion from the organisation and from the party, Shakir Pashov has begun a factional battle against the better Gypsy communists. During the quarter, Pashov sent about 160 reports to all the presidents of the Gypsy organisation in the country. In these statements, he defended himself by saying that he was not guilty and so on. In the neighbourhood of Brick Factories, home to about 500 Gypsies and to himself, he made great efforts to separate these Gypsies from the other Gypsies in Sofia and to oppose them against each other. For example, on St George's Day, their holiday, Pashov wanted to organise big celebrations in the Brick Factories neighbourhood and to attract the Gypsies to his side. He also tried to organise a Gypsy music group in order to undermine the authority of the Theatre *Roma*. [...]

2. WITH REGARD TO CONTINUING SURVEILLANCE

A) The Durak active surveillance operation on Shakir Mahmudov Pashov was opened on May 8, 1950, based on the fact that the object headed the Muslim organisation *Istikbal* in the past. As of today, he was expelled from the Gypsy organisation and from the Bulgarian Communist Party as a former collaborator of the police and has engaged in a factional struggle. The nature of the surveillance operation is to establish his enemy's activity and hand him over to the court. The object is under surveillance by agent Melnik.

[...]

8. NEWLY OPENED ON FILES

A/ Judas surveillance record on the person Emin Eminov Yumerov, opened on April 29, 1950. He is the former director of the Theatre *Roma* and close to Shakir Mahmudov Pashov, with whom he runs a factional group which fights against the progressive elements of the minority. During the quarter, measures were planned and carried out, such as the referral of an agent and intelligence search from department "B". Additional implementation measures will be planned for the next quarter.

[...]

10. GENERAL ASSESSMENT OF THE WORK WITH REGARD TO THE GYPSY MINORITY

During the reporting period of the second quarter, the work with the Gypsy minority achieved good results. Since there had been no work on this object, it was necessary to recruit a qualitative and quantitative intelligence agency with which we could quickly penetrate this minority and start operations [3]. Thus, during this quarter, two agents and an informant were recruited, through which we will be able to closely monitor the activity of the objects who are under surveillance. The operations during the quarter included: one active surveillance, one preliminary surveillance, and 1 OND; some of the persons detected in these operations were identified and studied, and they will be placed under surveillance in the current quarter. However, in terms of the intelligence and information apparatus, it is necessary to recruit more agents and informants in order to be able to cover the object of the Gypsy minority comprehensively. They must be recruited from the close environment of the reactionary elements, and especially those objects who are under surveillance, so we can uncover their enemy goals and intentions.

[…]

Compiled OR … [signature] (…).

Notes

1. Regarding the accusations against Shakir Pashov for cooperation with the police before September 9, 1944, see more details below.

2. For Nikola Terzobaliev in more detail (see Marushiakova & Popov, 2022).

3. This is another confirmation of the fact that the State Security began to work actively on the Gypsy issues only at the end of 1950 and on a relatively limited scale (judging by the number of operations).

Source: AKRDOPBGDSRSBNA, f. 13, op. 1 a.e. 774, l. 30–32.

13. Information Note from the State Security (1954)

Strictly confidential!

INFORMATION NOTE

Re: SHAKIR MAHMUDOV PASHOV, born on October 20, 1898, in Sofia, living [in] Sofia, 144 Emil Markov Street, Krasno selo [neighbourhood], ironworker by profession, non-partisan (former a member of the Bulgarian Communist Party and an MP), accused of being an agent provocateur.

In Department II of the State Security, there is a letter from the Directorate of the People's Militia from 1950 to the Cadres Department of the Central Committee of the Bulgarian Communist Party, which states that the Directorate has materials revealing that SHAKIR MAHMUDOV PASHOV was a secret collaborator of the police, before September 9, 1944. The inspection found the following:

In 1951, SHAKIR M. PASHOV was arrested by the Metropolitan Department [of] the Ministry of Internal Affairs, where he was investigated because he cooperated with the police. The investigation established that SHAKIR MAHMUDOV PASHOV originates from a craftsman Gypsy family. His lucrative occupation (ironworker) raised him economically, and he became popular among the Gypsy minority, which he headed. PASHOV's political activity consisted of unprincipled drifting among various political parties without a clear political outlook. He was guided by his personal interests.

In 1930, PASHOV left for Turkey without regular documents with a friend of his. They were deported from Turkey according to the established rules. They brought him to the Police Directorate in Sofia. Here at the police, PASHOV has signed a declaration of cooperation with the police.

During 1941-[19]44, PASHOV maintained close ties with the police agents IVAN RACHEV and the chief of the 10th police station, NIKOLA SHTERKOV. PASHOV indicated to them progressive Gypsies, who were then interned and sent to brutal labour [1].

After September 9, 1944, PASHOV skilfully concealed his past activities and once again stood at the head of the Gypsy minority and was elected an MP to represent them. As an MP, he took secrets from the National Assembly, which he gave to pronounced enemies – the followers of Nikola Petkov [2].

Pursuing egotistic career goals, PASHOV stopped at nothing to achieve them. He has wrongly accused and slandered progressive Gypsies who have hindered him in some way in his career advancements. He pursued an incorrect nationalist policy among the Gypsy minority. For his cooperation with the police and subversive activities among the Gypsy minority, in 1951, SHAKIR M. PASHOV was sent to a labour camp for one year. Considering that the case of his cooperation with the police was already acted upon, I SUGGEST discontinuing the work on this report.

Agreed. Suggested.
Head of Department I: ... (signature). Investigator: ... (signature).

February 13, 1954.

Notes

1. This refers to the practice of labour mobilisation following the Law on Labour Obligation, adopted by the government of Alexander Stamboliyski as early as 1920.

2. This refers to the supporters of the 'Bulgarian Agricultural People's Union – Nikola Petkov', who were in opposition to the Communist Party when Shakir Pashov was an MP.

Source: CDA, f. 2124 K, op. 1, a.e. 108107, l. 3–4.

14. Information Note from State Security (1959)

INFORMATION NOTE

for SHAKIR MAHMUDOV PASHOV, born in November 1897, in the city of Sofia (re letter No. 1104, dated December 24, 1958, of the Central Committee of the Bulgarian Communist Party).

From the examination of the police materials for SHAKIR MAHMUDOV PASHOV, the following was established:

1. On April 16, 1925, he was detained by the police in Sofia. In his testimony, Pashov wrote that the reasons for his detention are unknown. He noted that he was not a member of either the Bulgarian Communist Party or the Bulgarian Agricultural People's Union but had been a member of the Democratic Party since 1921.

Until the time of the railway strike, he was working in the railway workshop in Sofia and was a member of the Railway Union, but then he resigned and opened a private iron workshop. During the 19th June coup in 1923, the same person, as a member of the Democrats, took part in night patrolling around Sofia. This was done by order of the club of the Democratic Party. It is not clear when he was released from the police.

2. On August 4, 1930, he wrote a statement to the police on the occasion of his return from Turkey. In his testimony, he noted that together with his friends Ivan Stoyanov and Vasil Peykov, they decided to go to Turkey to look for work since they were unemployed. Crossing illegally into Turkish territory, they were detained by the Turkish authorities and handed back to Bulgaria. It is not clear how long he stayed at the police.

3. After September 9, 1944, there were reports about him that he had been a secret collaborator of the police in the past. Because of the above, in 1951, Pashov was detained by the authorities of the Ministry of Internal Affairs, and in the course of the investigation, the following was established: [...] [1]

Because of his above activity, Pashov was sent to the Belene labour and educational residential institution, where he stayed from September 10, 1951 to August 10, 1953.

Sofia, 13 January 1959.

Head of Department: ... (signature). Head of Section: ... (signature).

Notes

1. The relevant passages from the previous State Security Information Note are repeated almost verbatim (see above).

Source: CDA, f. 2124 К, op. 1, a.e. 108107, l. 1–2.

15. Report Note (1981)

To: Comrade Lazar Prichkapov, Head of the Propaganda and Agitation Department of the Central Committee of the Bulgarian Communist Party.

REPORT NOTE

Re: The funeral of Shakir Mahmudov Pashov from Sofia.

The funeral took place on 7 October this year in the cemetery of the Malashevtsi neighbourhood.

About 130–150 people attended the funeral, primarily Bulgarian Gypsies from all areas of Sofia. From the neighbourhood organisation [of the Bulgarian Communist Party] in Druzhba Housing Complex, in which the deceased was a member, two people attended the funeral – the secretary of the Party bureau and another bureau member. The latter delivered a speech in the ritual hall on behalf of the communists and the public from the neighbourhood. In his speech, the speaker emphasised that the deceased had been a member of the Bulgarian Communist Party since 1919 and had actively participated in the struggle against fascism and capitalism, for the happiness of his proletarian brothers, that he had been elected as a member of parliament as a communist twice – in 1931 and 1945, and for services to the people he was awarded many medals, including the Georgi Dimitrov medal. The speaker did not mention anything about his national origin and his activities as the head of the Gypsy Theatre *Roma* and editor of the newspaper *Upbringing* [2].

Mustafa Aliev, director at Bulgarian Television, also spoke in the ritual hall. He called the deceased "Our Father", the founder of the progressive movement of the Gypsies in Bulgaria; emphasised that his life – the life of a communist fighter for the people's happiness – is and will be an example for the living; that his work will live on.

Tihomir Tairov gave a speech at the grave. He also focused on his activities as the head of the Gypsy cultural and educational organisation, calling the deceased the "progenitor" of the progressive movement of the Gypsies in Bulgaria.

Both Mustafa Aliev and Tairov emphasised that the deceased was faithful throughout his life to the cause of the Bulgarian Communist Party. He worked actively to turn the decisions of the Bulgarian Communist Party into action for the happiness and well-being of the entire Bulgarian people. Before placing the deceased in the grave, a ritual was performed according to the dogmas of Islam – in a special room, the deceased corpse was washed, and then openly, in front of all present, the hodja pronounced the prayer appropriate for the occasion with chanting and kowtow.

Gospodin Kolev [1].

October 8, 1981.
Sofia.

Notes

1. This report was prepared by Gospodin Kolev, who at that time worked in the apparatus of the Central Committee of the Bulgarian Communist Party (for more details, see Marushiakova & Popov, 2022).

2. Significantly, the speaker did not use the original name of the newspaper *Terbie* (in Turkish) but its translation into Bulgarian.

Source: CDA, f. 16, op. 89, a.e. 139, l. 44–45.

16. Remembrance (1982)

On October 5, 1982, one year had passed since the death of

SHAKIR MAHMUDOV PASHOV

Let everyone remember the organiser of the Gypsy Cultural-Educational Organisation in Bulgaria, the creator and organiser of the newspaper *Romano esi.*

The founder of the Central Gypsy Theatre *Roma.*

The communist, anti-fascist and fighter against Capitalism and Fascism.

The first Gypsy MP in the Grand National Assembly.

The man with a big heart.

We give a bow!

Notes

1. This is an obituary on the occasion of the first anniversary of Shakir Pashov's death (see Illustrations).

2. It is not written on behalf of whom the obituary was printed.

Source: ASR, f. Shakir Pashov.

ANNEXE NO. 2

Shakir Pashov – The Apostle of the Roma in Bulgaria (1898–1981)

Lilyana Kovacheva

Preface

It is impossible to make a real analysis of the origin and development of the Roma movement, Roma organisations, Roma public figures, leaders, and politicians in Bulgaria without exploring the life and work of Shakir Pashov, his experience in raising the culture and education of the Roma community.

Shakir Pashov "awakened" the sense of Roma identity among the Roma in Bulgaria and fostered their sense of belonging to the Roma ethnic community. It is since the time of Pashov that the Roma community has been trying to find its place among the other ethnic communities in Bulgarian society.

Shakir Pashov was a candid person with an open and rich soul and with a cheerful character who was loved and respected by the Roma and non-Roma. His words – simple and ordinary, filled with humaneness, touched the most intimate corners of the Roma soul. His words revived the faith of the Roma in goodness and justice. He was an extremely strong-willed man who did not give in to difficulties and was able to defend his positions. He sold his motorcycle to secure funding for the first Gypsy Theatre *Roma* in Sofia. Deportations and camps did not break his spirit; he continued to believe in his ideas and to follow them.

In 1931, Shakir Pashov gave the initiative for the establishment of the first national Gypsy educational and cultural organisation and became its leader. The purpose of this organisation was to work for the improvement of the culture and the education among the Roma population in Bulgaria. At that time, the newspaper *Terbie* was issued with Shakir Pashov as editor-in-chief.

After September 9, 1944, Shakir Pashov was the first Roma elected as a representative of the Roma population in the Bulgarian Parliament in 1947. He was the founder of the first Gypsy Theatre *Roma* in Bulgaria and gave the initiative for the establishment of the first Gypsy School (in the Fakulteta neighbourhood in Sofia). As a Member of Parliament, he constantly travelled around the country, met many Roma and helped set up local Gypsy groups which were actively involved in the socio-political life of the country. He visited villages

 | DOI:10.30965/9783657790302_005

and towns, speaking to the Roma about the things he believed in and about his dedication – to explore the origins of our culture and to present it to others. In other words, to believe in ourselves and to respect ourselves so that others would respect us too. This was his main life goal, and it remains relevant today.

In his lifetime, he faced mean lies and vile insinuations by some Roma people, who slandered him out of envy. He was interned several times because of their false reports. In the end, their lies were exposed, and Shakir Pashov was rehabilitated. On his deathbed, his "friends" asked for forgiveness.

May his memory be bright!

Shakir Pashov's Childhood And Adolescence

"Oohh, it is so cold" said old Pemba through gritted teeth in mid-October, "aahh, it's going to be very cold this winter. Deep snow will fall outside."

"Get up, my dear, get up, my little grandchild, it is daylight outside already, your grandfather has sore feet. Go to the shed to fetch some chaff, light a fire and warm up our souls. You know, do not you, we will put the stick in the middle to make a hole in the chaff and light up the fire."

"I am sleepy, Granny ..."

"Get up, lazybones, eat my daughter-in-law's ..."

"I will get up, Granny, just do not hit me."

"Just do not slam the door hard so that you do not wake your aunt, she hasn't slept all night, poor thing. She was in a lot of pain last night, poor her, she will give birth these days."

"Here, my son, close the hole so the fire can light up. Put the jug of water on top of the stove so that it can heat and that we can wash ourselves."

"Come, Granny, the water is warm already, should I pour for you to wash your face?"

"Go on, my son. Dear Lord, protect all of us from troubles and evils, give health and luck to all, and to us. Please, help my poor daughter-in-law give birth without difficulties, and please heal my ill husband. Come on, son, wash yourself, grandma will pour water for you. Now, take the porridge out of the cupboard so that it can heat up until your grandpa gets up for breakfast. Neno, son, can you see why the dog is barking outside? Who is coming?"

"Granny, grandmother Nadira is coming."

"Well, son, let her come in, God has sent her, she is coming with His luck, I hope she has a "light" leg."

Nadira was Pemba's younger sister and the most beautiful girl in the mahala. When she appeared on the square, on weddings, everyone – men and women, young and old, turned to see her and could not take their eyes off her. Murat, with the black moustache, from the Dzhambazi Roma, liked her very much. He was ready for anything for her, he loved her more than anything in the world, but they were not destined to be together. Unfortunately, he was from the Dzhambazi, while Nadira's grandfather, the old Ibrahim, was from the Blacksmiths. The two clans did not get along with each other at all. Grandpa Ibrahim did not want to hear anything about Dzhambazi, let alone become related to them. When they happened to meet in the tavern, the grandfathers of Murat and Nadira always argued over something, sometimes they even got into fights. Murad, however, liked Nadira terribly and wanted her to be his wife.

Once in the mahala, musicians from far away came for a wedding. With them also came Ferat, the famous cornet-player, from the neighbouring village. When he saw Nadira, he lost his mind and his words. Two days later, he sent his parents to speak to her parents and to ask for her hand. Old Ibrahim agreed to give Nadira as a wife to Ferat but far away from the mahala so that Murat would not see her. They organised the wedding in a week. Exactly on the day of the wedding, Murat hanged himself in grief over Nadira. He could not come to terms with the thought that his beloved was with another man …

Pemba thought to herself, "Now she has six children – four boys and two girls. She grew older too, poor thing, but one could still see the beauty in her youth. Also, she dresses well, no woman from the neighbourhood has such clothes and gold jewellery; she wears the best headscarves. In her youth she was beautiful, strong, healthy, tall, slender – walking down the street, the ground trembling under her feet. Her husband, besides being a good musician, was also a good singer. In his songs, he was singing about Nadira's beauty. His most popular song was called "Nadira, my beauty" …"

"Aay, my sister, what are you doing, why don't you come home, I dreamt of you last night, when I woke up, I said to myself: "I will go to Pemba's today to see how they are, what they are doing, to make sure they are okay" …"

"What can I do my sister, I have problems, your brother-in-law is ill, your sister-in-law, Eda, is pregnant, Mahmud's wife is expected to give birth any day now, I do not go anywhere, I am at home all the time. And how about you? How are you? How is my brother-in-law, how are the children? Well, it is not nice to be married away from your loved ones, but such is fate."

"Well! What can I tell you, sister, your brother-in-law is fine; he often gets invitations to play music to weddings and christenings. He plays, he sings, he earns money, we are fine, we cannot complain, we do not lack anything, we have everything we need. But sister, I have one great pain and sorrow, and she looked toward the child."

"Neno, oh dear, go to your mother, son, your grandmother Nadira will tell me something, and children should not hear such things."

"When my daughter was 12–13 years old, the women in the neighbourhood always said to me, "Nadira, you have a beautiful daughter, I will take her as my daughter-in-law, and we will connect by marriage." They said this at weddings, in the public bathroom, or in the laundry. Now, my Zhemila is 16 years old, no one opens their mouths, let alone a door, to ask for her hand. If she does not get married in the next year or two, she will grow old, and it will become more and more difficult for her to get married. I am awake during the nights, I cannot sleep, I have such issues. I never expected that to happen to my daughter. I see in the mahala girls who are uglier, invalids, but they are married, while my Zhemila is not. My soul is aching when I look at her. Sister, what should I do?"

"Oh Lord, that is the devil's work!"

"I took her to Nazhiya, the fortune-teller, to hear what she would see. What can I tell you, as soon as she took the cards out it turned out from the first time that there is black magic on her not to get married. Her path to get married was closed. We need to break this black magic, if not – I will be so ashamed, sister, I will die young."

"Don't worry, Nadira, listen to your sister, I will take you to the sister of my mother-in-law. The woman is a widow, you will give her two levs, it is not much money, you will buy her a beautiful headscarf with lace. She knows all the herbs, she has helped many people and she will help us. We will ask her to collect 41 herbs, to boil them in a cauldron, she knows how. With this water, she will give our Zhemila a bath, entirely naked, as she came out from her mother. You should throw the water into the river, in a place where the river makes a turn. The water will take all the evil away. When we cleanse her of the black magic, we'll need to unlock her luck so that her way to get married would open again. You will go to the priest and give him five levs, then ask him to give you the key to the church on the day of the church holiday of Saint Mina. Zhemila should open the door of the church in the early morning and should say, "As the church door opens, so should my luck of marriage open too", and she should enter the church first, with her right foot, after her should enter the priest. Do this! And if they do not come to your place to ask for Zhemina's hand in two weeks, you can spit on me!"

"Oh dear, may you stay alive for easing the burden on my soul, my sister. I will do all of that. I will do all that you told me."

"Come now, sit down to eat with us, and after that you can go home."

"I ate quite well, it was really tasty. All right, stay in good health, may God protect you from bad things. If things happened, as you said, and I marry off my Zhemila, I will hold a big wedding and will slaughter a cow. Murzho will be the best man at the wedding. We will eat and drink to our hearts' content, while our enemies, let them die. Those who do black magic, let them not see the light of day, let them bury their children in the black earth, far from this home. All right, stay in good health. May God protect you."

"May the great Lord protect you too."

Pemba thinks to herself, "Merciful Lord, take away the pain from the heart of my sister, let her marry off her daughter, let her have grandchildren, one after another. Let her forget her pain. Why is this bitch barking?"

"Ooh, it is freezing cold outside. Inside it is nice and warm. Mom, where is my aunty Nadira? Neno told me she had come. I was rolling out the dough for *banitsa*, I baked it, and I am in a hurry to bring it while it is warm so that you can help yourselves."

"Argh, daughter, your aunt Nadira came, she was here, but she has left just now. She has big issues. And you, daughter, how are you, what are you doing?"

"What can I tell you, whether magic was done to us, whether we caught the evil eye, I don't know, but we don't have luck. Ever since I found dirt from the cemetery thrown in front of our door, we have not been doing well. I and my husband are always arguing and picking on each other. He goes to work but he does not earn anything. The other men, the neighbours, even though they leave for work after him, they manage to find work. It has been already a week that he leaves the house empty-handed, and he enters it the same way. Yesterday, I went to the church to light candles for health and good luck. I brought holy water. Mom, you had given me one herb, we were doing very well while we had it. Do you still have some it for me?"

"Listen, daughter, your neighbours are envious that you and your husband live well, so they do not wish you well. They do their work through magic – water sleeps but the enemy does not. Whoever casts spells on you, let these spells come back to them. That one, with the big head – Dacha, she wanted so much her daughter to marry your husband. I don't know, I haven't seen it, I hope I don't take a sin on my soul [for making a false claim/accustion]. Whether it is her, God will show us. Before she dies, she will eat her own shit and then she will be punished. Doing magic is the most sinful thing in the world, daughter, and the Lord punishes it severely. Here, take this herb and you should collect water from three fountains. The fountains should be facing the sun at sunrise. You should put the herb in a pot and fill it with the water collected from three fountains. You should leave the pot in the open sky, under the stars, for three days. Make sure that the cats do not jump over it because that it is not good. On the fourth day, collect the water in a bottle. Early in the morning, before your husband goes to work, sprinkle him with that water. With the same water, you should spray the four corners of the room and the beds. If there is any magic, it will break. You should give a piece from the herb to your husband, to put in his pocket so that money come there. And listen, daughter, what I will also ask you – tomorrow, after your husband goes to work, come here to clean the house. We should clean everything in the house because any day now my daughter-in-law will give birth, people will come to visit us and we should not be ashamed."

"All right, mother, I will come. Now call my father to have some *banitsa* while it's warm."

"Right, I will look for your sister-in-law, Eda, and tell her to come and eat too."

One morning, on October 20, 1898, the old Pemba went to bring lunch to her husband and her son in the smithy. When she returned, she found her daughter-in-law, Eda, curling up on the bed in strong pregnancy pain. She immediately put a jug of water to heat up. She prepared the swaddling clothes and told Neno to call the local midwife.

"Ha, it's a boy, grandma's sweetie, grandma will eat his bottom, what a handsome boy is my grandson!"

The families of the couple gathered to think about the name of their grandson.

"How about naming him Shakir, after his father's uncle?" Eda's mother said.

"May he be alive and healthy and may he grow up with his name. In-laws, you know that it isn't good to announce the child's name until we have the christening. Please, make sure not to mention his name to your relatives until the third night when we do the christening. In the night, the fairies will decide his fate and how his life would go."

Three days later, all the relatives of Eda and Mahmud gathered to celebrate the christening of their firstborn son, Shakir. They ate, drank, and had fun all night long. Everyone blessed the newborn baby:

"May he grow up in great health and become an educated and a great man. May he make his parents happy and find a good wife."

All the people that were blessing the baby thought that Amin Kushi would hear them and pass on their wishes to the fairies at that very moment. Shakir's mother did not sleep all night long as she wanted to hear what fate the fairies would decide for her child, but she could not hear anything.

At the age of one year and two months, Shakir made his first steps, and there was an event to celebrate the occasion. The two grandmothers and the aunts kneaded three large breads. Shakir's mother placed on a three-legged table in front of the house an accordion, a clarinet, a pair of scissors, a ball, a rope, and a pencil. If the child grabbed first the accordion and the clarinet, that would mean he would become a musician. If he grabbed the scissors, he would become a tailor, if it was the ball – he would become a football player, the rope – a porter, and if he grabbed the pencil – that would mean he would become a big man, a learnt man – a teacher or a banker. Grandmother Pemba took him three metres away from the three-legged table and let him go to touch the objects all by himself. When the first time little Shakir caught the ball, everyone applauded and said he would become a footballer. However, the second and last, third time, the little boy grabbed the pencil, and everyone rejoiced, applauded and said that Shakir would become a learned man.

When Shakir turned seven, his father Mahmud built a house in the Konyovitsa Gypsy mahala in Sofia. His sister and brothers were born in the same place. Later, when his grandfather died, his father took over the smithy in Sofia's city centre all by himself. People from the villages came to the smithy to shoe their horses and to order hoes and spades, axes, coppers, etc. Mahmud liked to communicate with Bulgarians from the villages. His best friend was Grandpa Georgi from the village of Chelopech. Every time he came to visit Mahmud, he always brought in his bag something from his village for the children – corn, beans, potatoes, apples, *rakiya*, walnuts. He spoke with Mahmud for hours about the hard life in the village, about the education of his brother's son and how he became a lawyer and a big man in Sofia. That is why Grandpa Georgi insisted that his son should study and become a learned man.

Impressed by the story of Grandpa Georgi, upon his return home, Mahmud told everything to his wife Eda while the young Shakir listened, his eyes and ears wide open.

One day, nine-year-old Shakir sat in the kitchen next to his mother and asked her what should be done if someone wanted to go to school. His mother looked at him in surprise, "Shako, why are you asking me that?"

"I want to go to school too, like my friend Sasho. He told me what they do there. They learn to read and write. I also want to learn. He showed me his primer and pointed my letter. I asked him about your letter and daddy's. Mom, I really want to go to school too."

At that time, it was not customary for Roma children to go to school. His mother stroked his head, bent down, and kissed him, "Son, sit down to eat and when your father comes back from work, we will see what he'll say."

Shakir looked forward to his father's return to find out what would happen with his studies. His mother, as she cleaned up the table after dinner, told her husband what Shakir had told her at lunch. His father was glad that Shakir wanted to study and immediately agreed to enrol him. He bought him nice clothes, a pencil, and a notebook and Shakir went to school. All Roma children mocked him, "You want to become a Bulgarian". Shakir replied to them that the school was very nice and if they wanted, they could enrol and learn to read and write. It was not easy for Shakir at school, but he liked it there. He graduated grade after grade until he graduated the eighth grade. All his Bulgarian classmates discussed where they would study after the eighth grade. He was saddened that only he would not continue studying further.

One evening he said to his father, "Dad, all my classmates will continue to study in the big schools – technical schools and secondary schools, and I want to study like them. What do you say about that?"

"Listen, son, it will be difficult for us – you and your siblings are now grown up, in two or three years you will get married, and I will have to organise weddings. I was waiting for you to finish school so that you can come to work with me and help the family. If you sign up to study again, we will need a lot of money – for textbooks, clothes, shoes. How would we cope?"

"Look, Dad, I will help you. I will come to your workshop after school. In the evening, I will study my lessons. You remember what your friend Grandpa Georgi has told you? He wanted his son to become a learned man."

"Okay, Shakir, if you help us, maybe it won't be so difficult for us. If you want so much to study, I will not stop you. Why should your life be more difficult than mine? What do you want to study, son?"

"Dad, my best friend will enrol in the school for machine-drivers. I also want to enrol in the same school."

"Good, son, I will tell your mother to come with you tomorrow and enrol you in that same school. Now, go to bed."

"Oh, dad, I love you so much! You must know, I shall never make you look bad" Shakir said and went to bed, however, he could not fall asleep as he was so excited that he would be a student in the "big school".

His father said to himself, "Thank you, Lord, for giving me such a good son. When he made his first steps, he grabbed the pencil. Perhaps such is his fate. What else can I do? Maybe this is your doing, Lord!"

As soon as Shakir enrolled in the railway technical school, the Roma children suddenly changed their attitude towards him and no longer mocked him. On the contrary, they talked about him with respect and high esteem. Since he went to the "big school", they sought his advice, and they considered him as a smart and knowledgeable man. His mother and father were proud of him. When people from Sofia and the countryside came to visit his parents, they talked for hours about their son, about his studies, and how much the teachers and his friends liked him. The news of Shakir spread around very quickly and his name became known in other towns. Those parents who were brighter spoke about Shakir to their children and gave him as a great example.

Shakir had many Roma friends from the neighbourhood where he lived and got along well with them, but he also had Bulgarian friends from the school and from them he learned new and different things. His best friend from school, and with whom he shared a desk in the classroom, was Stefan, a good boy who respected Shakir and the two friends helped each other a lot.

One day, on their way out of school, Shakir and Stefan witnessed an unpleasant sight on the street. One of Shakir's neighbours, who was quite drunk, chased his wife, cursing her and when he caught her, he started hitting her wherever he could. Shakir rushed to tear them apart.

"Uncle Dzhago, don't do it! It's not good to beat your wife. Do you hear me?", and Shakir grabbed Dzhago's hands so that he could not hit his wife.

At that moment, his wife ran away. Now, Dzhago got angry and started hitting and kicking Shakir. Shakir pulled away from him and went to his friend Stefan who was standing on the sidewalk.

"What did you do? Why did you try to interfere?" said Stefan.

"Don't you see he is drunk? He could hit her badly, she could fall on a rock and die."

"And what if he hit you and you fell on a rock and died? What would happen then?"

"In that case, my father would kill him!"

"Do you realise now? You were going to be in the cemetery, your father in prison, and all of this because of a drunk man. Is that what you want?"

"No, Stefan, I am a Gypsy, you see. I love the Gypsies and I cannot stand by idly, don't you get it?"

"Right, but would your father or you behave as he did? He got drunk and chased his wife down the street to beat her. As far as I know your family, you will not behave in such a fashion. Do you know what the problem of the Gypsies is – that they are not educated enough. So, if you want to help your people, help them get educated and to study like you. You see, everyone at school knows that you are a Gypsy, but everyone respects you and accepts you normally because you are like us. You dress well, you live like us. If the other Gypsies were like you, they would be concerned with other problems and they would not behave in such ways. Your people see that their lives are hard and at the same time they give birth to so many children. You see, our families have fewer children and you have more, why is that? Don't be angry at me, Shakir, you are my good friend, your family is also good, you are not like other Gypsies. You are my friend and I respect you, and that is why I tell you all this. If I have offended you, please excuse me."

Shakir listened to him thoughtfully with his head bowed.

"Yes, Stefan, maybe you are right."

Shakir graduated from secondary school and made his parents and all his relatives very happy. On Shakir's graduation, the whole family gathered to celebrate this important event. Everyone ate, drank, and had a lot of fun.

His mother got up early and began to prepare his breakfast. She waited for Shakir to wake up and to have his breakfast. Pouring warm milk into his glass, his mother said, "Son, it is such joy and pride for us that you graduated from school. I and your father are so proud of you. May you be alive and healthy."

Shakir Pashov's Youth and Marriage

"Listen, Shako, your father and I talked last night. It is time for you to get married and for us to have a good wedding before you go to the army. The time of your sister has come too. A good family wants her hand. They are from our guild, they are blacksmiths. However, you are the older child, and your sister cannot get married before you do. Your father and I liked a girl for you. If you want, we can go to ask for her hand from her father by Sunday. Your aunt hinted to her mother that we should become family, just to see how she would react, and she replied, 'If the young people like each other, we, the old ones, cannot do anything'. Her parents will agree. She is a very good girl; she also went to school and finished the fifth grade. She is smart and clean. She does not go out, she stays at home throughout the day and cleans, washes, irons, and cooks. She is aware of her obligations in the house. Her father doesn't drink, her mother speaks a bit too much, but she will learn to behave as we teach her, she will learn our ways. I will love her as my child and as I love you, for the sake of you. I will take her to the market, and I will buy her *shalwars* that no woman has ever worn. Whoever glances at her once will turn to see her again. The best musicians will play at your wedding. We will hold a wedding like no other in the mahala. While I am still healthy, while God keeps me on my feet, I will raise your children – your and your sister's. After that, if I die, I will close my eyes in peace."

"Mother, at school I met a Bulgarian girl, she likes me very much and I like her, but she is afraid to tell her parents because they do not like Gypsies."

"Oh, son, it is better for me to die! I don't want to hear such words from you. You will bring shame on us in the mahala, people will be laughing at us! As long as I am alive, a Bulgarian woman will not enter my house! She will not let me look after your children she will not speak to them in our language. She will not come with you to our weddings. I know my uncle Feros' son, Adem. He married a Bulgarian woman, and she did not let him come to his father's funeral, to honour his death. Adem is handsome, white, he speaks Bulgarian well and his wife hides from her relatives that he is a Gypsy. When he goes to the market with his wife, and when he sees one of our people, he turns his head to the other side so that they wouldn't speak to him in Romanes. Bulgarians are hard-hearted, they are not compassionate like us. The Lord has so commanded – the lamb should be with a lamb, the pig with a pig. You cannot have a lamb and a pig living together in one sheepfold. Listen, son, you should get this Bulgarian woman out of your head. Forget her. We will take one of our girls, the girl that your aunt spoke about is a good one. I like her as a daughter-in-law as well. She is prettier and better than the Bulgarian. She is going to make our house prettier."

"Mother, is she the daughter of Pata, Sabria?"

"Yes, son, she is. Do you like her? She is pretty, isn't she? With that long black hair covering her back, her smile shines like the sun ..."

"I saw her yesterday at the market. She was with her mother. She turned, looked at me, and smiled shyly; her cheeks burning like red apples. She is a beautiful girl and I think she will be a good bride."

"I'll send your aunt by Sunday to ask her parents when I and your father could go their place and ask for her hand. This week you must work hard with your father to earn money because we will have big expenses. We should make bread for the bride, we need money for food and drinks, clothes for your sister, your father, for you, for me. With God's help, everything will go well. My sister will sew, by herself, a pair of shalwars for the bride. I sewed for her bride and now it is her turn to sew for mine. Your father's friend – Grandpa Georgi, promised to give a demijohn of *rakiya* for your wedding, he makes it himself, it's made of plums."

Two weeks later, Sabria was brought home, her mother-in-law met her at the door, and before she entered the house, she carried a loaf of bread under one arm and a bottle of water under the other for luck to everyone in the house, and for bread and water.

In the evening, the young men who were already married gathered to talk to Shakir and to tell him 'this and that' for the first wedding night. The old woman, in turn, went to Sabria and took her rings and earrings off, and gave her a new white shirt. They told her what to do, her mother-in-law gave the bride last instructions and advice, and finally left her alone in the room. Shortly afterwards, Shakir joined her in the room while the rest of the relatives stayed to hear the drum. After midnight, Shakir went out, and his mother, along with two other elderly women (Sabria's aunt and sister-in-law), entered. After carefully examining Sabria's white shirt, one of them sprinkled rakiya on the red spot and said, "The girl is good, she is pure, let them beat the drum to let the people know about her honour. Send a message for her parents to come."

Was it found that the girl was not virgin, she would be returned to her parents. There would have been no drum nor a wedding. Such a girl was treated as married, and she could not marry a bachelor.

Shakir's whole family started preparations for the wedding. Relatives came early in the mornings and left late in the evenings. Aunts sewed crowns on which they wrote "Mashallah" with colourful sequins.

On Friday afternoon, the women of both families gathered at the house of the groom. A young bride, whose parents were alive, put henna on the bride while the other women sang a ritual song. Young unmarried girls took the bride's wedding clothes on plates and arranged in a row, carrying them around her house while dancing. Then, they took the clothes bought by the groom's mother-in-law and took them to his home, dancing on the way. The next day, on Saturday, the mothers of the newlyweds prepared sweet bread and after the *gilin banya* [washing of the henna from the bride's hair and hands], they handed out pieces of the bread to the women who were outside the public bath. The vessel for the *gilin banya* should be provided by the husband's mother and should remain to be used by the bride. Women from both families sang old songs during the bath. The musicians waited in front of the public bath and as soon as the bride appeared outside, they started playing. Then, the mother-in-law led the *horo* dance towards the public square. Late in the afternoon, the musicians roamed the streets while playing music while the groom went from house to house with a bottle of *rakiya*, decorated with a wreath of flowers and cinnamon, and invited relatives to the wedding. For the rest of the guests, the drummer was hitting the drum in the middle of the public square and shouted, "Hey people, Mahmud is has a wedding party for his son, Shakir, tomorrow (Sunday) and he invites everyone who'd like to attend, eat and drink."

The actual wedding was on Sunday. At 11 o'clock, the bride was dressed up, made up, powdered, and waited for the groom to come with the godparents and the flag-bearer to pick her up. The mother of the bride led the *horo* dance, and dancing, she led the bride towards the house of the in-laws. At the door of her house, the mother of the boy was waiting for the bride and her family, and when they arrived, she put a horse harness on the newlyweds, which signified that the couple would pull the family load together. She broke off a piece of bread, dipped it in honey and gave it to them with the words, "May your family life be as sweet as the sweetness of the honey." And she ushered them into the house. At noon, the bride, held by two bridesmaids, walked around the neighbourhood with the musicians while the others danced around them [this is the so-called first *alay*]. After that, they changed the blue shalwars of the bride with pink ones, danced a *horo* in the town square and led her on a second *alay* around the mahala. Then, they loaded the girl's presents in carts and went around the whole mahala so that everybody could see the presents made by the bride's mother and father. At around 3 pm, the third, and last, *alay* took place around the mahala – this time the bride wearing white shalwars.

In the middle of the tour, the young men lowered the flag to take off the three apples nailed on its top. They were usually painted in yellow or in white bronze. He, who managed to take the apples first, would soon get married. The apples were then cut and shared with the youth so that they could get married too. From 4 pm to 6 pm a beautiful *horo* dance was performed on the square and the relatives from both sides danced together with the newlyweds. After 6 pm, the wedding guests began to arrive in the tent, which was set up for the occasion of the wedding. The father-in-law greeted the arriving guests with a bottle of rakiya and received congratulations on the wedding. When young people came, they were immediately served drinks and food, music played, and people danced. At about 9 pm, the bride and her mother-in-law walked across the tables to receive greetings. The bride kissed the hands of the guests and gave them shirts (which were respectively suitable for men and women). The guests, in turn, gave the young family either gifts (cups, spoons, forks and plates, blankets, sheets, etc.) or money, which were all immediately announced. The closer family members donated pillows, quilts, mattresses, etc., and all guests ate and drank until the morning.

It was not long after the wedding when Shakir was summoned for military service. He left his young, beautiful wife with his father and mother and went to the army. The first year was very difficult for everybody. During the second year of his military service, Shakir and Sabria had a baby boy. They named him Alcho, after Shakir's grandfather. It was such a joy. Not long after, another child was born. Shakir went home every week. While he served in the army, his mother and his mother-in-law took care of the children. Thank God, one fine summer day Shakir returned home. He started going to his father's workshop, and they worked together. He worked harder than his father, and he kept telling him, "Dad, you worked hard while you were young. You also worked while I was in the army. Now you should rest. I will work as I am young and healthy."

"You speak well to me, son, but what can I do? I cannot just sit at home. My friends pass through the workshop, they come to see me, and my time quickly passes this way. I will come to work too, but I will do the easier work and you the harder."

"All right, dad, as you say. I will not challenge you, just like you didn't when I said that I wanted to study. Dad, you took care of my wife and children, while I was in the army and you could not help my sister. Now that I am here, I want you and me to help my sister a little. My brother-in-law is a good man, but he may hint to her one day that you are only helping me. I see they have now started building a small house. I will buy them the doors for the house, while the windows could be from you."

"Great, son, I am very glad to hear that from you. You warm my soul when I hear how worried you are about your sister. I wanted to suggest to you to help her too, but you did it yourself. Your sister took great care of your wife and children while she was in the army. She was coming to see your children all the time and always brought them milk. Even though she is building a house, she is thinking about your family".

Young Shakir went to work, took care of his family and relatives, and they all respected him very much. They were proud of Shakir. They used to say to their Bulgarian colleagues that they have a relative who is very educated, that he could drive a train, that he was a "big man", very handsome, that he looked like a Bulgarian and dressed like one, and that he did not look like a Gypsy at all. When they used to have problems, Shakir relatives went to him to ask for his advice on what should they do.

Shakir Pashov's First Public Appearances

In the summer of 1919, when Shakir returned from the Great War, along with several other friends, he decided to form a group attached to the Socialist (Communist) Party, which would be dedicated to working with the Gypsy population. Shakir was appointed as secretary of the group. In 1919, he worked for the railway and drove a train. He became even closer to the Socialists, who were his colleagues. They organised strikes demanding higher wages and better working conditions. Not only their demands were not granted, but the organisers, among them Shakir Pashov, were also fired. He did not lose his hope and was even more motivated to defend the Communist principles because they were in the interest of the poor, and the Roma were the poorest strata in the society.

In 1920, Pashov and his group joined a strike of unemployed people. Their demands were for shelter for the homeless people. They gathered Roma, who did not have homes, and joined the protest. Mounted Police suddenly appeared and chased the demonstrators away with batons and whips. After the protest was put down, the police searched for Shakir and his friends because they were the organisers of the strike among the Roma population. Pashov and his group had progressive ideas and thought differently from the rest of the people. They wanted people to be treated equally without a division between rich and poor.

One evening, on his way home, Sabria told Shakir that at noon the police had walked down their street and stopped in front of their home. Looking at their house, the policemen exchanged some words with each other, but Sabria could not hear what they were talking about. Shakir listened to her and did not say anything.

The next day he met some of his political friends and told them what his wife had told him. They advised him to leave Sofia. Three days later, Shakir went to the town of Kyustendil, where he worked as an ironworker in the construction of the local bank. He worked there throughout the summer of 1923 while his family stayed in Sofia. While in Kyustendil, after work, he went to the Gypsy mahala, where he met with progressive Roma, who shared his ideas. He managed to form a group. In this group, the most prominent were Arso, Zhesari, Demir and Zuche. During their meetings, Shakir told them about the real situation of the Roma. If they failed to organise, it would be very difficult for them to improve their lives or to get any rights. His friends from Sofia, and in particular his "teacher", as Pashov himself called him, Valcho Ivanov, were all very pleased with his work with the party. In the larger cities, there existed already political Roma party groups which have played a major role in the development of the education of Roma in Bulgaria and in the promotion of their culture.

During the bomb attack in the St Nedelya church on April 16, 1925, Shakir Pashov was detained and taken to the police, where he was brutally beaten, and then taken to Konstantin Fotinov school together with all other detainees. He was detained there for three months, and after his release, police agents followed him everywhere he went. Shortly before the bomb attack, Shakir had resumed work in the railway, but after his arrest, he was expelled from work. The police always came to the mahala accompanied by Roma, who cooperated with the police. These 'collaborators' told on and betrayed their neighbours and friends, even their own relatives. These were the so-called *topachi* who took the police to the houses of those Roma who were wanted for interrogations, arrests, or evictions.

One morning, a policeman from the Third District Department appeared in the Gypsy mahala *Konyovitsa* looking for Shakir Pashov. His collaborator Ismail, a Rom, was walking next to the policeman. When he saw Shakir's wife, he quickly told her in Romanes, and in a harsh voice, to go and tell her husband to run away because the police had come for him. The policeman asked Ismail what he had said to the woman, and Ismail responded that he had asked her the way to Shakir's house. He and the policeman took the long route around the mahala before they got to his house so that Shakir could escape. In the meantime, jumping out of the window, Shakir managed to escape through the backyard, and he went to his party comrades – Alexandar Lambrev, Nikola Milev and Angel Boyadzhiyata – and told them that the police were looking for him at his home. His friends advised him to spend some time out of the country until the police forgot about him. Two days later, Shakir left for Turkey, where his sister was married. There, he met with Roma from former Yugoslavia and in their conversations, he wanted to find out how they lived there, what they did for a living, etc.

He returned from Turkey four years later, in 1929, and began to work seriously with his comrades in the political group. Throughout his life, Shakir tried to be useful, with whatever he could, to help the Roma community. For instance, he organised them to vote in elections and to take part in the International Labour Day -- 1st May, manifestations. His political group was leading in the organisational work among the Roma population. In 1931, Shakir Pashov and his friends registered a cultural and educational organisation. Pashov had heard that Tsar Boris III wanted the Roma to have their own organisation. When the Tsar's son, Simeon, was born, all ethnic groups in the country – Turks, Armenians, Jews, etc., made performances in front of the Tsar's Palace, dressed in their national costumes, to greet the Tsar for his newborn son. Shakir Pashov, in turn, organised a group of young Gypsy girls who wore white *shalwars* in black dots and beautiful colourful Turkish headscarves. Singing and dancing, the Gypsy group was the last group to greet the Tsar. Noticing the last group, the Tsar's mother inquired about their nationality. The Tsar signalled to them to remain at the spot (all previous groups performed for 5 minutes, while the Gypsy group remained in front of the palace for 15 minutes). The Tsar's mother told him that she liked best the last group because they seemed the merriest people. The next morning, royal envoys met with the leaders of the Roma group that had performed in the congratulatory procession and gave them a cash prize to support the activities of the ensemble. Shakir Pashov was invited as the leader of the group. The Roma used the money from the prize for sewing new dance costumes – shalwars and headscarves for the girls and sleeveless tops and colourful shirts for the boys.

Later, in 1946, when Georgi Dimitrov, who also had great respect for Shakir Pashov, attended a performance by the Gypsy ensemble, he personally greeted his friend and expressed his approval. Years later, when Pashov asked Georgi Dimitrov for money to set up a Gypsy theatre, he made sure to support the theatre. Shakir had many Bulgarian friends who respected him and appreciated his work but also he had many Gypsy friends as well.

During the mobilisation in the Second World War, Shakir Pashov, who had good friends and influence among the military commissions, advocated for the release from labour mobilisation of the Roma, who were the only men in their families. That is why many Roma respected him in the past, and those who are still alive, keep good memories of him. There were, of course, people who envied him for the respect that he enjoyed.

One morning, Shakir's wife went to see her mother. She was pregnant with her fifth child. They already had three boys – Alcho, Neno, Stefko and one girl – Pata. Sabria wanted another girl so that Pata could have a friend. The merciful God heard her request and two months later she gave birth to a baby girl named Imet.

"Listen, daughter' said Sabria's mother, "your husband has the reverence of many people, but his work is such that some Roma envy his position even though they are not qualified to do his work. Our son-in-law has a good appearance, he was born under a lucky star and many Bulgarians like him. He is a well-mannered and educated man. He knows how to dress well and how to treat people, and he is aware of Bulgarian manners. He is a handsome man with a beautiful soul. Bulgarians are not crazy. They are not stupid, and they know what they are doing to give him such a job which is not just for anyone. I have heard that there is a black, fat Roma. People don't like him. He envies Shakir and goes to the police to snitch on him with base lies, get him in prison, and take his place. Do tell your husband that he has enemies who wish him bad! He should be aware of them so that there are no accidents, and your children should not suffer."

"I will tell him, mother, he works all day long in the workshop with his father. He leaves early in the morning and returns late in the evening. Yesterday, I went to bring him lunch, many people go there – Bulgarians and Gypsies. The Bulgarians, always nicely dressed, bring some booklets and tell him to hide them. He should open his eyes well for another person who would bring the rest of the booklets. If this person did not come, Shakir should burn the booklets and do not let the police capture them because many people from the group might end up in prison. When I heard this, I got very scared, mother, but I will tell him what you told me. I know he is a smart man and that he knows what he is doing."

"Tell him, daughter, he would know how to defend himself. Oh, my dear grandchildren, look how much they have grown, my sweet grandchildren. Grandma will now lay the table and serve some of the delicious *sarmi* [stuffed grape or cabbage leaves]. See what your grandfather has brought for you from the village! We went to the village last week. Your father and brother worked digging the gardens of the Bulgarians, and I and your sister-in-law cleaned their windows and washed their carpets in the river. The woman gave me some corn, apples, walnuts and two knitted sleeveless tops."

The old woman went into the other room, brought the knitted tops, dressed her grandchildren, and kissed them.

"Granny, these vests are so nice! Did Grandpa bring some for mom and dad?" Alcho asked his grandmother.

"When he goes the next time, he will bring some to your parents. Why are your eyes closing, my daughter? Did you not sleep last night? Come, lay down to rest."

"Well, mom, what can I tell you … Last night I couldn't sleep, the little one caught a cold, and she coughed all night long. Her throat got sore, and I rubbed her with *rakiya* so that she could warm up. She finally got some sleep at dawn, but she is still coughing."

"Do you know what you should do, daughter? You should put to boil walnut shells, add ten hot candies, and leave them to boil for ten minutes. You will then wait for it to cool down and then give your daughter to drink the water. I will give you some of the walnuts that the woman from the village gave to me. Wait for me to bring it to you. Then, you will break them and give the nuts to your children to eat, and the shells you will boil."

Sabria went home and waited for Shakir to return and tell him what her mother had learnt. Shakir listened to her carefully and said, "Listen, Sabria, I have not done anything I should be afraid or ashamed of. I have always tried as much as I can to help the Roma. I have never hurt anyone."

Later on, Shakir started building a house in the Brick Factory neighbourhood in Sofia [today Gotse Delchev neighbourhood], in the then Gypsy neighbourhood called *Boyana*. He wanted his fifth child to be born in the new house.

Three-four years have passed since Ismet's birth, and it was time for Shakir and Sabria to start looking for a wife for Neno, their second son (Alcho was already married). The other children have also grown up. They were all married and had children. Life was hard for both Bulgarians and Gypsies after WWII because people were very poor. Despite the famine, Shakir's united family had been doing well before one 'black' morning police knocked on their door.

The Unhappy Years of Shakir Pashov

Internment (1951–1953; 1959–1962) and Rehabilitation

Shakir Pashov's youngest son-in-law, Tsetso, worked for the police as a supplier. His task was to buy kitchen products such as vegetables, fruits, meat, etc. One day he saw the 'fat black man' entering the chief's office. Tsetso approached the chief's door and bent down, pretending to clean his shoes, hoping to hear what the Roma man would say to the Bulgarian. After hearing the conversation, Tsetso did not go straight home as usual, but went to Shakir's place.

"Listen, dad, what I have to tell you ... I will tell you what the situation is, so that you know who is plotting against you." [Tsetso said to Shakir].

"I told Shakir what my mother had told me about this man two or three years ago, but he didn't listen to me then. He told me he hadn't done anything wrong to anyone," said Sabria.

"Don't be angry! I will tell you again, I have no reason to be afraid. All calumny he uttered against me is about things he had committed himself. People know him, and they know me as well. My consciousness is clear. I leave myself to the will of my God, who sees everything and knows everything. I will not get after him, but my good Lord will not pardon him."

In less than two or three weeks, Shakir Pashov was already in trouble, and it was the beginning of the hard period in the life of this wonderful person. One 'black' morning for the Pashov's family, as Shakir's granddaughter, Snezhana, described it, the militiamen brought a summons for Shakir Pashov. This happened on April 7, 1950 and he had to report to the militia chief. This was the beginning of his misfortunes.

When Shakir presented himself to the militia chief, the latter told him, "Look, I know you very well, I know your job. I know that you are a decent and honest person and I respect you very much. Two weeks ago, two of your people, Gypsies, came to me with a denunciation against you. I told them that I did not believe mere words and that I wanted proof. They returned two days later with the signatures of some Gypsies and photos of you with some women. With these documents, I am obliged to initiate proceedings against you. If I don't, they will go to my boss and then I will have problems. I don't want to lose my job and the bread for my children. I want you to understand me well. I see that they are disgusting people and want to harm you, but there is nothing I can do."

"Listen now to what I have to tell you. I understand you very well, but I also want you to listen to me very carefully and to remember. The proof that the Gypsies brought you has the signatures of their relatives and friends, I know them by name, and everything they said about me is a lie. The story with the photos is fabricated, look at the photos well and you will notice that they are from two days ago. When you told them you needed proof, they made that filth up. Listen, I have been a worthy citizen all my life. I have been honest and respectable in my life and work. Sooner or later, the truth will prevail."

An investigation was launched. Each night, relatives, neighbours, and friends came to Shakir's home. They were very angry, but there was nothing they could do. In anger, they uttered heavy swearing for those who had slandered Shakir. He was sent to a camp on Belene Island where he was kept for almost two years. In 1956, after the April Plenum of the Central Committee of the Bulgarian Communist Party, Shakir was rehabilitated by the Government. When he reconnected with old colleagues and friends, they told him who had slandered him and brought about his troubles.

The years after 1959 saw the second 'black period' in Shakir Pashov's life. One day he received a message that he and his family would be interned in the village of Rogozina, in northern Bulgaria, for three years, from 1959 to 1962. In the morning, all their neighbours, friends, and relatives came to see them off. Everyone cried and gave them something for the trip. Shakir's aunt was the oldest woman in the neighbourhood and she cried the most. She swore day and night on those who had harmed Shakir. She used to take her headscarf off, drag it on the ground, and tell strong curses. She said the curse would reach their enemies because Shakir was with a pure soul.

"May death not come to their houses; may they agonise thrown out on the road. May they suffer from an incurable disease and not find a cure anywhere. May all those, who fabricated the slander against Shakir, die in excruciating pains", she cursed.

Shakir Pashov sent letters to his relatives and friends telling about his new neighbours in the village of Rogozina, and the good relations they had. They soon became friends. Shakir and his family left good memories in the people from the village. Three years later, when it was time for the Pashovs to leave for Sofia, their friends and neighbours sent them away with tears in their eyes. Their granddaughter, Snezhana, explained that they brought many golden pendants as gifts for their grandchildren. Relatives and neighbours rejoiced, especially the elderly women, and they came to kiss Shakir's hands and to thank him for the good things he had done for them and for their children. They blessed him and wished him long life, "Shakir, son, may God bless you. While you were here, we saw many good things from you. My husband had recently passed away and you helped my son remain home during the war mobilisation. I don't know how we would have coped if it weren't for you. You did good to us, child, we will never forget it. You should see now, those who are in your place – the miserable things they do to people instead of helping them. They moved the Gypsies away from the city centre to the Filipovtsi outskirts. If they like a young woman, they would intern her husband and would humiliate her. I am sorry, son, for telling you these things, but to me, you are like my child. These nasty people brought many Gypsy families to tears, but these tears will not bring them good. Remember what I tell you. I have seen many things in this life."

"Some of his political comrades avoided him for another three years and they kept at a distance. They did not even greet him, and my grandfather was not taking this easy", Snezhana said. "As people say, sooner or later, the truth comes out, and so it was with Shakir. After six years of torment, slander, and persecution, his name was cleaned up", she continued.

One evening Pashov invited his whole family for dinner – daughters, sons, in-laws, and grandchildren. Sabria prepared a delicious *banitsa, sarmi,* and stuffed peppers, and they all ate and drank to their hearts' delight. During the dinner, Shakir told them, "Listen, my children, I've had good and difficult periods in my life. I've had many happy moments but also many dark ones. When I finished my education, when I got married, when my children were born, when I married them off, the birth of my grandchildren – all these were the happiest moments in my life. The difficult moments are not few either. After six years of vilification with lies and slander, the time has come to get rid of this disgusting stain. Listen to what I have to say now – the most difficult moment in my life so far remains my conversation with my non-Roma friends. They said to me, "Shakir, your people, the Gypsies, the people you care for so much and for whom you worked for so many years, they were the ones who betrayed you. All the slanders and lies that caused you so much harm and suffering did not come from the Bulgarians, but they were fabricated by your people, by the Gypsies". This is what has depressed me most of all. When I found out about this, I was so ashamed and humiliated that I'd rather the earth opened and swallowed me."

Snezhana is Shakir's youngest daughter's daughter, who took care of her parents until their death in their home in Druzhba Housing Complex in Sofia, block 6, where Shakir received housing in 1970. To this day, many of his grandchildren, as well as many other Roma, live in the same block. She explained, "[My grandfather] felt offended by the people who did harm to him, his trust was lost, but this did not stop him from working for the Gypsy cause and did not crush his will to help the Gypsies who were in need. He did his work with so much love that it made him the first Gypsy MP. As such, he made the first sod of the Gypsy School in the largest mahala [in Sofia], *Fakulteta*. He met many Gypsies from the country and abroad. He wrote articles about the origin of the Gypsies and about their culture in the Gypsy newspaper *Neve Roma* (*New Roma*). He gathered young boys from Gypsy neighbourhoods and organised football tournaments. He worked hard to create a Gypsy theatre. He attracted other Roma in this work as well, such as Angel Blagoev (Simo Blagoev's father), Emin Eminov (Sasho Emilov's father), Neno's son, Neno, was the cashier of the Gypsy Theatre. For a short time, he achieved many things, and the respect for his personality was restored. Shakir was happy because he was respected by the people; he had overcome the isolation from the time of his internment on the Belene island and resumed contacts with the Gypsies from other towns in the country as well as outside the country. When his enemies realised that everything around him went smoothly, they felt envious and started plotting new attempts to ruin his reputation through denunciations, slanders, and plots. When the denunciations against him had piled up, his party comrades reported to Karlo Lukanov (Andrey Lukanov's father) who ordered an investigation and a report on the case to be handed to Shakir."

Snezhana also recalled, "I was born in 1949. I was ten years old when we had a small house near my grandfather's house in *Boyana* neighbourhood [today Gotse Delchev neighbourhood]. In 1970, they demolished our houses, and in return, we got apartments in the Druzhba Housing Complex. We, the grandchildren, were all around our grandparents. One morning, our grandmother served us hominy for breakfast. We had just finished eating and we started looking for our schoolbags to go to school when militiamen stormed inside and started looking for something. My grandmother was a fearless woman, she started shouting and arguing with the police. She told them, 'Aren't you ashamed of what you are doing in front of the children, you will frighten them, see how they are trembling. We are not criminals, we are not murderers, we never killed anyone, why are you treating us like that?'

They turned around, saw us, and asked grandma why we were not at school. Grandma replied, 'Can't you see they are with their bags, ready to go out.' We got frightened, they tied grandpa's hands and took him to the militia, we all started crying. Later, my mother told us that some Gypsies slandered my grandfather to harm him because they envied him. We know very well who these people were because the Bulgarians revealed them to my grandfather and my grandfather told us. They had caused a lot of misery to my grandfather, they harassed him a lot, but they received what they deserve from God. My grandfather died a natural death and lived until old age, as the old woman had blessed him. The slanderers died violent deaths, on the roads and from severe incurable diseases, as the old women had cursed them. They had told the police that my grandfather kept in his home portraits of Tsar Boris and Tsaritsa Joanna. That was true and I remember these portraits. Grandpa respected the Tsar because he helped Grandpa's Gypsy organisation financially. Two days before the police arrived, Grandma hid the portraits in the attic. The militiamen turned the house upside-down; they searched everywhere but found nothing. I don't know exactly what they did, but two days later they interned my grandfather to Belene island.

My grandfather told us that he saw more kindness from Bulgarians than from Gypsies. Grandpa was one of a kind, and such a person will not be born soon, he had a wonderful soul. He was a very disciplined and responsible man. He cared a lot about his appearance, he always went to work in a suit and a tie, his shoes were always polished. I was still small, but I remember. I was impressed by the fact that my grandfather would not go for a coffee just anywhere – his favourite place was the cafeteria of Balkantourist restaurant, today's Hotel Sheraton, across from the Central Department Store. My grandfather had many friends – when he returned from the village of Rogozina, he received letters from friends for months almost every day. I still keep his correspondence, photos and the newspapers in which he had published articles in one big sack. Even in his old age, he often arranged his archives.

He was very happy with us when we received good grades in school. He always told us how important it is for a person to be educated and hardworking. While he was alive, he always organised the people living in the block to clean the entrances and the areas around the block. He organised *Subbotnik* almost every Saturday. The neighbours in the Druzhba Housing Complex liked him very much. He organised excursions for them. He took them most often to the Rila Monastery. No matter what problems they had, the neighbours always came to him for advice. You wouldn't find anyone who would say that my grandpa did them harm. Roma and non-Roma alike loved him.

He died at the age of 83, of natural death, because he had a pure soul and a good heart. The old women never cursed him. There were many people at his funeral, among them the old [Yashar] Malikov and Manush Romanov. Manush cried a lot, he gave a funeral speech, asked for forgiveness and promised at his grave to write a book about his life and to take revenge on those who slandered him. He called my grandfather Pasha. The people who had harmed my grandfather died like dogs, the curses of the weeping old women reached them. There were also many non-Roma at my grandfather's funeral. We received condolence telegrams, wreaths, and flowers from many respectable people. People had high esteem for him."

Documentary Testimonies about Shakir Pashov

A RESTLESS MAN

I know he is seventy-five, but looking at him, he looks younger. There is a sense of strength in his large figure, unbent with the years. He speaks calmly, a little slowly, but clearly and meaningfully.

I am listening to his life-story – difficult, tense, with a lot of bitterness, and I am thinking – about what has urged him to live restlessly, to take risks, to 'look' for trouble. When he was young, he had a profession, which could provide him with, if not rich, a tolerable and peaceful life. However, this was not what the young Shakir Pashov was striving for; and what his soul was longing for.

The revolt in him was ignited by the Communists, their ideas of brotherhood and equality for all workers. Life itself brought him to the communists and to their ideas – on the one hand, as a worker, he felt the oppression of capitalist exploitation, and on the other hand, he felt sorrow for the Gypsies, who were doomed to exploitation and discrimination. That is why Pashov devoted his whole life to the idea to unite the Gypsies in Sofia with the struggles and the ideals of the working class; to arouse in them anger and hatred towards the oppressive capitalists; and to urge them to become fighters and workers.

The main events in the struggles of the working people in our country in the twenties are also events in the personal life of Shakir Pashov.

1919. Our people remember that this was the year of the great railway strike – a heroic battle of the Bulgarian working class for a better life. The locomotive driver, Shakir Pashov, who has already linked his life with the Communist Party, was among those who were actively involved in organising and conducting the strike. This was also his first major appearance as a class-conscious worker and his first participation in the battles of the working class.

The strike was suppressed with cruelty and with blood. The bourgeoisie did not recognise the right of workers to fight for a better life. Shakir Pashov also received his 'award' – he was fired. However, this did not frighten young Shakir, and neither did it weaken his devotion to communist ideas. His alert mind, relatively high culture, the lively feeling of a public figure all acted together to win the sympathy of the whole Gypsy population in Konyovitsa neighbourhood. A Party group had already been formed there.

Bulgarian workers welcomed heartily the Great October Socialist Revolution. When, as a result of foreign intervention and the internal counterrevolution, the economy of the young Soviet State was so destroyed that the Russian people began to starve, in Bulgaria, a popular movement for aid collection emerged. Among the funds that went from Bulgaria to the fraternal Soviet side was the modest help which was sincerely given by the Gypsies from Sofia. The organisers of the relief action were Gypsy communists.

1923. The September Uprising, as is well known, was not declared in Sofia. But the reactionary Government launched a chase against all progressive people across the country. Shakir Pashov was forced to flee from Sofia and hide.

1924. The founder of the Bulgarian Communist Party, Dimitar Blagoev – the Grandfather, died. After the pogrom inflicted on the party during the September Uprising, Dimitar Blagoev's funeral became an impressive demonstration of the workers. It showed both enemies and friends that working-class Sofia was not broken. Among the wreaths that were laid on the Grandfather's grave there was also a wreath from the Gypsy population, which was laid by girls in traditional Gypsy costumes. The organiser of this demonstration and the link between the Gypsy population and the Communist Party was comrade Pashov. He was a candidate for MP in the unified list of the Communists and Farmers. However, the Fascist Government did not allow the elected people's representatives to enter the National Assembly.

1925. Arrests and pogroms against the Communists took place again. Among those arrested was Comrade Pashov. After his arrest, he left the capital again to protect himself from the blows. When he returned to Sofia in 1929, the Bulgarian Workers' Party had already been established as the legal organisation of the illegal Communist Party. Shakir Pashov contacted the party comrades again and gave the initiative for the publication of the newspaper *Terbie* (Upbringing). The newspaper was an edition of the Cultural-Educational Organisation of the Gypsies in Bulgaria, and it was under the strong influence of the Bulgarian Workers' Party. The fact that after the military-fascist coup in 1934, the last issues of the newspaper were published almost illegally reveals its nature.

The liberation of our people from monarchist-fascist slavery on September 9, 1944, was welcomed by Shakir Pashov as his personal victory and as something that had been desired and expected for a long time. His dream was to see the life of the Gypsies transformed; Gypsies to become respected, equal members of society, as well as active participants in the building of our socialist homeland. The Government has given every member of our society the opportunity to do what they can; it values people for their qualities, regardless of their ethnic origins. The Gypsy population needed to give up some of their old habits and overcome the feeling of inferiority imposed by the bourgeoisie in order to demonstrate their qualities and virtues. This task was undertaken by the most active members of our population, including Shakir Pashov, with all his restless temperament. A Gypsy theatre was founded, a newspaper was published, and meetings and rallies were convened. The Government appreciated his activity and devotion to the cause of socialism and opened the way for him to the supreme governing body, the National Assembly, giving him the authority of a legislator and a member of the country's governance.

Everyone has great moments in their life that they discuss with pleasure; this was also the case with Shakir Pashov. Oddly enough, Shakir Pashov's most cherished memory is not from the time when he was an MP, which was undoubtedly a peak in his public activity. Instead, he considered that the greatest moments of his life were his meetings with the leader and teacher of our people, Georgi Dimitrov.

He himself finds it difficult to explain Georgi Dimitrov's charismatic presence. Perhaps it is due to his revolutionary zeal or the warm and human attitude that the leader has shown to Shakir Pashov and his comrades – without a trace of arrogance, just respect and love towards anyone.

Seventy-five years is the age at which a person has the right to a well-deserved break after a restless working life. At this stage, it is natural that people tend to have a diminished interest in the surrounding world because their need for personal care increases. This, however, was not the case with Shakir Pashov. When he retired, nobody could stop him from being a public figure, which he was throughout his life. He then worked actively in the organisation of the Fatherland Front in the neighbourhood, and he enjoyed observing the development of the Gypsy population, its increasingly active participation in the building of Socialism – with each new technician, doctor, teacher, or engineer. These educated young people, active builders of our socialist homeland, were the dreams-come-true story of his long and troubled life.

Source: Ivan Vapirev // Вапирев, И. Неспокоен човек. *Нов път*, an. 16, No. 11, November 1, 1974, pp. 1–2.

Instead of Conclusion: Shakir Pashov – Life and Work

The history of the Roma movement for civic emancipation in Bulgaria is inextricably linked with the name of Shakir Pashov. For presenting his personality, public and political activities over the years, in addition to the usual historical archives, we also used his rich personal archive preserved by his successors (ASR, f. Shakir Pashov), as well as the memories about him in the oral history of the community. Among the variety of historical sources, the place of the manuscript entitled *History of the Gypsies in Bulgaria and Europe: Roma* (Пашов, 1957) should be specially noted. This manuscript is not a rigorous scientific study in the academic sense of the word. Much of it is based on the author's memories of events in which he was a major participant. Although not credible in some specific details and interpretations, in many other respects, Shakir Pashov's memoirs are a unique source. They offer a perspective on the historical processes 'from within', from the community's point of view. This particular perspective may be, to some extent, distorted by the vicissitudes of the time but is nevertheless an authentic and indispensable source. In this case, there is a historical narrative reflecting the spirit of the era and presenting the vicissitudes of the author's historical destiny and the Roma community as a whole, of which he is the leading representative.

Shakir Mahmudov Pashov was born on October 20, 1898 (ASR, f. Shakir Pashov) in the village of Gorna Banya (today, a district of Sofia). In various documents from the 1920s and 1930s, his surname is also written as Pashev, including by himself. This is not a mistake, but two different forms (Pashev and Pashov) of the family name originating from the personal name Pashí, a common name among the Gypsies in Sofia at the time. He belongs to the Erli Roma group, who have lived for centuries in Sofia and in the surrounding villages, and their first documented presence there is from the 15th century in the Ottoman Empire (Marushiakova & Popov, 2001, p. 21). Probably, he came from a family of hereditary blacksmiths and ironsmiths. Throughout his life, he made his living mainly on ironwork, and these skills have helped him in difficult times of his life.

Shakir Pashov received a relatively good education, especially considering that, at the time, most Gypsies were illiterate or with very basic education. In the last decades of the 19th century, there was a Turkish school in Sofia with more than 100 Gypsy children, five of whom were even sent by the Islamic religious community to Istanbul to continue their education (Пашов, 1957, p. 80).

In 1905 the Turkish school ceased to exist, and Gypsy children began to enter Bulgarian schools. After completing his primary education, Shakir Pashov graduated from a vocational school for railway workers. His father worked for many years on the construction of railways in the new Bulgarian state (Ibid., p. 30), so it can be said that Shakir Pashov was a hereditary proletarian.

In 1915, Bulgaria entered the First World War on the side of the Central Powers, and Shakir Pashov was mobilised and sent to the front in Macedonia. His participation in the War should be especially noted because this turned out to be a factor of crucial importance for his further public activity in the field of Roma civic emancipation. Shakir Pashov was well aware of this, so in the Preface to his manuscript, he included a poetic account of the time when he fought on the front with his comrades – eight other Gypsies from Sofia. After a heavy battle, they had a long conversation about the need to "organise our Gypsy minority". During this conversation, he promised, "if I return home alive and well, I will write the history of the Gypsies in such a way that it will be retold by the generations"; and the Foreword ends with the words "I have fulfilled my duty" (Ibid., p. 6).

The essence of the changes in the civic consciousness of the Gypsies in Bulgaria because of their participation in the First World War was captured precisely by Bernard Gilliat-Smith (writing also under the pseudonym Petulengro), who, before the War, was in diplomatic service in Sofia. His narrative about the language of the Gypsies in Sofia, in fact, reflects the changes that occurred in their lives after the War:

> This […] was due, I think, to the effects of the First Great War. Pashi Suljoff's [the primary respondent of B. Gilliat-Smith, from whom he recorded language and folklore materials – authors note] generation represented a different "culture", a culture which had been stabilised for a long time. The Sofia Gypsy "hammal" [porter] was – a Sofia Gypsy "hammal". He did not aspire to be anything else. He was, therefore psychologically, spiritually, at peace with himself. […] Not so the post-war generation […] who could be reckoned as belonging to the proletars of the Bulgarian metropolis. The younger members of the colony were therefore already inoculated with a class hatred, which was quite foreign to Pashi Suljoff's generation. […] To feel "a class apart", despised by the Bulgars who were, de facto, their "Herrenvolk", was pain and grief to them. (Gilliat-Smith, 1945, pp. 18–19).

After Bulgaria's withdrawal from the First World War in 1918, Shakir Pashov returned home from the front. He initiated the creation of the Sofia Common Muslim Educational-Cultural and Mutual Aid Organisation *Istikbal – Future*, which was officially registered on August 2, 1919 (CDA, f. 1 Б, op. 8, a.e. 596, l. 69; Marushiakova & Popov, 2021, pp. 79–83). According to the founding statute of the organisation, Shakir Pashov was its Secretary, and the Chairman was Yusein Mehmedov. This assignment of the positions in the organisation is understandable, having in mind the traditional norms in the community, which mandated that the elderly members are the most respected ones, while Shakir Pashov was then only 21 years old (i.e. he had just reached the age of majority according to the legal norms of the time). In this way, a specific dualism was established in the organisation: The Honorary Chairman speaks mainly to his community and works on its internal problems; while the young and educated secretary takes over the external contacts and works with the society, particularly the state and municipal institutions.

The creation of the organisation *Istikbal* marked the beginning of a new stage in the development of the movement for Roma civil emancipation. As this new stage did not come in a void, we need a short flashback to the first steps in this direction.

After the Russian-Turkish War (1877–1878) and the subsequent San Stefano Peace Treaty, Berlin Congress and the adoption of the Constitution of the Principality of Bulgaria (known as the Tarnovo Constitution) in April 1879 in Tarnovo, the new Bulgarian state was created. The Tarnovo Constitution recognised Bulgarian citizenship for all residents of the country (i.e. including Gypsies) and their civil equality: Art. 57 ("all Bulgarian subjects are equal before the law") and Art. 86 ("voters are all Bulgarian citizens who are over 21 years of age and who enjoy civil and political rights") (Конституция, 1945). Only two decades later, however, it became clear that the new state did not consider all its citizens as equal, as stipulated in the legislation. On May 3, 1901, the 11th National Assembly (at its 61st extraordinary session) discussed and voted on the Law on Amendments to the Electoral Law, which contained essential amendments and additions directly related to the electoral rights of the Gypsies. The government coalition between the Democratic Party and the Progressive Liberal Party, led by Petko Karavelov, proposed the amendments. According to the new edition of the provisions of this law under Item 2 of Art. 4 and Art. 7 (People forbidden to vote), the text reads as follows: "In that number the non-Christian Gypsies, as well as all those Gypsies without any fixed abode" (Държавен вестник, 1901, p. 3). In this way, Muslim Gypsies were deprived of voting rights (at that time, the majority of Gypsies in Bulgaria) as well as nomadic Gypsies (more precisely, those without administrative registration). After a parliamentary discussion, despite the objections raised, the law was voted almost unanimously, with 90 votes pro, out of 96 (Стенографски дневници, 1901, p. 258–260). Only the representatives of the leftwing political parties voted against it, including the Bulgarian Workers'

Social-Democratic Party (the future Communist Party). The amendments of the Election Law immediately came into force by Decree No 271 of Prince Ferdinand I (Държавен вестник, 1901, p. 3).

The reaction of the Gypsies, however, surprised Bulgarian society. Immediately after the adoption of the amendments to the Electoral Law, an improvised Gypsy conference was held in 1901 in Vidin in protest against the restriction on the electoral rights of the Gypsies (Marushiakova & Popov, 1997, p. 29). Even more surprising was that the Gypsies launched a real campaign denouncing the amendments. They were supported by Dr Marko Markov, an ethnic Bulgarian, a lawyer, a famous and eccentric public figure at that time. He was born in Tulcea (now in Romania), studied at Robert College in Istanbul, and continued law studies at the Universities of Bern and Zürich in Switzerland. Subsequently, he defended his doctoral thesis at the University of Liege in Belgium. In the 1880s, he was one of the forerunners of the future communist movement in Bulgaria (Стоянов, 1966, p. 213–220).

The idea for the civic emancipation of the Roma and their struggle for equal civil rights, however, can not not be considered to have been imported "from the outside", by non-Roma. Along with Dr Marko Markov, leaders of the protest initiative were Gypsy men – Ramadan Ali, a *Muhtar* (representative of the Mayor for the Gypsy mahala, appointed by the municipal authorities) in Sofia and Ali Bilyalov, his assistant (second Muhtar). Initially, they drew up a petition demanding equal voting rights for the Gypsies. They presented the petition to the Speaker of the National Assembly, and since no response was received, they decided to hold a Gypsy Congress in order to make the Gypsy demands more convincing (Вечерна поща, 1905a, p. 2).

In the newspapers, the Congress in Sofia was referred to as 'Tsiganski' ('Gypsy' in Bulgarian). At the same time, the organisers spoke of it as a 'Coptic' congress, and the speakers called themselves 'Copts' and 'Coptic population'. This is easy to understand, considering the dominant idea in the Bulgarian society (among Roma as well) at that time that the Gypsies originated in Egypt as the descendants of the ancient Copts, which is directly related to the most commonly used designation of Gypsies as 'Kıpti' (i.e. Copts) in the official records from the Ottoman Empire (Marushiakova & Popov, 2001).

The Congress was held in the San Stefano pub, in the centre of Sofia, on December 19, 1905 (see the published materials in Marushiakova & Popov, 2021, pp. 33–56). According to the organisers, the Congress was attended by "40 to 50 delegates" who came from "all major cities of the Principality" (in fact, apart from the participants from Sofia, the only other delegation present was from Plovdiv). The organisers had previously sent letters to about 20 cities and small towns in Bulgaria, but during the Congress, supporting telegrams arrived also from other locations (Vidin, Silistra, Varna) who had learned from the newspapers about the Congress (an indication that there were already people among the Gypsies in Bulgaria, who read the press). Dr Marko Markov was the elected Chairman of the Congress and presided over its meetings. Ali Bilyalov from Sofia, Ali Mutishev from Plovdiv, Iliya Uzunov, Ali Mola, Riste Mustafa, and Evtim Ikonomov participated in the leadership of the Congress. (Вечерна поща, 1905b, p. 2). After two days of discussions, it was decided to send a telegram with the decisions of the Congress to Prince Ferdinand (Ibid.). A delegation led by Dr Marko Markov was tasked with presenting the Congress petition with the demand for revoking the amendments, which deprived the Gypsies of voting rights, to the Deputy Speaker of the National Assembly, Dobri Petkov (Вечерна поща, 1905c, p. 2).

The development of civic consciousness among the Gypsies in Bulgaria is only one aspect of the process of their social integration. However, to finish this long process successfully, a move in the same direction from the other side is also necessary. Bulgarian society also needed to open up for the Gypsies and their aspirations for equal status within the Bulgarian nation. In the case of the violated civil rights of the Gypsies, the reaction of politicians, the media, and the Bulgarian public opinion pointed to something quite clear – the legitimate citizenship demands of the Gypsies were not only rejected but also ridiculed. That is why there was no response from state institutions (National Assembly and the Prince) either to the Congress petition or to the telegram sent to the Palace.

This reaction of the Bulgarian public opinion to the Gypsy Congress and to the subsequent public campaign for the restoration of their voting rights once again confirmed the lack of desire on the part of Bulgarian society to accept the Gypsies and their legitimate civil demands. The materials published in the press at the time are a typical illustration of the Bulgarian (and Balkan) contemptuous attitude towards the Gypsies. The main (and, in fact, the only) discourse in the press regarding the Gypsy Congress is the irony. Simeon Radev, a famous public figure, publicist and editor-in-chief of one of the most popular newspapers at the time, *Vecherna poshta* (Evening Mail), set the tune within the first article on the topic. He begins his article with a fictional quote by Karl Marx about the role of the Gypsies in the Russian and world revolution. He sarcastically presents the international dimension of the forthcoming Congress in Sofia (Вечерна поща, 1905a, p. 2). Only knowledgeable readers will note that the quote is fake, as Marx died more than two decades before the Russian Revolution in 1905.

All other press reports on the Congress were dominated by the same ironic discourse; some of them even resorted to deliberately distorted language in the presentation of speeches by Gypsies participating in the Congress. To the personal appeal on the part of Dr Marko Markov to Simeon Radev for helping the Gypsies regain their civil rights, the latter responded with "irresistible laughter" (Вечерна поща, 1905b, p. 2). This discourse persisted when Dr Marko Markov attempted to organise a public campaign in support of the Congress's demands and in defence of the constitutional rights of a significant part of the Bulgarian citizens. At the beginning of 1906, he delivered several public speeches in various cities of the country, such as Ihtiman, Pazardzhik, Plovdiv and Varna (see the published materials in Marushiakova & Popov, 2021, pp. 56–62). Because of this public activity, he was subjected to constant ridicule, or in the best case, a refined irony, and he was nicknamed 'The Gypsy King'. The press even expressed doubts about his mental health, which prompted him to call for a duel Krastyo Stanchev, the editor of the newspaper *Kambana* in 1908 (the duel did not take place) (Каназирски-Верин, 1946, p. 79). Eventually, unable to endure such public attitudes, Dr Marko Markov left the capital Sofia and settled in Ruse. In 1915, Andreas Scott Macfie (also writing under the pseudonym Mui Shuko) met him there and handed him a Manifesto on the struggle of the Gypsies for their civil rights (Mui Shuko, 1916, p. 138). This Manifesto is unfortunately not preserved (or at least we could not find it). Until the end of his life (1939), Dr Marko Markov lived in Ruse. Apparently disappointed with his failure to influence Bulgarian society and its attitude towards the Gypsies, he quit his public activities.

The public reaction to the Gypsies and their aspirations for civil equality in the instance of the Electoral Law is a typical illustration of the attitude towards the Gypsies in Bulgaria (and, in general, on the Balkans). The perception of the Gypsies as a part of the Bulgarian nation has already been permanently established in the public consciousness, with a specific position attributed to them in categorial and axiological terms. The Gypsies are still perceived as a collective unity with a defined categorial status, but with new axiological dimensions – in the eyes of the Bulgarian masses, the Gypsies are not equal citizens. Moreover, this inequality is of a different order compared to the attitude towards other ethnic communities – even though all others are 'foreign' and some are even 'enemies', they are still comparable as a category to the Bulgarians. The Gypsies, on the other hand, are a community of another kind, known a priori to be inferior and not comparable to the Bulgarians. Insofar as the Gypsies are subjected to any value assessments at all, the opinion towards them is often rather disparaging (at least, as far as they know "their place" in Bulgarian society and do not seek to move away from it). That is why the civic aspirations of the Gypsies remained without serious consideration, and nobody cared to discuss whether or not their constitutional rights to vote were truly violated. To put it in brackets, the best illustration of this initial inequality could be found in Simeon Radev's memoirs about his childhood in the town of Resen (today in the Republic of Northern Macedonia):

> There were some wealthy people among the Gypsies. The Zizovtsi family lived not far from us. At Easter, we sent them red eggs; on St George's Day, we used to receive from them a piece of roast lamb. This put my mother in great difficulty. We, the kids, didn't want to eat meat sent by the Gypsies. My mother used to say that it was a shame and a sin to throw it to the dogs (Радев, 1994, pp. 222–223).

In the new national context of the independent Bulgarian State, some forms of the community's public life, inherited from the Ottoman Empire, were preserved and developed. Since the time of the Ottoman Empire, the Gypsies have entered into the system of ethnically distinct guilds (professional associations, called here with the Turkish term *esnaf*) and created their own, Gypsy esnafs (see Marushiakova & Popov, 2016a for more details). After establishing the new Bulgarian State, the Gypsy guilds changed their forms and social functions according to the new conditions. This is not just about their legitimation under the conditions of the independent Bulgarian State, such as the transformation of the old Porter's Esnaf in Lom into a professional association in 1896 (Тахир, 2018), but also about the creation of new associations, such as the Porter's Association *Trud* (Labour), founded in Kyustendil in 1901 (the flag of the Association is still preserved), and the First Sofia Flower-selling Association *Badeshte* (Future) headed by Ali Asanov, founded in Sofia in 1909 (Тахир, 2018). Moreover, this period saw the creation of officially registered public organisations for the defence of the Roma social positions as an ethnic community in Bulgarian society.

An essential historical source for this process is the *Statute of the Egyptian Nation in the Town of Vidin*, published in the form of a booklet (Устав, 1910; see also Marushiakova & Popov, 2021, pp. 69–76). This historical document referred to the Roma as *Egiptyani* ('Egyptians' in Bulgarian), which directly correlates with Kıptı (i.e., Copts, as in the Ottoman Empire), and the Congress in 1905 used this designation too.

The creation of this organisation is a significant step forward in developing organisational forms in the process of Roma civic emancipation in Bulgaria (Marushiakova & Popov, 2017a, pp. 42–46). The Statute describes already-known practices for selecting a Chair (called *Muhtar*), his assistant, and his councillors. This practice continued as part of the local administration in other places in the country too. Such an example is provided in Sofia, where Ramadan Ali held this post for almost two decades, since 1888, when he was unanimously elected (by 230 votes) by the Gypsies in the Gypsy mahala as their leader, having served previously as deputy of the former Muhtar, Ibrahim Mustafov (DA Sofia, f. 1 K, op. 2, a.e. 1848, l. 1–15). In addition to the already established matters in the Statute, there are several new and meaningful points. The first thing to note here is the name itself – this was already not just about one Gypsy mahala but the entire "Egyptian Nationality" in the city and the region, i.e., the Gypsies are represented in it as a collective entity on an ethnic basis. The Statute promotes the "Egyptian Nationality" representatives in charge of communicating with the authorities on behalf of the community. Starting with Art. 1, the primary function of the Statute is as follows: "In respect of the old custom" (that is, following the norms which remained since the time of the Ottoman Empire), the organisation establishes and regulates not only "its rightful relationships in the society" (i.e. the public positions and attitudes of the Gypsies in the new realities), but also "among themselves" (i.e. within the community itself, which is undoubtedly a new moment in its development).

Moreover, in Art. 2, it is explicitly highlighted that the rules and regulations of the Statute concern "all the Gypsies in the neighbourhood", and if there are no other alternative formations, it applies to the whole constituency. There is an evident desire for the new organisation to be set up on a large scale and to include the entire "Nationality" in the region. It envisages organisation on a hierarchical, vertical structure in which the leaders (the so-called *Tseribashi*) of individual urban Gypsy neighbourhoods and rural Gypsy communities will coordinate their activities with the 'Muhtar of the township'. However, for its part, the Muhtar shares its power functions with those of the Supreme Council, which is the "supreme body" (i.e. the original formula of parliamentary democracy and the separation of powers are evident). In doing so, the governing bodies (the Muhtar and the Supreme Council) assume specific responsibilities and obligations, such as to protect the "common moral and material interests of their compatriots", to solve internal problems in the community, etc. (Устав, 1910, pp. 6–7).

The Statute has an interesting stipulation that the voters and those who run for election shall "preferably" be included in the voter registers for the municipal elections (in other words, voting is allowed for the unregistered ones as well). At first glance, this requirement is discriminatory against the Muslim Gypsies who were deprived of voting rights by the amendments to the Election Law of 1901 (see above). The actual situation, however, is noticeably different from the legal norms. As demonstrated by the founders' names, most of them were Muslims, including Gyulish Mustafa, the Chair of the Constituent Commission of the Vidin organisation (recorded as a "reserve sergeant," i.e. he was previously on regular service in the Bulgarian army). His deputy had two names, a Muslim and a Christian (Ahmed Neyazimov and Tako Munov), which is an indication of his recent baptism. Notably, among the 19 members of the Commission, the members with Muslim names, who were listed in the Statute, were significantly higher in number than those with Christian names (Ibid., p. 15). It would have been illogical for the founders to set such a restrictive criterion themselves if they were indeed deprived of suffrage. Hence, it is clear that the law stipulations do not always apply in reality (at least in the local municipal elections).

Regarding the above-mentioned *Statute of the Egyptian Nation in the Town of Vidin*, it is impressive that some of its specific formulations sound quite up-to-date, as if they were written by our contemporaries. For example, Art. 10 shows that one of its main goals is to "awake civil consciousness among the people" (the emphasis on the civic awakening comes to underline their position as an equal part of the Bulgarian society and the Bulgarian civil nation). As one can see from the Statute, it uses the terms 'Tsigani' (Gypsies) and 'Egyptyani' (Egyptians) synonymously and interchangeably. The preference for the appellation 'Egyptians' is obvious, and this is not only because it signifies their Egyptian origin (based mainly on the Holy Scripture) – so well-known and spread in Bulgaria, but also because it would be much more prestigious for them and their social status to be recognised in society as the heirs of an ancient civilisation and high culture. That is why the Statute pays so much attention to the stamp with its iconography. The *Gergyovden* (St George Day) is the organisation's annual holiday, and the organisation's seal depicts the image of St George "on a horse with a spear in his hand, stuck in a crocodile, and behind his horse the royal daughter" (Ibid., pp. 11–12). It reveals connections with Ancient Egypt and emphasises relationships with Christianity which is the "dominant religion" in the new Bulgarian state, according to the Tarnovo Constitution.

In this case, we see an indication of the standard processes that went on in the emerging nations in Central and South-Eastern Europe. It is a common feature that the basic national narratives about the origins of the nation were created and reproduced at the artistic-pictorial level with symbolic significance (in this way, a new ethnonational symbolism is created).

The Statute of the Egyptian nationality in the city of Vidin is the only known historical evidence of the existence of this organisation. We can assume that it existed only for a relatively short period. The organisation probably ceased to exist soon after its establishment, when the period of military conflicts in the Balkans began, which included the two Balkan Wars (1912 – 1913) and the First World War, and the State mobilised many Roma as part of the Bulgarian army.

Concerning the practice of the municipal authorities to appoint Roma representatives promoted by the community itself in the Gypsy mahalas (which can be considered as a rudimentary form of internal national autonomy), this legacy of the Ottoman era was actively practised in the first decades of the new Bulgarian State.

The situation changed in the 1920s and 1930s when city mayors started appointing their deputies in the Gypsy neighbourhoods without holding internal elections. We can provide an illustration from Ferdinand city (today Montana), which was preserved in the local archive. After the election of a *Cheribashi* in 1927, in response to the Gypsies' request, the municipal council adopted a decision according to which the appointment of a 'mayoral deputy' (this is the new term in the Bulgarian language, which replaced the Turkish *Cheribashi* in new Bulgarian state) to their neighbourhood, "a person from the mahala, with Mohammedan faith", should be done only following the mahala representatives' recommendation (DA Montana, f. 3 К, op. 1, a.e. 25, l. 61). Despite this decision, over the next two years, the city mayor fired three mayoral deputies and appointed new ones in their place (DA Montana, f. 79 К, op. 1, a.e. 32, l. 15; a.e. 34, l. 20; a.e. 35, l. 30).)

In this way, the mayoral deputy institution became hostage to political strife (each new authority appointed its own deputies), and its functions gradually diminished. In fact, the transition to a Gypsy civic movement after the First World War was made by the younger generation, who wanted to replace the old Muhtars (or Cheribashis) with new civil committees to take over their functions and were looking for other forms of community representation in the municipal and central government authorities.

In this socio-political context, the emergence of the Sofia Common Muslim Educational-Cultural and Mutual Aid Organisation *Istikbal – Future* was a logical event revealing the transition to a new, crucial stage in the Roma civil emancipation process. In this new stage, the primary aspiration of the community was for an equal position in society. The early attempts to realise a real (not existing on paper only) Roma emancipation relied on the existing institutions which were inherited from previous eras, preserved and developed in the new social conditions (as in the case of the muhtars). In the new stage, the old forms changed according to the conditions and requirements of the new historical realities and they were filled with new content. The main reason for this development is contextual, namely, the complete and significant changes in the socio-political realities after the First World War, which inevitably affected the Gypsies, an ethnically distinct segment of society. The participation of the Gypsies in the wars (the two Balkan Wars and the First World War), along with all other Bulgarian citizens, developed and strengthened their sense of belonging to the Bulgarian civil nation. The new realities after the war, when the Roma became "second-class citizens" once again, prompted them to launch an organised struggle for changing the position of their community in the larger society, as Shakir Pashov explicitly emphasises more than once in his manuscript. Thus, it turns out that the inclusion of the Gypsies in the Bulgarian army (for more details, see Иванова & Кръстев, 2014) has led not only to the strengthening of their national civic identity but also to the development of the civil emancipation processes among them. This is not a specific Bulgarian phenomenon but a common development in the region of Central and South-Eastern Europe. Similar processes in one form or another occurred with the Roma in other countries (see more details on similar processes and phenomena in the region Marushiakova & Popov, 2021).

When studying this new and extremely important stage in the development of the Roma civic emancipation, one must consider a characteristic feature of the source base. Shakir Pashov's memoirs, as one of the main sources for this period, need further verification through comparison with other sources dealing with the described events. These memoirs were written in the 1950s (dated 1957), during the period of communist rule, after the end of his political career. Logically, he strived to attune his memoirs to the new, ideological reading of history, leading to the creation of a new historical narrative. Even excluding the other factors (such as fear of new repressions, striving for political rehabilitation, etc.), which undoubtedly (at least to some extent) influenced him in the preparation of the manuscript, it is unconditionally clear that without conforming to the dominant new historical discourse, he could not hope to have the manuscript published (despite his best efforts, however, the manuscript was never printed). For these reasons, in his memoirs, he nowhere mentions the creation of the Sofia Common Muslim Educational – Cultural and Mutual Aid Organisation *Istikbal – Future*, which was created on his initiative, and he was a leading figure in its activities. As one can learn from the archival documents (CDA, f. 1 Б, op. 8, a.e. 596, l. 69), the organisation *Istikbal* was defined as 'Muslim' and although the membership was open to all Bulgarian citizens (Art. 4) its primary purpose was "to organise the Muslims in one common organisation which helps the poor in times of illnesses, accidents, death and others" (Art. 2). At first glance, the organisation *Istikbal* could be a typical Muslim charitable organisation, at least according to its Statute. At the same time, the Statute revealed that the organisation originated from already existing professional organisations and charitable associations (Art. 8), including, in addition to the old forms of community life, also new elements of civic activities, such as "To fight for their moral, material and educational-cultural upbringing" (Art. 2). Moreover, although the Statute does not mention the word

'Gypsies' even once, it explicitly emphasises that it is "strictly non-partisan" (Art. 6). At the same time it envisaged facilitating the contacts of the members with the official administration (Art. 26). This means that the new organisation had ambitions not only to solve the problems within the community (Art. 27), but also to function as its representative within the Bulgarian Society, and to develop (among other things) also as a modern Roma civic organisation.

The most crucial goal of the organisation *Istikbal*, stipulated in its Statute and made evident by its subsequent actions, was to secure the participation of the Gypsies in the governance of the Muslim religious community in Sofia as well as in the management of Islamic properties. At that time, after the Russian-Turkish war and the expulsion of Turks from Bulgaria, only a small number of ethnic Turks were left in Sofia, but they did not allow the inclusion of the Gypsies in the governing bodies of the local Muslim community. This struggle for Gypsy participation in the Muslim religious communities (respectively, participation in the management of Islamic properties) has its historical roots. As early as 1895, the new Bulgarian State adopted Provisional Rules for the Election of the Boards of Trustees of Muslim Municipalities. The Rules explicitly stated that "Gypsies cannot be voters, nor can they be elected because, according to the Sharia rules, they shall not take any participation in the governance of the Muslim religious affairs" (Вълков, 2020, p. 349).

During the Gypsy Congress in 1901, in his speech, the delegate from Plovdiv, Ali Mutishev, made a vague attempt to distinguish between 'Copts' and 'Gypsies'. In his opinion, there was a difference between the two groups. Later on, he went on saying that 'Gypsies' were poor 'Copts' (Вечерна поща, 1905b, p. 2). This statement also raises issues that have had an impact on the Roma movement in Bulgaria for decades and continue to be relevant today. It is about the public demonstration of a Turkish ethnic identity on the part of large sections of Turkish-speaking Muslim Gypsies, as well as the prohibition of Gypsies (even those who declared as Turks) to participate in the governance of the Muslim communities and religious property, regardless of the fact that there were no 'real' (i.e. ethnic) Turks in a given settlement.

The circumstances that led to the creation of the organisation *Istikbal* become clear if the processes are viewed precisely in this Muslim religious (and property) context. In the same year, 1919, immediately before its establishment, the Bulgarian State adopted a new Statute for the spiritual organisation and governance of the Muslims in the Kingdom of Bulgaria. With this Statute, the management of the *waqfs* (Muslim religious endowment) was assigned to the elected boards of the Muslim religious communities. In addition, the Gypsies "who have a permanent residence and are literate in Bulgarian and Turkish" were granted electoral rights (Вълков, 2020, p. 349). The direct consequence of these legal changes is clearly stated in the Statute of the organisation, in which the desire "to give a new life to the Muslim religious community" is stated as a particularly important goal (Art. 25). Although, according to its Statute, the organisation *Istikbal* is formally a Muslim charitable organisation without clearly expressed ethnic dimensions, in practice, its activity over the years (it existed until the Second World War) was primarily oriented in the field of Roma civil emancipation. The struggle for participation in the governance of the Muslim religious communities and their properties can be interpreted as an expression of this aspiration.

According to Shakir Pashov, the first public appearance of the new Gypsy civic movement was the meeting of the "progressive youth" (progressive here implies attachment to the communist ideas) in 1921. They elected a delegation and managed to meet with Prime Minister Aleksandar Stamboliyski, the head of the Bulgarian National Agricultural Union. In addition to Shakir Pashov himself, this delegation included the Chairman of the organisation Yusein Mehmedov, Yusein Bilalov, Rashid Mehmedov, Redzheb Yuseinov, Muto Bilalov and Bilal Osmanov (Пашов, 1957, p. 101). At this meeting, the delegation raised the issue that the Gypsies were stripped of voting rights in 1901, and the prohibition against voting remained in force despite amendments to the 1919 Election Law which introduced mandatory voting for all Bulgarian citizens (Държавен вестник, 1919, p. 1).

Prime Minister Stamboliyski promised to restore their voting rights and, according to Shakir Pashov's statement, at the next session of the National Assembly, he tabled a "proposal for the restoration of the voting rights of the Gypsies, and with the support of the Communist MPs, the law was passed". The debates in the Bulgarian Parliament on this amendment to the Electoral Law are instructive. Prime Minister Aleksandar Stamboliyski, in response to a remark made by the opposition, justified the voting rights of the Gypsies with their participation in the Bulgarian army during the two Balkan wars and the First World War (Дневник, 1923). Eventually, the Electoral Law was changed, and the electoral rights of the Muslim Gypsies were restored. The only ban that remained was on the vote of the Gypsies who did not have a permanent domicile (i.e. the nomadic Gypsies).

As demonstrated in this case as well as in many other instances (both before and after), the main argument that the Roma used in the process of their civil emancipation was their participation in the wars. This is the most convincing proof of their national civil identity and the most serious challenge of the stereotype that the Gypsies (in a new time Roma) do not have a homeland, which is widespread until today, including the academia.

The reasons why Shakir Pashov apparently "omitted" mentioning the early activities of the organisation *Istikbal* are quite clear. It stands to reason that in his memoirs, written at a time when the struggle to limit the role of religion (and especially of Islam) was an essential element of state policy, Shakir Pashov did not want to associate his past with this organisation. The easiest way to do this was not to mention its creation and existence in the 1920s. That is why he indicated May 7, 1929, as the date of its creation. He attributed the struggles for "civil and political rights of the Gypsy minority" in the 1920s to the Society *Egipet* (Egypt), which according to him, was linked with the Communist movement in Bulgaria at that time. In Shakir Pashov's words, the Society *Egipet* was founded in 1919, after he returned from the front. Its members were "a major part of the Gypsy intelligentsia and all the progressive youth". The aim of the association was "to raise its members and the entire Gypsy minority in cultural and educational terms, and, above all – to work for the political and civic awakening of the Gypsy minority". It is difficult to answer definitively the question of whether this Gypsy organisation really existed. On the one hand, we could not find any other historical evidence to confirm its legal registration (except Shakir Pashov's memories). Still, on the other hand, a youth association with the name 'Egypt' could have existed without legal registration.

However, in another autobiographical document, written in 1946, about the influence of communist ideas among the Gypsy youth in Sofia, Shakir Pashov did not mention the Society *Egipet*. In this document, he asserted that the young communists in the Gypsy neighbourhood had their own flag, "red, under the name Napredak [Напредък – 'Progress' in Bulgarian]" (CDA, f. 1 Б, op. 6, a.e. 235, l. 6), but the name of youth society that existed at the time was actually *Napred* (Forward). The popularity of communist ideas among the Gypsies in Sofia (or at least among some of them) at that time is beyond doubt. Representatives of the Gypsy youth were actively involved in political struggles, and there were victims among them. During the so-called Socialist era, there was a commemorative plaque in honour of Ibrahim Kerimov (or, according to other data, Ibraim Kyamilov), who was shot dead by the police on the street in Sofia during a demonstration organised by the Communist Party in 1919 (Неве рома, 1957e, p. 2). Ironically, after 1989, during the "democracy period", this plaque was removed because it was considered a legacy of Communism.

Shakir Pashov himself, at this time, was actively involved in the Communist movement. He was a member of the Communist Party (at that time named the Bulgarian Workers' Social-Democratic Party – narrow socialists) since 1918 (or since 1919 according to other data) (CDA, f. 1 B, op. 6, a.e. 235, l. 6; ASR, f. Shakir Pashov). The Gypsy Communist Society (regardless of whether it was formally registered, under what name, or whether it existed informally) had about 50 members in its initial composition. A few months after the establishment of the Society *Egipet*, its members decided to join the newly transformed (and renamed in 1919) Bulgarian Communist Party. According to Shakir Pashov, the merging of the Society *Egipet* into the Party was carried out in a solemn setting, in the Club of the society, on 51 Tatarli Street. At the merger, the management of the society consisted of the following nine members: Asen Totev, Shakir Pashov, Yusein Bilalov, Mancho Shakirov, Mustafa Saydiev, Demir Yasharov, Mancho Arifov, Ali Yasharov and Ramcho Shakirov. Very soon after its creation, the society already included more than 50 members. The flag of the Society *Egipet* was kept in Yusein Bilalov's home, and it was used in the May 1st demonstrations in 1920. In 1924, the Society *Egipet* organised the mass participation of Gypsies (including Gypsy women dressed in their traditional suit, the shalwars) in the mourning procession at the funeral of Dimitar Blagoev, the founder of the socialist (later communist) movement in Bulgaria, and laid wreaths on his grave.

At the end of 1919, Shakir Pashov, who at that time was working as a railway worker in the Bulgarian State Railways, became actively involved in the transport workers' strike, organised by the Bulgarian Communist Party. He was fired because of that (Нов път, 1974, p. 1–2), and, as he wrote elsewhere, he left the Bulgarian State Railways system and started working in his father's workshop (CDA, f. 1 B, op. 6, a.e. 235, l. 6–7). In 1922, Shakir Pashov was elected a delegate to the Fourth Congress of the BKP, which was held in Sofia at the Renaissance theatre, and was attended by many guests from abroad, including Clara Zetkin as a representative of the International Communist Movement (ASR, f. Shakir Pashov).

However, we should note that in some cases, Shakir Pashov deliberately "decorated" his autobiography (written in the late 1960s) with additional details highlighting his leading position in the communist movement. For example, his claim that in the parliamentary elections held in 1924, he was elected a Member of Parliament from the United Front (a political coalition between the Bulgarian Communist Party and the left-wing of the Bulgarian Agricultural People's Union) cannot be valid because, in 1924, no parliamentary elections were held.

The political situation in the first half of the 1920s in Bulgaria was characterised by intense, even fierce political struggles, which had an impact on the Gypsies. The left-wing Bulgarian Agricultural People's Union, led by Aleksandar Stamboliyski, implemented an agrarian reform thanks to which many Gypsies living in the rural areas received their own land. After the military coup, which took place on June 9, 1923, some of the Gypsies became involved in the armed resistance of the Bulgarian peasants in defence of the legitimate government. As a result of the suppression of the resistance, the Gypsies Asan Lalchov from the village of Dragor; Ali Durakov and Muto Asanov from the village of Karabunar, Pazardzhik District, were killed (Генов et al., 1968, pp. 22–24). Gypsies from North-Western Bulgaria also joined the September uprising in the fall of 1923, which was organised by the Bulgarian Communist Party and the left-wing of the Bulgarian Agricultural People's Union. Seven Gypsies were killed in the attack on the army barracks in Lom (Романо еси, 1946g, p. 2). During the suppression of the uprising, the Gypsies Shinko Kalishev and Biryam Aliev from the village of Milin Bryag; Yusein Abdulov from Berkovitsa; Mecho Demov Gyulov from the village of Yalovo; Nano Banov Munov from the village of Doktor Yosifovo; Dervish Bayramov from the village of Archar; and Veli and Kurto Mangovi Seferovi from the village of Gradeshnitsa were killed (Генов et al., 1968, p. 20). On the eve of the September uprising, Shakir Pashov was wanted by the police and fled to the town of Kyustendil, where he worked as a plumber on the construction of public buildings, leaving his wife and three young children in Sofia without a livelihood. He returned to Sofia only after the brutal suppression of the uprising (ASR, f. Shakir Pashov).

On April 16, 1925, the military wing of the Bulgarian Communist Party organised an assassination attempt at the St Nedelya cathedral. The purpose of this terrorist attack was to liquidate the country's military and political elite, and it left many casualties among the ruling elite. Authorities responded with massive brutal repressions against their political opponents and killed hundreds of Bulgarian Communist Party and Bulgarian Agricultural People's Union activists and some prominent left-wing intellectuals. Shakir Pashov was arrested immediately after the attack and spent several months in various police stations and military barracks. After his release, he remained under surveillance by the police, who repeatedly searched his house. That is why he decided to immigrate. He crossed illegally the border to Turkey, where he lived on various types of unskilled labour in Istanbul and Izmir and did not return to Bulgaria until 1929. However, the organisation *Istikbal* did not cease its activities after Shakir Pashov's immigration. By participating in the elections for the leadership of the Sofia Muslim religious community, and in particular of the Waqf Board of Trustees, the Gypsies from Sofia hoped to "take it over" from within and have the chance to control and use the Muslims' real estate (waqf estates) in order to solve the problems of their own community. As early as 1923–1924, the Chief Mufti (the religious leader of the Muslims in Bulgaria), Suleiman Faik, repeatedly pleaded with the Bulgarian authorities not to allow Gypsies in the elections into the Boards of Trustees of Muslim municipalities, using various arguments. He claimed that the Gypsies were "deprived of any culture" and "unfit for any creative work", so "with their negligence and disregard for religious canons and dogmas, they lose the right to be guardians of other Muslims and the handing over of waqfs and Lord-pleasing establishments to them is clearly inadmissible". He stressed that the Gypsies were fewer in number than the Turks but were concentrated in important Muslim centres such as the cities of Sofia, Plovdiv, Vidin, and Stara Zagora, where they constituted a majority. If they were eligible to run in the board elections, they "would win the most important Muslim [religious] communities ... and thus would ruin these properties in the shortest possible time" (Вълков, 2020, p. 349).

In 1925 (before Shakir Pashov' immigration), the Muslim religious community of Sofia held elections for a Board of Trustees of the school that was governed by it. A school board consisting of Muslim Gypsies was elected, including Rashid Mehmedov, Chair; Redzheb Yuseinov, Vice- Chair; Shakir Pashev, Secretary; and Members – Mustafa Enkekov and Malik Omerov. This Board of Trustees was affirmed by the Sofia Municipality, but the Muslim religious community, which was supposed to provide guarantees for it, refused to do it). The Gypsies from Sofia overcame various obstacles in their effort to take control of the school (and other Islamic properties); some of them even managed to show official documents issued by the Sofia municipality that they were Muslims and ethnic Turks (i.e. they were ready to declare another ethnic identity in public), but encountered opposition from the leadership of the Sofia Muslim community.

These struggles resulted in the opening of a dossier by the Ministry of Foreign Affairs and Religious Denominations in 1926 and a lawsuit against the Ministry of Justice in 1927 for the Sofia Muslim community's refusal to hold elections for a Board of Trustees of the Sofia mosque (Романо еси, 1946a, p. 2). In response to the aspirations of the Muslim Gypsies to participate in Muslim religious boards, the first national congress of the Turks in Bulgaria, held 31 October – 3 November, 1929, in Sofia, decided that "the Muslim Gypsies cannot participate in elections" for trustees of religious communities because these "purely Turkish national possessions" are inherited from the ancestors of the Turks (Şimşir, 1988, pp. 89–90). In this way, the religious communities manifested themselves as religious institution, uniting the Turkish minority in Bulgaria and excluding other Muslims (in this case, the Gypsies in particular).

In this situation, after his return to Bulgaria, Shakir Pashov resumed the active work of the organisation *Istikbal*. According to his memoirs, this happened on May 7, 1929, when "the first organisation of the Gypsy minority in Sofia was founded, which unites all former societies (*londzhi*) in the organisation *Istikbal*". Shakir Pashov asserts that the organisation numbered 1,500 members, a significant number for that time. The Chair was Yusein Mehmedov (the old Chair when the organisation was registered in 1919); Shakir Pashev, Secretary; and Yusein Bilalov, Member." In this case, however, there was no setting up of a new organisation but a renewal of the old one, which preserved not only the name and the governing body but also its seal, which (as will be discussed later) was used until the end of 1930.

As it is obvious, the new generation in the civic movement relied on the existing, older forms of community organisation in the Gypsy neighbourhoods, namely the so-called *londzhi*. The londzhi originated from the Gypsy guild's (*esnaf*) associations (and preserved their terminology); they have lost their former professional bases but retained the functions of mutual aid. The organisation *Istikbal* tried to take on some of their functions, particularly the charitable work and the support of members in emergencies (especially in funerals which involved many expenses), but this was not enough for the community. That is why some of the londzhi began to function as charitable, civic associations and sought formal registration (how many of them managed to do so is difficult to say). The institution of the londzhi has proved to be highly sustainable over the years, although the Communist regime has restricted their activities. In Sofia, the londzhi continue to exist to this day while their actions are already entirely controlled by women.

In the same year, another Gypsy organisation was founded, the Association *Vzaimopomosht* (Mutual Aid), chaired by Rashid Mehmedov. It also included some of the londzhi. In addition to these two large organisations, the Gypsies in Sofia maintained professional guilds of blacksmiths, tinsmiths, and small traders (junk dealers). They (at least according to Shakir Pashov) were also members of the organisation *Istikbal*, together with the Youth Cultural and Educational Association *Naangle* (Forward) and the Sports Association *Egipet* (Egypt); in our opinion, Shakir Pashov was probably confused about the names of the two organisations because the name 'Naangle' is associated with the sports organisation in many other sources. In 1930, the two major Gypsy organisations and all others merged under a common name, *Istikbal* (Future). The new (actually old, but with a new format) organisation was headed by Shakir Pashev, two Vice-Chairs (Redzheb Yuseinov and Rashid Mehmedov), two Secretaries (Ahmed Sotirov and Ramcho Shakirov), and Members – Yusein Bilalov, Emin Eminov, Raycho Kochev, and others (Пашов, 1957, pp. 103–104).

In the 1930s, the organisation *Istikbal*, already headed by Shakir Pashov, developed its activities in the two main directions defined at its inception. These activities were provisionally differentiated as religious and civic ones, but in fact, they intertwined and complemented each other over the years.

Religious activities were not successful. The struggle for the admission of the Gypsies into the governance of the Muslim community and, respectively, of its religious properties continued for a long time. In 1930, a lawsuit against the non-admission of Muslim Gypsies in the governance of Muslim religious institutions was filed with the prosecutor at the Sofia District Court on behalf of the Muslim Gypsies in Sofia. The case was eventually lost at the Supreme Administrative Court. It is indicative that in his article, Hyusein Bilalov, who described these struggles (Романо еси, 1946a, p. 2), did not mention the word 'Gypsies' a single time, i.e. in the strives for inclusion into the Islamic boards (and property), the Gypsy ethnic identity was consciously bypassed.

However, the activities of the organisation *Istikbal* were by no means limited to the struggle for a place for the Gypsies in the Muslim religious community. The State Archive in Sofia keeps a poster entitled: *Moods and Truths. To the Attention of our State, the Sofia Municipal Administration, and the Society*. It is signed by the Sofia Common Muslim Educational-Cultural and Mutual Aid Organisation *Istikbal – Future* (i.e., we see here the old name from 1919) (DA Sofia, f. 1 K, op. 2, a.e. 831, l. 625–625об); see Annexes 1). The poster is dated March 6, 1930 and was prepared in response to the publications in the press about the forthcoming displacement of the inhabitants of the Gypsy neighbourhood in Sofia (80–100 families). In response to this "lawlessness", the organisation stated that the Gypsy neighbourhood could not be considered a "nest of infectious diseases" (as described in the press) because "no resident of the neighbourhood is registered in any hospital in Sofia"; that "we are the strictest observers of morality" and that in the Morality department of the Police Directorate "there is not a single Gypsy woman among the registered prostitutes"; that maintaining street cleanliness is an obligation of the city authorities, which they do not fulfil due to "criminal negligence". The poster also notes that the people from the neighbourhood (i.e. Gypsies) make their living from "skilled labour" of "blacksmiths, basket makers, livestock dealers, musicians, porters, shoemakers, etc.", which is beneficial for all inhabitants of Sofia.

Furthermore, it especially underlines that "we, as equal citizens of our equally dear for everybody homeland Bulgaria, participated with honour and courage in the wars [the two Balkan Wars and the First World War – authors note], in which Bulgaria was involved, on an equal footing, and we all made dear sacrifices". The organisation quotes the paragraph from the Constitution: "all Bulgarian citizens are equal before the laws of our country", and "property rights are inviolable". Further it requests the establishment of a joint commission with representatives of the neighbourhood to identify the illegal settlement of "comb-makers, sieve makers, beggars, and others, who arrived from the countryside" (Ibid.).

We should note that the poster's text uses both terms, 'Muslims' and 'Gypsies' (with the predominance of the former), without opposing them. In this way, for the first time, the organisation *Istikbal* de facto declared itself a representative of the Roma community in the public space and thus became a political subject in the struggles for the civic emancipation of the Gypsies.

In his Autobiography, Shakir Pashov described how, after returning from Turkey, he became a member of the Workers' Party (a legal, political structure of the Bulgarian Communist Party, established in 1927 after the banning of the Bulgarian Communist Party in 1924) and formed a "Gypsy Party group". In 1931, he became "Chairman of the Gypsy Cultural and Educational organisation in Bulgaria" and founded the "first Gypsy newspaper in Bulgaria" *Terbie* (Upbringing), which "fought for the cultural and educational uprising and political consciousness of our tobacco workers in Bulgaria" (ASR, f. Shakir Pashov, a.e. Autobiography). The actual course of events, as it appears in other historical sources, however, reveals a more or less different picture. The newspaper *Terbie*, which would have been an invaluable source, was not preserved in the Bulgarian libraries, and copies were not found elsewhere. According to known data, the newspaper was published between 1932 (or 1933) and 1934 (the latest one being No. 7 from May 6, 1934), in 7 editions with 1,500 copies each. Issue No. 2 from February 27, 1933, states that Shakir M. Pashev is the Editor-in-chief, and the newspaper is published by the Mohammedan National Educational and Cultural Organisation. Issue No. 6 states that the newspaper is an organ of the Common Mohammedan National Cultural and Educational Union in Bulgaria, and its Editorial committee includes: Shakir Mahmudov Pashev (Editor-in-chief), Asen Gotov and Demir Yasharov (Иванчев, 1966, Vol. 2, p. 398; see also Marinov, 2021, pp. 51–56).

To put it in brackets, the newspaper *Terbie* was not the first Gypsy newspaper in Bulgaria. In the 1920s and 1930s, the following newspapers were published: *Светилник* (Candlestick), *Bulletin of the Gypsies' Mission in Bulgaria: Народът, който се нуждае от просвета чрез Евангелието* (Bulletin of the Gypsies Mission in Bulgaria. A Nation that needs Enlightenment through the Gospel), and *Известия на Циганската евангелска мисия* (News of the Gypsy Evangelical Mission). The first of them was published in the town of Lom in 1927, and the other two in Sofia in 1932–1933, and their Editor-in-chief was Pastor Petar Minkov (Иванчев, Vol. 1, 1962, p. 363; Vol. 2, 1966, p. 264; Vol. 3, 1969, p. 6; see also Marinov, 2021, pp. 37–51). All of them are related to the so-called New (Evangelical) Churches which started spreading among the Gypsies in Bulgaria at that time (for more details, see Славкова, 2007; Marushiakova & Popov, 2021), and their activities led to the establishment of the Gypsy Evangelical Baptist Church in the village of Golintsi (today Mladenovo neighbourhood in Lom) and the Gypsy Women's Christian Society *Romni* (Roma Woman) (Ibid.). At the beginning of the 1930s, when the newspaper *Terbie* was already in print, the society in Bulgaria was shaken by a big public scandal connected with the propaganda of the evangelical church among the Gypsies in Bulgaria. Henry W. Shoemaker, a famous American folklorist, was appointed extraordinary plenipotentiary minister (i.e. ambassador) of the USA to Bulgaria (1930–1933). In this position, he became the 'Honorary Patron' of the Gypsy Evangelical Mission established in 1932 (CDA, f. 264 K, op. 2, a.e. 9385). However, the activities of the Mission met with opposition from the Bulgarian Orthodox Church. In a letter to the Holy Synod, dated May 25, 1933, Neophyte, Metropolitan of Vidin, stated:

> We are surprised by the fact that this Gypsy mission was allegedly under the auspices of the American plenipotentiary minister, Mr. Shoemaker! Because we did not know until now, and even now, we do not allow the possibility that a political representative of great power can put himself at the service of reckless propaganda and openly patronise it. (Ibid., l. 3).

It seems unlikely that Shakir Pashov was unaware of the existence of Gypsy newspapers published by Evangelical churches; moreover, in 1947, in his capacity as a Member of Parliament, he visited Golintsi to quell the scandals among the Gypsy population there (see below). Presumably, when he wrote his book in the 1950s, he did not want to publicly advertise the presence of followers of the Evangelical churches among the Gypsies because of the atheist policy of the authorities in Bulgaria at that time.

Information about the contents of the newspaper *Terbie* is available, apart from Shakir Pashov's memoirs, from only two other independent historical sources. One of them is the already quoted article by (H)Yusein Bilalov, *From the Life of the Sofia Muslim Confessional Municipality – Sofia* (Романо еси, 1946a, p. 2), a reprint of the article first published in the newspaper *Terbie*, in which the emphasis is on the struggle for participation in the management of the Muslim religious community (and its properties). The second source is the article *Gypsies and the Gypsy Question* by Nayden Sheytanov, an amateur researcher of the Gypsies, which was published in the mainstream press (Мир, 1934, p. 3). As pointed out by Sheytanov, the newspaper *Terbie* devoted a great deal of space to the struggles of the Muslim Gypsies for access to the governance of the Islamic religious communities and property. In this field, it left behind their ethnic identity. At the same time, the newspaper publicly presented the new 'national' concept of the Gypsy community. It systematically used the terms "our nation", "our national movement", and "our national consciousness", illustrating the Gypsies' national identity. It referred to the Gypsies as "descendants of the great King Pharaoh" and appealed to them: "Do not neglect your family, your faith, your traditions", "You must proudly call yourself a Gypsy!" (Ibid.).

It is obvious that the Roma historical narrative at that time continued to be dominated by the "Egyptian version" of their origin; it began to give way to the "Indian version" only in the 1950s, when the Gypsies became aware of the latter and under the influence of the first wave of Indian films shown in Bulgaria. The Indian version is already prevalent in Shakir Pashov's manuscript. The newspaper *Terbie* covers the strategic plans and concrete actions aimed at advancing the Roma civic emancipation movement to a new, national level. Indicative in this respect is the call to the Sofia Gypsies "to self-organise as soon as possible in order to give pace to all Bulgaria, so that […] we have representatives of our interests" (Ibid.), which can be interpreted as a desire for political representation of the Gypsy community. The newspaper reflects the specific attempts in this direction, such as the organisation of a fair in the village of Dolna Kremena, Vratsa region, as well as the effect of these activities, revealed in letters from the cities of Sliven, Vratsa, the village of Galiche, etc. (Ibid.).

New moments in the development of the civic consciousness of the Gypsies were also their appeals to the Bulgarian State for an active policy for the social integration of the Gypsies. The main argument was the realities in other countries worldwide: "Why Gypsies in Turkey are not at such a low stage as we in Bulgaria? […] In Europe, especially in Austria, Hungary, Romania, Poland […] and in Soviet Russia, legislators undertook to create a series of laws assisting [the Gypsies], both materially and in terms of culture and education" (Ibid.). These statements are propaganda which does not correspond to reality because, in other countries, the situation of the Gypsies was no different than that in Bulgaria. At that time, there was no affirmative policy towards the Gypsies, except in the USSR (see Marushiakova & Popov, 2021).

According to Nayden Sheytanov, the newspaper *Terbie* cooperated with the "Romanian and Hungarian Gypsies" (Ibid.). In fact, from today's point of view, we cannot be sure whether such cooperation took place or whether this was a mere propaganda trick. Nevertheless, it shows a clear consciousness of the cross-border unity of the Gypsy community. In his memoirs, Shakir Pashov devoted much space to the newspaper *Terbie* and the critical role it played in the "upbringing and cultural and educational enlightenment of the Gypsy population in Bulgaria" as well as generally, in raising the civic consciousness and national civic identity of the Gypsies. In his words, "the newspaper *Terbie* truly raised the national and patriotic feeling of the Gypsy minority, but it fought resolutely against its chauvinistic feelings […] [and] was working towards an enlightened patriotism, and against uneducated fanaticism and chauvinism" (Ibid.). The newspaper was circulated throughout the country. For that purpose, many people were organised in Vratsa, Lom, Oryahovo,

Pleven, Plovdiv, Kyustendil, Stara Zagora, Ruse, Shumen, Burgas, Pernik, Sliven and many villages.

The first step for organising the Gypsies in the country and creating a national Gypsy civil organisation was the Conference, which took place near the Mezdra Station on May 7, 1932. The Conference was organised on the initiative of the Gypsy organisation in Vratsa. The organisers were Nikola Palashev and Sando Ibrov. The Conference was attended by delegates from the whole Vratsa region, including from the villages Montana, Oryahovo and the villages around it, Byala Slatina, Pleven, Lom, and Cherven Bryag. The Sofia delegation was headed by Shakir Pashov and included Emin Eminov, Naydo Yasharov and Ali Yasharov. According to Shakir Pashov, the Conference decided that the common Organisation *Istikbal* should lead all Gypsies in Bulgaria, and its newspaper *Terbie* "would penetrate as an enlightening beam to the last hut of the entire Gypsy minority in Bulgaria" (Пашов, 1957, p 105).

In several autobiographies, written at different times, as well as in the manuscript published in this edition, Shakir Pashov wrote neutrally "the Gypsy Cultural and Educational Organisation" without giving the exact names of the organisations he has in mind, i.e. Sofia Common Muslim Educational-Cultural and Mutual Aid Organisation *Istikbal – Future*, Mohammedan National Educational and Cultural Organisation and Common Mohammedan-Gypsy National Cultural-Educational and Mutual Aid Union in Bulgaria. This "omission" of the exact names was made deliberately – to avoid mentioning their definition as 'Muslim/Mohammedan' and all religious activities. Nevertheless, when he wrote about the 1930s, he noted his ties with the organisation *Istikbal* whose connection with Islam is not so visible by its title.

This is the reason why in his memoirs, Shakir Pashov consciously linked all activities in the field of Roma emancipation in the early 1930s with the organisation *Istikbal*, including the publication of the newspaper *Terbie*. In fact, the leading organisation in these processes was the new organisation established in 1931 and led by him, which in various sources is called 'Mohammedan National Educational and Cultural Organisation' (Иванчев, 1966, Vol. 2, p. 398) or 'Common Mohammedan National Cultural and Educational Union' (Мир, 1934, p. 3). No documents about its registration have thus far been discovered. Still, in 1933 this organisation was restructured, and Shakir Pashov tried to register it, a fact that he also consciously "omitted" in his memoirs.

The minutes from the meeting for the establishment of the organisation with the name 'Common Mohammedan-Gypsy National Cultural-Educational and Mutual Aid Union in Bulgaria' have been preserved. From the minutes, it became clear that on December 25, 1933, in Sofia, a Constituent Assembly was held with Chair Ramcho Shakirov, Vice-Chair Demir Yasharov, and Secretary Slavi Iliev, at which the Board of Directors of the new organisation was elected with members: Shakir M. Pashev (living at that time on 80 Konstantin Velichkov Street), Rashid Mehmedov, Bilyal Osmanov, Slavi Iliev and Mehmed Skenderov; and Substitute Members – Ramcho Shakirov and Mladen Spasov. The management board elected the President of the Union – Shakir M. Pashev, Secretary of the Union – Slave Iliev, and Treasurer of the Union – Mehmed Skenderov. Control Commission, Enlightenment Council, and Religious Council were also elected (CDA, f. 264, op. 2, a.e. 8413, l. 27–28; Marushiakova & Popov, 2021, pp. 86–93). At this Constituent Assembly, the Statute of the Common Mohammedan-Gypsy National Cultural-Educational and Mutual Aid Union in Bulgaria was discussed and adopted. (CDA, f. 264 K, op. 2, a.e. 8413, l. 7–12, 15–20, 21–26 [3 copies]; see also Marushiakova & Popov, 2021, pp. 86–94). In the Statute of the new organisation, there are many new and important elements compared with the Statute of the organisation *Istikbal*. The name itself explicitly emphasises that it was a union of the Gypsies in Bulgaria, i.e. it already had the ambition to work on a national scale along with separate subdivisions in the country and to be representative of the whole community. This was explicitly stated in the beginning of the Statute, in the chapter about the purpose of the Union, "to organise all Gypsies (Mohammedans and others) in their national belonging in Bulgaria" and "to create an organisation for the preservation of the material and spiritual interests of this nation in the country, but also a mutual aid institute through self-help" (Art. 1), as well as to work "for the cultivation of civil virtues in the motherland – Bulgaria" (Art. 2). The new Union had ambitions to unite all existing forms of Gypsy organisations (civic, mutual aid, sport, etc. including the professional associations), without infringing on their independence (Art. 3).

Moreover, the Union even left its door open for international participation, allowing the inclusion of "our co-nationals" from other countries (Art. 3). This possibility remained at an abstract level, however, it reveals the emergence of a Gypsy trans-border identity (or at least indicates the presence of such aspiration). The tasks that the Union defined for itself go far beyond those of the organisation *Istikbal*. By its very design, it was, to a much greater extent, a modern Gypsy civic organisation with three directions – cultural and educational, religious, and urban development.

The interesting point is that the Statute of the Union envisages, "if the laws permit, the opening of private schools" (Art. 2). Apparently, this article presumed the successful completion of the long struggle for control by the Gypsies over the Islamic religious community in Sofia and its properties. According to the legal norms at the time, only religious communities had the right to open their private schools, and the control over the Islamic religious community would have made it possible for the Gypsies to establish a private Gypsy school (perhaps several ones in the future).

It is worth noting that the new Union declared St Gheorghe's day as its patron saint's day (although almost all of its founders were Muslims). This fact continued the tradition of ethno-national symbols, which started at the Vidin organisation (see above). Having in mind the dichotomy community – society, such symbols did not contradict the national civic identity of the Gypsies, which was clearly expressed in the Statute itself.

In April 1934, the Common Mohammedan-Gypsy National Cultural-Educational and Mutual Aid Union in Bulgaria submitted documents for registration with the Ministry of Internal Affairs and National Health as required by law (CDA, f. 264, op. 2, a.e. 8413, l. 1). Following the military coup on May 19, 1934, a new government headed by Kimon Georgiev, came to power. It banned all political parties and organisations and their newspapers. On that occasion, Shakir Pashov wrote a new letter to the Ministry of Internal Affairs and National Health, emphasising that the Common Mohammedan-Gypsy National Cultural-Educational and Mutual Aid Union in Bulgaria unites legally registered organisations such as the Blacksmiths' association, the Tinsmiths' association, the Society *Egipet*, the organisation *Istikbal*, the Mutual Aid association. It is an organisation "without any party affiliation", and its goals "do not contradict any law in our country". Therefore, he asked for approval and legalisation of the Statute (Ibid., l. 14). The Ministry sent the Union's documents to the Department of Religions with the request for an opinion. The Department returned a resolution: "this Statute SHOULD NOT BE AFFIRMED because the organising of the Gypsy Muslims in our country is influenced by foreign factors" (Ibid., l. 14). Thus, finally, the registration of the Common Mohammedan-Gypsy National Cultural-Educational and Mutual Aid Union in Bulgaria was rejected (Ibid., l. 2).

As can be seen from these materials, the reason for the refusal to register the Union was not because it is a 'Gypsy' organisation, but because it is a 'Muslim' one, and as such, it can be used as a channel of "foreign influence" (foreign in this case means Turkish – authors note). Paradoxically, Nayden Sheytanov used the same argument in his article mentioned above, in which he explicitly warned the "competent and responsible" (i.e. the authorities) that the Common Mohammedan National Cultural-Educational Union in Bulgaria was meant to become a centre attracting the Gypsies in a "common front" of the Muslims in Bulgaria (Мир, 1934, p. 3). Nayden Sheytanov's interpretation, in fact, gave an argument to the authorities to reject the Union's application for registration, despite the fact that the Union's Statute introduced the term

'Gypsy' and its goals extended beyond the religious dimension, compared to the Statute of the First Union. The historical irony is that Sheytanov used this insinuation to call on the Bulgarian authorities for greater attention to the Gypsies and their problems. The outcome, however, had been contrary to his intention (i.e., we have once again evidence that scholars must be cautious in their texts because it is possible that they will be used against the subject of their research). The implication of the Gypsies in general anti-Muslim (actually anti-Turkish) discourse of the state policy was not new for Bulgaria. This approach is characteristic of the entire history of the new Bulgarian State. Its most striking manifestation is the so-called Revival Process in the 1980s, when the Communist regime forced all Muslims, including the Gypsies, to change their Muslim (Turko-Arabic) names with Christian (Bulgarian) names. The Gypsies were renamed not because they were Gypsies but because they were Muslims (in fact, the changing of names for the Gypsies began as soon as the 1960s).

Shakir Pashov has repeatedly written that after the coup of May 19, 1934, the organisation *Istikbal* was banned by the authorities and ceased its activities (see published here manuscript of Shakir Pashov; Неве рома, 1957f, p. 4). In this case, he referred to the rejection of registration of the Common Mohammedan-Gypsy National Cultural-Educational and Mutual Aid Union in Bulgaria (which he did not mention in his memoirs). In any case, there are some documentary pieces of evidence suggesting that the organisation not only continued to exist after 1934 but even wrote formal letters to the local and national authorities on the organisation's letterhead and used its stamp, one of the letters (published above) being addressed to the Police Department itself. Probably because of these contacts, which his detractors could interpret as cooperation with the authorities, he preferred to present his activities during the second half of the 1930s without mentioning the allegedly "closed" organisation. Despite this, in his memoirs, he praised the activities of the organisation, explicitly noting that "the organisation *Istikbal* played the role of an official institution, the only one representing the Gypsy minority before the legitimate authorities in Sofia" (Ibid.). These activities took place precisely during the period in which, according to Shakir Pashov's allegation, the organisation had been forbidden.

In 1934, Shakir Pashov worked as a machine mechanic in the municipal technical workshop. He was fired on January 1, 1935, because he participated in the strike organised by the Workers' Party (ASR, f. Shakir Pashov, a.e. Autobiography). After his dismissal, he made his living in his small ironwork workshop located in the area of Positano Street. At that time, he lived with his family in the largest Gypsy mahala in Sofia, known as 'Konyovitsa and Tatarli' on Klementina Boulevard (today's Alexander Stamboliyski Boulevard), across the Jewish mahala. In 1943 (or 1944), the family moved to the so-called *Boyana* mahala, known also as *Tukhlarna* (Brick Factory), pronounced *Tu'la mahala*, which was located around today's Gotse Delchev Boulevard.

During this period, Shakir Pashov actively worked among his community. In his memoirs, he paid particular attention to the struggles of the organisation *Istikbal* against some traditional customs of the Gypsies in Sofia. He devoted a whole chapter of the manuscript in the present edition, entitled *Habits and Customs, and the Fight against the Harmful Ones*. In this chapter, he focused on the customs and rituals of paying for the bride; the circumcision of boys; and the wearing of shalwars by the women, all of which Shakir Pashov described as harmful to the Gypsies. We cannot avoid the fact that these customs are linked (including in the eyes of the surrounding population) with Muslim traditions. Clearly, the emphasis on these aspects of the work of the organisation was influenced by the spirit of the time in which he wrote the memoirs. However, this was not the author's primary approach because he raised no single concern (not to mention disagreement) about other Muslim traditions, such as those at funerals, which were very strong at the time (including the obligatory presence of an Islamic cleric).

The apparent need to support Gypsy families in organising funerals is reflected in the Statutes of the Sofia Common Muslim Educational-Cultural and Mutual Aid Organisation *Istikbal – Future* and of the Common Mohammedan-Gypsy National Cultural-Educational and Mutual Aid Union in Bulgaria. It also was one of the reasons for the establishment of other organisations, for example, the Gypsy Cultural-Educational and Posthumously-Charitable Association *Butlaches* (Virtue) in 1939 (CDA, f. 264, op. 5, a.e. 1109, l. 3–5). Moreover, Shakir Pashov himself mentioned in his memoirs as an important fact that the organisation *Istikbal* owned a funeral car and that it helped poor Gypsy families in need to cover the funeral expenses. So, it is logical to assume that Shakir Pashov truly believed that the customs and rituals he mentioned were "harmful" as they created obstacles to the development of the community, as well as to its successful social integration and civic emancipation, and therefore fought against them.

It is clear that the development of the leading Gypsy Organisations (the Sofia Common Muslim Educational-Cultural and Mutual Aid Organisation *Istikbal – Future* and the Common Mohammedan-Gypsy National Cultural-Educational and Mutual Aid Union in Bulgaria) during the interwar period constantly oscillated between the ethnic and the religious dimensions. We should keep in mind that these two dimensions often overlapped in the Balkans, and hence, they were interchangeable. The Gypsies were not an exception in this respect;

moreover, these processes were most pronounced among them, which leads to the so-called preferred ethnic identity (communities of Gypsy origin publicly demonstrate or actually experience a Turkish ethnic identity) (Marushiakova & Popov, 2015a, pp. 27–33).

In any case, regardless of the specific circumstances, these ethnic and religious identities were superimposed on the Bulgarian civic national identity. This multidimensional identity is reflected in the names of the organisations – most of them are in Bulgarian, with fewer words in Turkish (*Istikbal, Terbie*) and in the Romani language (*Naangle, Butlaches*). The identity negotiation is especially visible in the Gypsy activists' struggle against the shalwars described above. On the one hand, by rejecting Gypsy traditions, which were interpreted as Turkish, the Gypsies aspired to establish a Bulgarian civic national identity in the public space. On the other hand, as Shakir Pashov himself wrote in his manuscript, the shalwars remained as a "valuable asset" and as a Gypsy national symbolism, which was demonstrated publicly only on certain special occasions. For example, many photos from the time show that during public celebrations until circa the 1960s, the Gypsies from Sofia walked in front of the officials' tribune dressed in festive shalwars (ASR, f. Photos, see also Illustrations in this book).

Another important event in the second half of the 1930s, to which Shakir Pashov paid special attention in his memoirs, was the organisation of a Gypsy Ball held at the City Casino, located in the centre of Sofia. It featured art scenes from *The Thousand and One Nights*, authored by himself. The director was Emin Eminov and ballet master Hyusein A. Bilalov. The Gypsy ball was attended by many people, very well received by the audience, and widely covered by the press in Bulgaria and abroad. From the descriptions, one can learn that the Gypsy Ball was opened by a mixed choir, which performed the Bulgarian national anthem, followed by traditional Gypsy songs; the dancer Anushka and the famous Gypsy singer Keva also took part in the Ball (Observer, 1937). The singer Keva sang in the popular At Keva's cabaret, located in the then-Gypsy neighbourhood. The place was frequently visited by the city's bohemians, and according to rumours, by members of the royal family as well (Тенев, 1997, pp. 225–227, 233–235). Keva had several phonograph records in the 1930s for the Balkan Records Company, which included the song *Telal Avel* (She Comes from Downside), performed in the Romani language. This was the first record of a song in Romani in Bulgaria (Димов, 2005).

At the Gypsy Ball, the Bulgarian Tsar Boris III was also invited, but while he did not personally attend it, he had sent money in an envelope for the poor Gypsies (ASR, f. Shakir Pashov). For obvious reasons, Shakir Pashov himself did not mention anything about this in his manuscript. In the memoirs, he also made a small factual error. According to him, the Gypsy Ball happened on 3 March (a national holiday of Bulgaria) in 1938 (see Shakir Pashov's monograph published here; Неве ром, 1957f, p. 4), but in fact, the ball was in 1937, as evidenced by many publications in the Bulgarian and foreign press.

In his memoirs, Shakir Pashov described how on 6 March 1938, the Gypsy neighbourhood was sealed off by the authorities due to press publications about the spreading of typhus among the Gypsies. The committee, set up on his initiative, made an address to the authorities demanding the end of the blockade as well as compensation from the state for workers' lost wages. However, he skipped the fact that on this occasion, it was the organisation *Istikbal* that set up the committee and issued a public declaration entitled *Clarification in Relation to the Publication in the Dnevnik Newspaper of False and Inaccurate Information About the Occurrence of Typhus Fever among the Gypsies* on 16 March 1938 (DA Sofia, f. 1 K, op. 4, a.e. 531, l. 5). It is clear from this declaration that such manipulations in the public space were not accidental but were part of an organised campaign, ongoing "for years" (Ibid.). In this case, the declaration pointed to a series of complaints to various institutions from the Bulgarian population in the neighbourhoods around the Gypsy quarter in 1937–1938 against the allegedly illegal settlement of Gypsies, violation of public order, poor sanitation, etc. (DA Sofia, f. 1 K, op. 4, a.e. 531). The petitioners demanded that the municipal authorities evict the Gypsies and "relocate and isolate them in the Gypsy mahala near the Faculty [of Agriculture of the Sofia University St Kliment Ohridski], where they can live in the same way as their fellow countrymen, and where they will be further away from us" (Ibid., l. 2). The purpose of this campaign is very transparent – to evict the Gypsies from the Gypsy neighbourhoods Konyovitsa, Tatarli and Batalova vodenitsa into the emerging new Gypsy neighbourhood Fakulteta (at that time in the outskirts of the city), and to buy their plots for little money. The declaration of the organisation *Istikbal* ends with an appeal to the Bulgarian authorities:

> We are Bulgarian citizens with Bulgarian spirit, we have left the bones of our fathers and brothers on the battlefields in the two wars, and today we are ready to make sacrifices for our homeland Bulgaria in which we were born, we live and enjoy all freedoms (Ibid., l. 5).

In the end, some of the residents of the Gypsy neighbourhoods Konyovitsa and Tatarli moved to the new Fakulteta neighbourhood, but the majority remained in their old homes.

To say in brackets, the attempts of the authorities to push the inhabitants of the Gypsy neighbourhoods Konyovitsa and Tatarli as far as possible from the city centre continued in the subsequent historical periods. In 1959, the communist regime decided to evict the Gypsies from there to the newly built dwellings next to the village of Filipovtsi (at that time outside Sofia). On this occasion, residents of the neighbourhood sent a complaint, addressed personally to the First Secretary of the Central Committee of the Bulgarian Communist Party, Todor Zhivkov, in which they wrote:

> Who made this decision and chose the village of Filipovtsi as the most suitable place for us? The houses there are just a little better than henhouses. Why is this being caused to minorities? Is this why we rejoiced and clapped our hands, and the fascists hated us until the last moment? Should they [fascists] return to power, they would slaughter us, the minorities, like chickens. We, the Gypsies in Bulgaria, have no country, no one to care about us, and no one to complain to. If comrade Georgi Dimitrov were alive, would this be the situation with the minorities? (CDA, f. 1, op. 28, a.e. 6, l. 3).

In the first years of our century, the Sofia Municipality began once again the preparations (accompanied by a public campaign in the media) for the eviction of the Gypsies in the Batalova Vodenitsa neighbourhood (without making provision for alternative housing). Human rights and Roma organisations took the issue to the European Court of Human Rights in Strasbourg in 2012. After the court decision, the eviction was stopped (at least for the time being).

In 1937, the Gypsy issue attracted public attention on another occasion. An article in the yellow press, entitled *The Gypsies will Organise Themselves*, reported that two young Gypsies, Ahmed Seizov and Petar Ivanov, were touring the country and trying (without much success) to organise the Gypsies into a union to become a member of the International Gypsy Union based in Hungary (Празднични вести, 1937, p. 2). The Bulgarian police investigated the case but failed to find persons with such names; the leadership of the organisation *Istikbal* also confirmed that such persons were not known in the Gypsy community (CDA, f. 370, op. 6, a.e. 745, l. 1, 3). Nor was there any information about the existence of any International Gypsy Union (neither in Hungary nor anywhere else in the world). Apparently, the article was a journalistic sensation which had nothing to do with reality.

The last written statement of the organisation *Istikbal*, for which historical evidence is preserved, is an official letter to the Police Directorate dated 18 July 1939, signed by Shakir Pashov and stamped with the seal of the organisation. Notably, in this letter, the Gypsy organisation demonstrated awareness of its obligations towards the Gypsy community as well as expectations for active state policy towards the Gypsies as part of the society and explicitly emphasised that the intervention of the state was crucial for the future of their people. This letter calls on the police to "take the most stringent measures against all Gypsy men and Gypsy women who roam in the night without any reason, especially those who are in an intoxicated state", and "do what you need to do to close down the Gypsy cabarets – the nests of immorality, that demoralise the Gypsy population and have a bad influence on the upbringing, especially of the youth and of the children in the neighbourhood" (DA Sofia, f. 1 К, op. 4, a.e. 683, l. 93).

There is no reliable historical evidence of Shakir Pashov's political and civic activities during the Second World War. Although Bulgaria was an ally of Nazi Germany (although Bulgaria did not send its army to the Eastern Front), partisan groups in the country launched an armed struggle led by the Communist Party. Shakir Pashov asserted that during this period, he was actively involved in the anti-fascist resistance, and his iron workshop, located at that time on 28 Serdika Street (in the centre of Sofia), was used as a communication point for the transmission of illegal materials and weapons (ASR, f. Shakir Pashov, a.e. Autobiography). However, there is no other historical evidence for these allegations, nor for the plan for a conference of the Gypsy minority prepared by him (with the approval of the illegal communist activists with whom he was in constant contact) to be held on September 5–6, 1944 (Ibid.).

At the beginning of September 1944, the political situation in Bulgaria radically changed. At that time, the Soviet army had already reached the Bulgarian border, and on September 5, the USSR declared war on Bulgaria; on September 9, a new government led by the Fatherland Front (a political coalition dominated by the Communist Party) came to power. According to Shakir Pashov, the very next day, he, together with several other Gypsy activists, appeared before the new authorities, from whom they received an order to establish a Gypsy organisation as part of the Fatherland Front; such an organisation was created, and it was headed by Shakir Pashov himself (Ibid.). There is also no other historical evidence for these events, and it seems highly unlikely that only a few hours after taking power, the creation of a Gypsy organisation was a matter of importance for the communist leadership. What is certain, however, is that Shakir Pashov, in the first days after September 9, supported the new government and organised mass public events with the participation of Gypsies.

Two photographs from September 1944 (ASR, f. Photos) documented these events. The first one shows a rally of Sofia citizens in support of the new government, with festively dressed Gypsy women in the first row carrying a poster, *Long live the Fatherland Front. Death to fascism. Gypsy Mahala – Sofia* (Ibid.). Another photo shows the manifestation of Gypsies in Sofia, in front of the Bulgarian Parliament, in which women dressed in festive "traditional" costumes (wearing shalwars), wear posters, *Enough with Racial Differences*, and the same poster as described above (Ibid.). This Gypsy manifestation is also presented in a painting by the famous Bulgarian artist Vasil Evtimov (1900–1986), dated 1944, obviously painted immediately after the manifestation (Галерия Лоранъ, 2014).

The end of the Second World War marked the beginning of a new historical era in which, under the influence of new social and political realities, the basic ideas and approaches of the Roma civic emancipation began to radically change. On 6 March 1945, before the end of the war, at 18 Tatarli Street, the United Common-Cultural and Educational Organisation of the Gypsy Minorities *Ekhipe* (Unity in Romani language) was established in Sofia. The creation of the new organisation was announced as the restoration of the old, "disbanded organisation *Istikbal*", with an emphasis on the continuity of the two organisations.

At the constituent assembly, the Statute of the old/new Gypsy organisation was presented, and its leadership was elected, including Shakir Pashev, Chair; Raycho Kochev and Bilal Osmanov, Vice-Chairs; Tair Selimov, Secretary; Demir Rustemov, Treasurer; and Members – Emin Eminov, Hyusein A. Bilalov, Sulyo Metkov, Resho Demirov, Ramcho Totev, Demcho Blagoev, Naydo Yasharov, Asan Osmanov (Palyacho), Asan Somanov, Ismail Shakirov, Shakir Meshchanov, Ali Mehmedov, Izet Salchov and Tseko Nikolov (Пашов, 1957, pp. 121–122).

According to its Statute (CDA, f. 1 Б, op. 8, a.e. 596, l. 50–52; Marushiakova & Popov, 2021, pp. 103–110), the organisation had the following tasks: a) to fight against fascism, anti-Gypsyism and racial prejudices; b) to raise the Gypsy nationality feeling and consciousness among the Bulgarian Gypsies; c) to introduce the Gypsy language among the Gypsy population as an oral and written language; d) to introduce the Bulgarian Gypsy minority to the Gypsy culture; e) to introduce to the Bulgarian Gypsies their spiritual, social and economic culture; f) to raise the economic status of all Gypsy strata in Bulgaria; g) to make physically fit the Gypsy youth in Bulgaria; h) to make the Gypsy masses productive; i) to consolidate and set up Gypsy institutes in Bulgaria; j) to enlighten the Bulgarian general public about the needs of the Gypsy population; k) to foster among the Gypsies aspiration for the creation of a national hearth in their own land.

The organisation had a national scope and a complex hierarchical structure and included local organisations. The Statute explicitly emphasised that the "eligible member could be any Gypsy at the age of 18 and above, regardless of sex and social status" and "all Gypsies with Mohammedan and Christian Orthodox religions without any differentiation" (Art. 2).

It is interesting to note that the very first task of the new organisation contains the wording "fighting […] antiziganism", which raises some questions. The concept of anti-Gypsyism, which is widespread these days, is not a product of the last few decades, as is often assumed (and even written in some academic works). It arose in the conditions of the early USSR as early as the 1920s in the circles of Gypsy activists. It became a key ideologeme through which the history of the Gypsies was explained in previous (before the creation of the USSR) historical eras (see in more detail Marushiakova & Popov, 2021, pp. 832–833). The question here is how Shakir Pashov, the main initiator of the creation of the new Gypsy organisation and the author (or at least one of the authors) of its Statute, could know this concept and from where he took the term anti-Gypsyism, which was previously unknown in Bulgaria (and was subsequently not used anywhere, including in the Gypsy press). We have no satisfactory answer to this question.

Another intriguing point in the Statute of the organisation *Ekhipe* is the emergence of ideas about the future development of the Gypsies as an ethnonation, or in other words, about establishing a nation-state (even if this was vaguely worded and presented as a matter of the uncertain future).

The Statute repeatedly emphasises the commitment to the "World Gypsy Movement", the "World Gypsy Organisation", and the "World Gypsy Congresses" (Art. 1, Art. 2, Art. 22, Art. 23), and, ultimately, as a distant perspective, the creation of an independent Gypsy state: "To create an aspiration in the Gypsies to build a national hearth in their own land" (Art. 3). At that time, a "World Gypsy Organisation" did not exist anywhere in the world, and it is unclear how Shakir Pashov and the Gypsy activists came up with these ideas, which occupied leading positions in the ideological platform of the new organisation. This could have been an expression of their wishful thinking aimed at activating the mechanism of the "self-fulfilling prophecy", or an analogy with the ideas of the world Zionism, which were especially popular at the time. Another possibility is that the Gypsy activists knew the ideas for the creation of a Gypsy state, launched publicly by the so-called Gypsy Kings from the "Kwiek Dynasty" in Poland, which was widely covered in the world media in the 1930s (see Marushiakova & Popov, 2021, pp. 599–650).

In any case, one of the leading national symbols of the future Gypsy state, the national flag, was already present in the Statute of the organisation (Art. 59). Neither its description ("The flag of the organisation is red with two white fields and with a triangle in the middle") nor its symbolism have a clear meaning. The date May 7th was declared a holiday of the organisation. In his memoirs, Shakir Pashov explained that the celebration of this date began in 1934 when the Gypsies laid a wreath on the grave of Redzheb Yuseinov, a longtime Vice-President of the organisation *Istikbal*. Since then, it has become a tradition for the Gypsies in Sofia to celebrate this date. However, he intentionally omitted to mention the fact that May 7 was the first day after St Gheorghe's day. This is when all Gypsies in Sofia (mostly Muslims) traditionally visit the cemetery to honour their deceased relatives. The fact that the Stature did not explicitly mention St Gheorghe's day, but only the date May 7, which was declared a holiday of the organisation, reveals an unwillingness to publicly acknowledge religious affiliation in the new conditions of the communist rule.

The Gypsy organisation was established with the blessing of the new government. In 1945, the Central Committee of the Bulgarian Workers' Party (Communists) discussed and adopted a series of reports on individual national minorities. The report on the Gypsy minority promoted the establishment of a Gypsy organisation that will "facilitate the educational, cultural ... and political struggle" among them (CDA, f. 1 Б, op. 25, a.e. 71, p. 5; Стоянова, 2017, p. 40). However, this does not mean that the organisation was a creation of the Communist party because the same report explicitly stated that "the initiative to organise the Gypsies comes from themselves" and emphasised that "our Communist comrades believe that such an organisation will allow them to keep the Gypsies under their influence" (Ibid.). The organisation's documents were probably not checked by the authorities (or the authorities did not pay much attention to them), which explains the presence in the Statute of the idea of a Gypsy nation-state and a World Gypsy Movement, which subsequently did not appear anywhere in the historical sources of that time.

The Statute of the organisation *Ekhipe* was to be adopted by the Second National Conference, which, however, had not been scheduled (Art. 61). Eventually, the conference did not take place, and "at a meeting" in 1946, it was decided that the mandate of the organisation's leadership would be extended "to emphasise the trust that this committee enjoyed in the Gypsy circles" as Shakir Pashov underlined in his manuscript. This meeting also made a decision about the publication of the newspaper *Romano esi* (Gypsy Voice), with Shakir Pashov as Editor-in-chief and Sulyo Metkov, Tair Selimov, Mustafa Aliev (later known as Manush Romanov), Hyusein Bilyalov and others as members of the Editorial Board.

The Statute of the organisation *Ekhipe*, at least formally, presented it as non-partisan and not tied to any political forces. However, Shakir Pashov himself, who re-established his membership in the hitherto illegal Communist Party (its official name at the time was Bulgarian Workers' Party – Communists), and after September 9, 1944, repeatedly emphasised in his memoirs that under his leadership, the organisation actively supported the state policy pursued by the Fatherland Front government.

The newspaper *Romano esi* started with state support and its first issue was printed out on the February 25, 1946. The newspaper was declared an organ of the United Cultural and Educational Organisation of the Gypsy Minority in Bulgaria, and its Editor-in-chief was Shakir Pashov. The newspaper reported that the Statute of the organisation was approved by the Minister of Interior, Anton Yugov, and the permission for the newspaper was given by the Minister of Propaganda, Dimo Kazasov (Романо еси, 1946c, p. 2). Its lead article was Yusein Bilyalov's speech on Radio Sofia, on January 14, on the occasion of St Basil's Day, "the national Gypsy holiday", with which the Blyalov made a de facto political proclamation on behalf of the organisation. The article described the hard life of the Gypsies in the past and the struggles of their organisation (the author implied organisation *Istikbal* without mentioning its name) for their civil rights and welcomed the civil liberties and social equality brought to them by the Father Front government.

Indicative of the spirit of the time is the end of the article:

> Long live the Fatherland Front! Long live the founder of the Fatherland Front, Georgi Dimitrov! Long live the allied peoples of the USSR, the United States and England! Long live the brave patriotic Fatherland Front's Army! Long live the People's Republic of Yugoslavia and Marshal Tito! Long live the Leader of the Soviet people, Generalissimo Stalin! Baxtalo tumaro Vasili! Happy St Basil's day! (Романо еси, 1946b, p. 1).

Active agitation in support of the Fatherland Front government continued to be a leading line in all subsequent issues of the newspaper *Romano esi*.

Meanwhile, the Communist Party continued to strengthen its power in the country; the parliamentary elections for the Grand National Assembly and the new constitution of the country were scheduled for October 1946. On August 4, 1946, an extended conference of the Gypsy organisation was held, which included "all chairmen representing various professional associations" (CDA, f. 1 Б, op. 6, a.e. 235, l. 5). In the minutes, the organisation was designated as the 'United Organisation of the Gypsy Minority for the Fight against Fascism and Racism'. There is no information whether the conference had adopted such a title change (most probably not); the newspaper *Romano esi* continued publication until 1948 as a body of the United Cultural and Educational Organisation of the Gypsy Minority in Bulgaria, and in this period, both the new and the old names were used in different combinations. The stamp on the document with the decision of the conference had the name 'All-Gypsy Cultural Organisation – Sofia' and depicted a five-pointed star with 1945 written as its founding year (Ibid., l. 4).

The conference emphasised that the Fatherland Front was "the only defender of the national minorities" and the proposed inclusion of a Roma community representative as a candidate in the Fatherland Front's election ballot for the Grand National Assembly. The delegates of the conference voted for three candidates in a secret vote. Shakir Pashev received 7 votes from 14 delegates; Tair Selimov and Hyussein Bilyalov received 3 votes each, and one ballot was declared invalid (Ibid.). It is noteworthy that the conference minutes were signed by 15 people, including a single Christian name (B. Naydenov) among all Muslim names. Presumably, a representative of the Fatherland Front participated in the conference, and the entire event was previously coordinated with the Fatherland Front (most likely on the initiative of the Gypsies themselves). The proposal for the conference was discussed in the District Committee of the Communist Party. According to the records from this discussion, Shakir Pashov's past activity as a member of the Communist party had not been as flawless and heroic as he himself presented it. For example, the records noted that after his two arrests (in 1923 and 1925), "he became somewhat frightened", or in 1931, when he was offered to as a Gypsy representative to become a candidate of the Workers' Party (Ibid., l. 9) for the municipal elections in 1931, "he promised to cooperate, but subsequently became frightened" (Ibid., l. 9). Nevertheless, the District Committee concluded that, "if it comes to electing a candidate from among the Gypsy minority, there is no one more suitable than him", and "from his inclusion in the Grand National Assembly as Member of Parliament, the Party will only benefit because this will raise the Party in the eyes of the Gypsy minority and … and will help the party strike roots [there]" (Ibid., l. 9–10).

In the Grand National Assembly elections, Shakir Pashov was placed at the bottom of the election ballot, and he was not elected. This mistake was corrected three months later, on February 28, 1947, at a meeting of the highest collective Party organ, the Politburo of the Central Committee of the Bulgarian Workers' Party (Communists). The issue was discussed as a second point on the agenda (usually, the items were ranked in order of importance). The decision of the Politburo on this issue reads:

> 2. Comrade Dimitar Ganev [who was appointed ambassador to Romania – authors note] should resign as an MP. Comrades Grigor Vrabchenski and Hristina Bradinska, who come right after him on the ballot, should quit, so that comrade Shakir Pashev (a Gypsy) could enter the Grand National Assembly. (CDA, f. 1Б, op. 6, a.e. 235, l. 1).

Apparently, the comrades in question had accepted the proposal (a possible refusal would have meant the end of their Party career), and Shakir Pashov became a regular member of the Grand National Assembly, which, at the end of the same year, adopted the new Constitution of the People's Republic of

Bulgaria (the so-called Dimitrov's Constitution). As an MP (using the possibilities that this position offered), he started vigorous work for the development of the Gypsy movement. In this regard, he used the support (and the administrative resources) of the ruling political coalition of the Fatherland Front (de facto of the Communist Party). In 1947, the National Committee of the Fatherland Front issued Circular No. 18, which ordered: "Cultural and educational associations of the Gypsy minority should be formed in all district and city centres with the full assistance of the district and city committees of the Fatherland Front" (Романо еси, 1947d, p. 2). Shakir Pashov himself enormously contributed to the establishment of these associations as subdivisions of the United Cultural and Educational Organisation of the Gypsy Minority in Bulgaria: "He constantly travelled in the remotest parts of the country to lift the spirits of the Gypsy minority and to get acquainted with the needs of our compatriots, who feel great joy from his presence among them" (Романо еси, 1948c, p. 1). For about a year, more than 90 Gypsy organisations had been established in the country (CDA, f. 1 Б, op. 8, a.e. 596, l. 61); in some places, such as the town of Shumen, there were two Gypsy organisations, one of which was named [Shakir] Pashov Gypsy Cultural and Educational Organisation (Демирова, 2017, pp. 70–72).

Along with the work for establishing and strengthening local Gypsy organisations in the country, Shakir Pashov was tasked with helping to solve various problems among the Gypsy population in his capacity as an MP. Such was the case in Ruse, where there were tensions after the refusal on the part of the local Turks to allow the participation of Gypsies in the management of the Muslim religious community properties (ASR, f. Shakir Pashov, a.e. Autobiography). Shakir Pashov has been familiar with this problem since the 1920s and 1930s. Another problematic case that required his intervention, together with another local MP, took place in the village of Golintsi (Ibid.). The details of this case are not known, but in all probability, the problems were related to the local Gypsies, who established their own Gypsy Baptist Church in the 1920s (Славкова, 2007, pp. 78–81; Marushiakova & Popov, 2021, pp. 152–153).

The lead direction in Shakir Pashov's work and the work of the organisation's leadership at the time was strengthening the unity of the Gypsy community, regardless of its internal heterogeneity. The very first edition of the newspaper *Romano esi*, wrote in the celebration speech on the occasion of the Gypsy holiday, St Basil's day, the following:

> There are still bad manifestations and irregularities in our organisational life in the relations between Christian Gypsies and Muslim Gypsies, but we hope that the power of the Fatherland Front will help us overcome some old understandings; eliminate the obstacles created by reactionaries in our circles; and work for

> the cultural raising of the Gypsies and the success of Bulgaria of the Fatherland Front. (Романо еси, 1946b, p. 1).

This theme was present on the pages of the newspaper also in later editions, taking on distinctly ethnic dimensions. For example, in 1947, Sakir Pashov addressed the readership of the newspaper, calling "those people among our compatriots who hide under the name of Bulgarians or Turks, to take off their masks and join our organisation to raise it to a higher level, because they are Gypsies by blood, they should not hide but respond to the invitation of our organisation, because they are responsible to their conscience" (Романо еси, 1947a, p. 1).

The only exception to this leading discourse is the attitude towards the Gypsy nomads:

> There are Gypsies among us, whom we despise, and who deserve despisal, and those are the nomadic Gypsies (wanderers) who do not have permanent residence and depend on their wives, who do palmistry, fortune-telling, and theft. That is why it is time for our country to deal with this issue as soon as possible and to take timely measures to limit the vagrancy (wanderings) and those [of them] wishing to settle to be provided with land and involved in useful community service. (Романо еси, 1946d, p. 2).

This attitude towards the nomadic Gypsies should not come as a surprise. In the process of Roma civic emancipation in the period between the two World Wars, throughout the region of Central, South-Eastern and Eastern Europe, the new Roma civic elite shared a similar attitude to the problem of Gypsy nomadism. Moreover, the Gypsy activists in the USSR had been calling on the Soviet state to sedentarise the Gypsy nomads for several decades (Marushiakova & Popov, 2020c, pp. 265–276). Ultimately, this idea found its realisation through the Decree of the Presidium of the USSR Supreme Council in 1956, followed over the years by more or less similar measures in all countries in the region of the so-called "Socialist Camp" (Marushiakova & Popov, 2008b).

As an MP, Shakir Pashov also put a lot of effort into the development of education and social and cultural life in the Gypsy neighbourhoods. In 1947, he managed to get special funding of over 3 million levs for the construction of a school in the Fakulteta neighbourhood. He personally made the first sod in the construction of the new building (ASR, f. Shakir Pashov, a.e. Autobiography) of the First Gypsy School, named after the famous Soviet pedagogue Anton Makarenko (AKRDOPBGDSRSBNA, f. 13, op. 1, a.e. 759, l. 145; Стоянова, 2017, p. 157–158). The adjective 'Gypsy' indicates that the school educated Gypsy children, but according to its program, it provided mainstream education. In the following years, such 'Gypsy Schools' were open in different places in the country – Varna, Berkovitsa, Sliven, Kyustendil, Lom, etc. (AKRDOPBGDSRSBNA, f. 13, op. 1, a.e. 759, l. 145). Similarly, the Gypsy Community Clubs established in the neighbourhoods developed various forms of social and cultural life – lectures for political education, literacy courses for adults, music and dance theatre groups, etc. (Стоянова, 2017, pp. 204–205). In Sofia, in 1946, the Sports society *Naangle* (Forward) was established (actually re-established) with its own football team. A photo of Shakir Pashov with the team has been preserved (ASR, f. Photos). The first official match between Gypsy teams in our country was played at the *Yunak* stadium in Sofia in 1947, with the two Gypsy teams of *Naangle* (Sofia) and *Boyan Chonos* (Vidin) playing against each other.

At that time, there was a serious debate among Gypsy activists, for which there is almost no historical evidence. An undated photograph shows six Gypsy young men holding a large poster with the inscription "Gypsy Alphabet". The graphics of the letters are obviously original creations of the authors, five of whom have their names written on the photograph: Tseko, Kune, Sulyo, Yashko and Yashar (ASR, f. Photos). We were able to identify with certainty only two of them, namely Sulyo Metkov and Yashar Malikov, while the rest remained unknown. In 1947, a short announcement was made on the pages of the newspaper *Romano esi* that the "draft of the Gypsy alphabet" would be published in the next issue of the newspaper and that grammar and dictionary of the Gypsy language were currently being developed (Романо еси, 1947c, p. 2). The same issue of the newspaper published Nikola Terzobaliev's polemical article, entitled *Is It Necessary to Have a Gypsy Minority Organisation* (Романо еси, 1947b, pp. 1–2), according to which "some of our compatriots question the use of having an [Gypsy] organisation if we do not have an alphabet" (and for Terzobaliev himself "the script is not our goal"). In the next issue of the newspaper, however, there is not a word on the subject of the Gypsy alphabet. It can be assumed with a high degree of probability that the idea of creating a written language of the Gypsies did not find support from the authorities supervising the organisation.

Shakir Pashov was especially proud of his role in the creation of the Gypsy theatre, to which he devoted a lot of space in his memories. The theatre united several music-, dance- and theatre-groups, which were based at the neighbourhood community centres in Sofia in 1947 (ASR, f. Shakir Pashov, a.e. Autobiography). It was set up after the direct intervention of the Communist Party and State leader Georgi Dimitrov, with whom Shakir Pashov had an old friendship:

> In 1923, during the elections for members of parliament, comrade Georgi Dimitrov, who was one of the candidates, visited the ballot boxes of the 3rd District Polling Station [...]. In a moment, the opposition group attacked him with fists, but our party group, which was there as agitators, immediately intervened, and we took comrade Dimitrov out of their hands as other comrades also came on the spot. We accompanied them to the tram, and he said to me, "Shakir, one day, when we come to power, you will be the greatest man, and for me, from the train station to the Palace, they will lay a carpet". When the glorious date, September 9, 1944, came and this came true, I became a Member of the Grand National Assembly, nourished by the ideas of the Party, because I had spent my whole life fighting for the victory of the Marxist ideas and in anti-fascist activities since 1919, and it is the same until today. (Ibid.).

Shakir Pashov visited Georgi Dimitrov in his office and proposed to him to create a Gypsy theatre modelled on the famous *Romen* Gypsy Theatre in Moscow, about which the newspaper *Romano esi* published a large article (Романо еси, 1946e, p. 1). Georgi Dimitrov was immediately ignited by this idea and ordered the allocation of 2 million levs in the budget with which the Central Gypsy Theatre *Roma* was established, with director Shakir Pashov (Ibid.). Under his leadership, the theatre presented its first performance, the play *Gypsy Rhapsody* by the Bulgarian writer Alexander Gerginov, in Sofia, in the spring of 1948 (Ibid.).

This is not the first Gypsy theatre in Bulgaria. A photo with the caption "Founders of the 1st Gypsy Theatre Group. Sliven. 24.03.1927" is preserved (ASR, f. Господин Колев). Written on the back of the photo are the names of the founders (12 men and 10 women) and the theatre directors (leaders), Ivan Kratsov and Yordan Chorapchiyata. It was obviously an amateur troupe which used to organise literary and musical social events (Сливенска поща, 1930, p. 2) and occasionally did theatrical performances, such as -- to name a few of them, the plays *Prodigal Son* (Сливенска поща, 1932, p. 2) *Golgotha* (Циганите, 1992, p. 7), and *Ruined Life* (Изток, 1941, p. 4).

The activity of the Gypsy theatre in Sliven was integrated with that of the Gypsy Community Centre based in the so-called *Gorna Mahala* (Upper Neighbourhood) in the city of Sliven in 1928 (Andral, 2000, p. 11; 2001, p. 96). In February 1939, the community centre was named *Knyaz Simeon Tarnovski* (Prince Simeon Turnovski) after the Bulgarian heir to the throne (Изток, 1939, p. 1). However, this renaming should not mislead us – at the centre of both Gypsy institutions (community centre and theatre) was the same circle of people who were closely connected with the youth Communist movement in Sliven at that time (see Marushiakova & Popov, 2022).

However, there are some differences in the repertoire of the two Gypsy theatres in Sofia and in Sliven. Before 1944, the Sliven theatre presented plays with a moralising character, which were widely distributed in the repertoire of amateur theatres in Bulgaria during that era, the purpose of which was to educate the Gypsies on the basic norms of social life. The premiere play, *Gypsy Rhapsody*, of the Sofia theatre was with an ethnic character. It was a free dramatic interpretation of Alexander Pushkin's famous poem *Gypsies*, combined with many Gypsy songs and dances (from today's point of view, the play would probably be criticised for exoticising the Gypsies). As a side note, its screenwriter Alexander Gerginov is known for being the first Bulgarian writer who made a successful business of literary work (Бенбасат, 2016, pp. 18–26). His novel *The Girl from the Gypsy Cabaret* (a typical boulevard reading) has undergone several editions and is perhaps the book with the highest print run in Bulgarian literature before 1944 (Ibid.).

After its establishment, the Central Gypsy Theatre *Roma* performed with great success for two months in the capital, and then, in the summer of the same year, it made a tour visiting various cities – Plovdiv, Stara Zagora, Yambol, Sliven, Burgas, Shumen, Tolbuhin (now Dobrich) and Varna –, and everywhere was greeted enthusiastically by the local audience (Пашов, 1957, pp. 127–128). Despite the successful tour, due to unresolved financial issues, Shakir Pashov had to give his watch and a golden ring in a pawnshop in the city of Varna to be able to buy train tickets so that the artists and musicians could go home (CDA, f. 1 Б, op. 8, a.e. 596, l. 37; Дром дромендар, 1998, p. 3). According to some testimonies (Дром дромендар, 1998, p. 3), at that time, Shakir Pashov wrote the theatre play *The White Gypsy Woman*, but it has not been discovered so far. Also, according to the memoirs of his contemporaries and his heirs, he wrote poems which have not been discovered either.

Shakir Pashov's success in the field of Roma civic emancipation, however, had a side effect that can be understood in the spirit of the times, given the specific historical context. In the second half of the 1940s, the so-called cult of the personality of Stalin already dominated in the USSR, and this model was transferred to other countries of Central and South-Eastern Europe with Communist parties in power, in which the personality cult for the local Communist leaders appeared. Expectedly, these processes trickled down to the lower levels, which resulted in a personality cult for Shakir Pashov's personality in the circles of Gypsy activism. This is most visible in the newspaper *Romano esi*, whose editor-in-chief was Shakir Pashov. The newspaper published texts (usually with solemn words and congratulations on various holidays) written by Shakir Pashov himself (Романо еси, 1948b) as well as articles dedicated to his personality such as "Leader and Teacher" of the Gypsies, who will "trace the path for our Nation" (Романо еси, 1948a, p. 2). Poems in his honour were also published, one of which ends with the words:

Long live Stalin, Tito, Dimitrov,
And the comrade [Shakir] M[ahmudov] Pashov! (Романо еси, 1948d, p. 4).

This poem gave rise to a widely known literary (and historical) mystification. In one of his books, the famous Bulgarian poet, satirist and dissident Radoy Ralin (pseudonym of Dimitar Stoyanov, 1922–2004) published a poem written by himself, the authorship of which he attributed to Shakir Pashov (Ралин, 1987, pp. 125–126). The text of Radoy Ralin's poem is interwoven with fragments of two naive poetic texts dedicated to Shakir Pashov (passage from which is quoted above), written by Sadak Ismailov and Aliya Ismailov from the village of Popitsa, district of Byala Slatina (Ibid.). We can only make guesses about Radoy Ralin's motives for this blatant falsification; the result, however, was a serious blow to Shakir Pashov's public image. Moreover, nowadays, this text continues to be actively used for mocking not only Shakir Pashov himself but also the Gypsies in general (see, for example, 168 часа, 2016), i.e. its public effect remains the same.

In 1948, there was a crisis in the Gypsy movement. The first signs of it appeared in the previous year with the publication of Nikola Terzobaliev's article *Is It Necessary To Have a Minority Organisation of Gypsies* in the newspaper *Romano esi*. The title indicated serious controversies among the Gypsy activists, not so much questioning the existence of such an organisation, but rather what it should do (Романо еси, 1947b, pp. 1–2).

These contradictions among the Gypsy activists were reflected in the results of the National Conference of the United Cultural and Educational Organisation of the Gypsy Minority in Bulgaria, held on May 2, 1948. The conference confirmed the organisation's commitment to the policy of the Fatherland Front, which at that time had already been transformed from a political coalition into a popular public organisation led by the Communist party. The close connection with the Fatherland Front had unexpected consequences both for the Gypsy organisation and for Shakir Pashov himself. The National Conference elected an Initiative Committee headed by Mustafa Aliev, with the mandate to lead the activities of the Gypsy minority until the First Congress of the organisation (which never took place). This change had obviously been planned in advance, as suggested by the fact that the issue of the newspaper *Romano esi*, published on the eve of the conference (Романо еси, an. 3, No. 10, April 30, 1948), included an Editorial Board with members Mustafa Aliev, Tair Selimov and Sulyo Metkov, in addition to the Editor-in-chief, Shakir Pashov. At the conference, it was also decided that the Theatre *Roma* would be under the direct control of the Minority Committee at the Fatherland Front's National Council (CDA, f. 1 Б, op. 8, a.e. 596, l. 63). These developments introduced two power centres in the Gypsy movement (Shakir Pashov and the Initiative Committee), which engaged in a fierce struggle against each other. The struggle involved submissions to various institutions with accusations against the opponents and the corresponding rebuttals. This led to a financial audit of the Theatre *Roma* (whose management was repeatedly changed and eventually taken over by Shakir Pashov's opponents), followed by a comprehensive audit of the organisation's activities, and in some cases, there were even physical fights (Ibid., l. 40; AKRDOPBGDSRSBNA, f. 13, op. 1, a.e. 774, l. 26–27).

The immediate reason for the mutual accusations had to do with the financial and artistic problems of the Theatre *Roma*; however, much bigger differences in the vision about the Gypsy movement transpired behind it. According to the inspection by the National Council of the Fatherland Front, there were two currents in the Gypsy organisation, one of which was headed by Shakir Pashov, and "the other current was led by young Communists who ruthlessly and unsystematically criticised his actions" (CDA, f. 1 Б, op. 8, a.e. 596, l. 62).

These "young Communists", affiliated with the Primary Party Organisation *Saliko* of the Bulgarian Communist Party, 3rd district, Sofia, sent a statement to the Regional Committee of the Party, with a copy to the Central Committee of the Party, accusing Shakir Pashov of disseminating among the Gypsies the "chauvinistic slander" that the new management of the Theatre *Roma* had "handed it over to the Bulgarians" (ibid.). The statement was, in fact, signed by the Secretary of the Gypsy minority's Party Organisation *Saliko*, Tair Selimov, as well as by the members of its leadership Lyubomir Aliev (former Mustafa Aliev, future Manush Romanov), Sulyo Metkov, Angel Blagoev and A. Osmanov (Ibid., l. 41).

The accusations against Shakir Pashov were an integral part of the file on the two "warring groups" in the Gypsy organisation, and on this grounds the State Security began an active investigation of Shakir Pashov, under the codename 'Durak' ('fool' in Russian) (AKRDOPBGDSRSBNA, f. 13, op. 1, a.e. 774, l. 27–28). In the course of this investigation, other allegations were added to his file. The most serious one was that an inspection of the documentation at the former police directorate revealed that in 1930, after his return from Turkey, Shakir Pashov had signed a declaration of cooperation with the police, and that during the Second World War he had assisted the authorities with the forced labour mobilisation of Gypsies from Sofia, showing them which Gypsies to be mobilised (CDA, f. 2124 К, op.1, a.e. 108107, l. 2). He was also accused of leading the Muslim organisation *Istikbal*, which had allegedly served the interests of Turkey, according to the authorities, as well as organising the Gypsies to give homage to the deceased Tsar Boris III at his funeral, in 1943 (AKRDOPBGDSRSBNA, f. 13, op. 1, a.e. 774, l. 27). A special focus in the accusations against Shakir Pashov was given to his actions as leader of the Gypsy organisation after 1945 and Member of Parliament when he allegedly pursued a "nationalist policy among the Gypsy minority" (CDA, f. 2124 К, op.1, a.e. 108107, l. 2). In addition, his file included an allegation that as an MP he issued state secrets and handed them over to Nikola Petkov supporters (Nikola Petkov was the leader of the opposition to the government of the Fatherland Front, hanged in 1947), which was not supported by any evidence (CDA, f. 2124 К, op.1, a.e. 108107, l. 2).

Shakir Pashov's attempts to defend himself and change the course of events were unsuccessful. He kept sending statements to various institutions (CDA, f. 1 Б, op. 8, a.e. 596) and at the same time was trying to secure the support of the Roma community; according to the State Security data, he sent over 160 letters to the Gypsy organisations in the country (AKRDOPBGDSRSBNA, f. 13, op. 1, a.e. 774, l. 30). However, these efforts proved futile. In the autumn of 1949, the City Committee of the Bulgarian Communist Party excluded Shakir Pashov from the Party (CDA, f. 1 Б, op. 8, a.e. 596, l. 1; Стоянова, 2017, p. 400). In the parliamentary elections on December 18, 1949, Shakir Pashov was not included in the election ballots; Petko Kostov Yankov from Sliven was elected in the National Assembly as a representative of the Gypsies (Personal communication with Gospodin Kolev, March 14, 2004).

In his memoirs, Shakir Pashov described the subsequent changes in the leadership of the Gypsy organisation:

> There were dissatisfied members of the minority, and unfortunately, young ones, pretending to have a higher culture. They undermined the general enthusiasm and planted a bomb under the feet of this activity to destroy everything that had been created so far, with so much effort. In 1950, in July, under pressure from these dissatisfied young people and to prevent a cleavage in our circles, the Sofia organisation and the Central Committee of all [local] organisations were ceded to the dissatisfied young people. The same, of course, happened with the Theatre *Roma*. (Пашов, 1957, p. 131).

Historical sources, however, reveal a quite different course of these events. On April 7, 1950, the Central Directorate of the Cultural and Educational Organisation of the Gypsy Minority in Bulgaria decided:

> The leadership of the Gypsy minority punishes Shakir Pashov by removing him from the post of Chairman of the Cultural and Educational Organisation of the Gypsy Minority in Bulgaria for his anti-people activity before September 9, 1944, as a police collaborator and for destructive activity after that date and excludes him from the ranks of the organisation forever. (AKRDOPBGDSRSBNA, F. 13, op. 1, a.e. 774, l. 30).

The general assembly of the Gypsy National Community Centre *9th September*, held on April 15, 1950, chaired by Lyubomir Aliev, condemned Shakir Pashov's activity as "harmful" to the Gypsy minority (Нево дром, 1953c, p. 3). This decision was publicly announced on May 2, 1950, on the front page of the newspaper *Nevo drom* (New Way) with Editor-in-chief Lyubomir Aliev, which succeeded the newspaper *Romano esi* as the organisation's publication. The same edition also announced that comrade Nikola Petrov Terzobaliev from the town of Sliven (for more details, see Marushiakova & Popov, 2022, pp. 81–89) had been elected as the new Chairman of the Gypsy organisation (Нево дром, 1950a, p. 1).

After the removal of Shakir Pashov, the fate of the United Cultural and Educational Organisation of the Gypsy Minority in Bulgaria is an unhappy one. The end of the organisation was predestined by the recommendations of the Fatherland Front's National Council representative following the inspection of the Theatre *Roma* in 1948. These recommendations proposed a complete structural change in the organisation involving the transformation of the Central Initiative Committee into a Minority Commission at the Fatherland Front's National Council, "to be instructed and led directly by the Fatherland Front's National Council". The same transformation applied to the district and city structures of the organisation. The Theatre *Roma* was to be placed under the direct authority of the Minority Commission and Fatherland Front's National Council (CDA, f. 1 Б, op. 8, a.e. 596, l. 62–63). The "young Communists" had their own contribution to the reformation (and de facto liquidation) of the Gypsy organisation, as illustrated by an extensive report written by Tair Selimov in 1950 in his capacity of instructor at the Fatherland Front's National Council. This report almost literally reproduced the recommendations of the Fatherland Front's National Council representative (AKRDOPBGDSRSBNA, f. 13, op. 1, a.e. 759, l. 147–148).

After the absorption of the local Gypsy organisations as Fatherland Front's sections, the logical outcome was that they were no longer identified as local "Gypsy" organisations but rather as territorial subdivisions of the Fatherland Front. This ultimately led to the end of the Gypsy organisation itself. Symbolically, the latest issue of the organisation's newspaper *Nevo drom* was the one that published the news about the removal of Shakir Pashov as leader of the Gypsy organisation.

The fate of the Gypsy theatre was similar. By Decision № 389 of November 25, 1949, the Secretariat of the Central Committee of the Bulgarian Communist Party proposed that the Central Gypsy Theatre *Roma* should continue its activities (there was also a proposal to disband it), but with the status of a "semi-professional" theatre as part of the system of the neighbourhood community centres (at that time organised on an ethnic basis) (CDA, f. 1 Б, op. 8, a.e. 596, l. 1–2). Thus, the theatre was transferred to the Gypsy National Community Centre *9th September* in Sofia, where his last production was *The Last Camp* by Vano Khrustalyov (a play from the Theatre Romen's repertoire) in 1950 (Нево дром, 1950b, p. 4). The new production that was underway, Ivan Rom-Lebedev's play *Heroic Poem* (Ibid.), was never realised, and in the early 1950s, the theatre gradually ceased to exist; its director Lyubomir Aliev took back his old name (Mustafa) and started working as a theatre director in the Turkish theatres in the towns of Haskovo and Kardzhali.

At that time, Shakir Pashov was under constant surveillance by the State Security (AKRDOPBGDSRSBNA, f. 13, op. 1, a.e. 759), and on September 10, 1951, he was interned in the concentration camp (officially 'Labour and Educational Dormitory') on Belene island, on the Danube, where he remained until August 10, 1953. (CDA, f. 2124 К, op. 1, a.e. 108107, l. 2). Despite the difficult conditions, he managed to survive thanks to his ironwork skills. According to the memories of his family, he was tasked with the maintenance of the tools used by the prisoners (mainly hoes), which secured slightly better conditions for him.

According to Shakir Pashov's file at the Ministry of Interior, the investigation of his alleged collaboration with the police was terminated, and on August 10, 1953, he was released from the concentration camp in Belene but was not rehabilitated (Ibid., l. 1–4).

After his return to Sofia, Shakir Pashov focused on the preparation of his book *History of the Gypsies in Bulgaria and Europe: Roma* published in this edition. The manuscript is dated 1957. The text is divided into separate chapters, and the logic of the internal structure is not always understandable. The style of the manuscript is generally uniform, but the presence of several more or less distinct segments, each with its own specific characteristics, is clearly visible.

It is interesting to note that for the first time in Bulgaria, he used the self-appellation of the community, Roma, in the title of the manuscript (although it is not clear why he put this part of the title in inverted commas). Throughout the text, however, Shakir Pashov adhered to the term 'Gypsies' ('цигани' in Bulgarian), which was common at the time and was used by the Roma themselves.

The first clearly visible segment of the manuscript is devoted to the origin, language and early history of the Gypsies. In this part, one can see the influence of the Bulgarian scholar Dr Nayden Sheytanov. He published the article *Contribution to the Speech of the Sofia Gypsies* (Sheytanov, 1932), and in 1955 submitted for review the manuscript of his book *Gypsies in Bulgaria: Materials on Their Folklore, Language and Way of Life* to the Ethnographic Institute with

Museum at the Bulgarian Academy of Sciences. This manuscript includes a Preface by Tair Selimov Tairov, who signed it as a "deputy of the working people at the Sofia City People's Council", i.e. representative at the municipal council of Sofia. After discussion, the Academic Council of the Ethnographic Institute with Museum at the Bulgarian Academy of Sciences decided not to publish the manuscript but to purchase it for its archive, where it can be found today (AIEFEM, No. 295 II; it was partially published in Марушиакова & Попов, 1994, pp. 18–48).

The part of the manuscript mentioned above is not entirely Shakir Pashov's original work. A significant number of texts are a repetition or (more often) paraphrase of parts or separate pages of Nayden Sheytanov's manuscript. They contain numerous references to scientific publications dedicated to the early history and language of the Gypsies in various foreign languages, which Shakir Pashov did not speak and could not have read independently. This fact notwithstanding, it would not be accurate to say that the manuscript is not Shakir Pashov's author's work. On the contrary, the entire composition of the text, with the selection of excerpts or citations from other authors, clearly shows that Shakir Pashov has thought through (in all probability in collaboration with Nayden Sheytanov himself) his author's text.

Nayden Sheytanov's influence on Shakir Pashov could also be perceived in another aspect. This is the radical change of Shakir Pashov's view about the origin of the Gypsies. In the 1920s and 1930s, Shakir Pashov adhered to the Egyptian theory. It was widespread in Bulgaria among the majority population and the Gypsies at that time. As can be seen from the newspaper *Terbie*, the historical narrative of the Roma at that time was still dominated by the "Egyptian version" of their origin, which is why they defined themselves as "descendants of the Great King Pharaoh." (Мир, 1934, p. 3). Gradually, the Gypsies (or at least some activists among them) became familiar with the factology of modern scientific knowledge about the Indian origin of the Gypsies. In the late 1940s, in a public speech, Shakir Pashov expressed his naive concept of Gypsy origin. It was based on etiological legends spreading among the Gypsies in Berkovitsa at the time: "Our minority lived in Bulgaria since the seventh century, where our ancestors were settled by the then world leader of the Gypsies, Berko, a dangerous opponent of the Indian Emperor Abdurrahman." (Романо еси, 1948b, p. 2). In his manuscript from 1957, Shakir Pashov already had adopted the modern concept of the Indian origin of the Gypsies, which was well known to Dr Nayden Sheytanov. This concept is presented extensively in his manuscript, although he made a compromise and tried to combine the two concepts by presenting Egypt as a "temporary station through which [the Gypsies] passed and travelled onward to Europe." The modern concept of Indian origin was widely spread among the Gypsies in the 1950s, under the influence of the first wave of Indian films shown in Bulgaria at that time.

The second clearly noticeable segments in Shakir Pashov's manuscript are the chapters dedicated to the traditional occupations (blacksmiths), way of life and folklore of the so-called Agupti (i.e. Egyptians) living in the Eastern Rhodopes. These parts are an almost verbatim transcript of Atanas Primovski's extensive study that had been already published. (Примовски, 1955).

Undoubtedly, the third distinguishable segment is the most interesting. It is Shakir Pashov's narrative about the origin and development of the Gypsy movement for civil emancipation in the first half of the twentieth century. It will not be an exaggeration to say that Shakir Pashov himself was the founder and primary driver of this process (at least from 1919 onwards). From this point of view, his book is significant not only as a historical source but also as the first attempt to understand and explain this movement from the position of an active participant in it. In this part, the book provides a reflection on historical circumstances "from the inside", from the community's point of view.

It is not possible to define the mechanism of cooperation between Shakir Pashov and Dr Nayden Sheytanov in the preparation of the book *History of the Gypsies in Bulgaria and Europe: Roma*. There is no doubt, however, that this was one of the first attempts for collaborative and reciprocal cooperation, which is very fashionable nowadays (Gay y Blasco & Hernández, 2020). It is difficult to understand Dr Nayden Shaytanov's motives for this cooperation, while Shakir Pashov's motives are quite straightforward. He was hoping that this book would provoke public (and political) rehabilitation of his overall activity in the Gypsy movement. Hence his attempts to create a narrative of the movement's history (even at the cost of omitting or manipulatively interpreting some facts) that would be accepted positively by the ruling Communist regime in Bulgaria.

Shakir Pashov sent his book to the Central Committee of the Bulgarian Communist Party for evaluation and approval. There was no response (or at least it is not known), and the manuscript sank into the party archives and remained unpublished. Nevertheless, Shakir Pashov received partial rehabilitation. He started working at the Gypsy National Community Centre *9th September*, chaired by Tair Selimov at the time (Неве рома, 1957a, pp. 1–2). In this capacity, he organised the amateur Roma Art and Music Group, led by Yashar Malikov, in 1956. In this way, he restored the Gypsy Theatre in a different form. In the same year, Shakir Pashov became a member of the Editorial Board of the newspaper *Neve Roma* (New Gypsies), which started to be published as the organ of the Gypsy National Community Centre *9th September* in the following year (Ibid., p. 137). Separate parts of his book appeared in the newspaper

(Неве рома, 1957c, p. 4; 1957f, p. 4). In the Brick Factory neighbourhood (or mahala Boyana), where he lived, Shakir Pashov organised the *Roma* Sports Sector (Неве рома, 1957d, p. 4). He also organised a Gypsy musical and artistic evening in the *Petar Beron* cinema. At a large meeting of young Gypsy activists, which was held in the Gypsy National Community Centre *9th September*, Shakir Pashov spoke about his memories from the early stages of the Gypsy movement, and after that, all participants laid a wreath at the Mausoleum of Georgi Dimitrov (Неве рома, 1957e, p. 1).

Soon thereafter, however, Shakir Pashov faced serious problems once again. The newspaper *Neve Roma* published an article, entitled *Do We Need an Organisation Now?* authored by Demir Shankov from Lom, a medical student in Sofia. The newspaper's Editorial Board proposed a meeting to discuss the article with the Gypsies at the grassroots level (Неве рома, 1957b, p. 1–2). At the end of 1957, the newspaper published Demir Shankov's report at the meeting "in connection with the restoration of the Gypsy cultural and educational organisation" (Неве рома, 1957g, p. 1). Apparently, this event was not coordinated with the institutions and approved by them because there has been no mention of a Gypsy organisation in the public space ever since.

The newspaper *Neve Roma* was discontinued, and in 1959 a new Gypsy newspaper, *Nov pat* (New Way), published by the National Council of the Fatherland Front, began to be issued instead. On the one hand, this undoubtedly increased the status of the Gypsy newspaper. On the other hand, the newspaper lost its independence and came under the direct control of the authorities. The newspaper has been published for 30 (sic!) years, even during the so-called Revival process (the forcible change of the "Turkish" names of Turks, Muslim Bulgarians and Roma with "Bulgarian" in the mid-1980s). Thus, it was the longest-running Roma periodical worldwide to date.

Following a letter from the Central Committee of the Bulgarian Communist Party, the Ministry of Interior started investigating Shakir Pashov in connection with this case. In 1959, the work on the case was terminated, and his file was finally closed (CDA, f. 2124 К, op. 1, a.e. 108107). However, he and his wife were expelled from Sofia to the village of Rogozina, in Dobrudzha, without the right to move to another place.

Shakir Pashov and his wife lived in the village of Rogozina for three years, from 1959 to 1962. A photograph of their stay there has been preserved, showing that they lived in a small, poor house, apparently in difficult conditions (ASR, f. Photos). According to the memories of Shakir Pashov's heirs, during this stay, his good command of the Turkish language and his ironmonger's skills greatly helped him. He made beds with iron springs, which he sold to the local Turks, who paid him with gold coins, and the family returned to Sofia with significant savings.

After Shakir Pashov returned to Sofia, he retired. In the late 1960s, due to the expansion of the capital city, the Gypsy mahala Boyana (neighbourhood Brick Factory) was eliminated, and its inhabitants were compensated with new apartments. Shakir Pashov moved to live in the newly built Druzhba Housing Complex (then Station Iskar). At his new residence, Shakir Pashov continued to be socially active, and for many years, served as a chairman of the local Fatherland Front organisation (ASR, f. Shakir Pashov, a.e. Autobiography).

At the same time, he fought for rehabilitation from his Party. In 1967, Shakir Pashov's membership in the Bulgarian Communist Party was restored (ASR, f. Shakir Pashov). However, the book *The Gypsy Population in Bulgaria on the Path of Socialism* (one of the authors of which is Tair Selimov Tairov), published in 1968, does not mention his name (Генов et al., 1968). His name reappeared in the public space, in 1974, in an article dedicated to him in the newspaper *Nov pat* (New Way), a Gypsy newspaper, which was published by the National Council of Fatherland Front (Нов път, 1974). In 1976, Shakir Pashov received the title "Active Fighter against Fascism and Capitalism", which gave him the right to a special pension as well as many other social privileges.

Shakir Pashov died on October 5, 1981, shortly before his 83rd birthday. There were no media reports about his death, and according to the memories of his relatives, only his relatives and a small number of close friends were present at his funeral; in front of his grave, Manush Romanov (Mustafa/Lyubomir Aliev) publicly asked forgiveness from the diseased. However, in his report, Gospodin Kolev, an instructor in the Central Committee of the Bulgarian Communist Party, reveals a different picture of Shakir Pashov's funeral. He wrote that there were about 130–150 Gypsies from all neighbourhoods of Sofia at the funeral. In the ritual hall, a representative of the Bulgarian Communist Party neighbourhood organisation, in which Shakir Pashov was a member, delivered a speech emphasising his merits in the fight against fascism and capitalism and for the happiness and prosperity of all his proletarian brothers, without mentioning his ethnic origin. In his speech, Mustafa Aliev called the deceased "Our Father"; he stressed that his life as a communist and a fighter for the happiness of the people would be an example for the living and that his work would live on. Before the body was laid in the grave, there was a ritual according to the dogmas of Islam – the corpse was washed, and at the grave, a hodja (imam) performed the appropriate prayer. Tair (already re-named Tihomir) Tairov also spoke at the grave, outlining Shakir Pashov's activities as the founder of the progressive movement of the Gypsies in Bulgaria and emphasising that throughout his life, he was faithful to the work of the Bulgarian Communist

Party and worked actively for the happiness and prosperity of all Bulgarian people (CDA, f. 16, op. 89, a.e. 139, l. 44–45).

One year after Shakir Pashov's death, a memorial obituary was published (according to the customs in South-Eastern Europe, such obituaries are displayed in public places). The obituary depicts a drawing of Shakir Pashov with clear symbolism – he is depicted sitting behind a desk, with a pipe in his mouth, behind him a bookshelf, on the desk in front of him a telephone, the manuscripts of four newspapers (*Terbie, Romano esi, Nevo drom* и *Neve Roma*), and the inscription *History of the Gypsies*. In contrast to customary practice, the obituary does not indicate on whose behalf it was issued, and this mystery remains unsolved to date. Supposedly, it was done by some of his closest collaborators. The text on it is as follows:

> Today, November 5, 1982, marks one year after the death of SHAKIR MAHMUDOV PASHOV. Let everyone remember the organiser of the Gypsy cultural and educational organisation in Bulgaria, the creator of the newspaper *Romano esi*. For the founder of the Central Gypsy Theatre *Roma*. For the communist-anti-fascist and fighter against capitalism and fascism. For the first Gypsy MP in the Grand National Assembly. For the man with the big heart.
> A bow! (ASR, f. Shakir Pashov).

Shakir Pashov lived a long and eventful life; he had passed through many vicissitudes and sometimes even oscillated in different directions. Invariable remains only the leading pillar in his social and political activity – the work for his community and the strife to steer and lead the community to its complete civic emancipation.

Elena Marushiakova and Vesselin Popov

References

Archives

AIEFEM. Архив на Института за етнология и фолклористика с Етнографски музей при Българска академия на науките (Archive of the Institute of Ethnology and Folklore Studies with the Ethnographic Museum at the Bulgarian Academy of Sciences): No. 295 II.

AKRDOPBGDSRSBNA. Архив на Комисия за разкриване на документите и за обявяване на принадлежност на български граждани към Държавна сигурност и разузнавателните служби на Българската народна армия (Archive of the Commission for Disclosure of Documents and for Declaring the Affiliation of Bulgarian Citizens to the State Security and Intelligence Services of the Bulgarian People's Army): f. 13, op. 1, a.e. 759; f. 13, op. 1, a.e. 774.

ARIM Sliven. Архив на Регионален исторически музей – Сливен (Archiv of the Regional History Museum – Sliven): Inv. No. 1437.

ASR. Архив на Дружество за изследване на малцинствата *Студии Романи* (Archive of the Minorities Studies Society *Studii Romani*): f. Gospodin Kolev; f. Photos; f. Shakir Pashov.

CDA. Централен държавен архив – Държавна агенция "Архиви" (Central State Archive – Archives State Agency): f. 1 B, op. 6, a.e. 235; f. 1 B, op. 8, a.e. 596; f. 1 B, op. 25, a.e. 71; f. 1 B, op. 28, a.e. 6; f. 16, Op. 89, a.e. 139; f. 264 K, op. 2, a.e. 8413; f. 264 K, op. 2, a.e. 9385; f. 264 K, op. 5, a.e. 1109; f. 370, op. 6, a.e. 745; f. 2124 K, op. 1, a.e. 108107.

DA Sliven. Държавен архив – Сливен (State Archive – Sliven): f. 879, op.1, a.e. 27.

DA Sofia. Държавен архив – София (State Archive – Sofia): f. 1 K, op. 2, a.e. 831; f. 1 K, op. 4, a.e. 531; f. 1 K, op. 4, a.e. 683.

Media

168 часа. (2016, April 10). Бутовски И. Героичните подвизи на първия ромски депутат.

Вечерна поща. (1905a, December 14). Радев, С. Конгрес на циганите в България.

Вечерна поща. (1905b, December 20). [No Author]. Цигански конгрес [– Първо заседание].

Вечерна поща. (1905c, December 21). [No Author]. Цигански конгрес – Второ заседание.

Дром дромендар. (1998, November). Колев, Г. Първият.

Държавен вестник. (1901, June 30). Закон за изменение на избирателния закон.

Държавен вестник. (1919, December 3). Закон за изменение и допълнение на някои членове от избирателния закон.

Изток. (1939, April 30). [No Author]. Подкрепете читалището ни!

Изток. (1941, February 23). [No Author]. Културна дейност в циганската махала.

Мир. (1934, May 5). Шейтанов, Н. Циганите и циганския въпрос.

Неве рома (*Нови цигани*). (1957a, January 14). Селимов, Т. Народното ни читалище и неговите задачи.

Неве рома (*Нови цигани*). (1957b, January 14). Шанков, Д. Необходима ли ни е сега организация?

Неве рома (*Нови цигани*). (1957c, May 1). Пашов, Ш. М. За произхода на циганите.

Неве рома (*Нови цигани*). (1957d, May 1). [No Author]. Хроника.

Неве рома (*Нови цигани*). (1957e, July 13 юли). Демчо. По пътя на Димитров.

Неве рома (*Нови цигани*). (1957f, July 13). Ш. П. Циганите в България.

Неве рома (*Нови цигани*). (1957g, December 19). [Шанков, Д.] Доклад.

Нево дром (*Нов път*). (1950a, May 1). [No Author]. [No Title].

Нево дром (*Нов път*). (1950b, May 1). От профкомитета при театъра. Театър "Рома" посреща Първи май с нови постижения.

Нево дром (*Нов път*). (1950c, May 1). Тасев, А. Годишно-отчетно събрание събрание на циганското читалище "9 септември" в София премина под знака на критиката и самокритика.

Нов път. (1974, November 1). Вапирев, И. Неспокоен човек. Очерк.

Отвътре / Andral / Inside. (2000, No. 7). [No Author]. [No Title].

Отвътре / Andral / Inside. (2001, No. 17–18). [No Author]. [No Title].

Празднични вести. (1937, January 11). [No Author]. Циганите ще се организират. Подетата иницатива. Изникналите пречки.

Романо еси. (1946a, February 25). [Билялов, Х.] Из живота на софийската мюсюлманска изповедна община – София.

Романо еси. (1946b, February 25). [No Author]. Слово по случай народния празник на циганското малцинство в България Св. Василий.

Романо еси. (1946c, February 25). [No Author]. Хроника.

Романо еси. (1946d, Mart 28). [No Author]. Из живота на нашите сънародници цигани в България.

Романо еси. (1946e, Mart 28). Яшко. Циганският театър "Ромен".

Романо еси. (1946f, May 1). Йолов, М. Г. Циганите от с. Голинци са стояли и стоят здраво на поста си.

Романо еси. (1947a, February 1). [Пашов, Ш.] Слово.

Романо еси. (1947c, February 1). Терзобалиев, [Н.] Необходимо ли е да имаме малцинствена организация на циганите.

Романо еси. (1947d, February 1). [No Author]. [No Title].

Романо еси. (1947e, September 9). Общо културно-просветна организация на циганското малцинство в България. Окръжно № 1. До всички околийски и градски комитети на Отечествения фронт.

Романо еси. (1948a, January 14). Николов, Вл. Г. Може би чудо!

Романо еси. (1948b, January 14). [Пашов, Ш.] Слово.

Романо еси. (1948c, January 14). Сотиров, Я. Кратки биографически бележки.

Романо еси. (1948d, April 30). Исмаилов, А. Цигани.

Сливенска поща. (1930, January 23). [No Author]. Хроника.

Сливенска поща. (1932, February 11). [No Author]. Хроника.

Циганите. (1992, December). [No Author]. Ромски театър преди 65 години.

Gypsy Newspapers

Newspaper *Светилник* [Candlestick]. Newspaper of the Evangelical Baptist Mission among the Gypsies in Bulgaria. Lom. Editor: Pastor Petar Minkov. An. 1, No. 1, January 15, 1927. In Bulgarian. Supplement *Романо алав* (Roma Word) in Romani language.

Newspaper *Bulletin of the Gipsies Mission in Bulgaria. Народът, който се нуждае от просвета чрез Евангелието* [Bulletin of the Gypsies Mission in Bulgaria: The People that Needs Enlightenment through the Gospel]. Sofia. No. 1, September 1932. In Bulgarian.

Newspaper *Известия на Циганската евангелска мисия* [Bulletin of the Gypsy Evangelical Mission]. Sofia. No data for No.No. 1, 2; No. 3, June 3, 1933. In Bulgarian.

Newspaper *Тербие* [Upbringing]. Newspaper of the Mohammedan National Cultural-Educational Organisation. Editor: Shakir M. Pashev. From No. 6: Newspaper of the Common Mohammedan National Cultural-Educational Union in Bulgaria. Editorial Board: Shakir Makhmudov Pashev (Editor-in-chief), Asen Gogov and Demir Yasharov. Sofia. No data for No.No. 1, 3, 4, 5; No. 2, February 27, 1933; No. 7, May 6, 1934. In Bulgarian.

Newspaper *Романо еси* (Gypsy Voice). Newspaper of the United Cultural and Educational Organisation of the Gypsy Minority in Bulgaria. Sofia. Editor: Shakir M. Pashev. An. 1 (1946), No.No. 1, 2, 3, 4 [No. 5 is missing]; An. 2 (1947) No.No. 6, 7, 8; An. 3 (1948–1949), No.No. 9, 10, 11. In Bulgarian.

Newspaper *Нево дром* (New Way). Newspaper of the Cultural and Educational Organisation of the Gypsy Minority in Bulgaria. Sofia. Editor: Lubomir Aliev. An. 1 (1949), No. 1–2; An. 2 (1950), No. 3. In Bulgarian.

Newspaper *Неве рома* (New Gypsies). Newspaper of the Gypsy People Reading Club *September 9* – Sofia. Editorial Board: [no names]. An. I (1957), No.No. 1, 2, 3, 4, 5, 6, 7, 8, 9, 10–12. In Bulgarian.

Newspaper *Нов път* (New Way). Newspaper of the National Council of the Fatherland Front. Sofia. Editorial Board [changing over the years, last Editor-in-chief Stoyanka Sokolova]. An. 1 – 30 (1959–1988). In Bulgarian.

Bibliography

Bataillard, P. (1872). Les derniers travaux relatifs aux Bohémiens dans l' Europe orientale. *Revue critique*, 2 (5): 191–218, 277–323. Paris: A. Franck.

Bataillard, P. (1875a). Sur les origines des Bohémiens on Tsiganes. *Bulletins de la Société d'anthropologie de Paris*, II° Série, 10: 546–557.

Bataillard, P. (1875b). Les Tsiganes de l'âge du bronze. *Bulletins de la Société d'anthropologie de Paris*, II° Série, 10: 563–595.

Bataillard, P. (1876). État de la question de l'ancieneté des Tsiganes en Europe. *Congrés international d'anthropologie. 8 Session* (pp. 321–385). Budapest: Franklin-Társulat.

Bataillard, P. (1878). *Les Zlotares dits aussi Dzvonkars. Tsiganes fondeurs en bronze et en laiton dans la Galicie orientale et la Bukovine.* Extrait des *Mémoires de la Société d'anthropologie de Paris*. Paris: Ernst Leroux.

Boué, A. (1840). *La Turquie d'Europe; ou, Observations sur la géographie, la géologie, l'histoire naturelle, la statistique, les moeurs, les coutumes, l'archéologie, l'agriculture, l'industrie, le commerce, les gouvernements divers, le clergé, l'histoire et l'état politique de cet empire.* Tome 6. Paris: A. Bertrand, 1840.

Brown, I. H. (1922). *Nights and Days on the Gypsy Trail: Through Andalusia and on Other Mediterranean Shores*. New York and London: Harper & Brothers.

Brown, I. H. (1924). *Gypsy Fires in America: A Narrative of Life among the Romanies of the United States and Canada*. New York and London: Harper & Brothers.

Dixon, W. H. (1872). La Russie libre. *Le tour du monde – nouveau journal des voyages*, No.No. 600–604.

Encyclopædia Britannica. Eleventh Edition. (1910–1911). London: Horace Everett Hooper.

Gaster, M. (1883). Ţigani ce si au mancât biserica. *Revista pentru istorie*, 1 (1): 469–475.

Gay y Blasco, P. & Hernández, L. (2020). *Writing Friendship: A Reciprocal Ethnography*. Cham, Switzerland: Palgrave Macmillan.

Gilliat-Smith, B. (1912). *E Devléskoro sfjato lil. E Ísus-Xristóskoro džiipé thai meribé e sfjatoné Lukéstar*. London: British and Foreign Bible Society.

Gilliat-Smith, B. J. (1945). Two Erlides Fairy-Tales. *Journal of the Gypsy Lore* Society, Third Series, 24 (1): 17–26.

de Goeje, M. J. (1903). *Memoire sur les migrations des Tsiganes à travers l'Asie*. Leide: E. J. Brill.

Hasse, J. G. (1803). *Zigeuner im Herodot, oder neue Aufschlüsse über die ältere Zigeuner-Geschichte: aus griechischen Schriftstellern*. Königsberg: Göbbels u.a.

Hovelacque, A. (1874). Crânes Tsiganes. Bulletins de la Société d' anthropologie de Paris, 2 (9): 396–398.

Ješina, P. J. (1886). *Romáňi čib, oder Die Zigeuner-sprache (grammatik, wörterbuch, chrestomathie)*. Leipzig: List & Francke.

Kanitz, F. (1882–1887|. *Donau Bulgarien und der Balkan: historisch-geographisch-ethnographische Reisestudien aus den Jahren 1860–1879*. Band 1–2. Leipzig: Renger'sche Buchhandlung.

de Kogalnitchan, M. (1837). *Esquisse sur l'histoire, les moeurs et la langue des Cigains, connus en France sou le nom de Bohémians; suive d'un recueil de sept cents mots cigains*. Berlin: Librairie de B. Behr.

Kopernicki, I. (1872). Über den Bau der Zigeunerschädel. Vergleichend. Kraniologische Untersuchung. *Archiv für Anthropologie, Völkerforschung und kolonialen Kulturwandel*, 5: 267–324.

Kovacheva, L. (2000a). *O rom dzhanel o drom*. Sofia: SCORPION

Kovacheva, L. (2000b). *Rom know the way*. Delhi: Kafla.

Krantz, A. (1580). *Germanicarum historici clariss. Saxonia: de Saxonicæ gentis vetusta origine, longinquis expeditionibus susceptis & bellis domi pro libertate diui fortiterq[ue] gestis*. Francofurti ad Moenum: A. Wechelumis.

Leland, Ch. G. (1924). *The Gypsies*. Boston & New York & Houghton: Mifflin Company.

Liszt, F. (1859). *Des Bohémiens et de leur musique en Hongrie*. Paris: Librairie Nouvelle – A. Bourdilliat.

Marinov, A. G. (2020). Images of Roma through the Language of Bulgarian State Archives. *Social Inclusion*, 8 (2): 269–304.

Marinov, A. G. (2021). Bulgaria. In R. B. Roman, S. Zahova & A. Marinov (Eds.) *Roma Literature and Press in Central, South-Eastern and Eastern Europe from 19th Century until the Second World War* (pp. 35–57). Leiden: Brill & Paderborn: Ferdinand Schöningh.

Marushiakova, E. & Popov, V. (1997). *Gypsies (Roma) in Bulgaria*. Frankfurt am Main: Peter Lang.

Marushiakova, E. & Popov, V. (2001). *Gypsies in the Ottoman Empire*. Hatfield: University of Hertfordshire Press.

Marushiakova, E. & Popov, V. (2008b). State Policies under Communism. In *Information Fact Sheets on Roma History*. Strasbourg: Council of Europe. Retrieved from http://www.coe.int/t/dg4/education/roma/histoCulture_en.asp.

Marushiakova, E. & Popov, V. (2009). Gypsy Slavery in Wallachia and Moldavia. In T. Kamusella & K. Jaskulowski (Eds.) *Nationalisms Today* (pp. 89–124). Oxford: Peter Lang.

Marushiakova, E. & Popov, V. (2011). 'Whom belong this Song?' How to research Romani Culture on the Balkans. *International Journal of Romani Language and Culture*, 1 (1): 54–65.

Marushiakova, E. & Popov, V. (2015a). Identity and Language of the Roma (Gypsies) in Central and Eastern Europe. In: T. Kamusella, N. Motoki & C. Gibson (Eds.) *The Palgrave Handbook of Slavic Languages, Identities and Borders* (pp. 26–54). London: Palgrave.

Marushiakova, E. & Popov, V. (2015b). The First Gypsy/Roma Organisations, Churches and Newspapers. In M. Kominko (Ed.) *From Dust to Digital: Ten Years of the Endangered Archives Programme* (pp. 189–224). Cambridge: Open Book Publishers.

Marushiakova, E. & Popov, V. (2016a). Gypsy Guilds (Esnafs) on the Balkans. In: H. Kyuchukov, E. Marushiakova & V. Popov (Eds.) *Roma: Past, Present, Future* (pp. 76–89). München: Lincom Academic Publishers.

Marushiakova, E. & Popov, V. (2016b). Roma Culture: Problems and Challenges. In E. Marushiakova, & V. Popov (Eds.) *Roma Culture: Myths and Realities* (pp. 35–64). München: Lincom Academic Publishers.

Marushiakova, E. & Popov, V. (2017). Commencement of Roma Civic Emancipation. *Studies in Arts and Humanities*, 3 (2): 32–55.

Marushiakova, E. & Popov, V. (2020). 'Letter to Stalin': Roma Activism vs. Gypsy Nomadism in Central, South-Eastern and Eastern Europe before WWII. *Social Inclusion*, 8 (2): 265–276.

Marushiakova, E. & Popov, V. (Eds.) (2021). *Roma Voices in History: A Source Book. Roma Civic Emancipation in Central, South-Eastern and Eastern Europe from 19th Century until the Second World War*. Leiden: Brill & Paderborn: Ferdinand Schöningh.

Marushiakova, E. & Popov, V. (Eds.) (2022). *Roma Portraits in History: Roma Civic Emancipation Elite in Central, South-Eastern and Eastern Europe from the 19th Century until World War II*. Leiden: Brill & Ferdinand Schöningh.

Mui Shuko [R. A. Scott Macfie]. (1916). *With Gypsies in Bulgaria*. Liverpool: Henry Young & Sons.

Obédénare, M. (1875). Sur les Tsiganes de la Roumanie. *Bulletins de la Société d'anthropologie de Paris*, 10: 597–603.

Paspati, A. G. (1870). *Études sur les Tchinghianés ou Bohémiens de l'Empire Ottoman*. Constantinople: A. Koroméla.

Pennell, E. R. (1893). *To Gipsy Land*. New York: The Century Co.

Pott, A. F. (1845). *Die Zigeuner in Europa und Asien. Ethnographisch-linguistische Untersuchung, vornehmlich ihrer Herkunft und Sprache, nach gedruckten und ungedruckten Quellen*. Teil I: *Einleitung und Grammatik*. Teil II: *Einleitung über Gaunersprachen, Wörterbuch und Sprachproben*. Halle: E. Heynemann.

Roman, R. B., Zahova, S. & Marinov, A. (Eds.) *Roma Literature and Press in Central, South-Eastern and Eastern Europe from 19th Century until the Second World War*. Leiden: Brill & Paderborn: Ferdinand Schöningh.

Shoemaker, H. W. (1924). *More Allegheny Episodes: Legends and Traditions, Old and New, Gathered among the Pennsylvania Mountains*. Altoona, Pa.: Mountain City press, Times-tribune company. Retrieved from https://catalog.hathitrust.org/Record/002705841.

Shoemaker, H. W. (1925). *The Tree Language of the Pennsylvania German Gypsies*. An address by Henry W. Shoemaker at the Clio Club, Williamsport, Pa., December 2, 1925. Retrieved from https://openlibrary.org/works/OL3967802W/The_tree_language_of_the_Pennsylvania_German_Gypsies.

Sinclair, A. T. (1915). *An American-Romani Vocabulary*. New York: The New York Public Library.

Sinclair, A. T. (1917). *American Gypsies*. New York: The New York Public Library.

Vulcanius, Bonaventura. (1597). *De literis & lingua Getarum, Sive Gothorum. Item de Notis Lombardicis. Quibus accesserunt Specimina variarum Linguarum, quarum Indicem pagina quæ Præfationem sequitur ostendit*, Leiden: Editore Bon. Vulcanio Brugensi, Lugduni Batavorum, Ex officina Plantiniana, Apud Franciscum Raphelengium.

***

Боров, С. П. А. (1870). Цигани. *Читалище*, 1 (6): 190–191.

Венелин, Ю. И. (1840). *Влахо-Болгарские или Дако-Славянские грамоты*. Санкт Петербург: Тип. Императорской Российской Академии.

[No Author]. (2014). Галерия "Лоранъ". Социалистическо или Тоталитарно изкуство. Retrieved from http://www.galleryloran.com/archive/news/socialistichesko-ili-totalitarno-izkustvo.

Демирова, Д. (2017). *Циганско/Ромско движение в Шумен. История и съвременност*. Дисертация. София: ИЕФЕМ – БАН.

Генов, Д., Таиров, Т. & Маринов, В. (1968). *Циганското население в НР България по пътя на социализма*. София: НС на ОФ.

Димов, В. (2005). Към изследване на записаната музика в България от първата половина на XX век: архиви и колекции. *Българско музикознание*, 1: 144–171.

[No Author]. (1923). *Дневник (стенографски) на XIX-то Обикновено народно събрание*. Трета редовна сесия. LIV редовно заседание, сряда, 21 февруари 1923 г. София: Народно събрание.

Захариев, С. (1870). *Географико-историко-статистическо описание на Татар-Пазарджишката кааза*. Виена: Л. Соммер и С-ие.

Зихровски, Х. (1956). *Индия без воал*. София: Отечествен фронт. [Bulgarian translation of Sichrovski, H. (1954). *Dschai Hind Indien ohne Schleier*. Wien: Globus Verlag]

Илиева, Н. (2012). Брой на ромската етническа група в България от Освобождението (1878 г.) до началото на XXI в. според Преброяванията (първа част). *Проблеми на географията*, 3–4: 61–79.

Иречек, К. (1876). *Исторія Болгар*. Одесса: Типография Л. Нитче.

Иречек, К. (1899). *Княжество България.* Част II. *Пътувания по България.* Пловдив: Христо Г. Данов.

Каназирски-Верин, Г. (1947). *София преди 50 години.* София: Българска книга.

Керим, У. *Песни от катуна. Стихотворения.* София: Български писател, 1955.

Керим, У. *Очите говорят. Стихове.* София: Български писател, 1959.

Ковачева, Л. (2000). *Ромът знае пътя. // O rom dzhanel o drom.* София: SCORPION.

Ковачева, Л. (2003). *Шакир Пашов. Апостолът на ромите в България. 1898–1981. // Shakir Pashov. O apostoli e romengoro. 1898–1981.* София: КХАМ – Слънце.

Ковачева, Л. (2020). *Фамилия Ковачеви, гр. Кюстендил.* София: Арт Медиа плюс.

Колев, Г. (2003). *Един циганин в ЦК на БКП. Преживелици, терзания, размисли.* София: Вини 1837.

Колев, Г. (2010). *Българската комунистическа партия и циганите през периода 1944–1989 г.* София: Център за публични политики.

[No Author]. (1945). *Конституция на Българското царство.* София: Държавно книгоиздателство.

Костенцева, Р. (1979). *Моят роден град София преди 75 години и после.* София: Отечествен фронт.

Марков. А. (1947). Нови документи по историята на северните павликяни. *Истина*, No. 1100.

Марушиакова, Е. & Попов, В. (1993). *Циганите в България.* София: Клуб '90.

Марушиакова, Е. & Попов, В. (Eds.) (1994). *Студии Романи. // Studii Romani.* Том 1. София: Клуб '90.

Мизов, Б. (2006). *Българските цигани (бит, душевност, култура).* Том 1–2. София: Авангард.

Младенов, С. (1927). *Увод в общото езикознание.* София: Художник.

Нягулов, Б. (2007). За историята на циганите/ромите в България (1878–1944 г.). In В. Топалова & А. Пампоров (Eds.) *Интеграцията на ромите в българското общество* (pp. 24–42). София: Институт по социология.

Нягулов, Б. (2012). Циганите/ромите. In Г. Марков (Ed.) *История на България.* Том 9. *1918–1944* (pp. 664–573). София: Тангра ТаНаКра.

Пашов, Ш. М. (1957). *История на циганите в България и Европа. "Рома".* София. Ръкопис. ASR, f. Shakir Pashov, a.e. Manuscript. 216 pp.

Попов, Р. (1991). *Светци близнаци в българския народен календар*, София: БАН.

Примовски, А. (1955). Ковачите агупти в гр. Мадан. *Известия на Етнографския институт с музей*, 2: 217–261.

Радев, С. (1994). *Ранни спомени.* София: Стрелец. [2nd ed.]

Ралин, Р. (1987). *Кадровикът Теофраст. Сатирични есета.* Пловдив: Христо Г. Данов.

[No Author]. (1932). *Сомнал евангелие (кетапи) (лил) Матеятар.* Накае дасиканестар романе чибате А. Атанасакиев. София: Американско Библейско дружество & Британско и чуждестранно Библейско дружество.

[No Author]. (1937). *Сомнал евангелие (кетапи) катаро Иоан.* Накае дасиканестар романе чибате А. Атанасакиев. София: Американско Библейско дружество & Британско и чуждестранно Библейско дружество.

[No Author]. (1901). *Стенографски дневници на XI Обикновено Народно събрание, I Извънредна сесия, LVIII заседание, 28 май 1901 година.* София: Народно събрание.

Стоянов, З. (1966). Социализмът в България. In Стоянов, З. *Съчинения.* Том 3. *Публицистика* (pp. 213–220). София: Български писател.

Стоянова, П. (2017). *Циганите в годините на социализма. Политиката на българската държава към циганското малцинство.* София: Парадгима.

Тахир, О. (2020). 122 години от рождението на Шакир Пашов – Апостолът на ромското движение в България. Retrieved from https://romastandingconference.org/122-godini-ot-rojdenieto-na-shakir-pashov-apostolut-na-romskoto-dvijenie-v-bulgaria/.

Тенев, Д. (1997). *Тристахилядна София и аз между двете войни.* София: Български писател.

[No Author]. (1910). *Устав на Египтянската народност в гр. Видин.* Видин: Божинов и Конев.

Шейтанов, Н. (1932). Принос към говора на Софийските цигани. *Известия на Етнографския музей,* 10–11: 227–254.

Шейтанов, Н. (1941). Произход и история на циганите. *Български народ,* 1: 79–81.

List of Illustrations

Cover: Gypsy demonstration in front of the National Assembly after September 9, 1944. The photo, in all probability, was shot in the early autumn of 1944 because the painting by Vasil Evtimov, which was painted after this manifestation (see above, page 222), is dated 1944. ASR, f. Photos.

On p. 22 is the title page of Shakir Pashov's manuscript

1. Caricature by an unknown author. *Вечерна поща*, December 21,1905, p. 1.
2. Caricature by Aleksandar Lambov. *Вечерна поща*, December 17, 1905, p. 1. The 'Sakantiya' (from the Turkish 'sakın'– do not) was the public nickname of Dr Marko Markov and in this case, it was used in the sense of 'trouble-maker'. The expression "Anlanda sivri sinek sandur – Anlamayana daul da zurna azdur" is a Turkish proverb "For the one who understands, even the mosquito is a *saz* (musical instrument), for the one who does not understand, both the drum and the zurna are not enough".
3. Cover of *The Statute of the Egyptian Nationality in the Town of Vidin* (Устав, 1910). The seal of the organisation is placed on the cover of the Statute.
4. Shakir Pashov as a soldier in the Bulgarian army during the First World War. ASR, f. Photos (courtesy of Lilyana Kovacheva).
5. Participants in the Constituent Congress of the Union of Gypsy Musicians. Sofia, 1920. ASR, f. Photos (courtesy of Lyudmila Zhivkova).
6. Gypsy Evangelical Baptist Church in Golintsi village (today Mladenovo district in Lom). *Светильник / Svetilinic* (Chișinâu), 1934, No.No. 6–7, p. 3.
7. Inscription on the back of the photo: "Photo of a group of Gypsy members of the RMS [Workers' Youth Union] – 1924. First row seated – 1. Todorka Doncheva. 2. Stefanka Panayotova. 3. [unknown]. 4. Sotirka Doncheva. 5. Kurti Dechev – the child. 6. Radka Kurteva. 7. Todor Ruschev. Standing women – 1. Sofka Pencheva. 2. Siyka Petrova" (ARIM Sliven, Inv. No. 1437). There is an obvious dating error in this description, because the Workers' Youth Union was established in 1928, i.e. the picture is not earlier than this year.
8. Inscription on the back of the photo: "The photo was taken [in] 1921 with a section of young Komsomol members from the neighbourhood, with the newspaper *Mladezhka iskra* (Youth Spark). From left [to right] standing are G. Nedev, Mihail Hristov, At. Vasilev, Mikhail Golemanov, Petar Todorov, Dimitar Vasilev. Sitting Veliko Nikolov, N[ikola] Terzobaliev, Kosta Marinov, Rusko Yovchev" (State archive – Sliven, f. 879, op.1, a.e. 27, l. 4). In this description, there is also an obvious error in the dating because the newspaper *Mladezhka iskra*, which is a printed organ of the Workers' Youth Union, began to be published in 1928, i.e. the photo was taken not earlier than this year.

9. Photo in the journal *Отвътре / Andral / Inside*, 2000, No. 7, p. 11. Explaining the photography: "Management of the chitalishe (community reading and cultural centre) *Knyaz Simeon Tarnovski*. Sliven, 1928. Standing (from left to right): Petar Takev (Takyoolu), Dimitar Budakov (Baraka), Tasho Chakmakov, Decho Kurtev (Papazoolu), Kuzman Mihalev, Krastyu Vachev. Seated (from left to right): Vasil Stambolov, Vasil Gochev, Yordan Kolev (Koloolu), Dimitar Zanzalov (Zanzala)". There is an error in the name of the *chitalishte* here, because Prince Simeon Turnovski, the Bulgarian heir to the throne, was born in 1937, and the community centre carries this name since 1939 (see above).
10. Photo in the journal *Отвътре / Andral / Inside*, 2001, No.No. 17–18, p. 96. Explaining the photography: "Management of the community centre *Knyaz Simeon Tarnovski*. Sliven, 1929. From left: Georgi Armanzov, Tasho Chakmakov, Mikhail Kuzmanov, Nikola Terzobaliev, [unknown], Mikhail Zanzalov, Vasil Chakmakov, Atanas Vasilev, Dimitar Kochev. Seated from left to right: Todor Keleshev, Gancho Vasilev, Todor Rusakiev". For the name of the community centre, see above.
11. Inscription on the photo: "Founders of the 1st Gypsy Theatre Company. March 24, 1927. Sliven". Inscription on the back of the photo: "First row seated, from left to right – Petar Vasilev, Kolinata (Nikola), Kratsov, Ivan Kratsov (director), Yordan Chorapchiatia (director), Armanzov". ASR, f. Photos (courtesy of Gospodin Kolev).
12. Inscription on the back of the photo: "Commemoration from the party USSR. May 17, 1941, Sliven. Petar Terzobaliev". Later addition: "The RMS [Workers' Youth Union's] Group in the Gypsy Quarter. 1941". ASR, f. Photos (courtesy of Gospodin Kolev, on the photo the last one in the first row).
13. Inscription on the back of the photo: "June 8–10, 1942. The Trial. The photography was taken by the police after the announcement of the verdict, on the June 10, 1942. Three of the kneeling and the first of the standing ones on the left are Gypsy members of Workers' Youth Union. The three Gypsy members of the Workers' Youth Union are Kiril Hristov, Petko Dimitrov, Kiril Kratsov (from left to right in the first row), and the last on the left in the second row is Gospodin Kolev. ASR, f. Photos (courtesy of Gospodin Kolev).
14. The exact date of the photo is uncertain, in all probability, it was taken in the first days after the September 9, 1944. The photography is from a solemn event in Sofia, perhaps the welcoming of the Soviet Army or (which is more likely) the sending of Bulgarian troops for participation in the war against Germany (the so-called Patriotic War). ASR, f. Photos.
15. Newspaper *Romano esi* (Gypsy Voice), No. 1, 1 February 1947, p. 1, with a photo of Shakir Pashov and his *Speech on the Occasion of the National Holiday of the Gypsy Minority in Bulgaria St Basil.*

Note. The illustrations also include photos that are not directly related to Shakir Pashov but reflect the spirit of the time, in particular the movement for Roma civil emancipation. The photo of Shakir Pashov's wife, Sabria, with two other women sitting on a glass of beer, we have added especially because of the increased interest currently in the subject of the double discrimination of Roma woman.

Illustrations

No. 1. Caricature of Ramadan Ali

No. 2. Caricature of Dr. Marko Markov

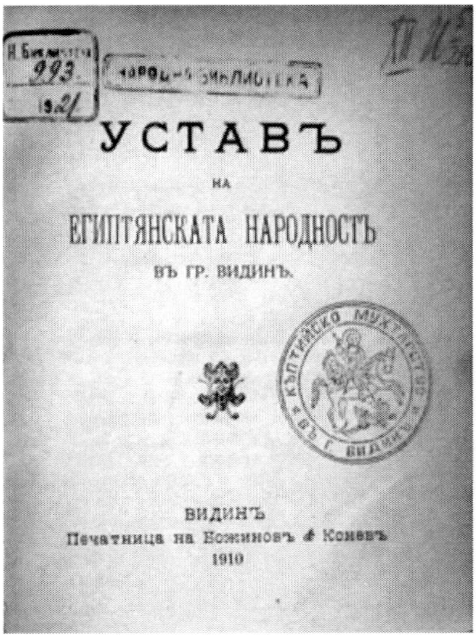
УСТАВЪ

НА

ЕГИПТЯНСКАТА НАРОДНОСТЪ

ВЪ ГР. ВИДИНЪ.

ВИДИНЪ
Печатница на Божиновъ & Коневъ
1910

No. 3. Statute of the organization in Vidin

No. 4. Shakir Pashov as a soldier in WWI

No. 5. Constituent Congress of the Union of Gypsy Musicians, 1920

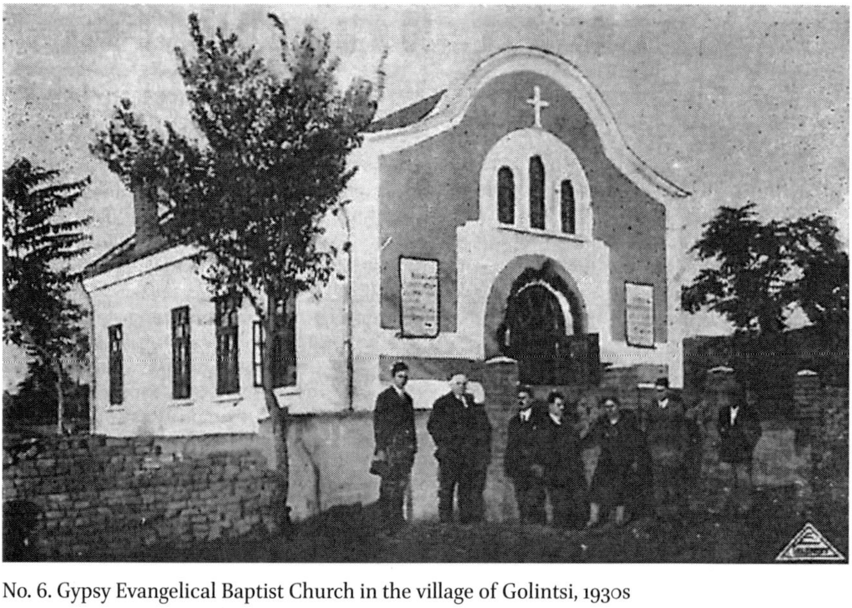

No. 6. Gypsy Evangelical Baptist Church in the village of Golintsi, 1930s

No. 7. Participants in the communist youth movement from Sliven, late 1920s

No. 8. Participants in the communist youth movement from Sliven, late 1920s

No. 9. The management of the Gypsy chitalishte in Sliven, 1928

No. 10. The management of the Gypsy chitalishte in Sliven, 1928

No. 11. First Gypsy theater in Sliven, 1927

No. 12. Young Gypsies from Sliven, members of the RMS, 1941

No. 13. Young Gypsies from Sliven, political prisoners, 1942

No. 14. Gypsy women from Sofia celebrate after September 9, 1944

ОД. I. СОФИЯ 25 ФЕВРУАРИ 1946 ГОД. БРОЙ 1

Излиза два пъти в месеца

Издава редакционен комитет

Редакция ул. Клементина 166

РОМАНО-ЕСИ

(Циган. глас)

Редактор: Ш. М. ПАШЕВ Тел. 2-17-55

Абонаменти за година 200 лева

Полугодина 100 лв.

Обяви за реклами по споразумение

Орган на общо културно-просветителна организация на циган. малцинство в България

Слово по случай народния празник на циганското малцинство в България Св. Василий

Уреденият радио-час от председателя Шак. М. Пашев по случай Народния празник на циганското малцинство в България Св. Василий 14. I. в 19 часа в студиото на радио-София. С участието на групата-музиканти „Фараоните" и певицатаЯ сиба при организацията на циг. малцинство. Словото се прочете от организатора Ю. Билялов

Драги сънародници цигани — християни и мюсюлмани!

За пръв път в България се дава такава свобода на циганското малцинство, за пръв път на нас циганите се дават пълни и равни права като граждани да участвуваме в културния, стопанския и политически живот на тази страна, която е и наша родина. И това ние можем днес да за- организираме издаването на наш вестник — „Народен будилник", вестник „Тербие", но бяхме наклеветени от наши сънародници реакционери и предатели пред страшната Дирекция на полицията. Вестникът ни беше спрян от тогавашното лъжедемократично правителство, организацията ни разтурена, а нашите ръководители разкарвани и тормозени из- ските цигани — християни и мюсюлмани.

Драги сънародници,

Народното представителство на Отечествения фронт ни даде право да възстановим нашата организация, на която сега е даден нов живот, разреши ни се да издаваме нашия будилник „Романо еси" — Цигански глас, който ще излезе в най-скоро време и ще бъде разпратен

Шакир М. Пашев

председател на циганското малцинство е роден в 1898 год. в София, през миналия период той е бил дълги години в борба за националното въздигане на своите сънародници от 1918 г. до днес, през 1933 год. бе председател на своите сънародници и редактор на вестник „Тербие" (Възпитание) и днес е редактор на в. „Романо-Еси" (циг. глас) като всички свои сили сложи за националното въздигане на своите сънародници, е упорит и с воля за преуспяването си за което и днес Отечествено-фронтовското Правителство ще подкрепи неговото голямо дело, за културно и посветно въздигане на сънародниците му.

No. 15. Newspaper Romano Esi (Gypsy Voice), 1947

No. 16. Gypsy participation in the festive manifestation on September 9, 1947

No. 17. Shakir Pashov, 1940s

No. 18. Shakir Pashov (in the middle) as a member of Parliament (1947–1949)

No. 19. Gypsy alphabet. Sofia, 1948

No. 20. Shakir Pashov as member of Parliament in Lom, 1947

No. 21. Shakir Pashov votes in the election, 1949

No. 22. Shakir Pashov receives a financial subsidy for the Gypsy Theater *Roma*, 1948

No. 23. Shakir Pashov at Gypsy conference in Sofia, 1949

No. 24. Poster for a performance of the Gypsy Theater *Roma*, 1949

No. 25. Mustafa/Lyubomir Aliyev (Manush Romanov) in the late 1940s

No. 26. Performance of the Gypsy amateur theatre *Roma* in Sofia, 1950s

No. 27. Poster of the Gypsy amateur theatre *Roma* in Sofia, 1950s

No. 28. Shakir Pashov with the Naangle football club in Sofia, 1950s

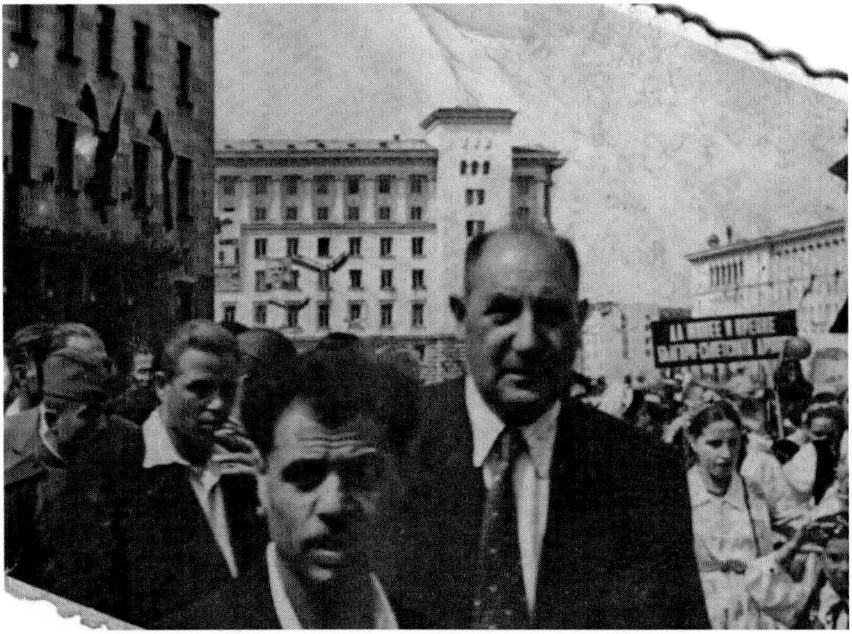

No. 29. Shakir Pashov at a festive manifestation in Sofia, 1950s

No. 30. Gypsy participation in a festive manifestation, 1950s

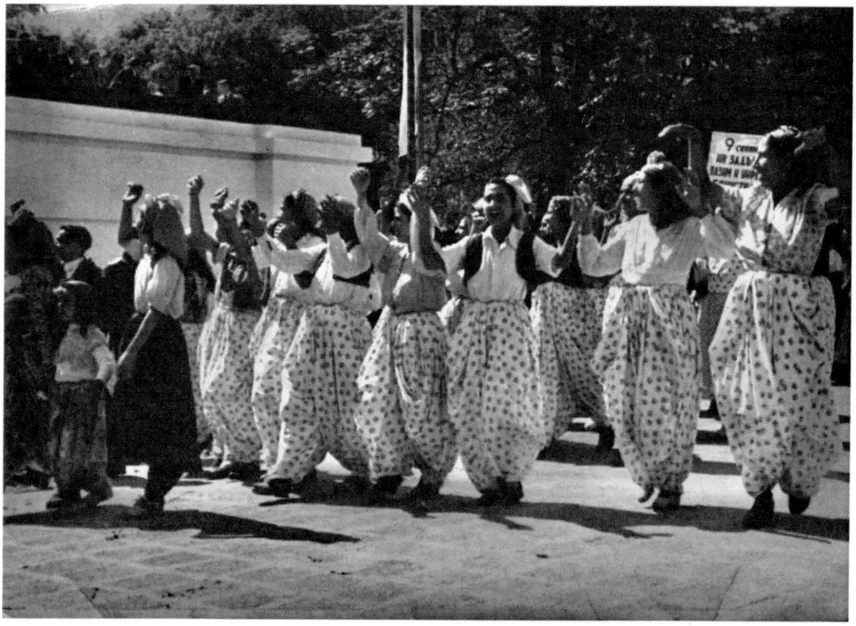

No. 31. Gypsy women in front of the tribune of the Mausoleum at a festive manifestation, 1950s

No. 32. Shock workers at the International Fair in Plovdiv, 1950s

No. 33. Shakir Pashov and his wife during his internment in the village of Rogozina (1959–1962)

No. 34. Gospodin Kolev at the Plenum of the Fatherland Front, Targovishte, 1963

No. 35. Shakir Pashov on vacation in Hisarya, 1970s

No. 36. Gypsy activist in front of the Mausoleum, 1973

No. 37. Family photograph of Shakir Pashov with his parents, 1940s

No. 38. Shakir Pashov's wife with her relatives, 1950s

No. 39. Shakir Pashov and his wife, "Brick Factory" quarter, 1950s

No. 40. Family photo of Shakir Pashov, 1960s

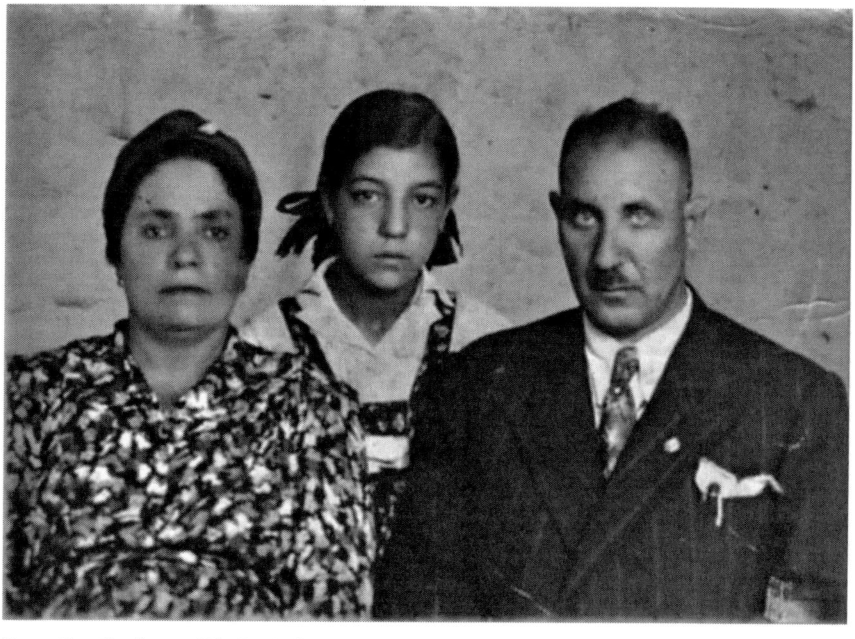

No. 41. Family photo of Shakir Pashov, 1960s

No. 42. Shakir Pashov and his wife on vacation, 1960s

No. 43. Shakir Pashov's family photography. Sofia, 1960s.

ЦК на БОРЦИТЕ ПРОТИВ ФАШИЗМА И КАПИТАЛИЗМА — БЪЛГАРИЯ

Серия С4 № 056657

Шакир Мехмедов Пашов

роден на 20.X. 1898 г.

гр. (с.) София

окръг

Саморъчен подпис

Притежателя на картата има право на:

— Пътуване с 50% намаление по железопътния, автомобилния и водния транспорт.
— Безплатно пътуване по трамвайната, тролейбусната и автобусната мрежа на градския транспорт.
— Безплатно ползуване на баните в страната.

(Постановление на ЦК на БКП и МС от 14 юли 1959 г.)

Утвърден на 2.VIII. 1976 г.
от Централния комитет на БПФК.

9.1.1977 г. Председател:

No. 44. Membership card of Shakir Pashov, 1977

No. 45. Shakir Pashov, 1981

тъжен помен

Изминаха 6 месеца от смъртта на непрежалимия ни съпруг, баща и дядо

ШАКИР МАХМУДОВ ПАШОВ

на 83 год.

Член на БКП от 1919 г. активен борец против фашизма и капитализма, редактор на вестници, депутат във Великото народно събрание, известен обществено-политически деятел до края на живота

Съпруже, тат о и дядо, ние пазим и ще пазим в сърцата си живия спомен за теб:

Опечалени съпруга деца внуци и близки

No. 46. Obituary of Shakir Pashov

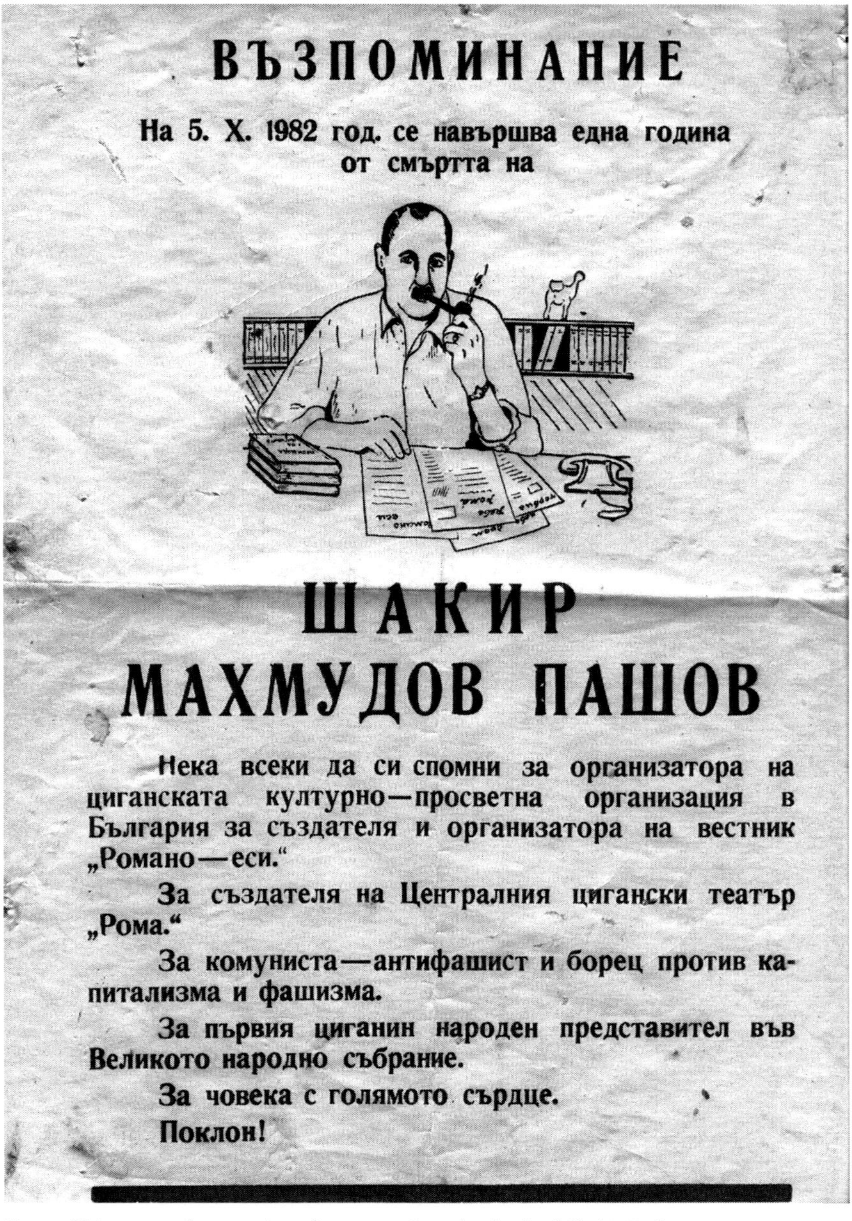

ВЪЗПОМИНАНИЕ

На 5. X. 1982 год. се навършва една година от смъртта на

ШАКИР МАХМУДОВ ПАШОВ

Нека всеки да си спомни за организатора на циганската културно—просветна организация в България за създателя и организатора на вестник „Романо—еси."

За създателя на Централния цигански театър „Рома."

За комуниста—антифашист и борец против капитализма и фашизма.

За първия циганин народен представител във Великото народно събрание.

За човека с голямото сърдце.

Поклон!

No. 47. Obituary on the occasion of one year since the death of Shakir Pashov